The Asset Protection Guide for Florida Physicians

Updated and Revised Edition

Adam O. Kirwan, J.D., LL.M.

ACANTHUS PUBLISHING

Boston, Massachusetts
www.AcanthusPublishing.com

Published by Acanthus Publishing
a division of The Ictus Group, LLC
343 Commercial St
Unit 214, Union Wharf
Boston, MA 02109

Written by:
Adam O. Kirwan, J.D., LL.M.

The Kirwan Law Firm
390 North Orange Avenue
Suite 2300
Orlando, Florida 32801
Phone: (407) 210-6622
Fax: (407) 540-9484
E-mail: akirwan@kirwanlawfirm.com
URL: http://www.kirwanlawfirm.com

Publisher's Cataloging-In-Publication Data
(Prepared by The Donohue Group, Inc.)

Publisher's Cataloging-In-Publication Data
(Prepared by The Donohue Group, Inc.)

Kirwan, Adam O.
The asset protection guide for Florida physicians / written by Adam O. Kirwan. -- Upd. and rev. ed.

p. ; cm.

ISBN: 978-1-933631-81-3

1. Physicians--Finance, Personal--Florida--Handbooks, manuals, etc. 2. Executions (Law)--Florida.
3. Debtor and creditor--Florida. 4. Finance, Personal--Florida. I. Title.

R728 .K57 2007
610.695

HG179 .K57 2007
332.024/0109759
ISBN 978-1-933631-86-8

This book is dedicated to my smokin' hot wife, Renée, my three wonderful children, Savannah, David, and Faith, and to all Florida physicians who continue to provide their valuable services to my family and the citizens at large despite these trying times.

Table Of Contents

PART II
The Flordia State Law Exemptions

PART III

Protecting Assets with Domestic and Offshore Entities

As I sat down at my word processor to write the first edition of this book in 2003, Florida physicians (and numerous physicians all over the United States of America) were in the midst of a medical malpractice insurance crisis, and there did not appear to be any light at the end of the tunnel. Three and a half years later, malpractice rates have slightly improved, however not to any meaningful degree. Other aspects have grown progressively worse.

It Goes From Bad to Worse.

The Florida "tort reform" bill that was passed into law has done little to nothing to reduce malpractice insurance premiums and the $500,000 cap on non-economic damages (which can be pierced and increased to $1,000,000 in cases of wrongful death, permanent vegetative state, and in some instances "catastrophic injury") still leaves Florida physicians open to large judgements given the fact that economic damages alone can easily reach the million dollar mark. This means that most physicians are left being able to afford only $250,000 / $750,000 coverage at best (if they can afford it at all), while the non-economic damages component of any potential judgement they face could eat up all their insurance coverage. The physician is then responsible for the remaining economic damages component, including the plaintiff's loss of income, medical bills, and ongoing care costs. To make matters worse, physician reimbursements continue to be reduced, leaving the professionals we entrust to care for ourselves and our loved ones in ever growing financial straits.

In 2004, Florida physicians fought the good fight and were successful at getting Amendment 3 passed, which amended the Florida Constitution to limit the amount of attorney's fees a plaintiff's attorney is allowed to receive in a medical malpractice law suit. The trial bar quickly responded that this limitation was every Florida resident's constitutional right, which he or she is free to waive if they see fit. On September 28, 2006, The Florida Supreme Court issued an opinion ruling that individuals may waive their "Amendment 3 rights," thereby allowing malpractice attorneys to charge their full fee.

The constitutional amendment battle also resulted in the passing of two other amendments, Amendment 7 and Amendment 8. Amendment 7 dealt with a patient's right to know about adverse medical incidents. The language of the amendment was drafted very broadly, allowing almost anyone to have access to the records of a health care facility or provider concerning "medical negligence, intentional misconduct, and any other act, neglect, or default of a health care facility or health care provider that caused *or could have caused* injury to or death of a patient." Thankfully, the enabling legislation that was subsequently passed seeks to protect the peer review process, however there is still significant contention about the constitutionality of this legislation. At least one judge, Judge Douglas from Columbia County, entered an Order relating to Amendment 7 and the enabling legislation. In that Order, Judge Douglas ruled that the enabling legislation is unconstitutional because "the legislature did not attempt to 'implement' Amendment 7 in enacting Section 381.028; they attempted to abolish it."

Whether the enabling statute will be held to be constitutional will most likely take a significant amount of time to finally determine. Several other issues related to Amendment 7 also remain unresolved. In the mean time, we will have to wait until the legislature and the courts address these numerous issues to know exactly what this Amendment will mean for physicians and hospitals.

Amendment 8 is best known as the "three strikes - you're out," rule which provides in relevant part that "[n]o person who has been found to have committed three or more incidents of medical malpractice shall be licensed or continue to be licensed by the State of Florida to provide health care services as a medical doctor." The good news is that an "incident of medical malpractice" does not include settlements, only (i) final judgments in a court of law, (ii) final orders of the Board of Medicine, and (iii) final decisions of binding arbitration proceedings. Unfortunately, Amendment 8 could have a serious detrimental affect on a physician's negotiating leverage in trying to settle a law suit.

Adding to the bad news, in 2004, the U.S. Chamber Institute for Legal Reform (which ranks states according to fairness of their legal systems) ranked Florida 38th in the nation. In 2005, Florida fell another four places to 42nd, meaning that only eight states are worse than the Sunshine State when it comes to fair legal systems.

Just when you thought it could not get any worse, a horrible piece of legislation ironically called the "Bankruptcy Abuse Prevention and Consumer Protection Act of 2005" was passed. This new law will, with rare exception, prevent physicians who end up on the wrong side of a medical malpractice judgement to use the bankruptcy laws to get rid of the judgement and obtain a "fresh start." Even worse, if you do end up in bankruptcy, many exemptions that allowed you to protect assets from creditors under Florida law may not be available to you in bankruptcy. If you stay out of bankruptcy, however these exemptions will continue to provide their intended protection. Therefore, there will now be many cases where you will desperately want to avoid bankruptcy because living with the judgement will be preferable to seeking a bankruptcy discharge. This new law will also make the asset protection process more complicated, which means that it will be more important than ever to use qualified legal counsel to assist you in the asset protection process.

And what of the promise for federal tort reform aimed at helping physicians? Good question. A piece of legislation that made bringing class action law suits more difficult was passed early in 2005, however the bill addressing the medical malpractice crises died an early death. On April 3rd, 2005, the Washington Post published an article entitled "President's Proposed Remedy to Curb Medical Malpractice Lawsuits Stalls" written by Jeffrey H. Birnbaum and John F. Harris. In this article, the authors state:

> Quick passage of the class-action bill, which Bush signed into law Feb. 18, was 'both good and bad news,' a senior business lobbyist said. It was good for industry that class-action legislation passed at all, he said, because it represented a small but meaningful victory over the hard-to-defeat plaintiffs' bar. But it was bad news, he added, because many lawmakers are loath to whack the powerful trial-lawyer lobby more than once in a single year.

All these events point to one conclusion: things are not getting better and Florida physicians need to protect their hard earned assets, because the calvary is not on its way to cure this difficult problem.

It appears that there may be some small reductions in medical malpractice insurance premiums, however the insurance is still expensive by any measure. Combine that with the fact that Florida's "tort reform" laws can still allow a plaintiff to obtain a multi-million dollar judgement, reimbursements are not getting any better, and the bankruptcy laws are no longer your friend, and you can see why asset protection planning will continue to be essential well into the future.

Be Smart and Protect Your Assets the Right Way.

A trend that has arisen since the medical malpractice insurance crisis started making the news is a proliferation of attorneys, financial advisors, and other professionals getting into the asset protection business after seeing there is a profit to be made. Unfortunately, many of these professionals lack the requisite skill in this area, or worse, have come up with a one size fits all solution which they are heavily marketing, and which provides the greatest benefit to the marketer rather than the physician engaging in the planning. The old adage "if it seems to good to be true, it probably is" is one you should take to heart before spending your valuable time and money on an asset protection plan.

Common sense should tell us that every asset protection technique, from the most simple to the most complex, has upsides and downsides. Unfortunately, since there is money to be made in this type of planning, many people offering assistance in asset protection planning focus purely on the upsides and fail to educate the people with whom they are working as to the downsides of a given technique. I have also searched the bookstores (and yes, the Internet too) to try and find a good book I could recommend to people interested in learning more about asset protection planning. What I found was a few good books written exclusively for lawyers and a proliferation of books written for non-lawyers that hype the need for asset protection and then fail miserably in providing the reader with any meaningful explanation of what real asset protection is.

My reason for writing this book is to hopefully shed some light on the admittedly confusing area of asset protection planning. It has been my experience in working with my physician clients (and in spending time over the years with my father-in-law, a radiation oncologist in the Port St. Lucie area, whom I love and greatly respect both as a person and a physician) is that physicians as a whole are intellectuals at heart. With this in mind, I have tried to keep this book both interesting and as academic as possible without turning it into a legal textbook. By educating you on the principal asset protection techniques and areas of law surrounding them, you will be able to make intelligent decisions on what form or forms of asset protection is best for you. It is also important to understand what this book is not. It is not a do-it-yourself book that encourages you to go out and become your own asset protection lawyer. As with medicine, the area of asset protection planning is a specialty filled with traps for the unwary, and while I will do my best to point several of them out to you, no book will be able to replace the assistance that a seasoned asset protection attorney will be able to provide. That being said, after you have read this book, you will be armed with enough information on the topic to accurately distinguish a real asset protection professional from a scam artist or a well meaning lawyer or advisor who is simply undereducated in this area of the law.

The book is organized into three parts. Part I is designed to explain some of the foundational elements of asset protection planning that will make understanding the asset protection techniques described later more understandable. I also discuss the process I call Integrated Wealth Planning to give you an idea of the type of comprehensive planning everyone should consider implementing. Part II delves into one of the three broad categories of asset protection planning, namely Florida state law exemptions and certain federal law exemptions. Parts III covers the remaining of two of these three broad categories, namely, domestic entities and offshore entities. Part III also provides an overview of certain techniques to protect your practice's assets, some of which are being heavily promoted, and, in my opinion, should be avoided altogether. I hope this book will serve you as a continuing source of information, because, whether you like it or not, if asset protection planning is not an integral part of your overall life planning, there may be a serious price to pay. Remember that if you fail to plan, you are really planning to fail.

Part I

Foundational Elements of Asset Protection Planning

Forgive me for starting this book on a philosophical note, however it is my sincere belief that each and every thing we do in life and each and every choice we make is not made to accomplish any thing, but rather to give us a desired emotional state. Right now, physicians face an awful realization. They have devoted a huge amount of their time, money, effort, and emotional energy to acquire the skills and experience to go out into the world as physicians, a vocation dedicated to helping and healing their fellow man. They have worked hard to earn a living to provide for their family and loved ones. Now, after making this huge investment, they are facing losing it all to a legal system run amok. In these trying times, more than anything physicians want to feel secure. Secure that everything they have worked for together with the financial security of themselves, their spouses, and their children will not be lost in an instant. Secure that they can continue to practice their art without being questioned or ridiculed for doing what they feel is best for their patients.

When it comes down to it, the process of asset protection planning gives physicians back their security. The feeling that they and their family and loved ones will be safe and secure and that as time passes, their lives as they know them will continue without an impending feeling of fear lurking around every corner.

That being said, Part I is designed to give you an overview of many important topics that constitute the foundation on which a strong asset protection plan is constructed. Chapter 1 provides an overview of the process I call Integrated Wealth Planning. Integrated Wealth Planning takes a holistic view of the planning process by effectively combining financial planning, estate planning, and asset protection planning to meet an individual's multi-generational goals and objectives. While it is possible to engage in pure asset protection planning without taking into account financial planning and estate planning considerations, the combination of these three disciplines results in a whole which is far superior to the sum of its parts.

Chapter 2 starts getting into the meat of asset protection planning by helping you identify your potential sources of liability, which are far more broad than the risk of being sued for medical malpractice.

Chapter 3 examines the unpredictable legal system that all of us live under on a day to day basis. This will hopefully broaden your awareness of the potential problems that you may someday face and give you an idea of the often unfair playing field on which disputes may have to be resolved.

Chapter 4 defines what real asset protection is, and, equally important, what asset protection is not.

Chapter 5 explains the confusing, yet vitally important, area of the law called Fraudulent Transfers. Without a keen understanding of the law of Fraudulent Transfers, a sound asset protection plan simply cannot be constructed. After gaining deeper insight into the law of Fraudulent Transfers, you will understand the legitimacy of this type of planning and why protecting your assets within the boundaries of law should be incorporated into everyone's long term planning.

Chapter 6 gives a very brief introduction to various types of insurance. It will also give you insight as to what you need to know when purchasing insurance and how using insurance can add value to your overall plan.

Chapter 7 gives a brief overview of the new "Bankruptcy Abuse Prevention and Consumer Protection Act of 2005." This horrible piece of legislation (which was Congress' gift to the credit card companies) changes the role bankruptcy plays in your asset protection plan, and it is important to understand when planning to protect your assets.

Finally, Chapter 8 provides an overview of the Florida malpractice insurance requirements (i.e., the financial responsibility obligations a physician must meet to maintain medical licensure) and the upsides and downsides of self insuring.

Reading each of these chapters will give you insight into what it takes to properly protect your assets and prepare you for learning about the various asset protection tools discussed in the balance of this book.

CHAPTER 1

Understanding the Integrated Wealth Planning Process

This chapter is designed to give you an overview of the complete planning process. Before we proceed, there are a few planning basics to keep in mind as you start to formulate your own personal plan. First, it is important to keep in mind as you read this book that every estate planning and asset protection planning technique you may consider has an upside and a downside. This is a theme that will be repeated many times throughout this book, at the risk of sounding like a broken record at times. I do this simply because it is important to understand this fact and the more you hear it, the more likely you are to incorporate it into your personal planning. Second, a basic building block in constructing an effective plan is flexibility. It has been said that the only constant is change. For this reason, it is always important to build flexibility into every legal structure you create. For example, there are ways to draft irrevocable trusts that can be modified over time despite their irrevocable nature and without compromising the tax and asset protection benefits. Next, although this should be so obvious as to eliminate its mentioning, any plan created for you or by you should be customized to meet your well thought out objectives, not to just fit within the options offered by the local attorney's software package. Customized drafting is becoming a lost art, however there are many competent attorneys who can help you in this regard.

Finally, keep the big picture in mind. Always identify what you want and why you want it before creating your plan. This is actually the most important part of the planning process. Many people take a "ready, fire, aim" approach to planning without taking the time to really solidify their true goals and objectives and the underlying motivations for why they want them. Understanding **why** you want something, in my opinion, is more important than **what** you want. The **why** first provides you with options. If you understand your true motivations behind a goal or objective, you are oftentimes able to come up with several options, while when you think of an isolated goal you usually stop there, leaving yourself disappointed if it does not come to fruition. The **why** also supplies you with the emotional drive to move toward your objectives and motivates you to revisit your plan from time to time to make sure you stay on track. Spending time clearly determining your goals and objectives and why you want them will be time very well spent. If you do not plan with the big picture in mind, you may create a plan that fixes one problem but inadvertently creates another.

The rest of this chapter will provide a brief overview of a process I have coined Integrated Wealth Planning. This holistic planning process effectively combines Financial Planning, Estate Planning, Asset Protection Planning, and other types of planning in a manner where each planning area is supported by and improved by the inclusion of the others. As you read, keep your personal situation in mind and take notes. These notes will be helpful in the future when we start discussing the various tools and strategies for protecting your hard earned assets.

The Integrated Wealth Planning Process and the Role of Asset Protection.

The Integrated Wealth Planning process begins by helping you discern the personal goals and objectives which are most important to you, and then building a plan to bring them to fruition. Once your personal goals are identified (which is a large part of the process), a total plan to accomplish them is built combining personal life planning, financial planning, estate planning, asset protection planning, and potentially other planning areas as well. In practice, a team comprised of your financial advisor, accountant, attorney, and other trusted advisors will work togther to bring the total plan together. As mentioned above, this section is included to give you some insight into what "big picture planning" involves. It would be a shame to implement a plan that protects your assets or saves taxes but ends up causing problems in some other area of your life.

Financial Planning

The first prong of the Integrated Wealth Planning process is a sound financial plan. A financial plan will help you determine things such as (i) how much you need to retire and maintain the economic standard of living that you have become accustomed to (or want to become accustomed to) in your retirement years, (ii) what do you need to maintain your current lifestyle and how will those needs likely change over time, (iii) what are your sources of current and future cash flow, and are they exempt (i.e., protected from creditors) or non-exempt (i.e., reachable by creditors), (iv) how much do you want to pass on to your children or other family members when you die, and (v) to what extent do you want to give to charity both during your life and upon death.

Please note that this plan should not initially focus on how your assets are invested or how much insurance you have, but rather be limited to a number crunching process to determine the economic feasability of attaining these enumerated goals. First, you determine (i) the things you want (i.e., to retire with an income of $400,000 per year adjusted for inflation, to send your kids to Harvard, take at least one vacation a year where you plan to spend $10,000, etc.), (ii) when you want them (i.e, you want to retire in ten years, your first child will be college age in four years with child number two just one year behind, etc.), and (iii) what it is you have right now. You then start the process of looking at what you need to accomplish financially in order to meet these goals taking into account things such as inflation, taxes, your current rate of spending/saving, etc. A plan like this will be a helpful tool in reaching your financial goals, keeping you on track over time, and allowing you to choose investment options that incorporate the proper amount of risk without jeopardizing the plan as a whole. If you already have enough assets to meet your goals and objectives, an intelligent plan will focus more on protecting what you have rather than taking unnecessary risk to grow it into something larger than what you need. Even if you do not see the immediate benefit in creating a financial plan, there are quantifiable benefits from both an estate and asset protection perspective.

Estate Planning

Next, your estate plan needs to integrate with the financial plan you have put in place. Note that the financial plan will not only help you identify what you own currently, but what you are likely to be worth if you live to your actuarially projected life expectancy. From this starting point, you can create an estate plan that will deal with issues during your life such as what would happen if you became disabled, who would care for your children if your spouse were not there, who would take care of you and watch over your assets, etc. Your estate plan will also address what happens upon your death. A good estate plan not only sets forth "who gets what," but also (i) strengthens your asset protection plan while you are alive and right thinking, (ii) reduces estate taxes at your death and income taxes during your life, (iii) incorporates business succession planning with respect to any business you may own (including your medical practice), and (iv) creates customized trusts for children, family members, and others that take into account who the beneficiary is and incorporates methods for ensuring they get the most from their inheritance. For example, you can create trusts for a surviving spouse or a child that protects the inherited assets from the claims of their creditors including a divorcing spouse. Trusts can also keep the inherited assets from being included in the child's (or other beneficiary's) estate. The consequences of this type of planning can be powerful for a child. For example, rather than taking assets out of the trust and then using them to purchase a home or start a business, if the trust is drafted properly, the child can buy the home or start the business within the trust. That means those assets can receive additional asset protection and potentially be passed on to future generations estate tax free regardless of how large they grow. Imagine if Bill Gates had created Microsoft within one of these estate tax protected trusts. All of his billions could pass to his child(ren) without being cut in half by the estate tax. If this sounds good, imagine if your parents changed their estate plan to create a trust like this for you. Trusts can also be drafted to provide incentives to children to work hard, do well in college, or accomplish any other objective you feel strongly about. You may even want to supplement your estate plan to provide moral guidance to children who may be growing up without you or simply let them know how much you love them.

Asset Protection Planning

Finally, the third integral part of the Integrated Wealth Planning triumvirate, asset protection, needs to be incorporated into the overall plan. The rest of this book will discuss the topic of asset protection in great detail, however I still wanted to point out that a brilliant financial and estate plan can be rendered worthless if your assets are taken by a judgement creditor. Likewise, a sound financial and estate plan can strengthen your asset protection plan. For example, if you have a financial plan that has determined that you need $4,000,000 to be able to maintain your current life style in your retirement years, that will serve to justify why you transferred that amount (or a lesser amount if you have not yet achieved that

$4,000,000 objective) to an asset protection structure. What if you were asked by a court someday "Why did you transfer $3,000,000 to your asset protection trust?" Which response sounds more defendable. (i) "Well, it was everything I own," or (ii) "I worked hard to get through college and earn grades that allowed me to get into medical school. I then spent the next four years of my life (and a considerable amount of money) learning how to be the best doctor possible. That was followed by starving through my residency, all so that one day I could practice medicine, help people, and earn enough so that my spouse and I could retire in comfort. I determined exactly how much money I would need to fund that retirement by working with various professionals to come up with a sound plan that incorporated financial planning, estate planning, and asset protection planning. I have been following that plan since its inception and can share it with you if you so choose." I know which response I would rather give.

The next benefit of a financial plan from the asset protection perspective is that a financial plan helps the asset protection attorney do what is called a solvency analysis. As you will read later when the topic of Fraudulent Transfers is discussed, if someone makes a transfer that renders them insolvent, the transfer is subject to being set aside or "undone" later as a fraudulent transfer. This can obviously have severe negative implications to an asset protection plan. There are two primary tests for insolvency and it is always best to pass both to ensure the strength of asset protection intended by a particular transfer. The first is "balance sheet" solvency which means that once a transfer is made, if you subtract your debts from the assets you have left you end up with a positive number. Certain modifications to a standard balance sheet analysis are typically made, however a financial plan that accurately lists all your assets is a great starting point. The second test is "an ability to pay your debts and obligations as they come due" test. Again, the cash flow analysis provided by a thorough financial plan provides valuable information in determining whether this test is met.

Another benefit of financial planning from an asset protection standpoint is garnered from understanding your cash flow. Some asset protection techniques (such as the family limited partnership) may protect your assets from the claims of creditors but may also have the effect of keeping the protected assets from you as well. Whether a technique like this is appropriate for you will in large part depend on your sources of cash flow and whether they are protected from the claims of creditors. For example, you may have protected wages and a disability insurance policy to replace that income in the event you are disabled (disability insurance payments are protected from creditors under Florida law). Maybe you have a large IRA or cash value in annuities or life insurance (all of which is protected under Florida law). On the other hand, you may not have readily available sources of exempt income. A sound financial plan will help you identify your sources of cash flow and give you the background to make sound planning decisions.

Estate planning also can help from an asset protection standpoint. In the event you can justify transfers to a legal structure that accomplishes estate tax benefits in addition to asset protection objectives, you will be better able to justify your actions in the event the transfers are later called into question by a judgement creditor.

In practice the Integrated Wealth Planning process may also entail planning that involves (i) the skills of professionals like business consultants, insurance professionals, and/or lending processional, and/or (ii) your own skills and abilities, those of your family, and those of other trusted individuals (i.e., friends, business associates, etc.). As mentioned above, this is just a brief introduction into the Integrated Wealth Planning process, however I hope it will provide you with some insight into the process you are most likely contemplating if you purchased this book.

CHAPTER 2

Identifying Your Sources of Liability

I do not believe in the scare tactics that many promoting the need for asset protection engage in, however I also feel I would be remiss if I did not cover some of the principal types of risk that all individuals potentially face. Although it may seem self-evident why physicians (and anyone else for that matter) should take active steps to protect the assets they have worked hard to amass, a preliminary overview of the types of liability we all face helps us with the first step in any intelligent asset protection plan; namely identifying the potential risks from which to protect ourselves. Physicians oftentimes focus solely on medical malpractice risks, forgetting that they are also (i) business owners, (ii) employers, (iii) board members, (iv) individuals perceived by the general public as "deep pockets," and (v) a class of individuals with one of the highest divorce rates. That being said, some broad areas of potential risk are:

1. Professional Malpractice;
2. Divorce;
3. Wrongful Termination of an Employee;
4. Sexual Harassment;
5. Discrimination in Hiring Practices;
6. Automobile Liability (including when someone else drives your car);
7. Liability from Owning Real Property (i.e., slip and fall, environmental, someone is attacked in your parking lot, etc.);
8. Damages caused by others (i.e., employees, children, subcontractor, joint-tenant, partner, etc.);
9. Liability as an officer or director of a company;

10. Contractual Liability (i.e., personal guaranties, leases, business agreements, etc.); and
11. Negligence (the number of negligence theories could fill volumes).

This list is certainly not comprehensive, however it will hopefully give you a starting place to examine your personal sources of liability. For example, if you enjoy investing in rental real estate, it will be helpful to learn about entities such as corporations, limited liability companies, and partnerships, and the benefits and detriments of each one. If you serve on the board of a local charity, you may want to consider donating your time without acting in a fiduciary capacity (remember that the board of directors can very easily be sued if there is any corporate mismanagement (even if you are unaware of it)). In short, the first part of any comprehensive asset protection plan is to first determine the problems or potential problems you may one day face. Once these are properly identified, then we can move on to the solution phase.

In helping my clients determine the potential ways they could be "shot at," I oftentimes tell them to start by creating two separate lists. The first list will set forth a complete summary of their assets. From this list we can determine whether something they own (i.e., real estate, a business, automobiles, etc.) could produce liability. In the second list, I have them write down where they spend their time on a regular basis. For example, a physician may pull out their calendar and determine that they spend a large part of their time practicing medicine, another chunk of time dealing with employees and administrative functions related to their practice, another chunk of time serving on the board of directors for a hospital or local charity, another chunk of time donating his or her services to providing medical care to the homeless, and another chunk of time flying his or her personal aircraft. By reviewing this second list, we can likewise identify which of their activities and relationships are potential sources of liability. For example, an employee could always sue for wrongful termination or sexual harassment (rightly or wrongly), the personal aircraft could be another source of liability, and so on down the list. I encourage you to create these two lists before you start the process of asset protection planning. You can either do it now or after you have completed the book, however I find that it is usually more helpful to create these lists first, because your mind will be better able to identify the best solutions for you as you read through the book if the potential problems are already resident in your consciousness.

Finally, you will want to try and estimate the amount of any potential liability you may be subject to. This is oftentimes difficult to do with any degree of certainty, however it is an essential aspect of planning since some potential liabilities can be easily insured against, while insurance is not an option (or only a partial option) with respect to other liabilities. For example, liability stemming from the practice of medicine could easily produce a judgement in excess of a million dollars. The cost of obtaining enough insurance to protect against the full amount of the potential liability is prohibitive assuming you can even obtain that much insurance in the first place. Given this fact, establishing a sound asset protection plan has become a necessity in today's environment.

Super Creditors

Before ending this chapter, I wanted to point out two of what I call "Super Creditors;" namely, the Internal Revenue Service and your spouse. The first of these super creditors is next to impossible to protect against unless you are willing to expatriate yourself (and even that has its problems). In addition, there are severe federal penalties for people (including attorneys and accountants) who help someone in protecting assets from the IRS. For that reason, in the event you want to engage in planning to shield assets from the IRS despite these warnings you will be doing so on your own. If you do find a professional willing to help you in this endeavor be extremely wary for they are most likely a con-artist or someone lacking the knowledge and skill to actually be of assistance.

With respect to the second of these Super Creditors (i.e., your spouse), it is possible to plan to keep assets from them in the event of divorce, but most of the techniques discussed in this book will not accomplish that goal. For example, the state law exemptions such as the homestead exemption, the wage exemption, the exemption for life insurance and annuities, and exemptions for IRAs and qualified plans do nothing to keep assets from a divorcing spouse. In the event you are already married, the best planning techniques typically involve offshore structures. In the event you are not yet married, there are domestic options that may be very protective. In the event you wish to engage in "pre-divorce" planning, make sure you are very specific in discussing these goals with the asset protection attorney. Otherwise, you may end up with an asset protection plan that is severely lacking with respect to the spousal creditor.

CHAPTER 3

The Unpredictable Legal System

In addition to the many areas of risk you may face over your lifetime, you may also have to deal with the United States "legal system" (note that I did not call it a "system of justice") which, in my opinion, is unfortunately flawed in many ways. At the risk of sounding somewhat jaded, the United States legal system is feared by a large portion of its citizens. I recently attended a continuing education seminar on asset protection and one of the speakers pointed this fact out. He said he had made this assertion in an interview for a local newspaper and was challenged by the reporter who did not share his viewpoint. I found his response to be very insightful. He said:

> "I spend a good part of everyday helping people create legal structures that they do not completely understand, that names a trustee they never met, using laws of countries they have never visited, and that hold their assets thousands of miles from where they live, and afterwards they feel comforted."

If you made the decision to spend your hard earned money to buy this book and further decided to take time out of your busy schedule to read it, you probably made these decisions, at least in part, out of fear; fear that you may one day be sued and your day in court will not produce a "just" result. Thankfully, a sound asset protection plan can quell this fear and let you sleep well at night.

Before proceeding I wanted to enumerate some of the flaws I believe exist in the United States justice system and that have lead to many American's fear of it. To be fair, however I want to acknowledge the fact that I am not going to spend any real time discussing possible solutions beyond giving you various tools to protect your assets. The process of making any meaningful change will need to resolve in part a conflict between cost, efficiency, and fairness, which is a daunting task.

This is not to say that the effort should not be made, just that this book is not the forum for such a philosophical discussion. That being said, some of the principal flaws are:

1. **Limited Number of "Good" Cases Compared to the Number of Attorneys.** The number of plaintiff's attorneys far outnumber the number of "good" cases out there. Therefore, there is always the temptation for a plaintiff's attorney to take on a case that lacks true merit if the attorney feels it could result in a settlement or is emotionally charged enough for a jury to sympathize with the plaintiff.

2. **Expanded Theories of Liability.** Plaintiff's attorneys are continually expanding theories of liability to reach the deep pocket. A plaintiff's attorney working on a contingency fee basis is not only looking for a case he or she believes could result in a settlement or a win, but also someone to sue who actually has the money to pay a judgement in the event they lose either by virtue of having insurance or simply by having sufficient assets. It is not uncommon for plaintiff's attorneys to simply "sue everyone involved." This tactic is in part brought about to ensure they have someone on the hook who can pay. I had a physician client who was sued (and who ultimately settled for full policy limits in the amount of $1,000,000) despite the fact that the physician had cured the plaintiff of cancer. The real bottom line as to why this physician was kept in the case was that the other doctor involved (who was really at fault) had little to no insurance or other assets to pay a judgement in the event the plaintiff won the case.

3. **An Inherently Flawed Legal System.** The newspapers are filled with cases that demonstrate that our legal system cannot be trusted to return fair, unbiased verdicts. You are all probably aware of the case brought by Stella Liebeck against McDonalds after she spilled a cup of hot coffee in her lap. The jury initially awarded Stella $2,900,000, which was later reduced to $640,000. That was not the end of the story, however. Rather than letting the case go to appeal, McDonalds settled the case for an undisclosed amount. Numerous other cases can be cited where the amount of the judgement seems outrageous in the context of the alleged wrong. In addition, once you have been sued, you have oftentimes lost. A case in point in the medical malpractice context is the case of Kurt Kooyer, M.D. Dr. Kooyer had moved to rural Mississippi to provide

medical services to the area's poor. One of Dr. Kooyer's patients, Hazel Norton, was prescribed the drug Propulsid which was later taken off the market after the drug was implicated in 341 cases of heart rhythm abnormalities. Of course, a class action law suit against the drug's manufacturer followed. Hazel Norton decided to sue Dr. Kooyer even though she never suffered any harm at all. In a later interview she stated that she decided to sue because, she said, "I might get a couple of thousand dollars." She then went on to admit "Actually, I didn't get hurt by Propulsid." Dr. Kooyer and his wife, also a physician who wanted to help the poor with her husband, ended up moving out of the state leaving just two physicians to serve a two-county area. Dr. Kooyer moved to Mississippi to help the poor, took a cut in pay to do so, and ended up having to defend a law suit where he did no wrong.

4. **The Jury of Your Piers.** It is a sad fact that the people that sit on the jury and decide the fate of the doctor being sued rarely constitute a true "jury of your peers." While I do not wish to belabor this point, it has been said that a "jury of your peers" is a group of people who were not clever enough to get out of jury duty. If this is true, then how can such unsophisticated people adjudicate a complicated medical malpractice case?

5. **Increased Complexity and Specialization.** I do not want to be too harsh when describing the intelligence of potential jurors because oftentimes intelligent people do make it on to a jury. This does not, however make these people your "peers." As an attorney, I am competent when it comes to understanding many complex legal issues, but that does not make me an engineering expert or able to understand the fine points of a medical malpractice case. In today's world where everything is becoming more complex and more specialized, it is more and more unreasonable to believe that twelve people off the street (even twelve reasonably intelligent people) can properly determine which side's experts are believable and which are not. Remember that the more complex the issues of a case are, the more an expert's ability to be convincing (even if he or she is wrong) will depend on his or her people skills and less on the actual information being attested to. Once an area of expertise becomes so complex that only other people who devote their lives to understanding the nuances and intricacies of the subject (i.e., other experts) can actually achieve a decent understanding of a particular set of facts in a case, the only thing a jury can really rely on to discern the veracity of what the expert is actually saying is the

credentials of the expert and his or her style in communicating the information. Therefore, a dishonest expert who has good credentials and an amicable disposition could easily be more convincing that an expert who is actually right but lacks the requisite people skills.

I recently heard of a study where jury members heard the testimony of two groups. The first group was made up of people who intentionally lied. The second group was made up of people who only told the absolute truth. Afterwards the jurors were asked to identify the liars. More than 50% of the time, the jurors identified the liar as the truth teller and vice versa. This study would seem to indicate that you are actually better off lying. Of course this is only one study and I do not know all the facts surrounding how it was conducted, but it is a bit unsettling to say the least.

6. **Result-Oriented Judges and Juries.** Unfortunately, the society in which we live is increasingly made up of people who refuse to take responsibility for their own actions and who cannot accept the fact that there are some things that even the most skilled physician just cannot prevent. In the event the facts of the case are emotionally charged, there will always be judges and juries who will want to "give them something" regardless of whether the physician did anything wrong. I recently had a conversation with a hospital risk manager who described a recent study that determined that in roughly 50% of all medical malpractice cases the outcome of the case was unrelated to actual fault. This study seems to back up my previous contention that judges and juries are swayed by more than the objective facts of a case. You also need to take into account the fact that most judges do not command large salaries and may be emotionally predisposed to consciously or unconsciously side with a financially challenged plaintiff rather than a doctor who is at least perceived to be financially well off.

7. **Outrageous Jury Awards / Jackpot Justice.** As mentioned above, the size of a particular judgement oftentimes bears little relationship to the actual damages suffered. Many cases are brought because the plaintiff sees an opportunity to cash in by suing a "deep pocket" defendant and as long as there is at least some colorable argument (which is a pretty low standard) it is oftentimes not difficult to find an attorney willing to file the suit. The media reports with alarming frequency cases such as the McDonald's hot coffee case, or someone

suing an airline because they were sat next to an overweight person, or someone suing fast food restaurants because they are obese. Even worse are the reports of the size of the settlements being made and the judgements being handed down.

At present, any meaningful tort reform seems unattainable in the state of Florida. The primary focus of Florida's "tort reform" legislation has been to place a $500,000 cap on non-economic damages (which, as mentioned earlier, can be increased to $1,000,000 in certain circumstances). This is not of much practical help to physicians, however since economic damages can still be very large depending on the age of the patient, the injury suffered, the cost of ongoing medical needs, and the patient's economic situation. In short, this legislation while better than nothing, should not cause you to forgo taking measures to adequately protect your assets.

8. **Traditional Insurance is Often Problematic.** Sadly, the medical malpractice insurance purchased by physicians to protect themselves in the event of a law suit actually can serve to attract the very same law suits since insurance companies are good payers (a source of "easy money") and have a pattern of settling rather than taking the suit. This willingness to settle stems from at least two large concerns. First, the insurance companies also recognize (and fear) the unpredictable nature of our courts. Second, they fear being sued for "bad faith" in failing to settle a law suit in the event they take the case to trial and lose. I will discuss the benefits and detriments of insurance (both medical malpractice insurance and other types of insurance) in greater detail in Chapters 6 and 8, however suffice it to say that using insurance alone as your asset protection plan carries with it significant risk (ironic isn't it).

As stated above, these are just some of the faults that exist in the United States legal system, and, unfortunately, I do not believe that there are any easy cures; the problems are systemic. To quote Randy Cassingham, the creator of the Stella Awards which recognizes and catalogs cases that illustrate various aspects of the runaway problems in our civil legal system, "It's definitely not just bad lawyers, or too many of them (though that's part of it). It's not just that the medical profession isn't weeding out bad doctors (though that's part of it). It's not just that insurance companies encourage frivolous claims and suits by making "nuisance" payments to make complainers go away (though that's part of it). And it's not just average citizens who refuse to take responsibility for their own actions and are convinced that "someone must be to blame" for every little thing that happens to them (though that's certainly part of it!)." Until reasonable steps are made to improve, at least to some degree, the unpredictable nature of our court system, asset protection planning will continue to make more and more sense to more and more people.

CHAPTER 4

What Asset Protection is and What it is Not

What Is Asset Protection Planning?

Before we proceed with a discussion of asset protection, it is helpful to define what is really meant by the term.

Asset protection planning is a process of using legal methods to organize your assets, affairs, and business structures, at a time when there are no legal actions pending, threatened, or expected, with the goals of:

1. Protecting your assets from loss in the event of any given peril; **and**
2. Reducing the likelihood of being the target of a law suit or other legal action which would require you to spend time and money, and put your emotional well_being at risk.

It is also important to understand what legitimate asset protection is not.

1. **Hiding Assets / Secrecy.** A proper asset protection plan will never rely on secrecy or hiding your assets. Relying on a plan that will require you to do anything but be 100% honest about what your assets are and the planning you have engaged in is not real planning and may have serious negative implications.
2. **Defrauding Existing Creditors.** The maximum benefit from asset protection planning is achieved if there are currently no lawsuits pending, threatened, or expected. This is not to say that you have no options once you are sued, however, if a creditor is on the horizon, your planning choices are significantly limited.

3. **Evading Payment of U.S. Income Taxes.** Many people look to foreign asset protection planning in hopes of avoiding paying income taxes. A proper foreign asset protection structure will be income tax neutral.

In short, legitimate asset protection planning is based on sound legal principals and does not involve creating complex plans simply for complexity's sake. A good plan will be user friendly to both you and the advisors who will be helping you properly maintain the plan over time. Finally, as mentioned above, a proper asset protection plan will never be based on you having to hide the truth about what the plan is and why you put it in place.

The benefits of a good asset protection plan include:

1. Removing the economic incentive to sue thereby deterring litigation in the first place;
2. Increasing the ability to force early and affordable settlements;
3. Placing the power back into the hands of the physician despite a plaintiff's attorney's ability to fund expensive litigation; and
4. Increasing a physician's options in the face of numerous possible perils other than malpractice claims.

In closing this chapter, asset protection planning should be thought of as an insurance policy that:

1. Covers all litigation risks;
2. Has low annual premiums and no deductibles; and
3. Contains few or no exceptions to coverage.

CHAPTER 5

The Law of Fraudulent Transfers

This chapter will explain the law of Fraudulent Transfers. In very general terms, fraudulent transfers are any transfers made with the intent to hinder, delay, or defraud a creditor. For example, you know you are going to be sued so you give all your assets to your spouse so the creditor cannot get at them or you sell your million dollar vacation home to your brother for a dollar. The fraudulent transfer laws were designed to give the creditor a means of undoing transactions like these.

Fraud vs. Fraudulent Transfer

The term "Fraudulent Transfer" seems to imply that if one makes a transfer to keep it from being seized by a creditor, that person is committing an act of fraud. Actually, that is not the case. Blacks Law dictionary defines fraud as a "knowing misrepresentation of the truth or concealment of a material fact to induce another to act to his or her own detriment." Committing fraud subjects the person who makes the misrepresentation or who conceals the material fact subject to liability for the loss suffered by the person who was lied to.

Fraudulent transfers, however, do not subject the person making the transfer subject to liability. In fact, the fraudulent transfer laws do not even prohibit transfers of property. Instead, the fraudulent transfer laws merely provide equitable tools and devices to return property to the name of the person who made the transfer so that the creditor can then reach it. Therefore, even though the word "fraud" appears in the term "fraudulent transfer," there is actually no element of fraud in the fraudulent transfer laws.

What Constitutes a Fraudulent Transfer?

Florida Statutes §726.105(1), describes what transfers are fraudulent with respect to **present** and **future** creditors (the distinction between present and future creditors will be described later in this chapter). In essence, a fraudulent transfer is any transfer of an asset made by a person:

1. With **actual intent** to hinder, delay **or** defraud a creditor; **or**
2. Without receiving something of equivalent value in exchange for the transferred property, and the person making the transfer:
   a. was engaged or was about to engage in a business or transaction for which his or her remaining assets were unreasonably small in relation to the business or transaction; or
   b. intended to incur, or believed that he or she would incur debts beyond his or her ability to pay as they became due.

Note that this is an either/or test. If you either (i) transfer property with the intent to hinder, delay or defraud the creditor (i.e., you know you are going to be sued so you give all your assets to your spouse so the creditor cannot get at them), **or** (ii) you transfer property and do not get back something of equal value (i.e., you sold your million dollar vacation home to your brother for a dollar) and after the transfer you are basically broke, then you have made a fraudulent transfer. This test applies regardless of whether the creditor's claim arose before or after the transfers were made. Please note that the above summary of Florida Statutes §726.105(1) is just that, a summary. In the event you wish to see the whole statute complete with legalese, you can view it by going to the Florida Senate's web site at http://www.flsenate.gov.

Factors to Be Considered In Determining Intent.

Since the first part of the legal test to determine whether a fraudulent transfer was made relies on whether you intended to hinder, delay or defraud a creditor, it is important to know how a court comes to that conclusion since mind reading is still an unperfected art. Florida Statutes §726.105(2) provides that consideration may be given, among other factors, to whether:

1. The transfer or obligation was to an insider (e.g., someone related to you, etc.);
2. The person making the transfer retained possession or control of the property after the transfer;
3. The transfer was disclosed or concealed;
4. The person making the transfer had been sued or threatened with a suit prior to making the transfer;
5. The transfer involved substantially all of the transferor's assets;
6. The person making the transfer absconded (i.e., left and hid);
7. The person making the transfer removed or concealed assets;
8. The amount received by the person making the transfer was equal to the value of the assets transferred;
9. The person making the transfer was insolvent or became insolvent shortly after the transfer was made;
10. The transfer occurred shortly before or after the person making the transfer incurred substantial debt.

The court can use any of these criteria (in addition to others not listed above) as circumstantial evidence that the person making the transfer had the intent to hinder, delay, or defraud a creditor and, therefore, that a fraudulent transfer was made.

Fraudulent Transfers as to Present Creditors Only.

The fraudulent conveyance rules provide another test if the creditor is a present creditor and NOT a future creditor. Florida Statute §726.106 basically states that:

1. A transfer is fraudulent if:

a. a transfer is made by someone and that person does not receive something of equal value, **and**

b. at the time the transfer was made the person was insolvent or the person became insolvent as a result of the transfer.

OR

2. (i) someone pays an existing debt to an insider (i.e., a related party), (ii) the person paying off the debt was insolvent at that time, and (iii) the insider had reasonable cause to believe that the person was insolvent at the time.

In essence, the whole notion of intent is disposed of. This is a principal reason why establishing your asset protection plan in advance of being sued is so important.

Present Creditors vs. Future Creditors vs. Possible Future Creditors.

The term "future" creditor, as used in the fraudulent conveyance laws, unfortunately leads one to believe that planning with respect to any possible creditor that may surface in the future, regardless of how remote that may be, is contemplated by the fraudulent conveyance laws. This is not the case. Courts and the fraudulent conveyance laws have made the distinction between present creditors, future creditors, and possible future creditors.

A present creditor is a creditor whose claim arose before the transfer was made. For example, if someone were to be injured on a piece of real estate and the owner of the property then starts transferring assets, the injured person would be a present creditor. Likewise, if a physician commits an act of malpractice and afterwards transfers property to his or her spouse, that patient could be considered a present creditor. Note that it does not matter whether or not a law suit has been filed or whether the physician was served with a notice of intent. Unfortunately, many people have mistakenly believed that as long as a law suit is not filed, their asset protection options are not diminished; this is an erroneous assumption.

The distinction between "future creditors" and " possible future creditors" was well stated by a legal authority on fraudulent transfers, Peter A. Alces. Mr. Alces stated that in order to be a future creditor (and, therefore, a creditor with greater rights under the fraudulent transfer laws) "it is necessary for a future creditor to establish a causal link between the fraudulent [transfer] and the injury suffered, that in order for there to be a 'future creditor' to who the [transferor] and [transferee] may be liable, the creditor must be reasonably foreseeable." In other words, if a creditor is not reasonably foreseeable in the immediate future, they are not a future creditor for purposes of the fraudulent transfer laws.

Therefore, the broad class of creditors that may materialize in the future, including, a physician's current patients, and anyone else for that matter, are " possible future creditors." It is with respect to this broad class that your asset protection options are wide open.

Fraudulent Conversions.

Just as with actual transfers of property, Florida law also encompasses in its body of fraudulent transfer law, conversions of non-exempt assets (i.e., assets that would be reachable by a judgement creditor) to exempt property (i.e., property that is exempt from creditors under some state or federal law). For example, later in this book I will discuss how assets held by a husband and wife as "tenants by the entireties" are exempt from the claims of creditors under Florida law. Therefore, if a physician were sued for malpractice and then changed the name on a brokerage account in his individual name (i.e., a non-exempt asset) to the name of the physician and his spouse, as tenants by the entirety (i.e., an exempt asset), the conversion of the brokerage account from an exempt asset to a non-exempt asset could be considered a fraudulent conversion with the creditor being able to undo the conversion and reach the assets. Likewise, transferring money into an annuity or life insurance product (both of which are exempt assets under Florida law) could also be set aside under similar facts.

Definition of the Term "Asset."

Another interesting aspect of the Florida fraudulent transfer laws is found in Florida Statute Section 726.102(2), the section that defines the term "asset." In order for the fraudulent transfer laws to apply an "asset" must be transferred. The term "asset' is defined as follows:
(2) "Asset" means property of a debtor, but the term does not include:

> (a) Property to the extent it is encumbered by a valid lien;
> (b) Property to the extent it is generally exempt under nonbankruptcy law; or
> (c) An interest in property held in tenancy by the entireties to the extent it is not subject to process by a creditor holding a claim against only one tenant."

Therefore, if an asset is considered to be exempt from the claims of creditors under another body of law, then the asset may be subsequently transferred without running afoul of the fraudulent transfer laws. This can be an important fact that can be added to an asset protection plan to give a second layer of security. For example, if tenancy by the entireties property is transferred to a Family Limited

Partnership or trust structure, it is harder for the creditor to unwind the transfer as a "fraudulent transfer" since what was transferred is not an "asset" for purposes of the Florida fraudulent transfer laws.

Statute of Limitations.

Like most law suits, a fraudulent transfer law suit must be brought by a creditor within a certain time frame (called the statute of limitations), otherwise the creditor is barred from suing. There are three distinct statutes of limitations depending on which fraudulent transfer test was failed.

1. In the event the transfer was made with the actual intent to hinder, delay, or defraud a creditor, the statute of limitations is four years after the transfer was made or, if later, within one year after the transfer was or could reasonably have been discovered by the creditor.

2. In the event the transfer was not made with the actual intent to hinder, delay, or defraud a creditor, the statute of limitations is simply four years after the transfer was made.

3. In the event the transfer was paying off an existing debt to an insider, the statute of limitations is just one year after the transfer was made.

The Validity of Asset Protection Planning.

A topic that goes hand in hand with the law of fraudulent transfers is the validity of asset protection planning. As you saw in the discussion of fraudulent transfers, we are free to engage in planning that protects our assets from "possible future creditors." Put another way, we as American citizens, do not have the legal obligation to amass our assets and hold them in a manner which is easiest for possible future creditors to reach them. Below I have listed several cases that back up this assertion.

In Re Oberst

Numerous cases have held that asset protection planning in advance of experiencing creditor problems is valid and acceptable. One such bankruptcy case, **In re Oberst**, stated:

"If the debtor has a particular creditor or series of creditors in mind and is trying to remove his assets from their reach, this would be grounds to deny the [bankruptcy] discharge. If the debtor is merely looking to his future well being, the [bankruptcy] discharge will be granted."

Riechers v. Riechers

Another case which demonstrates the legitimacy of asset protection planning is the case of **Riechers v. Riechers**. Between 1984 and 1988, three separate malpractice lawsuits had been filed against Dr. Riechers. After experiencing these problems, Dr. Riechers began to consider asset protection planning to preserve the family assets, and ultimately formed an offshore asset protection structure. In discussing the legitimacy of his offshore planning and whether the assets in the structure were reachable by Dr. Riechers divorcing spouse, the court stated:

> "Assuming arguendo, that this Court had jurisdiction over the corpus of the Riechers Family Trust, which it does not, a cause of action would not [be permitted] to set aside the trust since the trust was established for the **legitimate purpose of protecting family assets for the benefit of the Riechers family members**."

Hurlbert v. Shackleton, Jr., M.D.

Finally, the Florida case of Hurlbert v. Shackleton, Jr., M.D., demonstrates the effectiveness of asset protection planning and how courts distinguish between "future creditors" and " possible future creditors."

Dr. Shackleton used to practice obstetrics, gynecology, and surgery but after receiving notice that his medical malpractice insurance was to be cancelled, he began a part_time general medical practice confined primarily to doing physicals, x_rays and tests, eliminating riskier areas of practice. About this time Dr. Shackleton began transferring assets that were in his name alone to himself and his wife, either as tenants by the entireties, or as joint tenants with right of survivorship. A little less than a year later, Dr. Shackleton allegedly committed malpractice during the treatment of his patient, Ms. Hurlbert. During a deposition, Dr. Shackleton was asked why he transferred various assets to him and his wife jointly; he responded "[b]ecause I wasn't able to get malpractice insurance, and I wanted to cover all the bases."

The trial court drew a distinction between "probable" and "possible" future creditors. The court classified Ms. Hurlbert as a "possible" future creditor, and then went on to say that it found no cases holding a transfer of assets to be fraudulent as to "possible" future creditors. The court went on to explain that under Florida's fraudulent transfer laws, where the creditor is not in existence at the time of the conveyance, there must be evidence establishing actual fraudulent intent by one who seeks to have the transaction set aside.

Though the facts of the case contained some additional twists and turns, the end result is that Ms. Hurlbert was unable to reach any of the transferred assets.

Conclusion.

The timing of the planning, the solvency of the person engaging in the planning, and ancillary reasons for engaging in planning, all play an important role in the efficacy of an asset protection plan. Therefore, the best time to establish an asset protection plan is before the creditor appears on the horizon. Just like with life insurance, once the terminal illness is discovered your prospects for getting good coverage will be bleak.

CHAPTER 6

Using Insurance to Protect Assets

The use of certain types of insurance as part of a comprehensive asset protection plan is essential. For example, Homeowner's Insurance, Property and Casualty Insurance, Umbrella or Excess Liability Insurance, Automobile Insurance, General Business Insurance, Professional Liability Insurance (e.g., medical malpractice insurance), Employment Practices Liability Insurance (i.e., insures you with respect to law suits for wrongful termination, discrimination, sexual harassment, etc.), and Directors and Officers Insurance, all can play a part in comprehensive asset protection planning. While insurance does not directly protect assets, it can cover some or all of the damages awarded a plaintiff in a suit against you and typically covers the cost of your legal defense. The fact that the insurance is considered easy money (i.e., extremely easy to collect) by plaintiffs and their attorneys can also provide an incentive for the plaintiff to settle, especially if the defendant's remaining assets are unreachable or very expensive to chase. Oftentimes, it is less risky to give the plaintiff some "go away" money to settle the case. Both sides have an incentive to settle since going to trial is both expensive and carries risk due to the unpredictable nature of the legal system. In addition, when you consider that the cost of defending a law suit could easily exceed $100,000, carrying insurance may make sense for the legal defense aspect of the coverage alone. Where insurance is affordable, adding it as part of your asset protection plan makes perfect sense.

There are also downsides to using insurance, especially if you use it as your sole means of asset protection. The obvious first downside is that it may be impossible to obtain or afford coverage that will adequately protect you from liability, especially with General Business Insurance, Professional Liability Insurance, Directors and Officers Insurance, and Property and Casualty Insurance. In all these cases, it is very possible to imagine a lawsuit that could result in a multi-million dollar judgement and it is usually not affordable (and sometimes impossible) to carry coverage that could pay the entire judgement if you lost.

Another problem with traditional insurance is that most policies contain numerous exclusions to coverage. You do not want home owners insurance that covers "injuries incurred from falling off the roof" if "injuries incurred from hitting the ground" is a listed exclusion. This is sometimes referred to as "porous" coverage and is not to be taken lightly. For example, in the medical malpractice insurance context, some common exclusions are as follows: (i) punitive damages or penalties, (ii) acts of certain employees unless they are specifically covered under the insurance policy, (iii) service provided to organizations other than the physician's practice (i.e., serving on the hospital board, etc.), and (iv) grossly negligent acts. While some of these items may not initially appear to cause any concern, closer examination reveals some potential problems. For example, a physician may believe that they would never do anything "grossly negligent," however, a jury of individuals who are not the doctor's peers will most likely be the ones making that determination. In addition, in the event an employee of the physician's practice does something "grossly negligent," the physician or the practice could be held responsible as the employer under a legal doctrine called "respondeat superior." Therefore, even though the physician may have done nothing wrong, they are still liable for a claim that is not covered under their insurance.

I want to make the point that exclusions from coverage are usually not a crafty way for the insurance company to avoid paying legitimate claims. Insurance companies make money by computing (through the law of large numbers) the likelihood of a particular "bad event" occurring, the average amount of the typical damages, the likelihood of a frivolous claim being made, the cost to defend against such a claim, etc. and then determining what an appropriate premium should be that allows these expenses to be met and still provide them with a profit. These computations are exact and, therefore, exclusions are oftentimes a necessity. Some of the reasons exclusions exist are (i) the particular risk is simply uninsurable, or (ii) the specific coverage is intended to be covered in another type of policy. You should seek out an insurance professional that can thoroughly explain the exclusions and endorsements on a policy, identify deficiencies in the policies and take pro_active measures to protect those assets that the insurance may leave unprotected.

One type of insurance that you should seriously consider purchasing is "excess liability insurance" which is also sometimes referred to as an "umbrella policy." These policies are usually sold with your homeowners insurance policy and are most often very inexpensive. They provide additional insurance coverage if someone is injured at your home or if you are in an automobile accident and are found to be liable. These policies are particularly valuable if you have titled property in the name of a lower risk spouse to protect them from the medical malpractice claims of the physician spouse (see Chapter 13 for a discussion of this asset protection technique). In the event the "lower risk" spouse is in an automobile accident and is found to be liable, that spouse's creditors could reach those assets. Therefore, having an umbrella policy that could pay an additional $1,000,000 to $5,000,000 in damages could be an effective and inexpensive means of protecting that level of personal assets. In shopping these policies, make sure you understand all the exceptions and make sure there are no "gaps in coverage." Most umbrella policies will start paying after $500,000 in damages. This usually does not pose a problem because many homeowners policies cover the first $500,000. If your homeowners policy only covers $300,000, for example, you would have to come out of pocket in the amount of $200,000 to cover the "gap" between what the homeowners insurance covers and where the "umbrella policy" starts coverage.

Two other types of insurance which are oftentimes overlooked are (i) Employment Practices Liability Insurance (sometimes referred to as an EPLI policy), and (ii) Crime Insurance. An EPLI policy covers numerous employment related risks such as law suits for wrongful termination, discrimination, sexual harassment, etc. A crime policy covers risks related to employee dishonesty like fraud, embezzlement, theft, etc. Both of these policies are typically very inexpensive and can pay for themselves many times over if you only used them once.

When buying any insurance policy always make sure that you have a clear understanding of its terms including all listed exclusions. Unfortunately, the source for understanding your policy is oftentimes the insurance agent who sometimes doesn't have much more knowledge of the technical points than you do. As eluded to above, there is a big difference between an insurance professional who really knows the ins and outs of the various policies available and what will best suit your individual needs and an insurance salesman who only knows enough to make a sale. Understand that there are many informed and moral insurance agents (I have had the pleasure of working with several of them) and they can be invaluable if you work with a good one. Ask lots of questions, press for details, ask what the policy does NOT cover, ask for the worst case scenario, and ask them to show you the actual language in the policy. If they are a true professional they will have no problem with answering your questions and helping you ferret out the issues. If you are uncertain you can always get a second opinion to be on the safe side.

In conclusion, utilizing insurance as part of your comprehensive asset protection plan can make imminent sense if the price is affordable and the coverage amounts and exclusions are reasonable and clearly understood by you. If you do not understand your insurance policies, you could be lured into a false sense of security only to find once the problem surfaces that your policies do not provide the protection you thought they did. If, on the other hand, your assets have been protected using other means, then insurance can ameliorate your plan's effectiveness as discussed above and if a problem surfaces with your coverage, your assets are still safe.

CHAPTER 7

The Bankruptcy Abuse Prevention and Consumer Protection Act of 2005 and its Effects on Asset Protection Planning

On April 20, 2005, George W. Bush signed the bankruptcy act into law. This new law substantially reduces an individual's ability to file for bankruptcy and obtain a fresh start. In the new spirit hiding the substance of laws by giving them names that intentionally muddy the waters of candor and truth, this horrible new act is named the Bankruptcy "Abuse Prevention" and "Consumer Protection" Act of 2005 (I'll refer to the act as "BAPCPA" for short).

My Short Political Rant.

I apologize for beginning this Chapter on a political note, but I feel compelled to give you some insight into this awful piece of legislation since there was so much deception in how it was sold to the American public. To start, lets address the obvious. What 'abuse' was this act intended to 'prevent?' The answer provided by politicians was that people are racking up large amounts of debt, filing for bankruptcy, and then going out and doing it again and again. This is just not the case. First, you can only file for bankruptcy once every six years, and once you file, it is next to impossible to withdraw. Second, once you have a bankruptcy on your credit report (let alone two), getting additional credit extended to you is difficult at best and always expensive. This argument is similar to the argument that the estate tax should be repealed in order to save the family farmer when there has never been a single family farm lost to the estate tax. There are several good reasons for repealing the estate tax, but this reason is unsubstantiated political rhetoric.

Next, how this act 'protects consumers' is beyond me unless you buy in to the argument that the already profitable credit card companies who charge high rates of interest and make huge sums on hidden junk fees are going to voluntarily reduce profits by lowering rates to consumers (I do not think I will be holding my breath). Many federal bankruptcy judges are also upset with the new law. One judge who was forced to dismiss a case where the debtor had otherwise filed for bankruptcy in good faith stated:

> "Apparently, it is not the individual consumers of this country that make the donations to the members of Congress that allow them to be elected and re-elected and re-elected and re-elected. The Court's hands are tied. The statute is clear and unambiguous. The Debtors violated the provision of the statute outlined above and are ineligible to be Debtors in this case. It must, therefore, be dismissed . . . . Congress must surely be pleased." In re Sosa, 336 B.R. 113, 115 (Bankr. W.D. Tex. 2005).

Make no mistake about it, BAPCPA is a gift from our elected representatives to the credit card companies in exchange for large campaign contributions.

As mentioned above, promises were made that BAPCPA would reduce interest rates and lower prices.

> "Have interest rates gone down? According to the Federal Reserve, interest rates on personal loans and credit cards are the same today as they were just before BAPCPA went into effect. What about credit card fees? For the three months ended September 30 of [2006], Citigroup reported it made $1.3 billion in fees on credit and bank cards, an 8% increase over the same time period one year previous. In October, Wells Fargo increased late fees on its largest credit card accounts 11%, from $35 to $39 for each late payment. What about the claim that the old bankruptcy law led to higher prices? The new bankruptcy law certainly has not stopped consumers from paying more for goods and services than they did one year ago. . . .

> [In addition,] read the quarterly financial reports of the publicly traded major consumer lenders. Almost every one reports larger revenues and profits in their credit card business since the new law was passed. American Express, for example, reported operating income of $956 million for the third quarter of 2006 alone, an increase of 10% from the previous year. Also for the third quarter of 2006, Wells Fargo reported an 11% rise in total net income, $2.19 billion." **Testimony before the United States Senate, Committee on the Judiciary**, Mr. Robert Lawless, Professor, University of Illinois College of Law, December 6, 2006.

The bankruptcy filing rate is a symptom; not the disease. The primary change over the last ten years that has lead to increased bankruptcy filings has been the way that credit is marketed to consumers. The credit card lenders, in particular, have become more aggressive in marketing their products, and a large, very profitable, market has emerged in sub_prime lending. Increased risk is simply part of the business model and as credit is extended to riskier and riskier borrowers, a greater number default when faced with a financial reversal. I am personally not opposed to companies engaging in the business of sub-prime lending if they think the financial rewards will outweigh the risk, however, buying legislators to pass laws that artificially reduce their risk in order to increase their profits is personally offensive.

In addition, these companies' success stems in large part to hidden fees, excessive interest rates, and penalties that are levied as often and for as many reasons as possible. The credit card companies "disclosures" are buried in fine print and written in legalese no normal American can comprehend without a lawyer. This country was founded on an entrepreneurial system that encourages its citizens to take risks and pursue the American dream. The bankruptcy laws were enacted to provide a fresh start to individuals who took these risks and failed. Under BAPCPA it no longer serves that purpose.

As mentioned above, although I do not feel that abuse is prevalent, true abuse could have been easily curtailed without the ridiculous, sweeping changes made under the new act. Consider that bankruptcy filings are a matter of public record and show up on an individuals credit report. It is certainly the right of any company that extends credit to deny credit to an individual who has filed for bankruptcy without exhibiting financial responsibility thereafter or deny credit to someone who has filed for bankruptcy more than once. This solution would not even require any law change, just a little fiscal responsibility on the part of credit card companies. If someone asked you for a loan and you can see from their credit report that they routinely do not pay their debts, aren't you being just a bit of an idiot for lending them money in the first place. If you think that this is just too much responsibility to place on the poor credit card companies, why not just change the law to only allow a bankruptcy once every ten years or limit a person to only two bankruptcy discharges in their lifetime? This eliminates the abuse problem without the draconian changes. Of course, the answer again is that curtailing real abuse was never BAPCPA's true objective.

I apologize again for starting this article on a political note, but this law hurts working Americans, furthers corporate greed, and hurts the true entrepreneurial spirit upon which this country was founded. I hope that you take note and get involved to help get this law repealed, or better yet, help get new legislation passed that makes the credit card companies take fiscal responsibility for engaging in sub_prime lending if they choose to do so and properly disclose all of the hidden 'junk fees that they presently hide in reams of unintelligible legalese. You may also consider sending a message to your representatives who voted 'yes' for this atrocity of a law by voting 'no' for them next election.

Brief Overview of Bankruptcy.

Before proceeding with a discussion of BAPCPA, I want to provide you with a very brief overview of how bankruptcy works and the interplay between the federal bankruptcy laws and the Florida state law exemption statutes.

Bankruptcy Code Section 541 - What Is Included in the Bankruptcy Estate?

Section 541 is the primary section of the bankruptcy code that defines what is included in someone's "bankruptcy estate." To understand why this is important, when someone either voluntarily files for bankruptcy or is forced into bankruptcy by creditors, the individual involved in the bankruptcy (usually called the "debtor") ceases to own most of their assets individually and instead something akin to a legal entity springs into existence called the bankruptcy estate. The person in charge of these assets is the bankruptcy trustee whose role is to collect and liquidate the property in the "bankruptcy estate" for the benefit of the debtor's creditors within the context of the bankruptcy laws. If Section 541 does not include an asset in the bankruptcy estate to begin with, then it is considered to be excluded and we do not need to worry about whether it is exempted under the federal or state exemption laws discussed below. For example, BAPCPA amended Section 541 to exclude 529 plans (i.e., a type of college savings plan) from the bankruptcy estate subject to certain limits (e.g., certain funds that were contributed not later than a year preceding filing of the petition, etc). Therefore, if you have a 529 plan to which you contributed (i) some assets before the one year period preceding your bankruptcy filing (the "Pre-One Year Assets"), and (ii) some assets within the one year period preceding your bankruptcy filing (the "One Year Assets"), then the Pre-One Year Assets would be excluded from the bankruptcy estate due to Section 541. The One Year Assets would not be excluded from the bankruptcy estate, but may be exempted under a particular exemption (such as is the case in Florida under Florida Statutes 222.22.

Bankruptcy Code Section 522 - What Is Exempted from the Bankruptcy Estate?

Once the bankruptcy estate is properly defined, Section 522 of the Bankruptcy Code then goes on to list several things that can be exempted or "taken back out" of the bankruptcy estate (this is a system that could only have been designed by lawyers). Section 522(d) lists numerous assets that are considered to be exempt (and, therefore, asset protected) under federal law. Each state also has a set of state statutes that also lists various assets that are exempt from creditors claims. People who file for bankruptcy in many states are given a choice as to whether they want to use the exemptions provided under federal law or those provided under state law (but you cannot choose both). Floridians, however, are not given this option. Florida Statutes Section 222.20 specifically states that Florida residents may not use the federal exemptions and are, therefore, limited to our state law exemptions. This is usually not a problem since Florida's state law exemptions are much more inclusive than the federal exemptions.

Certain provisions under Section 522 (i.e., federal law) apply even if someone chooses to use the state law exemptions, or, as in the case of Floridians, that choice was made for us. For example, the provisions of BAPCPA that limit the ability to fully exempt your homestead under certain circumstances will apply even though Florida law typically exempts the full value of your homestead. If you stay out of bankruptcy altogether, however, the new bankruptcy laws have no effect and Florida's state law exemptions remain unaffected by BAPCPA.

How the Acts Affects Asset Protection Planning.

At the heart of BAPCPA are new rules that prevent most Americans from filing for Chapter 7 bankruptcy. Chapter 7 is the type of bankruptcy most individuals think of when they think of bankruptcy; namely, the ability to keep your 'exempt assets' and eliminate or 'knock out' their existing debt in order to obtain a fresh start. Under BAPCPA, if an individual voluntarily files for bankruptcy, most people will be forced into Chapter 13 or Chapter 11 where they will lose more of their assets, contribute most of their earnings to the bankruptcy estate, and live at close to poverty levels while the lion's share of their income will go to pay creditors for a period of 5 years. This being the case, it will be significantly more advantageous for most individuals to avoid bankruptcy altogether. In other words, bankruptcy's purpose is no longer to provide you with a fresh start. Lets first look at how BAPCPA operates.

The "Means Test" Means that Working Physicians Cannot Seek the Protection of Bankruptcy if They are Sued.

Under BAPCPA, granting someone a full Chapter 7 "discharge" (i.e., wiping out their debt) is considered to be "abusive" if the person fails the Means Test. The actual computations involved under the Means Test are too complicated to fully describe here, however, anyone that earns more than thirty-seven thousand five hundred dollars ($37,500) per year will be subjected to the Means Test. This means that most physicians will no longer be able to use bankruptcy to rid themselves of an oppressive medical malpractice judgement. The test does applies a six month look back period to determine your income, so if you have the ability to retire (or go without working for several months), you may be able to meet the Means Test and qualify for Chapter 7 bankruptcy. There may also be a 'back door' into Chapter 7 even if you fail the Means Test; this is discussed at the end of this Chapter.

Changes to Exemptions.

BAPCPA, also made changes to many exemptions, most notably the homestead exemption (remember that the United States Constitution contains something called the Supremacy Clause which states that in the event of a conflict between federal law (like the bankruptcy laws) and state law (even a state constitution), the federal law prevails). Before providing a summary of these changes, however, I want to reiterate an important point; namely that these changes only apply if you are actually in bankruptcy. If you are not in bankruptcy, BAPCPA does nothing to reduce the application or effectiveness of Florida's state law exemptions. At the end of this Chapter, I will discuss the effects of a creditor forcing you into involuntary bankruptcy and how you may be able to lessen the likelihood of this happening.

BAPCPA's Effect on the Homestead Exemption.

1. **$125,000 Cap.** Probably the most publicized aspect of BAPCPA was a $125,000 cap on the amount someone could protect in their homestead. Thankfully, BAPCPA still allows Florida's unlimited homestead exemption if the homeowner has lived in their home for at least 1,215 days (i.e., 40 months or three years and four months) before filing bankruptcy. If the homeowner has not met this 40 month ownership requirement, they are limited to a $125,000 homestead exemption.

2. **Exceptions for Certain Types of Liability.** In addition to the $125,000 cap discussed above, there are also exceptions for individuals convicted of any of the crimes listed below. In such an event, the homestead exemption is limited to $125,000. The enumerated crimes are:

   a. Any violation of State or Federal securities laws;
   b. Fraud, deceit, or manipulation in a fiduciary capacity;
   c. Any civil remedy under the RICO laws; or
   d. Any criminal act, intentional tort, or willful or **reckless** misconduct that

caused **serious physical injury or death** to another individual in the preceding 5 years.

This last exception may have serious implications to physicians. First, while most physicians are not likely to engage in willful or reckless misconduct, whether or not they meet this standard will be up to a judge or jury to decide. In the event a physician has significant equity in their home, it would not be hard to envision a plaintiff's attorney making the argument that a physician acted recklessly. Second, remember that an employer can be responsible for the acts of their employees, so in the event a physician were held liable for the willful or reckless acts of an employee, there may be an argument that the physician employee could not protect home equity above $125,000.

3. **The New 10 Year Lookback Rule**. Finally, in an attempt to prevent people from transferring assets into their homestead prior to filing for bankruptcy, BAPCPA adopts a new ten year lookback rule that renders "unexempt" (i.e., available to creditors) any amount that was fraudulently transferred into a homestead (i.e., paying down a mortgage, purchasing a new home, improving a home, etc.). Whether a transfer is fraudulent will be determined under criteria similar to that discussed in Chapter 5.

The New "Two Year" Rules.

Under the old bankruptcy law, a bankruptcy trustee could set aside (i.e., ignore and bring back) transfers of property made within one year of filing for bankruptcy. Under BAPCPA, (i) this one year rule has been extended to two years, and (ii) the definition of fraudulent transfers now includes transfers to insiders (such as owners of a business) made within the two year period. These "insider transfers" also include payments made under employment agreements that are not made in the 'ordinary course of business.'

Another new 'two years rule' now applies in determining whether someone who moved to Florida will be able to avail themselves of Florida's generous state law exemptions. Under BAPCPA, you now have to have resided in Florida for 730 days before filing for bankruptcy in order to benefit from Florida's state law exemptions. If you have not resided in Florida for at least two years, the place where you were domiciled for the 180 day period immediately preceding the 730 day period (i.e., days 731 through 910) will be considered your domicile for purposes of determining which state's exemption laws will apply to you. If you did not reside in any one place during that 180 day period, then the place you resided the longest during that period will be considered the domicile for these purposes. While these rules were intended to prohibit someone from being able to move to Florida to take advantage of its generous state law exemptions, consider the following:

Dr. Gray lives in Nebraska. A judgement was recently handed down against her and she wishes to avail herself of Florida's state law exemptions. She moves to Florida and resides there for 91 days. She then moves back to Nebraska and resides there for 730 days. She then files for bankruptcy. Dr. Gray has not resided in Nebraska for the 730 day period prior to filing for bankruptcy so she is not considered to be domiciled in Nebraska for bankruptcy purposes. If we then look at the 180 day period immediately preceding the 730 day period, we see that she lived in Florida for 91 days and Nebraska for 89. Dr. Gray appears to be entitled to Florida's state law exemptions.

I doubt congress intended this result, but under a strict reading of the statute, this is the correct result. Consider someone who wanted to be considered a resident of Delaware, Nevada, Alaska, or any other state with favorable asset protection laws. The wait may be a little longer but if you can move to another state for more than three months, you may still be able to forum shop.

BAPCPA Addresses Asset Protection Trusts and "Similar Devices".

Unlike under the old bankruptcy law, self-settled asset protection trusts (like Delaware Asset Protection Trusts and Offshore Trusts; see Chapters 19 and 20) are now specifically mentioned under BAPCPA. Any assets fraudulently transferred to one of these trusts within the ten year period prior to filing for bankruptcy will be included in the bankruptcy estate and, therefore, subject to the claims of creditors. This 10 year "clawback" provision requires actual intent to defraud in order for any such transfer to be considered a fraudulent transfer. The addition of this provision may actually bode well for those individuals with the foresight to create these trusts early on. First of all, by transferring assets to a self-settled trust early on and at a time when there are no creditor problems looming, the likelihood of a court finding that the assets were transferred to the trust with an actual intent to defraud is significantly reduced, thereby ensuring their protective nature even in the bankruptcy setting. Second, once the ten year period has elapsed, the assets are forever beyond the reach of creditors even in bankruptcy. In establishing these asset protection trusts, care must be given to (i) careful drafting of the trust agreement and other elements of the structure, (ii) funding the trust in a manner that reduces the likelihood of a future fraudulent transfer action, and (iii) documenting the non-asset protection advantages provided by the trust.

Unfortunately, this new provision did not limit its scope solely to asset protection trusts but instead also included other "similar devices." It is unclear exactly what is meant by the term "similar device" however, some commenters have suggested it may include transfers to business entities such as family limited partnerships and even retirement plans. Only time will tell how broadly the term "similar device" will defined by the courts in applying the 10 year clawback provision, however, two important points need to be made. First, the earlier you establish your asset protection plan the better off you will be. If the term "similar device" is defined broadly, you will have started the clock running year running. In addition, by establishing your plan early on, the "actual intent to defraud" standard will be harder to meet. Second, since this provision only applies if you are in bankruptcy, planning to avoid being forced into involuntary bankruptcy also becomes an important part of your overall strategy.

Retirement Plans and IRAs.

BAPCPA may actually have provided some benefit in the area of retirement plans and IRAs. First, BAPCPA applies to a broader range of retirement plans than under the old bankruptcy law and, while not completely resolved, most likely provides protection to retirement plans that do not cover any non-owner employees (see Chapter 10 for a more complete discussion).

BAPCPA also added a limit to the amount that is protected under IRAs. Under BAPCPA, IRAs are protected up to $1,000,000 PLUS any amounts rolled over from qualified plans such as 401ks. Since it is highly unlikely that any individual would be capable of amassing a full $1,000,000 in an IRA given the relatively small contribution limits, this limit should not pose problems for most Floridians. Another benefit is that if you ever move to a state whose laws do not protect IRAs, filing for bankruptcy would be an option to protect these valuable assets. Obviously, this would only make sense if there were relatively few non-exempt assets and you were able to qualify for Chapter 7 bankruptcy under the Means Test.

Involuntary Bankruptcy.

I am sure that you can see by now that the purpose of BAPCPA was NOT to prevent abuse and it was NOT to protect consumers; it WAS a gift by congress to the credit card companies in exchange for large campaign contributions. If you are an American who works for a living, you can see that the bankruptcy laws will prevent you from obtaining a fresh start regardless of the reason for your financial woes, even a judgement for medical malpractice based on thin evidence. I have mentioned this before and I will continue to mention it again and again throughout this book; if you are not in bankruptcy, none of the provisions of BAPCPA will apply. Since the bankruptcy laws no longer serve the purpose of providing hard working people a fresh start, your best bet will usually (but not always) be to avoid ending up in bankruptcy in the first place. Of course, you will not file for bankruptcy unless you can be certain that you will pass the Means Test (as would be the case if you recently retired and have protected your assets). A creditor, however, may attempt to force you into bankruptcy if they feel doing so will free money that is otherwise protected under state law.

> Suppose that Dr. Jones moved to Florida last year and has not lived in his $800,000 homestead for the full 40 months required under BAPCPA. I am assuming that his homestead meets all the requirements for it to be exempt under Florida's constitution. Someone has just obtained a large judgement against him. Since Dr. Jones is not in bankruptcy, his homestead is completely protected and the creditor is left unpaid. If Dr. Jones were in bankruptcy, however, only $125,000 of his homestead would be protected and $675,000 would be available to the creditor. Therefore, the creditor would much rather see Dr. Jones in bankruptcy than out in the 'real world.' In the event that Mr. Jones (i) had lived in Florida for the requisite period 40 month period; (ii) had not fraudulently transferred assets into his homestead within the last 10 years, and (iii) there are no other BAPCPA exemption issues with respect to his other assets, then involun-

tary bankruptcy is of no real use to the creditor (and may even be detrimental).

In fact, involuntary bankruptcy petitions are on the rise.

The bankruptcy law allows a creditor to force a debtor into bankruptcy under certain circumstances. Below is a brief discussion of the involuntary bankruptcy process and some planning measures that can be implemented to reduce the risk of being forced into an unwanted bankruptcy.

The 12 Creditor Rule. If you have less than twelve creditors, then a single creditor with a claim of $12,300 or more has the standing (i.e., the right) to attempt to force you into bankruptcy by filing an involuntary bankruptcy petition with the court. If, on the other hand, you have twelve or more creditors, then three creditors with aggregate claims of $12,300 or more must join forces in order to have standing to file an involuntary bankruptcy petition against you. Obviously, if you have a single judgement creditor and all your other creditors are being paid on time, it is highly unlikely that two of these satisfied creditors are going to join forces with the judgement creditor, especially since doing so may mean that they will receive less then the full amount that is owed to them. This could very well be the result since the bankruptcy estate (which is comprised of all your non-exempt assets) is divvied up among the creditors and then your ongoing obligation to all creditors is discharged (i.e., forgiven). Since the judgement creditor is likely to be owed the largest amount, they may receive the lions share of the bankruptcy estate leaving the rest of the creditors with little or nothing. In addition, if one or more creditors file an involuntary bankruptcy petition and you are successful in defending against it (i.e., you successfully stay out of bankruptcy), the creditor(s) can be made to pay your costs and attorney's fees in addition to compensatory and punitive damages. Just one more reason not to join the party.

Given this fact, it may be worthwhile to ensure that you have at least twelve creditors if being forced into bankruptcy would free up assets for a creditor to take under the new BAPCPA regime. You could do so by acquiring additional credit cards provided that (i) each card has more than a *de minimis* balance, and (ii) that the debt is continuous. What constitutes a *de minimis* debt is obviously subject to some interpretation, however, an amount of roughly $2,000 per credit card should be very difficult to consider *de minimis*. Utilities and credit cards similar to an American Express card that you are required to pay in full each month are oftentimes not counted as creditors since they are not continuous and ongoing. In the case of In re Smith, a Florida bankruptcy court stated "In [the Denham case], the Debtor claimed to have eighteen creditors, seventeen of whom held small, insignificant debts which were customarily paid monthly. The Denham Court held that small current debts **which are contracted to be paid monthly** cannot be used by an alleged Debtor to increase the number of his creditors to greater than twelve in an effort to defeat an involuntary petition by a sole creditor."

I hate to suggest rewarding the credit card companies who are at the heart of this abusive piece of legislation being passed in the first place, so to the extent there are other legitimate debts you can establish (i.e., car loans, debt to your practice or other businesses, etc.) I recommend you do so first. Any loan between you and a related party or a business entity that you are an owner of must always be fully documented using a promissory note, should bear a commercially reasonable rate of interest, and should have payment terms similar to third party lending transactions. Some commentators have stated that you can wait until the creditor has already been identified before creating these additional creditors. While I do not know of any authority that specifically contradicts them, I think the safer method is to establish these credit relationships over time (i.e., not all at once) and before the 'bad thing' happens to avoid an argument that you acted in bad faith and, therefore, the 'new creditors' should be ignored.

Defending Against an Involuntary Bankruptcy Petition. If you have been unsuccessful in preventing an involuntary bankruptcy petition from being filed against you in the first place, you need to understand some ways you could argue that the petition should be dismissed. In order for a creditor to force someone into bankruptcy, each creditor filing a petition must first prove that their claim is not the subject of a bona fide dispute. Therefore, if an involuntary bankruptcy petition were to be filed against you and you can provide a legitimate defense, even if your prospects of prevailing on that defense are tenuous, then you may be able to disqualify their claim and, therefore, get their petition dismissed. In cases where you can raise a dispute about the amount owed or show there is a genuine issue of material fact that is still unresolved in your case, you may very well be able to get the creditor's petition dismissed. If you can still legitimately appeal a judgment, the creditor(s) are not likely to proceed with an involuntary bankruptcy petition.

Second, each creditor wishing to force you into involuntary bankruptcy must show that you are generally not paying your non-disputed debts and obligations as they come due. Courts have oftentimes defined "generally not paying" to mean that the debtor is regularly missing a significant number of payments that are significant in relation to the debtor's overall financial situation. Although the court will examine a number of factors, this means that if you are paying all of your ordinary commercial debts and obligations as they come due (such as your utility bills, mortgage, credit card payments, etc.) but are just not paying the single judgement creditor's claim, you may be able to have the involuntary bankruptcy petition dismissed.

Third, under BAPCPA, before anyone is allowed to **voluntarily** file for bankruptcy (assuming, of course, the means test is met), they are first required to seek credit counseling and show proof of completion to the court. There have been several cases since BAPCPA has been enacted where debtors who have otherwise filed in good faith have had their bankruptcy dismissed solely due to a failure to obtain this required counseling (so the court seems to be taking it seriously). Under a literal reading of BAPCPA, the law does not distinguish between **voluntary** and **in**voluntary bankruptcy when it comes to applying the credit counseling requirement. Therefore, if a creditor is trying to force you into involuntary bankruptcy, technically you are required to voluntarily attend and complete the required credit counseling. If such a creditor asked you to cooperate in this regard and you flatly refused, they may have their petition dismissed, and be forced to pay your costs, attorney's fees, and maybe even penalties. No court opinion has yet to be issued on this issue, but it seems that many judges hate BAPCPA as much as the rest of us (except, of course, the credit card companies).

Finally, although the Means Test is generally a test that must be passed before one is permitted to file a **voluntary** bankruptcy petition, a local bankruptcy attorney told me that he thinks that there may be an argument that a technical reading of the Means Test will preclude a creditor from forcing someone who would otherwise fail the Means Test into involuntary bankruptcy. If he is right, then you have a clear cut method of staying out of involuntary bankruptcy. If he is not right, then consider this. If bankruptcy would help you (i.e., your assets are substantially exempt or protected), however, you are ineligible to file for Chapter 7 due to the Means Test, consider the following:

First, you would borrow money from a friendly party (lets call him Joe Friendly). This loan would be fully documented by a promissory note and other relevant legal documents. This loan would also bear a commercially reasonable rate of interest. Second, you would default on your loan to Joe by missing several payments. Third, Joe would file an involuntary Chapter 7 bankruptcy petition against you. Finally, you would agree to Joe's petition, and there you are in the Chapter 7 bankruptcy you wanted but were precluded from obtaining due to BAPCPA's Means Test. Thanks, Joe.

As a quick aside, a creditor cannot force you into a Chapter 13 bankruptcy which requires you to include your income in the bankruptcy estate. The reason for this is that it violates the thirteenth amendment to the United States constitution which abolished involuntary servitude (i.e., slavery). This same reason would most likely prohibit an involuntary Chapter 11 bankruptcy since BAPCPA now requires someone in Chapter 11 to include their income in the bankruptcy estate.

As you can see, the involuntary bankruptcy law is complex and a complete discussion of its intricacies is beyond the scope of this book. If you find yourself facing the need to avoid being forced into involuntary bankruptcy, you will be best served by hiring a good bankruptcy attorney who can help you negotiate the land mines raised by BAPCPA.

Conclusion.

As explained above, the bankruptcy laws are no longer the friend of the working person. The new law now prevents you from obtaining a fresh start even if the reason for your financial woes stems from ill health or an unwarranted judgement. While I am disgusted by congresses' greed and willingness to enact legislation that is bad for the very people they are supposed to be representing in exchange for the almighty campaign dollar, BAPCPA is now a reality that must be taken into account when engaging in asset protection planning. Given the fact that in most cases you will no longer be able to seek the refuge of a Chapter 7 bankruptcy if you find yourself on the wrong side of a judgement, asset protection planning is more important than ever. In addition, given the new time requirements set forth under BAPCPA, you will be rewarded by starting your asset protection planning sooner. The longer you wait, the fewer your options may actually be.

CHAPTER 8

Florida Malpractice Insurance Requirements and the Upsides and Downsides of Self Insuring

Florida Malpractice Insurance Requirements.

Florida law requires physicians to meet one of the following obligations in order to obtain and maintain medical licensure:

1. Obtain malpractice insurance in an amount not less than $250,000 per claim with a minimum aggregate of not less than $750,000 (if the physician has hospital staff privileges), or obtain malpractice insurance in an amount not less than $100,000 per claim with a minimum aggregate of not less than $300,000 (if the physician does **not** have hospital staff privileges).
2. Establish and maintain an escrow account in the amounts set forth above.
3. Obtain an irrevocable letter of credit from a financial institution in the amounts set forth above.
4. With respect to every adverse final judgment against a physician, agree to:
   a. Pay the lesser of:
      i. the amount of the judgment plus any accrued interest, or

      ii. $250,000 ($100,000 for physicians without staff privileges); and
   b. "Prominently display" a sign "noticeable by all patients" informing them that the physician does not carry malpractice insurance (the wording of the sign is provided in the statute);
   c. Provide a written statement to each patient to sign, again informing them that the physician does not carry malpractice insurance.

This final option is often referred to as "going bare" or self-insuring.

Should I Self-Insure?

This decision requires a careful cost-benefit analysis by each physician. The factors that must be weighed are listed below:

Insurance is "Easy Money"

Malpractice insurance is a double edged sword. It pays for the legal costs of defending a law suit and protects personal assets to the extent of the policy limits. Contrarily, it represents the easiest pot of money for a plaintiff's attorney to reach. If the policy limits are high enough, it will always make financial sense to sue you.

Hospital Privileges

Some hospitals require malpractice insurance to maintain staff privileges even though Florida law gives you the option to self insure. If it is necessary to your practice to maintain staff privileges at such a hospital, your real choice becomes whether to carry minimum coverage or something more. As the malpractice insurance crises has worsened, however, several hospitals loosened this requirement.

Managed Care Providers

Certain managed care providers require physicians to maintain malpractice coverage. The decision to continue the association with the managed care organization will depend upon the profitability of the relationship. The current dearth of malpractice insurance availability for some specialists will force managed care organizations to rethink their insurance requirements.

Cost vs. Coverage

Self insurance is usually inappropriate for the physician who does not practice in a high risk area and has traditional malpractice insurance limits that are likely to cover the amount of any foreseeable judgment, however the physician's personal assets must be adequately protected from an outlandish judgment. On the other hand, self insurance may be economically sound for the doctor who works in a high risk specialty and pays exorbitant amounts for minimum coverage. For example, a physician who pays premiums of $200,000 a year will save $600,000 (which he can place in a reserve fund) if he escapes suit for three years.

Cost of Litigation

A physician who self insures will be responsible for providing for his/her own legal defense in any malpractice suit. Any physician who has confronted litigation understands that plaintiff's attorneys may attempt to inflate your legal expenses to force an unfavorable settlement. Also remember that even if you do not carry malpractice insurance and are otherwise uncollectible, you can still end up in litigation.

Understand Your Policy

Before paying large sums for a malpractice policy, it is important to fully understand what you are buying. Take the time to read the policy's exceptions to coverage, the applicable deductibles, and whether the policy is a "Claims-made" or "Occurrence" type policy.

Asset Protection Plan

While it is my opinion that establishing a sound asset protection plan has become a necessity in today's litigious society, if you do not have a sound asset protection plan in place and do not plan on creating one in the near future, the cost of insurance will almost always be preferable to losing your life's savings if sued.

Conclusion.

The decision to self-insure is oftentimes not an easy one and requires taking many factors into consideration. To help with the decision making process, let me give you two quick examples. The first example is the perfect candidate for self-insuring and the second example is the perfect candidate for carrying at least \$250,000/\$750,000 coverage.

> Example 1: Dr. Parker has been a neurosurgeon for twenty years and has a couple of nuisance law suits in his past. He just received his medical malpractice insurance renewal notice and sees that his new premium will be \$185,000 per year. Dr. Parker has a net worth of \$15,000,000, \$8,000,000 of which is liquid. Dr. Parker has a solid asset protection plan in place.

In the above example, if Dr. Parker is sued, he can pay for his own legal defense and pay the \$250,000 necessary to continue to practice medicine and his family will not starve or suffer severe consequences. In the event Dr. Parker is not sued and continues to practice medicine for another ten years, he will have over $2,250,000 in the bank (assuming a 4% interest rate). Although paying $400,000 to $500,000 is never pleasurable, Dr. Parker would have to be sued five times over that ten year period and be found liable every time, in order to suffer a financial loss (which is highly unlikely).

> Example 2: Dr. Octavious is a family practitioner who has a very small net worth and a family that depends on him for their support. He can obtain $1,000,000/$3,000,000 coverage for the cost of $10,000 per year. To date, Dr. Octavious has not taken the time to think much about asset protection and the few assets he has are exposed to creditors' claims.

In example 2, Dr. Octavious would suffer considerable hardship in the event he were sued. He could not afford to pay for a good defense lawyer nor could he afford to pay the $250,000 necessary to keep his license if he lost such a case. Dr. Octavious would be foolhardy to not purchase at least $250,000/$750,000 coverage since it is so inexpensive and the consequences of not having it are so grave.

I hope these two examples help with your decision making process.

Part II

The Florida State Law Exemptions

Planning with state law exemptions can provide solid asset protection in many cases and in some cases (as with the Florida homestead exemption) can even provide planning opportunities that other methods of asset protection cannot. Before proceeding with an analysis of the major exemptions available to you as a resident of Florida and an American citizen, it is helpful to know what is meant by the term "exemption." Most exemptions that will be discussed in the following chapters have their genesis in one of three bodies of law: (i) Florida Statutes, (ii) the Florida Constitution, and (iii) federal laws such as the federal bankruptcy laws. These laws exempt certain assets from the claims of creditors and, therefore, provide people with a legally supported means of protecting assets. Florida residents enjoy some of the most generous exemptions in the United States; so generous in fact that Florida has earned itself the nickname "The Debtors Haven." One downside to keep in mind while reading through these exceptions is that despite Florida's strong public policy in favor of "debtor friendly" laws, these laws are potentially subject to change by the Florida legislature, Florida courts, and even the federal legislature or judiciary. If a change in the law is made that converts a previously protected class of assets to something that can be reached by a creditor, the consequences could be significant, especially if the law change does not incorporate some form of "grandfather" provision (i.e., a provision that grants continuing protection to assets protected prior to the law change).

Part II will begin to delve into the meat of how to protect your assets by explaining these important state law exemptions one by one.

Chapter 9 will discuss the unlimited homestead exemption which will be of interest to anyone who owns their own home.

Chapter 10 will discuss the exemptions that protect qualified plan assets (i.e., 401Ks, profit sharing plans, money purchase plans, etc.) and IRAs.

Chapter 11 will cover the very important Florida wage protection statute and provide instructions on how to keep your earnings free from the claims of creditors.

Chapter 12 will discuss a special type of co-ownership available in Florida called "tenants by the entireties." As you will learn in this chapter, there are upsides and downsides to the protection offered by TBE, however, there are also some planning strategies to help mitigate the downsides.

Chapter 13 will discuss gifting as a means of protecting assets and something I call "I Gave it to my Spouse" planning. As with TBE, there are upsides and downsides to this method of protecting assets and some ways to mitigate the downsides.

Chapter 14 will discuss the exemption for life insurance and annuities and how these financial products can be used to protect assets. The upsides and downsides of this type of planning will also be discussed.

Chapter 15 will discuss miscellaneous state law exemptions not covered by the preceding chapters in this Part II.

So, without further delay, on to the exemptions.

CHAPTER 9

The Florida Homestead Exemption

The Homestead Exemption is found in the Florida Constitution and is based on the public policy that the family home is sacred regardless of the financial condition of the owner. Florida is one of only a handful of states that have an unlimited exemption. In other words, if your home meets certain criteria, it will be protected from creditors regardless of how much it is worth. This is a powerful exemption, however, it is not without its "traps for the unwary." I have met with many clients whose home is not fully protected who mistakenly thought it was due to a misunderstanding of the law. This Chapter is designed to un-muddy the homestead protection waters and provide you with the knowledge necessary to receive maximum benefit from this valuable exemption.

Homestead Requirements.

An obvious starting point to discussing the homestead exemption is to read the actual language of Article X, Section 4 of the Florida constitution which grants the Florida homestead exemption:

> "(a) There shall be exempt from forced sale under process of any court, and no judgment, decree or execution shall be a lien thereon, **except** for the payment of taxes and assessments thereon, obligations contracted for the purchase, improvement or repair thereof, or obligations contracted for house, field or other labor performed on the realty, the following property **owned by a natural person**:

(1) a homestead,

(i) if located outside a municipality, to the extent of one hundred sixty (160) acres of contiguous land and improvements thereon, which shall not be reduced without the owner's consent by reason of subsequent inclusion in a municipality; or

(ii) if located within a municipality, to the extent of one_half (½) acre of contiguous land, upon which the exemption shall be limited to the residence of the owner or the owner's family;

(2) personal property to the value of one thousand dollars.

(b) These exemptions shall inure to the surviving spouse or heirs of the owner."

The underlined language was added to emphasize certain aspects of the exemption which will be discussed more fully in other parts of this chapter. Now that we have read the exemption, lets proceed with an analysis of what is required to benefit from this exemption.

First, it is interesting to note that the plain language of the Florida constitution does not define the term "homestead." Florida case law, however, has held:

> "In order to qualify his or her property with homestead status, the party seeking the protection of the exemption must have an actual intent to **live permanently on the property and actual use and occupancy of the property**. The mere intent to make the property one's homestead in the future is legally insufficient to entitle a person to a constitutional homestead exemption."

In other words, your homestead is your primary and permanent place of abode and does NOT include a vacation home or any other residence.

Next, there are three primary requirements that must be fulfilled in order to garner the protection of the Florida homestead exemption; namely (i) the residency requirement, (ii) the acreage requirements, and (iii) the ownership requirement. Each of these requirements is discussed in the following paragraphs.

Residency Requirement.

The first requirement to obtaining the benefits of the Florida homestead exemption is that one must be a resident of the state of Florida. In general, in order to be considered a resident of the state of Florida, an individual must maintain a residence in the state and intend to reside in Florida on a permanent basis. For bankruptcy purposes a person must be a Florida resident or domiciliary for the 730 day period preceding the filing of the bankruptcy petition, in order to exclude the homestead for his or her bankruptcy estate. In addition, courts have held that in order to be considered a resident for homestead purposes, a resident alien (i.e., a non-United States citizen residing in the United States) must possess a permanent visa.

Acreage Requirement.

The next, and commonly misunderstood, requirement is that the homestead must fit within certain acreage limitations. In the event you live within city limits (i.e., a municipality) your homestead property must be one-half acre or less in order to be fully protected. In the event you live outside the city limits, the acreage limitation is expanded to 160 acres. This seems rather straight forward, however, there are a few additional points to consider.

What Constitutes Homestead Property?

The first of these points is what is actually included as part of the "homestead property." Below I cover some common questions that have been asked by my clients over the years relevant to this issue.

1. **The Adjoining Lot.** Assume you own a home and have purchased the adjoining lot to serve as an "excess side yard" to your home. Is the adjoining lot part

of your protected homestead? The court answered this question NO in the case of In re Estate of Ritter. It is interesting to note, however, that one of the facts that the court appeared to have given considerable weight to was that the adjoining lot was not fenced in with the residence. Had the home owner constructed a fence around the adjoining lot, thereby making it look and feel as part of the residence, the lot may very well have been protected. The moral of this story is to fence in any adjoining lots you may have. This will strengthen your ability to protect them as part of your homestead.

2. **The Contents of the Homestead.** Another important fact to point out is that the contents of your home are not protected; only the land and the actual structure. For example, the Renoir hanging over your solid gold mantel place is not protected, however, your solid gold mantel place would be. The mantel is protected because it is a fixture (i.e., something permanently affixed to the structure you call home). Maybe it's time to buy that solid gold commode you've had your eye on (I say this only partially with tongue in cheek). In the event your home furnishings are comprised of antiques or other high value assets, you will need to consider them as unprotected assets that need to be integrated into some other facet of your comprehensive asset protection plan.

3. **Mobile Homes, Modular Homes, Co-Ops, and House Boats.** Florida Statutes Section 222.05 reads as follows: "Any person owning and occupying any dwelling house, including a **mobile home** used as a residence, or **modular home**, on land not his or her own which he or she may lawfully possess, by lease or otherwise, and claiming such house, mobile home, or modular home as his or her homestead, shall be entitled to the exemption of such house, mobile home, or modular home from levy and sale as aforesaid." Therefore, under certain circumstances (i.e., the mobile home or modular home is used as someone's permanent place of residence and is permanently connected to utilities) then such a home will be exempt even though the mobile home user is not the owner of the land on which the mobile home sits. With respect to house boats, the courts are split as to whether or not a boat used as someone's permanent residence can receive homestead protection. Because this is a "grey area" of the law with some cases holding that boats cannot receive homestead protection, it is best to explore other means of protecting this asset rather than relying on homestead protection. Finally, courts have also extended homestead protection to fractional interests in property, long term leases, and co-operative

apartments.

4. **Business Improvements.** In the event your homestead is located outside of the city limits, then improvements used in an ongoing business are also protected. These might include barns, storage buildings, silos, etc. In the event your homestead is located inside the city limits then Florida's constitution states that "the exemption shall be limited to the residence of the owner or the owner's family." In other words, no business improvements.

What If My Home Sits on More than One-Half Acre and I am Within City Limits?

Some of you reading this book may be doing so from within your full one acre home that lies within city limits. If so, you are probably wondering what part, if any, of your homestead is protected from creditors. When someone's homestead exceeds one of the two acreage requirements (for the rest of this section I will assume the half acre limitation has been violated), three outcomes are possible.

1. **The Homestead is Fully Protected.** If at the time you purchased your home the property was part of the unincorporated county (i.e., outside a municipality) and the city later annexed your home so that your home is now within city limits, your homestead is most likely fully protected. This stems from the fact that the acreage limitation may not be reduced **without the owner's consent** by reason of subsequent inclusion in a municipality. So if you never consented, your home is safe. Note, however, that if you sell your home to someone, the buyer does not continue to enjoy your "grandfathered" status.

   The homestead may also be fully protected if it is owned by husband and wife jointly as tenants by the entireties (see Chapter 12 for a discussion of tenancy by the entireties ownership) and the creditor only has a judgement against one of the spouses. For example, if a physician is sued for medical malpractice and loses, the judgement creditor will only have a judgement against the physician and not his or her spouse. Therefore, the homestead will be protected by the tenancy by the entireties law, not the homestead exemption.

2. **The Homestead is Partially Protected but the Creditor Cannot Force a Sale of Your Home.** In the event your property can be subdivided into a half acre lot and a second lot **and the second lot is actually useable by the creditor**, then you may keep your half acre homestead and forfeit the remaining lot to the creditor. It is very important to understand that oftentimes this is not a viable option due to the physical layout of your property and/or zoning laws that require minimum lot sizes. Therefore, if you own a home situated on one acre and you happen to live in an area where the minimum permissible lot size is one acre, even if your house was situated so that the lot could actually be physically divided in a manner in which the creditor could receive a full one-half acre lot, since the zoning laws would prevent them from being able to use the lot for residential purposes, a physical partition of the land would not be an available option. Likewise, even if the zoning laws were not an issue, but your home is located smack in the middle of a one acre lot, you would not be permitted to carve off strips of your lot that totaled one-half acre, since the creditor could not practically use that land.

3. **The Creditor Can Force a Sale of Your Home and You will Receive Part of the Sales Proceeds.** The final outcome (if the preceding two options were not available) would be a court ordered sale of your homestead with you receiving a portion of the sales proceeds that represented the protected half acre. For example, if your home sat on 3/4 of an acre and a court ordered the sale of your home, you would receive 2/3 of the sales proceeds since one-half acre is two-thirds of a three quarter acre lot. This forced sale of a homestead was first sanctioned by the court in the case of **Englander v. Mills**. In the subsequent case of **In re Quraeshi**, the court clarified that if a homestead is subject to a mortgage and that homestead is ordered to be sold, what you are entitled to is the relevant percentage of the **net** sales proceeds, NOT the **gross** sales proceeds. Note that this case also limits your ability to argue that the half acre with the residence should be allocated to you (which is obviously much more in your favor) with the balance being allocated to the creditor.

The Ownership Requirement.

While there are a few limited exceptions (i.e., a 99 year lease, for example), in order to garner the protection of the Florida Homestead Exemption, you must be the legal owner of the property. Remember that the Florida Constitution protects property that meets the acreage requirements discussed above **and** that is **owned by a natural person**. Up until very recently, whether or not you could lose your homestead protection by holding your residence in your revocable trust, was a "grey area" and, therefore, some advisors counseled their clients to do just that. Unfortunately, while the issue is not yet black and white, a somewhat recent bankruptcy case entitled **In Re Bosonetto** decided on December 12, 2001, confirmed my fear that a person who owns their homestead in a revocable trust may lose their constitutional homestead protection despite the fact that (i) they are the sole trustee of the trust, (ii) the sole beneficiary of the trust, (iii) vested with the right to terminate the trust at any time and take back the property, and, therefore, the only "real" owner of the property. While it is my opinion that this case constitutes bad law, it is, nonetheless precedent and should be taken very seriously. The loss of your homestead could be devastating. Since the Bosonetto decision, there has thankfully been a few cases that have reached an opposite conclusion (i.e., that a homestead held inside a revocable trust are considered protected), however, these cases have not had the effect of technically overturning Bosonetto. More good news came in the form of Florida's new trust code. Effective July 1, 2007, Florida Statutes Section 736.0505 now provides the following statutory rules:

"(1) Whether or not the terms of a trust contain a spendthrift provision, the following rules apply:

(a) The property of a revocable trust is subject to the claims of the settlor's creditors during the settlor's lifetime to the extent the property would not otherwise be exempt by law if owned directly by the settlor.

While this new statute does not end the problem by itself (since it could be argued that the homestead is still not "owned by a natural person," it still adds an additional argument that a revocable trust is really an estate planning tool and should be considered an extension of the "natural person."

Despite the trend away from the Bosonetto case, if you do not currently hold your home directly in your name(s), I still recommend that you seriously consider taking steps to doing so as soon as possible. Also note that holding your home in a "family limited partnership," limited liability company, corporation, or other legal entity will also cause you to lose your Homestead Exemption (in addition to being a very bad idea for other tax and non-tax reasons). If you do hold your residence in a legal entity, make sure to seek the advice of a competent tax attorney or CPA before attempting to retitle your property in order to avoid any unnecessary income tax consequences.

Exceptions to the Homestead Exemption.

Now that we have examined the basic requirements that must be fulfilled in order to garner the protection of the Florida homestead exemption, it is important to understand some exceptions to the protection offered by the homestead exemption. As noted above, the Florida constitution contains the following three major exceptions:

1. The home is not protected from forced sale from tax liens;

2. The home is not protected from a purchase money mortgagor (i.e., the bank who gave you the money to buy your home); and

3. The home is not protected from creditors who have provided materials and labor to improve the home.

Each of these exceptions make perfect sense since (i) every property owner is required to pay real estate taxes (and, as mentioned above, if you do not pay your income taxes, the IRS is a super creditor), (ii) the lending institution that loaned you the money to purchase your homestead should not be barred from collecting that money by the homestead exemption, and (iii) people who provide goods and services to improve your homestead should likewise be able to collect their fees notwithstanding the homestead exemption.

The Sale of Homestead Property. Are the Proceeds Exempt Too?

The general rule in Florida is that once a homestead is sold, the protection offered by the constitutional homestead protection disappears and does not extend to the sales proceeds. This being said, an important exception to this rule is where the sales proceeds are reinvested in another homestead IF, and only if, certain affirmative steps are taken. Prior to the Florida Supreme Court case of **Orange Brevard Plumbing & Heating Co. v. La Croix**, this result was uncertain, however, the language of this important case (quoted below) provides a useful guide on how to effectively roll the sales proceeds from the sale of an old homestead into a new homestead without subjecting them to the claims of creditors.

"After a full consideration of the applicable authorities representing both views on the issue before us, and in recognition of the liberal interpretation of the homestead exemption to which this court is committed, we hold the proceeds of a voluntary sale of a homestead to be exempt from the claims of creditors just as the homestead itself is exempt **if, and only if,**

1. The vendor [i.e., seller of the homestead] shows, by a preponderance of the evidence an abiding good faith intention prior to and at the time of the sale of the homestead to reinvest the proceeds thereof in another homestead **within a reasonable time.**
2. Moreover, only **so much** of the proceeds of the sale as are intended to be reinvested in another homestead may be exempt under this holding. Any surplus over and above that amount should be treated as general assets of the debtor [i.e., if you buy a less expensive home, any sales proceeds left over after the sale are reachable by creditors].
3. We further hold that in order to satisfy the requirements of the exemption, the funds must not be commingled with other monies of the vendor but must be kept separate and apart and held for the sole purpose of acquiring another home. The proceeds of the sale are not exempt if they are not reinvested in another homestead in a reasonable time or if they are held for the general purposes of the vendor."

Therefore, so long as (i) care is given to document your intention to purchase another Florida homestead within a reasonable time frame, (ii) the new Florida homestead is at least as expensive as the sales price of the old homestead, and (iii) the sales proceeds are kept in a separate bank account earmarked for the purchase of a new Florida homestead and no other moneys are added to that account, then the entire amount received from the sale of the old homestead can be protected from the claims of creditors (assuming a new homestead is purchased in the near future). If you move out of state, however, the sales proceeds may very well be reachable by creditors. Just one more reason to live in sunny Florida.

In addition, it is important to understand that under the implications of changing homesteads under the new bankruptcy laws (please read Chapter 7 for an overview of this new law). For example, in the event you have lived in your present homestead for greater than the 1,215 day period necessary to avoid the $125,000 cap and then sell your present homestead and buy a new homestead, (i) the equity from your first home can be rolled over into your new home, and (ii) you are starting a new 1,215 period with respect to any new equity that is acquired in the new homestead. If you have not yet lived in your present homestead for at least 1,215 days and have significant appreciation in your homestead, you may want to consider living there for the time necessary to meet this 1,215 day rule before putting your home on the market. Knowing these rules may prove to be very important if you ever found yourself in bankruptcy.

Homestead Exemption vs. Fraudulent Conveyance.

The issue of whether someone could intentionally convert non-exempt assets (i.e., assets that would be ordinarily reachable by a creditor) into an exempt homestead was always a grey area of law since courts have warned on several occasions that the homestead exemption should not be used as a tool to defraud creditors. The Florida Supreme Court, however, allowed an individual to do just that in the case of **Havoco of America, Ltd. v. Elmer C. Hill**. The following question was certified to the Florida Supreme Court by the Eleventh Circuit:

> Does Article X, Section 4 of Florida Constitution exempt a Florida Homestead where the debtor acquired the homestead using non_exempt funds with the specific intent of hindering, delaying or defrauding creditors in violation of Fla. Stats. 726.105, 222.29 or 222.30?

The Florida Supreme Court answered this question YES.

Elmer C. Hill, a resident of the state of Tennessee, had been sued and a judgement was entered against him on December 19, 1990 (the enforcability of the judgement had been delayed, however, until January 2, 1991). Mr. Hill, knowing that the creditors would be able to reach a large sum of personal assets, purchased a Florida homestead to keep those assets from his creditors on December 30, 1990 (just a few days before the judgement became effective). Of course, the creditors claimed that converting his non-exempt assets to an exempt homestead should be considered a fraudulent transfer (or technically a fraudulent conversion). As stated above, the Florida Supreme Court held that despite the fact that Mr. Hill purchased the homestead with the **specific intent to hinder, delay, and defraud** his creditors (you may remember that language from the previous discussion on fraudulent transfers), his home was not reachable by his creditors because (i) the facts did not fall into one of the three exceptions to the Homestead stated in the Florida Constitution, and (ii) the Homestead Exemption is constitutional while the fraudulent conveyance laws are merely statutory (i.e., the legislature does not have the power to deprive Florida residents of a constitutional right by enacting a statute).

In addition to allowing someone to shelter unprotected assets by buying a new home at the eleventh hour, this case also seems to permit an individual to pay down an existing mortgage to protect those assets after a creditor has been identified (or a law suit has been filed) and avoid the consequences of the fraudulent transfer laws. A person may similarly be able to ameliorate the value of their homestead (i.e., add a new room, put in a pool, etc.) to shelter assets from a known creditor.

The bankruptcy laws do pose a couple downsides. First, a special provision of the law (i.e., Bankruptcy Code § 727(a)(2)) allows a court to deny a bankruptcy discharge (i.e., allows the debt to continue even after bankruptcy rather than extinguishing the debt) if the person going through bankruptcy transfers property within one year of filing the bankruptcy petition with intent to hinder, delay, or defraud a creditor. The court may also issue additional sanctions such as prohibiting the person from filing for bankruptcy again for a prolonged period of time. Second, under the new bankruptcy act, there is now the new ten year look back rule that will subject any property fraudulently transferred into a homestead within ten years from the date a bankruptcy petition is filed to being reached by creditors. This rule only applies in bankruptcy, so if you can avoid ending up in bankruptcy for a ten year period after you transfer property into your homestead this rule will not work against you. If you are forced into bankruptcy through an involuntary bankruptcy, the Elmer Hill technique will not provide any benefit.

It is also important to note that two cases decided in 2002, have placed significant importance on the timing of the judgement in relationship to when the homestead is established. Take, for example the case of **In Re MacGillivray**. In this case decided on October 29, 2002, a judgement was filed against a Mr. Thomas

MacGillivray back on April 7, 1998. Almost two years later, Mr. MacGillivray purchased a residence in Jupiter, Florida. Roughly six months after the purchase of the residence, Mr. MacGillivray filed for bankruptcy. The court held that since the homestead was purchased after the judgement was recorded, the Florida homestead exemption did not prevent the judgement from creating a lien on the property and, therefore, the property was not exempt from the claims of the creditor. Note that in the case of **Havoco v. Hill** discussed above, Mr. Hill purchased the property just before the judgement became enforceable. Timing really is everything.

Likewise, in the event you buy a home but do not move in and use it as your "permanent place of abode" and later, a judgement is entered against you, moving into the home and making it your permanent and primary residence **post-judgement** will not provide the property the protection of the Florida homestead exemption. The homestead must be established prior to the recording of the judgement.

Finally, I want to point out that there is a series of cases that permit a court to impose what is called an "equitable lien" on homestead property in the event an individual acts "egregiously, reprehensibly, or fraudulently" prior to establishing their homestead. An equitable lien gives a creditor the right to receive payment if and when the homestead is sold, but not the right to force a sale of the homestead. Examples of egregious, reprehensible, or fraudulent conduct may include using assets obtained through illegal or fraudulent means to purchase the homestead. In the event the conduct rose to an extreme level, it may be possible for a creditor to actually force a sale of the homestead.

Homes Under Construction.

Property on which you plan to build a home or even property on which you are currently building a home is not protected by the Florida homestead exemption. Therefore, during the construction phase, it may be wise to use some other means to protect the land such as by titling it as tenants by the entireties (discussed in Chapter 12) if possible.

The Question of Whether to Have a Large or Small Mortgage on Homestead Property.

Many professionals are divided on the issue of whether someone engaging in asset protection planning should maintain a large mortgage on their homestead or whether they should maintain a large amount of equity in the homestead. Unfortunately, the answer to this question depends on many financial, tax, and asset protection variables so a black and white answer is not possible. Determining the correct answer for you will involve some value judgements and may end up landing somewhere between these two extremes. Below I have tried to summarize the upsides and downsides of both extremes.

1. **Asset Protection Considerations.** The primary upside to maximizing the equity in your homestead (i.e., maintaining a small or no mortgage) from a pure asset protection standpoint is that the homestead laws in the great state of Florida are very strong as evidenced in the previous sections of this chapter. Your home equity, therefore, is very safe (assuming a stable real estate market). The next considerations of which to be cognitive in deciding whether or not to pay off your mortgage are:

   a. How well protected the mortgage proceeds are in the event you choose to carry a mortgage; and
   b. How confident are you that Florida's unlimited homestead exemption will continue into the future.

   If you personally believe that future bankruptcy law changes are unlikely to ever affect the strength of the homestead exemption beyond what they have already done, and/or you do not feel the alternative methods of protecting your assets are as secure given your particular situation, then maximizing your home equity would make perfect sense. If, on the other hand, you are fearful that the homestead exemption may one day suffer in effectiveness due to future legislative action, and/or your other means of protecting assets given your personal facts and circumstances are very strong, then maintaining a low mortgage balance would make perfect sense. If you have not done so already, you should also read Chapter 7 for a discussion of the new bankruptcy law's effect on homestead property. For example, if you have lived in your homestead for less than the required 1,215 day period and are fearful of being forced into bankruptcy, then you would not want more than $125,000 in home equity. Likewise, if you are comfortable with the potential risk of not receiving a discharge in bankruptcy associated with paying off an existing mortgage with non-exempt (i.e., unprotected assets), then using that strategy as part of your overall asset protection plan would be a good option.

Another point to consider is that Florida law allows a married couple to own bank accounts and brokerage accounts as "tenants by the entireties" (see Chapter 12), a form of ownership that protects the property from the claims of a creditor who only holds a judgement against one spouse. If one spouse is sued and the couple wishes to use tenancy by the entireties property (I will call this TBE property, for short) to pay off the mortgage, the potential negatives of using non-exempt assets to pay off a mortgage "after the fact" will likely not apply since the creditor would not have been entitled to the TBE property in the first place. This is just one example of how the TBE form of property ownership can be helpful in asset protection planning.

2. **Financial / Tax Considerations.** Another main area to consider is the financial benefit of maintaining a mortgage. In the event you can obtain a mortgage at a good or excellent interest rate, maintaining a large mortgage may have some real economic benefits. First, at the time the first edition of this book was written, Americans were enjoying the lowest interest rates in decades. Second, home mortgage interest is tax deductible which is meaningful for those individuals who elect to itemize deductions on their tax return and is increasingly beneficial for those people in the highest income tax brackets. For example, if you can obtain a 30 year fixed mortgage for 5.5% and happen to be well into the top marginal income tax bracket of 35%, the effective interest rate (i.e., the real interest rate you are paying taking into consideration your tax savings) would be in the neighborhood of 3.5%. If you invested the mortgage proceeds and received a rate of return greater than 3.5% (say 5%), the difference of 1.5% is profit to you. Another advantage is that even if interest rates on bonds are low and volatility in the stock market has scared many investors away, if you can lock in 3.5% money that can be used over the next 30 years, there will assuredly be many opportunities during that time frame to profit from this interest rate arbitrage. Likewise, in the event home mortgage interest rates were to increase to a point where it would be difficult to receive a return on your money greater than the effective, after tax interest rate, paying off your mortgage would make imminent financial sense. While a qualified and honest financial planner or investment professional will be a great help to you in making this analysis given your risk tolerance and financial objectives, less than honorable people in the financial services industry may encourage

you to maintain a high mortgage balance regardless of the interest rate on your mortgage, especially if they are paid a percentage of the assets you have invested in the market or, even worse, if they are the ones getting paid to help you obtain the mortgage in the first place. Just make sure you understand the math behind what you are doing and be realistic with respect to the projected rate of return on invested assets.

Another financial issue in the decision of whether or not to carry a large mortgage balance is that of liquidity. It may simply not be prudent or practicable to use your home equity as a "bank account" since you may need access to that money for emergencies or simply to support your lifestyle. Since lines of credit typically bear a much higher rate of interest than a standard home mortgage, accessing your home equity, if needed, may be an expensive proposition.

3. **Emotional Considerations.** A final consideration in deciding how large a mortgage balance you wish to maintain has nothing to do with money, taxes, or asset protection. Many people are deeply comforted knowing that they have their home payed off regardless of the potential for profitable interest rate arbitrage. I am a strong believer that if the planning you are engaging in does not provide you with a deeper sense of security and comfort, you should continue your quest to find a planning solution that allows you to sleep well at night. Failure to take your emotional considerations into account is foolish, and any professional who tries to coerce you into a planning strategy that ignores these factors should be dismissed and replaced with someone more sensitive to these important issues (provided they also have the requisite technical skill).

Planning Recommendations.

1. **Fence in Adjoining Lots.** In the event you own an adjoining lot that you use as an extended yard, you should seriously consider fencing it in so that the lot appears to the rest of the world to be part and parcel of the primary homestead property. Failure to do so may result in the loss of that lot in the event a creditor obtains a judgement against you.

2. **Do Not Hold Your Homestead in Your Revocable Trust.** For the reasons explained above, in the event you currently own your home in your revocable

trust, take steps to retitle it in your individual name(s) (use TBE ownership if you are a married couple). Failure to do so could result in the loss of your home and there are very few upsides to having your revocable trust own your homestead property.

3. **Own Property as Tenants by the Entireties.** Married couples should own their homestead as tenants by the entireties. This is the default type of ownership in the state of Florida, so if your current deed reads John Doe and Jane Doe, husband and wife, you already have TBE property. Beware that if you purchased your home jointly before you were married and then subsequently married, you do NOT have TBE property and you should sign a new deed to give you the added protection of TBE ownership.

4. **Married Couples Should Consider Insurance to Protect Homestead Property that Exceeds the Acreage Requirements.** The insurance planning strategy discussed in detail in Chapter 12 on Tenancy by the Entireties ownership should be considered in the event a married couple owns their homestead as TBE and the homestead property exceeds the constitutional homestead requirements. Therefore, in the event one spouse has a judgement against him or her, and the other spouse dies, the insurance proceeds can be used to buy the homestead and hold it in a special type of trust designed to keep it from the claims of the judgement creditor. Note that this does not protect the asset as much as it replaces it, because the sales proceeds received by the surviving spouse with the judgement will be reachable by the judgement creditor.

5. **Consider Using a Delaware Qualified Personal Residence Trust to Protect Homestead Property that Exceeds the Acreage Requirements.** A Qualified Personal Residence Trust (sometimes called a "QPRT") is a specialized trust where one transfers a residence to the trust, and reserves the right to live in it for a set period of time (called a "term"). After the term expires, the house passes to someone else (typically children or a trust created for their benefit). There are estate planning benefits associated with QPRTs, however, they are considered Self-Settled Trusts which carries with it various creditor protection problems if it is created under the laws of Florida (see Chapter 19 for more details). If, however, you create a QPRT under the laws of Delaware, you may be able to avoid the Self-Settled Trust problems and protect a homestead that is otherwise unprotected under Florida law.

6. **Understand Your Mortgage Options.** Make sure you fully understand your options with respect to how big a mortgage to carry on your homestead. As mentioned above, this decision will be based on a combination of asset protection, financial, tax, and emotional considerations. All of these should be discussed with your asset protection attorney with input from your accountant and financial advisor.

7. **Increase the Value of Your Homestead Using Non-exempt Assets If You Are Sued.** In the event you are sued and have unprotected (i.e., non-exempt) assets that may be subject to the claims of the would-be judgement creditor, you should consider engaging in "Elmer Hill" type planning to shield those assets on an "after the fact" basis.

8. **Understand the Implications of the New Bankruptcy Laws.** Please read Chapter 7 for a discussion of the new bankruptcy law's effect on homestead property. While this new act will only affect you if you end up in bankruptcy, it needs to be understood and taken into account when constructing your asset protection plan.

Conclusion.

The Florida homestead exemption is a powerful tool in your arsenal of asset protection strategies, but there are many considerations and traps for the unwary. This Chapter has armed you with the knowledge to make informed decisions about planning to protect your home and you should use this knowledge in discussing your options with your asset protection attorney. Your home is sometimes your largest asset and usually represents financial and personal security from an emotional standpoint. Do not let it go unprotected.

CHAPTER 10

Protecting Retirement Plan Assets

Whether or not retirement plan assets are protected from the claims of creditors is possibly one of the most important questions for a physician to clearly understand and, unfortunately, it is one of the most misunderstood areas of asset protection planning. This stems in large part from the fact that the law in this area has historically been very complex and has required an understanding of numerous bodies of law and how they overlap and interrelate.

Since the first edition of this book was published, the enactment of the new bankruptcy act and a new Florida statute has helped simplify the complexity in this area and has also broadened the protection to include more types of retirement plans and add clarity as to what is needed to ensure they remain protected over time. While I generally feel the new bankruptcy act is a horrible piece of legislation, this is one area that it has admittedly helped.

The Legal Analysis.

The first question that needs to be answered when determining whether a particular retirement plan of yours protected, is whether or not you are in bankruptcy? If you are not in bankruptcy, Florida state law exemptions will determine whether your retirement accounts are protected. If you are in bankruptcy, the federal bankruptcy laws will provide the basis for the exempt or non-exempt nature of your retirement plan. As discussed in Chapter 7, if one or more of your retirement plans (maybe IRAs) would be protected under Florida state law but unprotected under the federal bankruptcy laws, you may want to consider taking affirmative steps to avoid being forced into involuntary bankruptcy in the future.

The Old Law.

Before I delve into a discussion of the present law, I want to give you a quick overview of the old law in order for you to better understand the changes brought about by the new laws. The analysis under the old law was complex and often gave people large headaches when trying to wrap their brains around all the relevant issues. The brief explanation set forth below is meant to give you a bird's eye view of the issues (remember that I have essentially condensed an entire Chapter of my last book into a couple paragraphs). If you are having problems understanding it, do not worry. It no longer applies.

The analysis started with Section 541(c)(2) of the bankruptcy code which excludes property from the bankruptcy estate (rendering it asset protected) if it is held in a trust which contains:

> "a **restriction on the transfer** of a **beneficial interest** of the debtor ...that is enforceable under **applicable nonbankruptcy law...**"

Since most retirement accounts are technically trusts, the next step was to see if such a restriction was present in the retirement plan at hand. Many (but not all) retirement plans are subject to The Employee Retirement Security Act of 1974 ("ERISA"). The United States Supreme Court held in the case of Patterson v. Shumate that if a retirement plan is subject to Part 2 of Title 1 of ERISA, then the plan would be exempt because ERISA Section 206(d)(1) requires it to contain a provision that prohibits the plan benefits from being assigned or alienated (i.e., transferred). If a retirement plan is subject to ERISA but not subject to Part 2 of Title 1, then it is not required to contain the "anti-transfer rule" and, therefore, is not a protected plan.

To muddy waters further, some plans that would ordinarily be subject to Part 2 of Title 1 of ERISA (such as 401k plans), were not required to contain the "anti-transfer" restriction if the only people participating in the retirement plans were owners of the business and/or their spouses. Whether the business in question was a corporation or a partnership also entered into the equation. Uncertainty also surrounded SEP IRAs (which are basically part IRA and part ERISA plan), SIMPLE IRAs, certain 403(b) plans, and KEOGH plans, to name few. IRAs were protected under Florida state law, however, in the event you moved to another state that did not protect IRAs, you could lose this protection since they were only nominally protected under federal law.

But wait, Florida Statute Section 222.21 provided that a retirement plan "that is qualified under section 401(a) [such as a 401k plan], section 403(a), section 403(b), section 408, section 408A, or section 409 of the Internal Revenue Code of 1986, as amended, is exempt from all claims of creditors of the beneficiary or participant;" wouldn't this statute provide protection under state law, even if a retirement plan was not subject to Part 2 of Title 1 of ERISA? Unfortunately, case law interpreting this statute held that the plan must **ALSO** be exempt under federal law (i.e., covered by Part 2 of Title 1 of ERISA) in order for the plan to be protected even though the statute itself did not explicitly state as such.

Finally, numerous cases interpreting the old statute held that in the event a retirement plan fails to meet the requirements for continued qualification under the Internal Revenue Code, any asset protection that would have ordinarily been afforded the plan disappears with the plan's qualified status. In many of these cases, the IRS had not taken any action to disqualify the plan, however, the court later determined that the plan in question was not properly maintained. Given the fact that the rules and regulations pertaining to retirement plans are highly complex, it is next to impossible for any lay person to accurately determine whether the plan is continuing to comply with all requirements imposed by law especially given the frequency in which the law in this area changes.

As you can see from this brief overview, given the numerous areas of law that had to be taken into account in determining whether a retirement plan was protected and the fact that there were oftentimes gray areas that were not directly addressed, planning in this area was complex and oftentimes included some degree of uncertainty.

The New Law.

Thankfully, the enactment of the new bankruptcy act and certain amendments to Florida Statutes Section 222.21, now makes determining whether your retirement plan is exempt much easier. In addition, more plans are now considered exempt.

The New Bankruptcy Act.

On April 20, 2005, George W. Bush signed the bankruptcy act into law (I will call refer to it as"BAPCPA" for short). While I generally feel the new bankruptcy act is a horrible piece of legislation, it admittedly did help eliminate much of the complexity and uncertainty when it comes to determining whether a retirement plan is asset protected.

Plans Only Need to be Tax Exempt.

The principal change made by BAPCPA is that "retirement funds to the extent that those funds are in a fund or account that is **exempt from taxation** under section 401, 403, 408, 408A, 414, 457, or 501(a) of the Internal Revenue Code of 1986" are now considered to be exempt from the claims of bankruptcy creditors. Now, rather than having to determine whether or not a specific type of retirement plan is subject to Part 2 of Title 1 of ERISA, the focus is on whether or not the plan is exempt from taxation. This is obviously a huge improvement over the old law. Because the ERISA analysis has effectively been eliminated, retirement plans that only cover owners should now be completely protected as well as single person 401k plans and Keogh plans. This also clears up the gray areas surrounding SEP IRAs, SIMPLE IRAs, and 403(b) plans, which are now clearly protected (SEP IRAs and SIMPLE IRAs even have a small advantage).

Requirement that Plans be Properly Maintained.

Another benefit bestowed by BAPCPA is that you can sleep a little easier with respect to whether your retirement plan is being properly maintained. BAPCPA added Section 522(b)(4) to the bankruptcy code which now provides that (i) if a plan has received a favorable determination letter from the IRS, the plan's funds shall be presumed to be exempt from the bankruptcy estate (i.e., they are protected). Even if a determination letter has not been obtained, the plan funds will be exempt if you can show that the IRS has not specifically determined that the plan is not in compliance, and either (i) the plan is in substantial compliance or, if it is not, (ii) you were not materially responsible for that failure. While this does not completely absolve you of the responsibility to make sure your plan is being properly maintained, it does significantly reduce the likelihood that a would-be creditor could effectively argue that your plan should lose its exempt status based on some technical issue of noncompliance.

Notwithstanding this new lower standard, I still highly recommend that you maintain a relationship with an attorney who specializes in ERISA and retirement plans who can inform you of any changes to the plan or methods of operating the plan over time. I will have more to say on this topic at the end of this Chapter.

IRAs.

Prior to the enactment of BAPCPA, IRAs were not specifically exempted under the bankruptcy code. This was not of much interest to Floridians since IRAs are exempt under our state law, and, therefore, exempt in bankruptcy as well. In 2005, the United States Supreme Court held in the case of Rousey v. Jacoway that IRAs were exempt since they were similar to other exempt retirement plans specifically set forth in Section 522(d)(10)(E) of the bankruptcy code (i.e., one of the exemptions provided for under federal law). Many individuals took this to mean that even in states where IRAs are not exempted under state law, IRAs were now completely beyond the reach of creditors. Unfortunately, this was not the case. Even though an IRA was deemed to be covered by the federal exemption statute (i.e., Section 522(d)(10)(E)) that section limits the amount exempted "to the extent reasonably necessary for the support of the debtor and any dependent of the debtor." What this amount would actually be is obviously subject to interpretation, however, one could certainly imagine a scenario where the entire IRA would not be protected.

BAPCPA now changes this result. Under BAPCPA all IRAs are now exempt under federal law, subject to certain rules and limitations. Because of a quirk in the way BAPCPA was drafted, IRAs are actually now protected under both federal law and Florida state law. Since the language of the two statutes are not the same (although they do share some similar elements), there may be some opportunity to argue that Florida's more generous law should prevail, however, these arguments are most likely tenuous at best.

The One Million Dollar Cap. The first, and arguably most publicized, of these limitations is the new $1,000,000 cap on the protection offered by IRAs. New Section 522(n) reads in relevant part as follows:

> "For assets in [traditional IRAs and Roth IRAs] [**but not including SEP IRAs and SIMPLE IRAs**], the aggregate value of such assets exempted under this section, **without regard to amounts attributable to rollover contributions** . . . , and earnings thereon, **shall not exceed $1,000,000** in a case filed by a debtor who is an individual, except that such amount may be increased if the **interests of justice** so require."

Therefore, IRAs are generally protected only up to $1,000,000. A big exception to this general rule is that amounts rolled over from certain other types of retirement plans to IRAs are not subject to this cap (see discussion below). There is also an argument, that since IRAs are protected under both federal law and state law, that Florida's exemption should be used which is obviously not subject to the $1,000,000 cap. I have not yet found anything that gives any insight into what would justify increasing the $1,000,000 to serve the "interests of justice." Only time will tell how these issues will eventually play out.

Rollovers: The first item to take away from the language of the new section is that amounts rolled over from qualified plans such as 401ks appear to be excluded from the $1,000,000 cap. Since the onus will rest with you to prove that amounts held in an IRA actually originated from an eligible rollover, it is recommended that any assets you roll over from one of these plans be held in a separate IRA and not commingled with other IRAs. For example:

> "Dr. Chrysostomos has a 401k plan at his present place of employment that has grown to $900,000. He also has an IRA he has been contributing to over the years with a balance of $350,000. Dr. Chrysostomos decides to open his own practice and leave his current employer. Upon leaving, he decides to roll the assets from his 401k to an IRA. Since he already has an IRA in place he decides to just roll the 401k assets into that IRA for simplicity's sake. He is not the best record keeper and ends up being sued several years later. Unfortunately, Dr. Chrysostomos loses his case and is now faced with a judgement creditor. His assets are all protected and he is ready to retire, so he files for bankruptcy to rid himself of the judgment. The creditor sees that his IRA is worth close to $1,500,000 and argues that he should be

> entitled to the $500,000 above and beyond the $1,000,000 cap. Dr. Chrysostomos now has to prove that $900,000 was rolled over from his old 401k plan in order to avoid losing $500,000, which may not be easy given the commingling and his poor record keeping. He now wishes that at the time of the rollover, he had opened a second IRA to receive the assets. If he had named that IRA the "Dr. Chrysostomos Rollover IRA" and saved the rollover documentation, he would have saved himself a lot of headaches and possibly even $500,000.

Typically, the best way to accomplish a rollover of assets from one plan to another is by way of a Trustee-to-Trustee rollover where the assets never pass through your hands. BAPCPA makes clear that the assets so rolled will not lose their exempt status in the process. Under some circumstances you may choose not to use the Trustee-to-Trustee method in which case you withdraw plan assets and must then deposit them in a another eligible plan in order to keep the assets from being taxed. BAPCPA also provides that the assets remain exempt even during the period they reside with you outside a retirement plan.

Another point on the topic of rollovers is that if you want to roll assets from a 403(b) plan or 457 plan over to any IRA, use a SEP IRA or a SIMPLE IRA since these IRAs are not subject to the $1,000,000 cap (see below). In addition, although most qualified plans will qualify for this rollover benefit, SEP IRAs and SIMPLE IRAs do not qualify. Therefore, if you roll a $1,200,000 401k plan into an IRA, the entire rollover IRA is protected since the rolled assets qualify for the rollover benefit. If you roll a $1,200,000 SEP IRA into a traditional IRA, however, the traditional IRA will only be protected up to $1,000,000 (maybe less if you have other IRAs), since rollovers from SEP IRAs and SIMPLE IRAs do not qualify for the rollover benefit as is the case with 401k plans.

There are still several unanswered questions regarding these new rollover rules. For example, if you rolled assets from a 401k plan to an IRA and then roll that IRA to another IRA, did you just blow your rollover exception and subject those assets to the $1,000,000 cap? What if you first rolled assets in a traditional IRA to a 401k plan, and later roll those assets back out of the 401k plan to another IRA. Do you get the full rollover exemption? And what if you die owning an exempt "rollover IRA?" Does you spouse continue to get the exclusion? Once again, it will take some time to ferret out the answers to these questions.

SEP IRAs and SIMPLE IRAs are not Subject to the Cap. Another thing to take notice of is that SEP IRAs and Simple IRAs have been specifically excluded from the $1,000,000 cap. Therefore, in the event you have one of these accounts and were considering rolling the assets over to a traditional IRA, you would be better served by NOT doing so and leaving those assets where they are. The general rule regarding SEP and SIMPLE IRAs is that you should either (i) keep assets in these types of accounts, and/or (ii) roll assets TO these types of accounts. If you roll assets FROM a SEP or SIMPLE IRA it does not appear to qualify for the "roll over exception" discussed above.

Under the prior law, there was a concern that SEP IRAs were not as protective as traditional IRAs and many individuals transferred these accounts to increase their protection. Now it appears that doing so has subjected those rolled assets to the $1,000,000 cap. This is one example of why you need to revisit your asset protection planning periodically to ensure that what you have done continues to be effective.

Florida Law.

Florida Statute Section 222.21. Florida Statute Section 222.21 is Florida's state law that protects certain retirement plans from the claims of creditors. State laws of this type are often referred to as "shield laws." Florida's shield law was amended in 2005 and now reads much like the new federal exemption for retirement plans. It reads in relevant part:

"[A]ny money or other assets **payable to an owner, a participant, or a beneficiary** from, or **any interest of any owner, participant, or beneficiary** in, a fund or account is exempt from all claims of creditors of the owner, beneficiary, or participant if the fund or account is:

1. **Maintained in accordance with a master plan, volume submitter plan, prototype plan, or any other plan or governing instrument that has been preapproved by the Internal Revenue Service as exempt from taxation** under s.

401(a), s. 403(a), s. 403(b), s. 408, s. 408A, s. 409, s. 414, s. 457(b), or s. 501(a) of the Internal Revenue Code of 1986, as amended, unless it has been subsequently determined that the plan or governing instrument is not exempt from taxation in a proceeding that has become final and nonappealable;

2. **Maintained in accordance with a plan or governing instrument that has been determined by the Internal Revenue Service to be exempt from taxation** under s. 401(a), s. 403(a), s. 403(b), s. 408, s. 408A, s. 409, s. 414, s. 457(b), or s. 501(a) of the Internal Revenue Code of 1986, as amended, unless it has been subsequently determined that the plan or governing instrument is not exempt from taxation in a proceeding that has become final and nonappealable; or

3. Not maintained in accordance with a plan or governing instrument described in subparagraph 1. or subparagraph 2. if the person claiming exemption under this paragraph proves by a preponderance of the evidence that the fund or account is maintained in accordance with a plan or governing instrument that:

a. **Is in substantial compliance** with the applicable requirements for tax exemption under s. 401(a), s. 403(a), s. 403(b), s. 408, s. 408A, s. 409, s. 414, s. 457(b), or s. 501(a) of the Internal Revenue Code of 1986, as amended; or

b. **Would have been in substantial compliance** with the applicable requirements for tax exemption under s. 401(a), s. 403(a), s. 403(b), s. 408, s. 408A, s. 409, s. 414, s. 457(b), or s. 501(a) of the Internal Revenue Code of 1986, as amended, **but for the negligent or wrongful conduct of a person or persons other than the person who is claiming the exemption under this section."**

The first thing to note is that since specific sections of the Internal Revenue Code are used to define which types of retirement accounts are protected, Florida Statute Section 222.21 now paints with a very wide brush exempting 401k plans, profit sharing plans, money purchase plans, Traditional IRAs, Roth IRAs, SEP IRAs, SIMPLE IRAs, 403(b) plans, Keough Plans, 457 plans, and even certain church and government plans. Note, however, that deferred compensation plans are NOT protected (see page for more information).

Second, Florida's new amended shield statute incorporates language that makes it hard for someone to reach the plan assets by arguing that the plan is technically not in compliance with the relevant Internal Revenue Code sections. As mentioned above and as further explained below, this should not be used as an excuse to be haphazard in properly maintaining your retirement plan.

Another benefit of the Florida shield statute is that retirement plans that are protected under federal law alone (such as would be the case for someone who lived in a state that did not protect certain retirement accounts) only offer protection while the assets are held in the plan. In other words, once distributions are made from the plan, the assets become reachable by the claims of creditors. The Florida shield statute cures this unsavory result by protecting distributions from retirement plans as well. In fact, the 2001 case of **In Re Ladd** states that if distributions are made from a retirement plan and are kept in a segregated bank account (i.e., a bank account that contains the distributions and ONLY the distributions), those assets continue to maintain their protected status. The same also holds true for IRAs.

Therefore, in addition to our beautiful weather and beaches, Florida residents also enjoy the significant benefits of the Florida shield statute. Although I have mentioned this fact earlier in this book, if your creditor happens to be a "Super Creditor" (i.e., the IRS or your spouse), the Florida shield statute provides no asset protection.

The Importance of Maintaining the Qualification of Your Retirement Plan.

After the enactment of BAPCPA the determination of whether or not your retirement plan is protected from creditors' claims will be based on its qualification under one of the enumerated sections of the Internal Revenue Code. Therefore, you have a significant vested interest in making sure your plan stays tax exempt for both tax and asset protection reasons. Thankfully, both BAPCPA and the amended Florida shield statute have made it more difficult for someone to reach the plan assets by arguing that the plan is technically not in compliance with the relevant Internal Revenue Code sections, however, it is still possible for a plan to cease to be in "substantial compliance" due to the complex nature of the rules and regulations pertaining to retirement plans and the fact that they change on a fairly regular basis.

One way to protect yourself, as mentioned above, is to maintain a relationship with an attorney who specializes in ERISA and retirement plans who can inform you of any changes that need to be made to (i) the plan, or (ii) the methods of operating the plan over time. In addition, with respect to certain types of plans, various reporting requirements need to be met (filing IRS Form 5500 for example). Failure to keep on top of these requirements can result in loss of asset protection for an otherwise qualified retirement plan even with the new lower standards.

One particularly dangerous area involves what are called "prohibited transactions." Examples of prohibited transactions include, (i) a sale or exchange, or leasing of retirement plan assets between the plan and any "disqualified person" (i.e., the plan owner, members of his or her family, certain legal entities owned in whole or in part by the plan owner or family members, etc.), and (ii) use of plan assets by or for the benefit of a disqualified person. This list is NOT all inclusive and various other acts of "self-dealing" can also cause a retirement plan to lose its qualification. For example, any traditional IRA established with a financial institution will typically be tax qualified and, therefore, protected, however once the IRA is established, if you, as the IRA owner, engage in a "prohibited transaction," the IRA will cease to be a qualified IRA **as of the first day of the tax year in which the "prohibited transaction" occurs.** This can obviously have devastating results if you happened to have been named in a law suit earlier in the year. In short, it is important to understand these rules especially if you own a "self-directed IRA" that can hold assets such as real estate and interests in closely held companies (i.e., companies that are not publically traded and in which you have any ownership interest or control over).

Anytime you want to engage in any transaction with the plan (i.e., selling property to the plan, loaning or borrowing money to the plan, purchasing real estate or investments other than publically traded stocks and bonds, etc.) make sure it is first discussed with and approved by your ERISA attorney **in writing** before proceeding. I have personally seen physicians engage in "prohibited transactions" with their retirement plans based on their own personal reading of the plan documents. Learn from their mistakes and don't risk jeopardizing one of your most important assets.

Conclusion.

BAPCPA and Florida's amended shield statute have taken much of the complexity out of determining whether or not your retirement plan is protected, but you still need to understand the exceptions, especially as they pertain to IRAs. If you take the time to understand the rules and properly maintain your retirement plan, however, your retirement plan can be an excellent asset protection tool.

CHAPTER 11

Protecting Your Wages

This Chapter provides a detailed explanation of the Wage Exemption granted under Florida law and will make you aware of some of the pitfalls that exist so they can be avoided in the future. It also provides you with instructions on how to create and maintain "wage accounts" to protect your future earnings from being garnished.

Benefits of Protecting Your Wages.

The benefits of having your wages exempt from attachment or garnishment by creditors are obviously significant. First, in the event you were ever sued for medical malpractice (or faced with some other judgement creditor), if you follow the procedures described later in this Chapter and establish and maintain a "wage account," your ability to continue to fund your personal asset protection plan after the law suit is filed will be significantly improved. If a wage account is not established, each transfer made after a potential law suit is identified may be subject to the fraudulent transfer laws with the creditor potentially being able to unwind those transfers and reach the transferred assets. Second, if a judgement was obtained by a would-be creditor, you will be in a much better negotiating position with your future earnings "off the table" so to speak. Since the cost of establishing a wage account is practically nothing, every physician who can effectively protect their earnings with a wage account has no excuse not to establish one.

Overview of the Wage Exemption.

Florida Statutes Section 222.11 provides that a creditor may not garnish or otherwise reach someone's "earnings" if that person qualifies as "head of family," unless they have agreed to the contrary in writing. This constitutes protection at the employer level (i.e., the creditor cannot force the employer to take a portion of your paycheck and pay it to the creditor). If the earnings are then "credited or deposited in any financial institution," the earnings that are payed out to you will be "exempt from attachment or garnishment for **6 months** after the earnings are received by the financial institution **if the funds can be traced and properly identified as earnings.**" If you are not a "head of family," only 75% of the earnings will be exempt (assuming the other requirements are met). In such a circumstance, it will be important to establish a history of receiving wages for federal tax purposes as opposed to distributions. If you do not do so (to save the 2.9% medicare tax, for example), you may not even be able to protect the full 75% mentioned above. While this statutory rule appears to be rather straightforward on its face, the case law interpreting the statute has created traps for the unwary.

Definition of Head of Family.

The first, and more straightforward, issue to address is the definition of "head of family." The Florida statute defines "head of family" as "any natural person who is providing more than one_half of the support for a child or other dependent." The term "dependent" is not defined in the statute, however, case law has held that any moral obligation to support another may be sufficient to satisfy the "head of family" requirement. Given this broad definition, spouses, minor and adult children, parents, and other family members for whom you provide more than 50% of their support would clearly qualify as dependants.

Definition of Earnings.

The second, and less straightforward, issue to address is the definition of "earnings." The definition provided by the statute is "compensation paid or payable, in money of a sum certain, for **personal services or labor** whether denominated as wages, salary, commission, or bonus." Case law interpreting this definition has held that "the fruits of someone's labor for the benefit of his family" is protected but **not** "income from passive sources, such as investment income **or return on**

capital." In short, the intent of the statute appears to have been to protect the classic "employee" who works for another to provide for his or her family.

The first exception to this rule which may not be readily apparent is that a sole practitioner cannot avail him or herself of the wage exemption despite the fact that they earn their money providing personal services. The court in making its analysis has focused on whether a person has an "arms length agreement" with the employer. Since a sole practitioner or a person who owns a controlling interest in the corporation or other legal entity that employs him or her cannot make an "arms length agreement," they lose the protection of the wage exemption. The court stated that people who run their own businesses have control over the timing and amount of their compensation and whether the monies they receive are classified as distributions or earnings. While I feel that this conclusion is bad law as it discriminates against heads of family who market their services directly rather than through employers, it has been upheld in several Florida court cases. Given this state of the law, there are two primary concerns that need to be addressed, both of which are listed below.

1. **Ensure that Payments Meet the Definition of Earnings.** Your first concern is whether or not the remuneration you are receiving are pure "earnings" within the definition of the wage exemption statute. Since earnings do not include "income from passive sources, such as investment income **or return on capital,**" any income you receive that is akin to business profits rather than "the fruits of **your** labor" should be segregated and distributed to you separately. Common examples of "business profits" in the physician context are (i) profits derived from the activities of physician assistants, physical therapists, and/or other staff members, and (ii) profits akin to "technical fees" such as fees for X-Rays. One possible way to reduce the amount of these distributions is to structure the practice accounting so that these business profits are first applied to pay practice expenses with the excess, if any, being distributed to shareholders in a separate check.

   Another issue of which to beware is the difference between "bonuses" (which are exempt) and "distributions" (which are not exempt). This is a common area of confusion since the distinction is rather technical in nature. A bonus is an amount paid to an employee as compensation **for personal services** above and beyond a base salary. A distribution is just that; a distribution of company profits to its shareholders. It is not uncommon for a physician practice to pay the physicians a reasonable salary and then distribute additional profits to save the 2.9% medicare tax which, unlike social security tax, is not subject to an earnings cap (i.e., social security tax is only paid on the first $97,500 of income in 2007 while the medicare tax is paid on **all** earned income). While this can often result in a nice tax savings depending on the size of your salary, the distribution will not be exempt as "earnings." Therefore, if you choose to engage in this tax savings strategy, do not deposit your distributions into your wage account. If there is any doubt as to whether bonuses or distributions are being paid, check with your accountant.

Remember that under the wage protection statute, earnings are "exempt from attachment or garnishment for six months after the earnings are received by the financial institution **if the funds can be traced and properly identified as earnings.**" The primary reason to segregate these non-personal income "business profits" or "distributions" is that if the assets flowing to the Wage Account (i.e., the account with the financial institution referenced by the statute) are a combination of "earnings" and "non-earnings," it may be difficult or impossible to accurately "trace" the deposited funds to "earnings." If that were the case, none of the assets in the Wage Account would be exempt from creditors. In case you are wondering, I will address the "6 month issue" later in the Chapter.

2. **Ensure that Sufficient Evidence Exists to Support Employee Status.** If you are an employee that does not have any ownership in the company that employs you, this section will not apply. On the other hand, if you are an independent contractor or if you do have an ownership interest in the company that employs you, you may not be an employee for purposes of the wage protection statute. If you are an independent contractor, recent case law has held against being able to protect your wages under Florida's wage protection statute. If you own an interest (but not a controlling interest) in the company that employs you, you need to adequately document your employee status. In short, the court will take a "totality of the circumstances" approach to determine whether your relationship with the employer (I will refer to the employer as the "PA" from now on) is similar to that of an employee or whether the PA is something akin to a conglomeration of separate sole practitioners or independent contractors. Courts consider several factors when determining whether

someone is an employee for purposes of the wage exemption statute. Below I have used the court's actual language in the bankruptcy case of **In re Montoya** to describe these factors and what the courts typically look for.

a. **Existence of an Employment Contract.** The court starts by explaining the importance of having an employment agreement:

> "The first factor is the existence of an employment contract itself. A contract is the best possible evidence of whether the contracting parties intended to form an employee-employer relationship or merely engage the services of an independent contractor. **Ware v. Money-Plan Intern, Inc.**. In this case the Debtor entered into an Employment Agreement with the PA which is quite comprehensive. The PA provides the Debtor with facilities, equipment and supplies and pays for his professional liability insurance, occupational license fees and many other expenses which would typically only be paid by an employer in an employee-employer relationship. The Employment Agreement gives the PA authority to establish policies and procedures to be followed in treating patients and to determine which patients the Debtor may treat. Additionally, the agreement establishes a fixed salary for the Debtor. The agreement itself is strong evidence that the parties intended to create an employee-employer relationship."

As the above language indicates, it is not only important to have an employment contract in place, but the employment contract should address certain key issues.

b. **Who Furnishes Tools and Supplies.** The Montoya court went on to describe the importance of having the PA supply the tools and supplies necessary for the employee to carry out his or her job.

> "Typically, an independent contractor furnishes his/her own tools and supplies whereas an employer generally furnishes any

> necessary tools and supplies for employees. In this case, the PA is responsible for providing medical facilities, offices, equipment, utilities, supplies and drugs which are necessary for the Debtor to use in the course of his employment. Additionally, the PA is responsible for providing all necessary support personnel. The Debtor is not required to purchase any supplies nor employ any other personnel. Thus, the PA's obligation to furnish necessary tools and supplies is further evidence that an employee-employer relationship was created."

c. **Right to Control the Progress of the Employee's Work.** The court then points out what it considers the most important factor in determining whether a physician will be considered an employee:

> "The next factor, and perhaps the most important factor, in determining whether a person is an employee or an independent contractor is the right to control the progress of work. Typically, an employer has a right to control the progress of an employee's work . . . As evidenced by the Employment Agreement in this case, the PA has the exclusive authority to establish the professional policies and procedures for treating patients. Through these policies and procedures the PA has the right to control the means by which the Debtor may treat his patients. If the Debtor is subject to control as to the means used in treating his patients, he is an employee. . . . Additionally, the Employment Agreement gives the PA the right to determine what patients the Debtor may treat. The Trustee has argued that the PA has not actually controlled or interfered with the Debtor's treatment of the PA patients. However, as stated by the Florida Supreme Court in **National Surety Corporation v. Windham**, "[i]t is the **right** of control, not actual control or actual interference with the work, which is significant in distinguishing between an independent contractor and a servant." The court held that the "right to control depends upon the terms of the contract of employment." Id. at 550. In this case, the Employment Agreement granted the PA the right to control the work of the Debtor regardless of whether the PA ever chooses to exercise that

right. Thus, the PA's right to control is an additional indicator of the existence of an employee-employer relationship.

d. **Method of Payment**. Next, the court addressed how the physician was compensated.

> "Turning next to the method of payment, the Debtor's compensation typifies that of an employee rather than that of an independent contractor. An employee is typically paid by time, whether it be by salary or by hourly rate, whereas an independent contractor is typically paid by the job. In the instant case, the Debtor is paid a straight salary by the PA. His salary remains constant regardless of how much money the PA is paid for his services or whether the PA incurs profits or losses. Thus, the Debtor's wages are indicative of that of an employee."

e. **Work is Part of Regular Business of Employer**. The final factor addressed by the court is whether the work is part of the regular business of the employer.

> "In the instant case, the PA is a professional association comprised of physicians engaged in the practice of medicine. The PA's sole enterprise is that of providing medical services. Therefore, the Debtor satisfies this test as an employee."

As indicated by the Montoya court, it is important to ensure you have the proper documentation in place to support the finding that an employer-employee relationship exists. Some physician practices I have worked with have not had any employment agreements in place (or had unsigned draft copies that were never finalized). I have worked with other practices that had employment agreements in place, however, the agreements did not meet all the criteria set forth by the Montoya court. I have also worked with physician practices that had shareholders' agreements in place (some that even addressed compensation issues), but no free standing employment agreements. In all of these cases, the physicians in these practices were placing the ability to protect their future earnings from being garnished at risk. I want to point out that in most cases, the attorneys advising the physicians who did have some legal work in place were usually well meaning attorneys who were only focusing on the corporate law issues and in most of these cases, that was the only thing they were hired to do. Putting that matter aside, in today's increasingly litigious society, physicians need to look at the complete picture and incorporate asset protection planning into their individual and practice planning. If you have not done so already, you should have your existing corporate documents, if any, reviewed by an attorney who concentrates their practice in the area of asset protection to minimize the risk of any unpleasant surprises in the event you are sued.

One More Reason to Have an Employment Agreement.

In a recent conversation I had with a creditors' rights attorney, he explained a rather innovative method of subverting the wage protection statute which he also stated he has successfully used against a physician. As far as I can tell, very few attorneys know of and are using this technique, and I have decided not to include it in this book for fear that it will do more harm than good. If a certain provision were added to a physician's employment agreement, however, he or she would have a good chance of defeating a creditor making this new argument. If you want to know more, please contact my office.

The Six Month Exempt Period.

Many people have questioned the importance of the wage account since, according to Florida's wage protection statute, the wage account only protects wages for a six month period. Despite this relatively short period of protection, the wage account is still a valuable tool for protecting assets for two reasons. The first reason has to do with the fraudulent transfer laws discussed earlier in Chapter 5. You may remember that an exception to the fraudulent transfer laws is a transfer of an exempt (i.e., protected) asset. Put another way, the fraudulent transfer laws do not generally concern themselves with transfers of protected assets since if the creditor is not entitled to it in the first place, who really cares what you do with it? That being the case, if you place your earnings in a wage account they are then classified as an exempt (i.e., protected) asset. Therefore, if you then make a transfer from the wage account (remember that you are now transferring exempt assets) to your spouse, an asset protection structure (i.e., a protective trust, a Family Limited Partnership, etc.), or to some other exempt asset (e.g., an account titled as tenants by the entireties, paying your mortgage, a life insurance contract, or an annuity, etc.) a creditor will have a hard time winning the legal argument that the transfer should be "undone" under the fraudulent conveyance laws, since they were never entitled to the transferred asset in the first place because it was exempt.

The second reason the wage account is important despite the relatively short six moth period stems from the fact that it is a **rolling** six month period and the exempt amount is determined on the FIFO (First In First Out) basis. This is best illustrated by an example. Suppose you deposit a paycheck in the amount of $5,000 into your wage account on January 1. Lets further assume that you need $3,000 of that deposit to pay for your living expenses. That leaves $2,000 left that needs to be withdrawn by July 1. Now lets assume you deposit your next paycheck on February 1, and again withdraw $3,000 to pay for living expenses. This second $3,000 withdrawal is actually comprised of the $2,000 from the January deposit, and $1,000 from the February deposit. Therefore, the remaining $4,000 in the wage account now needs to be withdrawn prior to August 1. If you carry this out to its logical conclusion, this means that as long as (i) you are constantly depositing paychecks and withdrawing living expenses, and (ii) the balance of the wage account is less than $30,000 in this example ($5,000 per month times six months), the entire wage account is protected. Again assuming this pattern of depositing $5,000 each month and withdrawing $3,000 each month, it would take fifteen months (not six) before some of the assets in the wage account began to lose their exempt status. Therefore, if you tend to spend most of your monthly earnings, it may take a long time to build a high enough balance in the wage account for assets to start becoming exposed to creditor claims.

If you do not spend a considerable portion of your monthly earnings on living expenses, it will be best to use your wage account as a conduit account. Again, let me use an example to illustrate. For purposes of this example, I will assume you receive one paycheck each month in the amount of $20,000, that you need $5,000 a month to pay your monthly expenses, and that you are accumulating the balance of $15,000 in an asset protection structure. Suppose you deposit your paycheck on January 1. Before the end of January (lets assume on January 7) you transfer the $5,000 needed to pay your monthly expenses to your checking account, and then transfer $14,000 to your asset protection structure. This leaves $1,000 in the wage account (to keep it open) that needs to be withdrawn by July 1. On February 1, you again deposit your paycheck and then make a transfer of $5,000 to your checking account and a transfer of $15,000 to your asset protection structure. The wage account is again left with $1,000 that needs to be withdrawn by August 1. If you repeat this pattern each month, the $1,000 left in the wage account will never become non-exempt (remember the FIFO method of determining the exempt amount), and the transfer each month to your asset protection structure will be a transfer of exempt (i.e., protected) assets that are not subject to the fraudulent transfer laws.

Do Not Place Non-Earnings Into Your Wage Account.

Although I have eluded to this earlier in the Chapter, I wanted to make clear that the **only** money that should be deposited into your wage account are your "earnings." Therefore, **distributions** from your practice or from other businesses you may have an interest in (perhaps you own an interest in a surgical center), should NOT be deposited in your wage account. If you win the local golf tournament, do NOT deposit your prize money in your wage account. If you get a rebate check from your recent purchase of a DVD player, do NOT deposit it in your wage account. Only your pay checks and true bonus checks should be deposited in your wage account. Remember the wage protection statute states that earnings deposited in a wage account will be "exempt from attachment or garnishment . . . **if the funds can be traced and properly identified as earnings.**" Therefore, the easiest way to ensure that you can trace the money in the wage account to your earnings is to not put anything other than earnings into it. Again, to maintain a clear, traceable record by means of your account statements, I also recommend not using a debit card or writing checks from your wage account. In the event you purchased a sweater from Target and later decided to return it, the account statement will show a credit to the account from something other than earnings. While a couple small things like this will not destroy the protection offered by the wage protection statute, remember that you are creating the evidence (your account statements) that may be later used in a court of law to prove that the money in the wage account was, in fact, pure earnings. Keeping this "evidence" easy to understand by having as few transactions as possible will only help you in the long run. Remember you may end up with a highly intelligent judge or jury who is committed to discovering the truth, but (believe it or not) this does not always happen.

Another way to further maintain good records that will be effective evidence if ever needed in court is to staple a copy of your pay stub to the corresponding statement each month. For example, if you are paid twice a month in the amount of $12,237.42, then the account statement for your wage account will show two deposits of $12,237.42 and you will have two pay stubs also reflecting the amount earned as $12,237.42 stapled to that statement. Each month, these will be filed in a special folder where you keep your important records.

Should the Wage Account Be Interest Bearing?

A question I am often asked when discussing wage accounts with my clients is whether the wage account should be interest bearing or non-interest bearing. The short answer is that it really does not matter, however, I still prefer it to be non-interest bearing. The issue that people are concerned about is that since we are trying to keep clean and easy to understand records where the only money in the wage account is traceable to earnings, the interest may cause the wage account to lose its effectiveness. In fact, the wage protection statute states "[c]ommingling of earnings with other funds does not by itself defeat the ability of a head of family to trace earnings." Therefore, since interest earnings would be relatively easy to distinguish from deposits, establishing an interest bearing account will not have the effect of destroying the protection offered by the wage account. That being said, if you are using the wage account as a conduit account as described above, or if you spend most of your earnings each month on living expenses, the balance in the account will be so low anyway that when coupled with the miserable interest rate being paid by most banks, the benefit of earning interest is probably so minuscule that it is outweighed by the benefit of maintaining easy to understand records.

Deferred Compensation Plans.

While a complete explanation of deferred compensation plans is beyond the scope of this book, it is important to understand a few of the principals that underlie their operation. First, at its core, a "deferred compensation" plan is simply an agreement between an employee and his or her employer to have the employer set aside a certain amount of the employee's earnings. Since you are only taxed on compensation you "receive," by postponing your receipt of the money, you also defer being taxed on that portion of your earnings. The full amount of the pretax earnings subject to the plan are then free to invest. There are numerous types of deferred compensation plans, but two requirements underlying all such plans are:

(i) you do not have free reign to pull out assets whenever you wish otherwise you have "constructively received" those assets (i.e., you have so much control over the money you are deemed to have received it), and (ii) the assets held in the deferred compensation plan have to be subject to the general claims of the employer's creditors (i.e., if the employer company is sued, the creditor must be able to reach the deferred compensation plan's assets). These two requirements do not bode well from an asset protection perspective.

But what if you are sued individually? Can your creditor(s) reach your deferred "earnings" held in the deferred compensation plan? Unfortunately, several courts have answered this question YES. First, deferred compensation plans do not qualify as protected "retirement plans" since they are not described under any of the relevant internal revenue code sections listed in the statutes that provide retirement accounts their protection. Second, the cases holding that deferred compensation plans are not protected have tended to give little consideration to the fact that the money held in them are "earnings." Instead, they choose to characterize these plans as unprotected savings accounts.

Therefore, if you participate in a deferred compensation plan and your employer is sued, your assets may be lost. In addition, if you are sued individually, the assets in your 'account' will be reachable by your creditors (most likely when you are entitled to receive them). In short, while deferred compensation plans may provide you with certain benefits, asset protection is not one of them.

The Two Income Family.

In the event both spouses work (e.g., a two physician family), the spouse that earns more money will generally be treated as providing "more than one-half of the support for a child or other dependent" and will, therefore, be treated as the "Head of Family" for purposes of the wage protection statute if the couple has dependant children. If the couple does not have children and the difference between the two spouses' salary is not significant, you can end up with the result that neither spouse is the Head of Family because neither spouse provides "more than one-half of the support for . . . a dependent;" in fact each spouse provides for the majority of their own support. This does not mean that a wage account is not worth establishing, just that 100% of the earnings may not be exempt.

In a two income family with more than one dependant child, there may be a means for both spouses to qualify as "Head of Family." The definition of "Head of Family" set forth in the statute reads as follows:

> "Head of Family" includes any natural person who is providing more than one-half of the support for a child or other dependent."

Assume that husband (Harry) and wife (Wilma) have two children, Stan and Susie. Harry and Wilma agree that Harry will pay for "more than one-half" of the support of Stan and Wilma will pay for "more than one-half" of the support of Susie. Assume that Stan and Susie each attend private grade school. Harry and Wilma each establish a wage account and maintain it as set forth in this Chapter. Harry and Wilma contribute equally to a joint checking account set up as Tenants by the Entireties (discussed next Chapter) from which all their day to day living expenses are paid. Each month Harry writes a check from his wage account to the private school to pay for Stan's tuition. Likewise, each month Wilma writes a check from her wage account to pay for Susie's tuition. Therefore, Harry is paying "more than one-half of the support for a child;" namely, Stan, and Wilma is paying "more than one-half of the support for a child;" namely, Susie. I am unaware of anyone who has tried this technique, let alone had it tested in a court of law, however, in the above example, both Harry and Wilma technically fall within the statutory definition of "Head of Family." Since this technique does not cost anything to implement and really only requires some additional record keeping in case you are ever called upon to prove your case if sued, it is definitely worth considering especially if both spouses earn a significant salary.

The Sole Practitioner / Majority Shareholder Physician.

As mentioned above, a sole practitioner cannot avail him or herself of the wage exemption despite the fact that they earn their money providing personal services. The court in making its analysis has primarily focused on whether a person has an "arms length agreement" with the employer. Since a sole practitioner or a person who owns a controlling interest in the corporation or other legal entity that employs him or her cannot make an "arms length agreement," they lose the protection of the wage exemption.

One possible way around this problem may be to have the corporation housing the physician practice owned by his or her spouse with the physician then being employed by the corporation. As will be discussed later in this book, it is possible for a non-physician spouse to own a medical clinic so long as the physician agrees to be responsible for certain responsibilities. Therefore, since the physician does not own an interest in the employer corporation, it may be possible for him or her to negotiate an "arms length agreement" with the employer. It is always possible that a court may hold that a physician is not really bargaining "at arms length" when their spouse owns the corporation, however, when I made this comment at a recent lecture to physicians, one gentlemen replied "you don't know my spouse!" All joking aside, if all other requirements for obtaining the protection of the wage exemption are met and the physician is not a majority (i.e., controlling) shareholder of the corporate employer, there is a chance the physician may be able to exempt his or her wages.

There is another technique that is beyond the scope of this book which would add additional certainty that the "primary person" with respect to a closely held business could still receive the benefits of Florida's wage protection statute. Anyone interested should feel free to contact me.

Waiving Wage Protection.

Florida Statutes Section 222.11(2)(b) reads, in pertinent part, as follows:

> "[E]arnings of a head of a family . . . may not be attached or garnished unless such person has agreed otherwise in writing. ..."

Note that most, but certainly not all, credit card companies and banks have added provisions to their loan documents that have you waive your wage protection. I note this for two reasons. First, if you are planning on borrowing money from a bank, individual, etc. review the loan documents and see whether or not this waiver exists. If it does, you may be able to negotiate the deal so that provision is removed or modified (i.e., only kicks in at a higher level of income). Second, if you are lending money to any Florida resident, you may want to add a waiver provision to protect your ability to garnish their wages if they default on the loan. In all cases, know where you stand so that you are not relying, one way or another, on a false belief that your wages are (or are not) protected.

How to Establish a Wage Account.

Opening a Wage Account is a simple procedure. You first start by opening a bank account with your local bank. The account can be any type, however, most of my clients open a checking account or savings account. In the event a physician is married, I recommend opening the account jointly between the spouses as "Tenants by the Entireties" to add additional protection (this will be discussed more thoroughly in the next Chapter). In the case of a single physician, the account would be simply opened in his or her name. Some banks allow you to name an account such as the "John Doe Wage Account." If your bank allows this, it may make the account statements better evidence by clearly establishing your intent to only deposit earnings in the account, however, if your bank does not have this capability, it is certainly not a requirement or a reason to change banks. Once the account is opened, you now have a wage account.

Once the account is opened, simply follow the recommendations described earlier in this Chapter; namely:

1. Only deposit earnings in the wage account;
2. If you are using the wage account as a conduit account, make the transfers each month to your checking account and to your chosen asset protected method of saving long term money (i.e., a tenancy by the entireties account, Family Limited Partnership, asset protection trust structure, etc.), leaving a small amount in the wage account to keep it open;
3. If you are not using the wage account as a conduit account (which I do not recommend), maintain adequate records so you can make sure that you do not have any money in the wage account that was deposited more than six months ago. A simple Excel spreadsheet works great for this; and
4. Each month when you receive the bank statement for the wage account, staple the corresponding pay stubs (if any) to the statement and store the bank statement in a safe place.

Conclusion.

Keeping your earnings safe from a creditor's reach is one of the most important pre-retirement aspects of your asset protection plan. Make sure you have employment agreements in place and have them reviewed to ensure they pass muster under the guidelines described earlier. You should then establish your wage account and properly maintain it as set forth above. Following these recommendations is both inexpensive and an effective means of accomplishing this important asset protection goal.

CHAPTER 12

Protection Offered by Joint Ownership and Tenants by the Entireties

This Chapter covers the form of joint ownership called Tenancy by the Entireties (sometimes referred to as "TBE" for short). I will also touch on another form of joint ownership called Joint Tenants with Rights of Survivorship (sometimes referred to as "JTWROS" for short), however, the majority of this Chapter will focus on Tenancy by the Entireties since that form of joint ownership is most protective. It is important to note at the outset that only married couples posses the ability to title assets as Tenants by the Entirety. Therefore, if you are single, understand that the majority of this Chapter will not pertain to you. That being said, owning assets as Tenancy by the Entireties can be an effective means for protecting assets but it is not without its downsides. First, I will give you a brief history of Tenancy by the Entireties. Next, I will provide a practical discussion on how TBE planning works to protect assets and how to properly establish TBE ownership with respect to various types of assets. Finally, I will discuss the downsides of TBE planning followed by concrete recommendations on how to mitigate those downsides when possible.

Explanation of Tenants by the Entireties

Historical Background.

The 2001 case of **Beal Bank, SSB v. Almand & Associates** (which is discussed later in this Chapter), provides a brief history of the tenancy by the entireties form of ownership.

"The tenancy by the entireties form of ownership dates back to the English common law and to a time when married women could not hold property individually. The historic basis for the tenancy was the assumed incapacity of married women to hold property individually. . . .

Florida's Constitution now expressly protects the equality of women by providing that "all natural persons, female and male alike, are equal before the law." Art. I, § 2, Fla. Const. Accordingly, if the sole foundation of the tenancy by the entireties doctrine was dependent on the fact that married women could not own property individually, the doctrine would have become obsolete long ago. Instead, however, the tenancy by the entireties as a form of ownership has survived and thrived even in present day:

> 'Whether or not incapacity was the supporting theory behind the tenancy as of 1776, subsequent reconsideration of [the] doctrine has led to development of the view that it ought to be based upon the intention of the parties, rather than upon any assumed incapacity of married women; and further, that concurrently, it ought to be based upon the simple fact that those who were married were to be considered as a unit . . . .'

Thus, the distinctive feature of a tenancy by the entireties, that husband and wife hold property as an indivisible unit, renders this form of ownership equally well-suited to the concept of modern-day marriage as a partnership between equals."

Distinction Between Tenancy by the Entireties and Joint Tenants with Rights of Survivorship.

Tenancy by the Entireties (sometimes called "TBE") is a type of joint ownership similar to Joint Tenants with Rights of Survivorship (sometimes called "JTWROS") that can only be entered into by a husband and wife. Before describing the creditor protection offered by TBE, it is helpful to first understand the JTWROS form of joint ownership. In the event two people (married or unmarried) own property as JTWROS, each owner (called a "joint tenant") is deemed to own an undivided one-half interest in the property (assuming each contributed equally to the purchase of the property) and each joint tenant is free to sell, gift, or otherwise transfer his or her interest in the property to whomever they please. Because each joint tenant is free to transfer their share of the property, the general rule is that a creditor of either joint tenant is fully able to reach that person's share of the property. The JTWROS form of ownership, therefore, does not offer much as far as asset protection is concerned.

Another principle feature of JTWROS ownership is that when one of the joint tenants dies, their interest in the property automatically passes to the other joint tenant without ever becoming an asset of their probate estate. Therefore, if one of the joint tenants dies at a time when they are being sued but before a the creditor can legally reach the property, the deceased owner's interest in the property passes to the other joint tenant free from the claims of creditors. Therefore, the only real asset protection offered by the JTWROS form of ownership is the ability to avoid a creditor by dying. As you may imagine, killing yourself is not a very popular asset protection technique.

Asset Protection Benefits of Tenancy by the Entireties.

As described above, when people normally own property jointly, each person is considered to own a percentage of the property (i.e., one-half in the case of two people owning a single piece of property). When property is owned by a married couple as TBE, a "legal fiction" is imposed and each spouse is considered to own the entire property and not a one-half interest. This distinction is significant from an asset protection standpoint. Assume that a husband and wife owned a piece of property as TBE and a creditor is able to obtain a judgement against husband alone. Since the judgement is not enforceable against wife, and since the TBE property is considered to be owned entirely by wife, the TBE property is not reachable by the claims of husband's creditor since that would be an injustice to an innocent person, namely wife. Likewise, if a creditor were able to obtain a judgement against wife alone, since the judgement is not enforceable against husband, and since the TBE property is considered to be owned entirely by husband, the TBE property is not reachable by the claims of wife's creditor since that would be an injustice to an innocent person, namely husband. As discussed more completely below, understand that if a creditor were able to obtain a judgement against both husband and wife, the asset protection benefits of TBE ownership disappear since there is no longer an innocent spouse to protect.

Establishing TBE Ownership.

In order to establish TBE ownership, the law requires that six characteristics, called "unities," are present at the time the title to the property or bank account is established. The six characteristics are:

1. Unity of possession (i.e., joint ownership and control);
2. Unity of interest (i.e., the interests in the property or bank account must be identical);
3. Unity of title (the interests must have originated in the same instrument);
4. Unity of time (the interests must have commenced simultaneously);
5. Survivorship (i.e., the property or bank account must pass to the survivor on the death of the first spouse to die); and
6. Unity of marriage (the parties must be married at the time the property became titled in their joint names).

This list may give the impression that establishing TBE ownership is complicated, however, quite the contrary is true. Below I discuss how to establish TBE ownership for real estate, bank and brokerage accounts, and personal property.

1. **Real Estate.** In the event a husband and wife purchase a parcel of Florida real estate (i.e., a home, office building, vacant land, etc.), if the deed is titled as "John Doe and Jane Doe, husband and wife" the law automatically provides for TBE ownership. Note that the deed does not have to contain the words "tenancy by the entireties," it simply has to list both spouse's names and it is best that it indicate that they are married. One potential trap for the unwary stems from the requirement that the six "unities" have to be present at the time the deed is signed. Suppose a house is purchased by an unmarried couple. Because they are not married, the property will be held by them as either JTWROS or as "tenants in common," another form of joint ownership that does not provide asset protection. If this couple is later wed, the subsequent act of getting married does not convert the property to TBE. Therefore, in the event you purchased property with the person with whom you are presently married, however, the property was purchased before you were married (being engaged does **not** count), you may want to sign a new deed transferring the

property from the two of you to the two of you. While deeding property that you already own to yourself may seem ridiculous, that is what is necessary to establish TBE ownership with its asset protection benefits.

2. **Bank Accounts / Brokerage Accounts.** The safest way to ensure that bank accounts or brokerage accounts will receive TBE protection is to have the bank or brokerage account signature cards marked "tenancy by the entirety" to expressly state your intent that you desire TBE ownership. In 2001, the Florida Supreme Court in the case of **Beal Bank, SSB v. Almand & Associates**, was asked to decide whether a creditor could garnish a bank account that was opened by a married couple despite the fact that the signature card stated that the account was held as JTWROS and not TBE. In answering this question, the Florida Supreme Court expressed three holdings. First, in the event all six "unities" (i.e., the six characteristics discussed above) are present when the account is opened, then in order for a creditor to be able to garnish the account, the creditor must prove that the account owners did **not** intend for the account to be owned as TBE. This shifting of the "burden of proof" to the creditor obviously makes it much harder for a creditor to garnish an account. Second, if the signature card for an account reads JTWROS, the Court held that that should not be considered an express disclaimer of TBE ownership. Finally, even if the signature card does expressly disclaim TBE ownership, the married couple can still offer evidence to prove that they actually intended TBE ownership despite the disclaimer.

   This was a wonderful case as far as protecting bank accounts where TBE is concerned, however, it is still best to insist on having the words "tenancy by the entireties" on the signature card. To quote the Florida Supreme Court in the Beal Bank case "we agree with the statement in [the earlier case of Hector Supply Co.] that an express designation on the signature card that the account is held as tenancy by the entireties ends the inquiry as to the form of ownership." Therefore, if you make sure those magic words "tenancy by the entireties" appears on the signature card, practically any argument the creditor may make to try and prove that you did not intend TBE will be rendered ineffective. A few of the large banks in Florida do not provide the option of titling certain types of accounts as TBE. I have actually had a conversations with their legal counsel on a few occasions. Interestingly, they usually start off with trying to explain that there are certain complex legal issues that make this necessary, however, not a single one of these lawyers (i.e., the banks own in house counsel) could ever explain exactly what these issues are. In short, these banks are placing their administrative convenience above allowing you an easy method of identifying your intent to create a TBE account. On way around this problem may be to give your account a name. Every bank I am aware of will let you name an account such as the "Smith Family Vacation Account." Therefore, even if you are forced by the bank to title the account as JTWROS, you could still name your account the "Bob and Mary Smith Tenancy by the Entireties Account." Your intent to create a TBE account would be hard to deny if this were done.

3. **Personal Property**. Personal property can either be titled (i.e., you have something in writing that indicates how the property is owned (like a stock certificate showing how shares of stock are owned)) or untitled (i.e., no such written document exists to memorialize how something is owned (i.e., bottles of wine, certain artworks and jewelry, furniture, etc.)). With personal property that is titled, it is best to have the words "tenancy by the entireties" appear on the title to ensure TBE ownership is established. With property that is generally untitled, it is possible to create your own written record. I will have clients sign an affidavit where they swear under oath that all of the personal property they own (i) met all six "unities" at the time it was purchased, (ii) was intended by the married couple to be owned as TBE when purchased, (iii) is still intended by the married couple to be owned as TBE, and (iv) that unless otherwise expressed to the contrary in writing, any future personal property purchased by the couple is intended to be held as TBE. This affidavit should then be dated and notarized. If you have an attorney create such an affidavit for you, make sure that as you purchase property in the future you are aware of the effect of the affidavit in the case that you do not want a specific piece of property to be held as TBE (i.e., perhaps you want it titled in the name of one spouse individually).

The 2002 case of Cacciatore v. Fisherman's Wharf Realty, held that just as is the case with bank accounts, Florida law is designed to create TBE ownership in personal property purchased by married couples, not just bank accounts. While this case is certainly helpful, it is still best to affirmatively state your intent in writing to reduce any argument by a would be creditor that you did not intend to own your personal property as TBE.

Limitations of Asset Protection Offered by Tenants by the Entireties

While owning property as Tenants by the Entireties may offer asset protection during a couple's married life, it does have some serious draw backs. These are listed below:

Joint Judgment. If a judgment is obtained against both spouses, TBE offers no asset protection because there is no innocent spouse to protect. Such may be the case if your automobiles are titled in both your names or if you are in an accident in a car titled in the name of your spouse. Judgements stemming from jointly owned property (including property owned as TBE) also pose similar problems. For example, assume you and your spouse buy a piece of rental property and hold it as TBE for asset protection purposes. Now assume a tenant slips and falls on the property, or is attacked on the property, or the roof caves in on the tenant, etc. If that tenant is successful in obtaining a judgement, it will be against the property owners, namely you AND your spouse. Now that the tenant has a judgement against both of you, all of your TBE property could be reached by the tenant creditor.

Death of Spouse. If one spouse dies, the property automatically passes to the surviving spouse and the asset protection benefits are immediately lost. Therefore, if you are being sued or if you have a judgement against you and your spouse then dies, you have two things to be sad about. You not only lost your spouse but all your TBE property is now instantly reachable by a creditor. If you have minor children, this could be particularly devastating. Remember that if you end up with all the property titled in your name with a creditor already identified, your asset protection planning options will not be plentiful.

Divorce. Divorce will destroy TBE and the related asset protection benefits. Therefore, in the event you and your spouse decide to divorce at a time when a law suit is pending or a judgement is outstanding, the divorce will have the effect of converting protected assets into unprotected assets. There may be some pre-divorce planning opportunities if both spouses cooperate, however, if the divorce happens to be bitter, this is something the spouse without creditor problems may use to their advantage in negotiating a property settlement.

Increased Estate Tax Liability. Because property titled as TBE automatically passes from one spouse to the other when the first spouse dies, the opportunity to use both spouse's unified tax credits (currently $1,000,000 per spouse) can be completely lost. In addition, other estate planning techniques (such as Family Limited Partnerships) cannot be used if your investment property is titled as TBE. Therefore, if your net worth is substantial enough to trigger estate taxation, titling your assets as TBE can be very costly from an estate tax perspective to your children or other heirs.

Liability Stemming from Real Estate. As mentioned above, in the event you own investment real estate as TBE, if liability results from the property itself (i.e., renter, visitor, trespasser is injured on the property, environmental liability, etc.) BOTH you and your spouse will most likely be sued. Since such a judgement will be against both spouses, all of your other TBE property will be reachable by that creditor.

Property Owned Outside of Florida. In the event you own real estate or other assets outside the state of Florida, you may not be able to protect those assets using TBE. The general rule is that the laws of the state where the property resides will determine (i) whether TBE is an available means of owning assets (i.e., some states do not have TBE ownership), and (ii) if TBE is an effective means of protecting assets since different states treat TBE differently. TBE is recognized in some form or another in Arkansas, Delaware, District of Columbia, Florida, Hawaii, Illinois, Indiana, Kentucky, Maryland, Massachusetts, Michigan, Missouri, New Jersey, New York, North Carolina, Oregon, Pennsylvania, Rhode Island, Tennessee, Vermont, Virginia, and Wyoming. But do not be lured into a false sense of security. If for example, you own a vacation home in North Carolina, you will need to have an attorney who practices in the area of asset protection, and who is admitted to practice law in North Carolina, give you an opinion on how protected TBE property is under North Carolina law. If you decide to plan for yourself in this area based on your understanding of Florida law, you may be in for a big (and bad) surprise if a creditor later tries to reach that property.

IRS Tax Liens. A recent United States Supreme Court case (i.e., **U.S. v. Craft**) held that property owned as TBE may not protect property from the claims of the federal government for taxes owed by one party. Although I personally feel this case represents bad law, it is just one more example of how the Super Creditor named the IRS will walk through most any form of asset protection technique.

Florida Cases. The case of **In Re Planas** caused great concern when it was originally decided in 1996. In that case, Chief Bankruptcy Judge A. Jay Cristol held that the protection offered by tenancy by the entirety is not available in the bankruptcy context if the married couple had any joint debt (i.e., a joint credit card, home mortgage, etc.). Fortunately, that case was later reversed (i.e., held not to be the law). The court held that Judge Cristol's interpretation of the TBE law would sacrifice the underlying intent of the law which is "to provide every spouse with the security that the family's entireties property cannot be reached by a creditor unless both spouses agree to become obligated to that specific creditor." The current state of the law provides that joint creditors are entitled to reach TBE property in a bankruptcy proceeding, however, all non-joint creditor's are prohibited from reaching TBE property. For example, assume a husband and wife owned $1,000,000 in TBE property and that is all they own. Further assume that they have the following debts: (i) a joint credit card with a $5,000 outstanding balance, (ii) a credit card in wife's name alone with a $10,000 outstanding balance, (iii) utility bills in husband's name alone in the amount of $3,000, and a (iv) judgement against husband for medical malpractice in the amount of $2,000,000. If husband and wife filed for bankruptcy, the only debt that could be satisfied out of their TBE property is the joint credit card. All of the remaining creditor's would most likely have their claims discharged in the bankruptcy proceeding and husband and wife could keep the remaining $995,000 in TBE property. This being the case, it may be wise to structure your debts in a manner that minimizes joint debt in favor of husband and wife each having separate debts (i.e., keeping individual credit cards as to husband and wife rather than joint cards, having utility bills in the name of one spouse but not the other, etc.).

As illustrated in the **Craft** case (see previous paragraph on IRS Tax Liens) and the above mentioned **Planas** case, one of the biggest downsides in using TBE ownership to protect assets is uncertainty as to what future courts may hold. In the event you choose to use TBE as part of your overall asset protection plan, take steps to make yourself aware of any changes in the law that could negatively affect you.

TBE Planning Musts

If you decide to use TBE ownership as a primary part of your asset protection plan, the following planning will help reduce some (though not all) of the negative consequences listed above.

Insist on Seeing the Words "Tenants by the Entireties" on the Signature Card. Although the Beal Bank case has given Florida residents some additional security that joint accounts established during marriage will most likely be considered to be held as TBE, the rule is not absolute. For that reason, it is best to make sure the words "**Tenants by the Entireties**" on the signature card of any account you open. Understand that many bankers have never heard of TBE and will tell you that a joint account is sufficient; rely on the advice of a bank teller at your own peril.
Real Estate Purchased by a Husband and Wife is Not TBE. As mentioned above, Florida real estate purchased by Florida residents who are husband and wife is assumed to be owned as Tenants by the Entireties. If you and your spouse purchased real estate **prior** to being married, beware that your subsequent marriage does not convert the property to TBE. If this is the case, a new deed must be properly signed and recorded in order to obtain the benefits of TBE.

Avoid Any Joint Debts. As mentioned above, if you are ever forced into bankruptcy, your TBE property may be available to pay any joint creditors. Therefore, to the greatest extent possible, you should not have any bills, credit cards, or other debt or obligation in the name of both of you and your spouse. If one spouse takes out a loan and the bank asks the other to cosign or guarantee that loan, try your best to refuse that request. If the spouse taking out the loan is the primary income earner, the bank will sometimes drop that requirement if they think they may lose the business over this issue.

Title Automobiles Properly. In the event you are ever in an automobile accident, the person you hit will be able to sue both the **driver** of the car and the **owner** of the car. Therefore, it is best to title the car that you primarily drive in your name and the car driven primarily by your spouse in your spouse's name.

Insure the Lower Risk Spouse Though an Asset Protection Trust. Assuming there exists a lower risk spouse (i.e., a home maker, etc.) and a higher risk spouse (i.e., a physician, business owner, etc.), one planning approach is to purchase insurance (term or otherwise) on the life of the lower risk spouse in an amount equal to the value of the property held as TBE (or greater to cover anticipated appreciation over time). This policy should be held in a trust that will remove the insurance proceeds from the taxable estate of the lower risk spouse and create a special trust benefitting the higher risk spouse while protecting the assets from the claims of their creditors. In this manner, in the event the lower risk spouse were to die while the higher risk spouse is being sued (or worse yet, after a judgement has been awarded against him or her), the assets held as TBE would indeed be subject to the claims of creditors, however, the death benefit provided by the insurance would replace the value of the assets now subject to loss. In the event a particular piece of property is something the higher risk spouse wishes to protect from seizure by a creditor, the trust could be granted an option to purchase the property at its fair market value which could be exercised by the trustee after the death of the lower risk spouse. Of course, this suggestion may not be an inexpensive one. If the annual cost of insuring the lower risk spouse is $4,000 per year, and if you plan to keep the insurance in place until retirement age (say 20 years), you will have paid $80,000 at the end of that period to protect the TBE assets. In contrast, a foreign asset protection structure may actually end up being much cheaper.

Use a Delaware Series Limited Liability Company to Hold Investment Real Estate. In the event you own investment real estate, you should consider titling that property in a Limited Liability Company (an "LLC") rather than as TBE. This stems from the fact that if liability ever stems from the property itself, the creditor will only be able to reach the assets in the LLC and not your other personal assets. If you have more than one parcel of property, you should consider using a Delaware Series LLC rather than a "typical" LLC. This is because if more than one parcel of property is held in the LLC and liability is spawned from one parcel, the creditor will be able to reach all of the property in the LLC, not just the property from which the liability arose. A Delaware Series LLC allows you to title multiple properties in a single LLC but still limit liability to the property that produced it. The Delaware series LLC is discussed in more detail later in the book.

Conclusion

Owning property as TBE can be an effective means of protecting assets, however, it is not without its downsides. A principal upside to using TBE ownership to protect assets is that it is cheap to establish, however, in the event of the death of a spouse, the loss of the ability to save on estate taxes may be very costly at the end of the day. Likewise, the use of life insurance to replace TBE property can also be costly. Whether or not TBE makes sense to you will require not only an analysis of your personal assets and risks, but also a cost / benefit analysis given your potential for estate taxes, the cost of insuring against loss of the TBE protection, and your risk tolerance regarding your personal assessment of the likelihood that your spouse will die once you have a creditor in sight. Remember that even if the risk of the "bad thing" happening is very small, if the negative consequences that could stem from that "bad thing" are considerable (i.e., losing all or a majority of your net worth), it should still be considered very risky.

CHAPTER 13

Asset Protection Through Gifting and I Gave it to my Spouse Planning

This Chapter will cover the topic of gifting as a means of protecting assets and something I call "I Gave it to my Spouse Planning." Neither of these are really state law exemptions, but I felt this was the best place to discuss them. These are typically inexpensive methods of protecting assets but they also carry with them some serious downsides. First, I will discuss gifting in general. Finally, I will spend the majority of this Chapter discussing "I Gave it to my Spouse Planning" together with a discussion of its downsides and planning strategies to minimize those downsides where possible.

Gifting as a Means of Protecting Assets.

Before discussing the topic of "I Gave it to my Spouse" planning, I want to discuss the general topic of gifting assets as a means of protecting assets. This discussion will focus on gifts to someone other than your spouse.

The primary consideration as to the efficacy of protecting an asset by giving it to someone else is whether the gift can be set aside (i.e., undone) by a creditor as a fraudulent transfer. This analysis was discussed in detail in Chapter 5. For example, in the event a gift was made at a time a creditor has already been identified, the transfer will most likely be subject to being set aside as a fraudulent transfer, and will therefore, be ineffective from an asset protection standpoint. On the other hand, in the event the "skies are blue" and there are no creditors on the horizon, then a gift of property to a child, family member, or other non-related person will most likely (but not always) place the gifted asset beyond the reach of the creditors of the person making the gift.

There are, of course other considerations to take into account when making gifts. Some of these are summarized below:

1. Gift Tax Consequences. Each United States citizen is entitled to make gifts in the amount of $12,000 to as many people as they choose each year without those gifts triggering gift tax. In the event you were to exceed that $12,000 amount then your $1,000,000 gift tax "unified credit" will be reduced. For example, in the event you made a gift of $102,000 to one person, $12,000 will be considered "gift tax free" and you would use up $90,000 of your unified credit leaving you with a remaining unified credit of $910,000. If, on the other hand, you made a gift of $1,612,000 to the same person, then $12,000 would be considered "gift tax free," you would use your entire $1,000,000 unified credit, and the remaining $600,000 would be fully taxable. Therefore, depending on the amount of the gift, gift taxes may be a considerable cost to protecting the transferred asset. Also note that if your plan is for the asset to be gifted back to you at some point in time in the future (which if proven could negate the asset protection contemplated by the transfer), the person making the gift back to you will also have to take the gift tax consequences into consideration (i.e., the IRS will not "net" the two transfers but will instead consider each a separate transfer with the gift tax implications described above).

2. Control. Another consequence of making gifts is that once the asset is gifted, you typically have to give up control over the gifted asset, which is typically something most clients I have worked with are not eager to do. If you do not part with control or if there is an implied promise that the property will be gifted back at sometime in the future, the gift will most likely be held invalid and a creditor could reach the property. Also consider the following. Suppose you make a gift of $500,000 to your responsible adult child and he or she is later sued or goes through a divorce. Since everyone is at some risk of being sued, the property may be protected from your creditor only to be subject to being taken by a creditor of your child.

   For this reason, making gifts in trust oftentimes makes the most sense. The trust can be drafted to give the donee (your child, for example) asset protection with respect to the gifted asset, and oftentimes can accomplish estate planning objectives. Family Limited Partnerships can also be used to make gifts. Gifts of Family Limited Partnership "units" can result in gift tax savings, provide some level of asset protection to the donee (if the partnership is drafted properly), and can even leave you with some control over the assets inside the partnership. In short, outright gifts are usually not considered a good asset protection technique.

3. Future Financial Stability. Even if you are comfortable making a true gift of property to a child or some other person, perhaps because you earn a good salary, remember the old maxim that the only constant is change. In the event that your financial circumstances change and you have given away a large part of your wealth, making a gift to protect assets may be a decision you live to regret.

"I Gave it to My Spouse" Planning.

Now that we have discussed gifting to non-spouse donees, the rest of the chapter will discuss the benefits and detriments of gifting assets to your spouse. As with owning property as tenants by the entireties, transferring assets to a lower liability spouse, is another inexpensive means of protecting assets. If the transfers are made at a time when there are no identified creditors, this planning can protect the property from liability of the higher risk spouse, however, as with TBE ownership, this type of planning carries with it some serious negative implications.

The Lower Risk Spouse Gets Sued. The first obvious problem with "I Gave it to my Spouse" planning is that there are a number of ways to get sued and the lower risk spouse may be at greater risk than initially contemplated. Remember that there is no such thing as a risk **free** spouse. I knew of a physician who had used "I Gave it to my Spouse" planning as his primary means of protecting assets, and ended up retiring after never being sued. Several years into retirement, his wife was in an automobile accident and a large judgement was given to the family of the person who was seriously injured in that accident. The physician and his wife ended up losing a significant amount of their total net worth due to the fact that the assets titled in the wife's name (remember she was the lower risk spouse) were completely unprotected from the claims of her creditors.

Divorce. With divorce rates at an all time high, gifting property to your spouse may give rise to some unexpected and unpleasant results. Property gifted to a spouse during marriage may give the donee spouse an advantage in a divorce proceeding. Under Florida law, if one spouse gives property to the other spouse, that transfer or gift does not convert the gifted property from "marital property" (i.e., property that is typically divided between the spouses upon divorce) to the "separate property" (i.e., property that is not divided between the spouses on divorce) of the recipient spouse. However, because Florida divorce law gives a judge the ability to make "equitable distributions" between the divorcing spouse's rather than mandating a 50%/50% split of the marital assets, it is not hard to imagine a judge using the gifts as evidence that the recipient spouse should be entitled to more than 50% of the marital assets. In addition, the laws of some states do convert "marital property" to the recipient spouse's "separate property" when inter-spousal gifts are made. Therefore, if you engaged in I gave it to my Spouse Planning, later moved out of Florida, and were divorced in your new state of residence, this type of asset protection planning could have a devastating result to the higher risk spouse who gave property to the lower risk spouse.

Loss of Control. Oftentimes the higher risk spouse is the spouse who principally makes decisions with respect to the management of the family investment portfolio. Once assets are transferred to the lower risk spouse, the higher risk spouse no longer has any direct control over the transferred assets.

The Lower Risk Spouse Dies. If you engage in "I Gave it to my Spouse" planning and the lower risk spouse then dies, it is not uncommon for the assets previously transferred to such lower risk spouse to return to the higher risk spouse in a manner that allows the higher risk spouse's creditors to, again, reach the assets. Even if the couple had engaged in estate planning, the trusts commonly established on the death of a spouse are typically drafted to reduce estate taxes, but not to provide any asset protection benefits to the survivor.

Increased Estate Tax Liability. In order to use both spouse's unified tax credits (currently $1,000,000 per spouse), each spouse must have a certain amount of property titled in their names (or the name of their revocable trusts). Therefore, titling a majority of assets in the name of one spouse can cause you to lose this benefit. In addition, it is typical for the higher risk spouse to end up with only qualified retirement assets in their name and all the "non-qualified" property to be in the name of the lower risk spouse. This can also cause negative tax consequences if the higher risk spouse dies first. Therefore, if your net worth is substantial enough to trigger estate taxation, engaging in this type of planning can be very costly from an estate tax perspective to your children or other heirs.

Encourages Negative Tactics. If the party suing can make the legal and collection proceedings exceedingly distasteful, the lower risk spouse may offer to give up assets just to stop the pain. Good plaintiff's attorneys know this and will use it to their benefit if they feel they can get results by doing so.

Negative Bankruptcy Implications. In the event you and your spouse are ever forced to file bankruptcy, the assets held in the name of the lower risk spouse are not exempt from creditor's claims (as is the case with TBE property).

Constructive and Resulting Trusts. There is a small likelihood that a creditor could argue that you did not really give property to your spouse but that they were holding it in trust for your benefit and, therefore, the creditor of the donor spouse should be able to reach the assets gifted to the donee spouse. This type of argument falls under two legal theories called "constructive trusts" and "resulting trusts." While a detailed discussion of them is beyond the scope of this book, I feel it would be difficult for a creditor to win on this argument. I do not know of any case where one spouse gave assets to the other and a resulting trust case was asserted by a creditor of the donor spouse. On the other hand, I have seen cases where inter-spousal transfers were respected from an asset protection standpoint provided they were not fraudulent transfers.

Minimum Planning

If you decide to use "I Gave it to my Spouse" planning to protect your assets, there are some minimum planning steps that should be considered to reduce some of the negative consequences that may flow from this decision.

Divorce. A **Post**marital Agreement can be drafted where the spouse's agree in advance of divorce as to how property will be divided regardless of whose name the property is titled in. If the spouses agree to a 50%/50% split, the lower risk spouse is not typically putting themself in a worse situation than if the transfer of property never took place. Therefore, there is oftentimes not the same political issues that surround typical prenuptial agreements. That being said, raising the issue of a potential divorce is rarely a fun conversation to have with your spouse. In order to increase the likelihood of a post-nuptial agreement being respected if a divorce does occur, it is imperative that the following three things take place: (1) there must be full and fair financial disclosure between the spouse's (i.e., you must tell each other everything you own and how much you earn), and (2) each spouse must be separately represented by their own legal counsel. Furthermore, if the suggestion of a post-nuptial agreement is not well received by your spouse, you may be lifting the lid of Pandora's box leading to a lack of trust between you which may even result in divorce in a worse case scenario (remember that a divorcing spouse is a Super Creditor).

Control and Death of the Lower Risk Spouse. It is highly advisable to add provisions to your existing estate planning documents (or to create them if you have not already planned your estate) to accomplish the following results:

1. Name both spouses as Co-Trustees of each other's revocable trust to allow the spouses to jointly manage the assets regardless of whose trust they are in. This has the benefit of allowing a spouse to continue to manage the trust assets even if the other spouse becomes incapacitated and without requiring the un-incapacitated spouse to obtain letters from physicians documenting the incapacity of their spouse as is typically required if the spouse is named as a successor trustee.

2. Prevent assets from returning to the spouse in a manner that can be reached by creditors by creating trusts that are designed to provide asset protection benefits to the surviving spouse. These trusts can be Florida trusts or can even be established under the laws of Delaware, Alaska, or Offshore.

3. Maximize estate tax benefits.

It is important to understand that while asset protection planning and estate planning do have common elements, having an estate planning attorney who does not devote a substantial part of his or her practice to asset protection planning make these changes could result in unsatisfactory consequences that may only be discovered after it is too late. I continue to see competent (and less than competent) estate planning attorneys make simple mistakes which can lead to significant asset protection problems.

Comparison of TBE and "I Gave it to My Spouse" Planning

As illustrated in this Chapter and the Chapter preceding it, TBE has an advantage if the lower risk spouse is sued. In addition, if your marriage is dissolved, the unequal division of assets that can occur with "I Gave it to my Spouse" planning will not be as large a concern. The principal benefit of "I Gave it to my Spouse" Planning is the ability for the high risk spouse to receive assets in the event of the lower risk spouse's death in a manner that will not subject those assets to the claims of their creditors. The largest downsides are that, unlike with TBE, a law suit brought against the lower risk spouse could cause a loss of all the assets titled in his or her name and the fact that a divorce could leave the higher risk spouse with the short end of the stick. You will need to base your decision on whether or not to use (i) TBE, (ii) "I Gave it to my Spouse" planning, or (iii) a completely different asset protection strategy, based on your own facts and circumstances / goals and objectives.

Conclusion

The principal benefit of using"I Gave it to my Spouse" planning is that it is cheap and easy to implement, however, there are several disadvantages that you need to be aware of before making the ultimate decision on how to protect your assets. If cost is the only factor taken into consideration at the outset, you may end up paying much more down the road. At a minimum, you should implement the planning techniques discussed above to mitigate some of negative aspects of "I Gave it to my Spouse" planning.

CHAPTER 14

Protecting Assets with Life Insurance and Annuities

This Chapter will discuss the generous asset protection afforded to life insurance and annuities under Florida law. First I will discuss the protective nature of these financial products and some of the ways that they can be used as part of your asset protection plan. I will then discuss some of the potential downsides posed by using life insurance and annuities if you do not understand the financial aspects of these vehicles.

Protection Offered by Life Insurance.

Before we proceed, it is important to understand a few general terms that I will be using in the foregoing explanation of the asset protection aspects of life insurance. First, the person who's life is insured is called the "Insured." The person (or people) who will receive money upon the death of the Insured is called a "Beneficiary." The money paid to the Beneficiary upon the death of the Insured is called the "Death Benefit."

There are two broad categories of life insurance; namely "term" and "cash value." Under a term policy, the policy itself has no intrinsic value other than the fact that a Death Benefit will be paid to the named Beneficiaries if the Insured dies during the term of the policy. Before moving on to an explanation of "cash value" policies, below is an example that describes a "term" policy and that also goes over the insurance terminology.

> Suppose Ichabod has a wife, Betty, and two lovely children, Colton and Cathy. Betty does not work outside the home, and therefore, does not earn a salary despite her valuable contribu-

tions to the family. Ichabod and Betty have some savings but not enough to pay all the household and living expenses if Ichabod were to die unexpectedly. Ichabod and Betty have done some financial planning and have determined that if they continue to save a certain amount each year, Ichabod could quit working in twenty years and he and Betty could retire comfortably. On the other hand, if Ichabod were to die unexpectedly, Betty and the kids would not be able to continue to maintain the lifestyle they currently enjoy. Ichabod decides to buy a term insurance policy that will pay Betty the amount of $2,000,000 if Ichabod dies anytime in the next twenty years. If Betty dies before (or at the same time as) Ichabod, the $2,000,000 will be paid to Colton and Cathy. To keep this insurance policy in force, Ichabod will pay the insurance company $2,000 per year for the next twenty years. If Ichabod stops making these payments, the insurance policy terminates. If Ichabod dies one day after the twenty year period expires, the insurance company will pay nothing. Ichabod is the owner of the policy meaning that he has the right to exercise control over the policy, including the right to change who the beneficiaries are.

Now lets review the terminology. In the preceding example:

1. Ichabod is the **Insured** (since the insurance policy pays the $2,000,000 if he dies).
2. Ichabod is the **Owner** of the policy (since he can exercise control over the policy).
3. Betty is the "**Primary Beneficiary**" (since the insurance company will pay her the $2,000,000 first, if Ichabod dies).
4. Colton and Cathy are the "**Contingent Beneficiaries**" (since the insurance company will pay them the $2,000,000 only on the contingency that Ichabod dies and Betty is also dead).
5. The $2,000,000 to be paid by the insurance company if Ichabod dies during the twenty year period is the "**Death Benefit.**"
6. The 20 year period that the insurance policy will be in effect (provided Ichabod pays the $2,000 each year) is called the "**Term**" of the insurance policy.
7. The $2,000 payment Ichabod must pay each year to keep the policy in force is called the "Premium."

Because the policy in the preceding example is a "term" policy, if Ichabod wanted to get any money from the insurance policy during the policy's twenty year Term, he would be unable to do so. In other words, the policy has no "cash value." The other large classification of insurance policies are called "cash value" policies. These types of insurance policies pay a Death Benefit to the named Beneficiaries, however, they also have an investment component. The Premiums paid by the Insured will be larger with a portion of the Premium covering the cost of the Death Benefit component of the Policy and the remaining portion of the Premium being invested. Therefore, the insurance policy has the potential to grow in value and can provide a source of money to the Insured in the future. An additional benefit of investing in cash value life insurance is that the assets invested inside the policy grow on a tax deferred basis and can actually grow tax free, if the policy is held until death. Also note that in some types of insurance policies, you have the option of investing the "cash value" in various "sub-accounts" within the policy. These sub-accounts are akin to mutual funds and can range from very conservative to very aggressive. It is important to understand that while these types of policies can produce investment growth, they can also suffer market losses that could cause the policy to terminate if the investment loss is substantial enough unless you are willing to pay more money into the policy.

These "cash value" policies come in numerous varieties such as "whole life," "variable universal life" (sometimes called VUL policies for short), and "universal life." There are also numerous "hybrid" policies that combine the features of these types of policies and some even pay dividends. A description of the differences in these types of policies is beyond the scope of this book, however, suffice it to say that the economics of how the "cash value" grows (or potentially declines) in value will vary depending on the type of policy you buy. A qualified insurance professional will be able to explain the differences and be able to tell you the upsides and downsides of the various types of insurance. If you decide to use life insurance as an investment vehicle, it is important to understand the economics of the policy including the policy's internal expenses, the manner in which the cash value is (or can be) invested, and whether the policy provides any "guarantees." If you have a need for insurance and make an intelligent choice with respect to which type of policy is right for you given your individual needs, investing in insurance can be a wise choice. On the other hand, if you do not understand your policy, and have not asked for a "worse case scenario" you may be in for an unexpected and unpleasant surprise down the road. For purposes of the following discussion, when I refer to "cash value" life insurance, I will be assuming a policy with "cash value" that the Insured will have the ability to draw upon.

Protection of the Death Benefit.

When discussing asset protection in the context of life insurance, there are two primary areas that need to be discussed. The first of these is whether the Death Benefit paid to the Beneficiary upon the death of the Insured will be subject to the Insured's creditors or whether the Death Benefit will pass to the Beneficiaries free from the claims of the Insured's creditors. The second area for discussion, is whether the "cash value" in a cash value type of insurance policy will be shielded from the claims of creditors. This next section discusses the first of these two issues.

The statute that prevents a creditor from reaching the Death Benefit of an insurance policy is Florida Statute Section 222.13 which reads in relevant part as follows:

> "Whenever any person residing in the state shall die leaving insurance on his or her life, the said insurance shall inure exclusively to the benefit of the person for whose use and benefit such insurance is designated in the policy, and the proceeds thereof shall be exempt from the claims of creditors of the insured unless the insurance policy or a valid assignment thereof provides otherwise. Notwithstanding the foregoing, **whenever the insurance**, by designation or otherwise, **is payable to the insured or to the insured's estate** or to his or her executors, administrators, or assigns, **the insurance proceeds shall become a part of the insured's estate for all purposes** and shall be administered by the personal representative of the estate of the insured in accordance with the probate laws of the state in like manner as other assets of the insured's estate."

To illustrate how this statute operates, assume that Ichabod in our previous example is a physician who has been sued for medical malpractice. Further assume that Ichabod lost his case and the plaintiff obtained a judgement against him in the amount of $3,000,000. Ichabod appeals the case and upon losing on appeal drops dead of a heart attack. The Death Benefit of $2,000,000 under Ichabod's insurance policy will be paid to Ichabod's wife and the judgement creditor will get nothing.

Review Your Beneficiary Designations.

Notwithstanding the general rule that the Beneficiary receives the Death Benefit under an insurance policy free from the claims of the Insured's creditors, the language in the above statute that I have underlined presents an exception to this general rule. Assume that Ichabod's insurance policy named his estate or his revocable trust as the Beneficiary instead of his wife. In that case, the insurance proceeds would be reachable by the judgement creditor even if Ichabod's will or revocable trust left everything to his wife. I do not think I have ever seen someone intentionally name their estate as the Beneficiary under an insurance policy, however, many insurance policies make the Insured's estate the default Beneficiary in the event no beneficiary is named or if the Beneficiary dies before the Insured and no Contingent Beneficiaries have been named.

For example, suppose Ichabod did not have any children and, therefore, only named his wife as the Beneficiary under his insurance policy. Assume that Ichabod's will left everything to his brother in the event his wife died before him or in the event he and his wife died simultaneously. Further assume that Ichabod's wife had died shortly before Ichabod. In this case, the Death Benefit under Ichabod's insurance policy would most likely be paid to his estate since no Contingent Beneficiaries were named. The judgement creditor would, therefore, be able to reach the entire $2,000,000 Death Benefit to partially satisfy their $3,000,000 judgement and Ichabod's brother would get nothing. Had Ichabod named his brother as a Contingent Beneficiary (or better yet, a trust for his benefit) after his wife, his brother would have received the entire $2,000,000 Death Benefit and the judgement creditor would have received nothing.

Next assume that Ichabod had named his revocable trust as the Beneficiary of his insurance policy on the advice of his estate planning attorney or insurance professional. Further assume that Ichabod's wife survived him. When Ichabod died, the insurance company would pay the Death Benefit to Ichabod's revocable trust, which, under Florida law, is liable to pay for the debts of Ichabod's estate, which would include the $3,000,000 judgement. Therefore, in the event you have named your revocable trust as the Beneficiary of any of your life insurance policies, you should consider naming new beneficiaries to avoid a creditor reaching the Death Benefit. Note that there is a way to ensure that the Death Benefit passes to your intended Beneficiaries in trust without generically naming your revocable trust. If this is important to you, discuss this with your estate planning attorney.

Death Benefit is Not Protected from the Claims of a Beneficiary's Creditors.

Before leaving the topic of protecting the Death Benefit of an insurance policy, it is important to note that the Death Benefit is NOT protected from the creditors of the Beneficiary receiving the Death Benefit.

> Returning to our example of Ichabod and Betty, assume that Ichabod's wife, Betty, had been previously sued for negligence in an automobile accident and the plaintiff had obtained a judgement against Betty in the amount of $3,000,000. Further assume that Betty is the Primary Beneficiary under Ichabod's life insurance policy. When Ichabod dies, the Death Benefit will pass to Betty free from the claims of Ichabod's creditors, however, once the money hits Betty's hand's, Betty's judgement creditor will be able to reach those assets. As explained in the Chapter on "I Gave it to my Spouse Planning," it is possible to draft your revocable trust to create an asset protection trust for the benefit of your spouse. Therefore, if Ichabod had the foresight to make changes to his revocable trust so that an asset protection trust would be created upon his death for the benefit of Betty when he died and if the named Beneficiary was that trust (i.e., the asset protection trust and not the revocable trust directly), the full $2,000,000 death benefit would be available to Betty but would not be reachable by Betty's creditor.

As explained above, it is not difficult to ensure your loved ones benefit from the Death Benefit payable under a life insurance policy, however, there are some traps for the unwary. Make sure you review your beneficiary designations to ensure that they properly coordinate with both your estate plan and asset protection plan.

Protection of Insurance Cash Value.

The next type of asset protection provided by life insurance is the protection of the policy's cash value. The Florida statute that provides this protection is Florida Statute Section 222.14 which reads in relevant part as follows:

> "The cash surrender values of life insurance policies issued upon the lives of citizens or residents of the state . . . upon whatever form, shall not in any case be liable to attachment, garnishment or legal process in favor of any creditor of the person whose life is so insured . . . unless the insurance policy . . . was effected for the benefit of such creditor."

In our previous examples using Ichabod and Betty, the life insurance policy was assumed to be a "term policy." In the following examples, I will assume that the insurance policy is a "cash value" policy meaning it has an investment feature and can provide cash flow to the Insured (i.e., Ichabod) while he is still living.

> Assume the same facts as used in previous examples except that Ichabod's insurance policy (i.e., the Insurance policy with a $2,000,000 death benefit) is a cash value policy that has an annual premium of $50,000 per year. Further assume that the Insurance policy has been in force for several years and the cash value (i.e., the amount of money that Ichabod could take from the policy if needed) has grown to $500,000 over the past several years. After Ichabod lost his law suit, the judgement creditor would not be able to reach the $500,000 in cash value. Even better, the cash value is not only protected if it stays in the policy but Ichabod is free to withdraw it and spend it without interference from his creditors.

In the case of **Faro v. Porchester Holdings, Inc.**, (Sept. 5, 2001), the Florida Fourth District Court of Appeals held that a Certificate of Deposit purchased with funds withdrawn from a cash value life insurance policy were exempt from the claims of creditors and could not be garnished. The court explained that because the statute states that "the cash surrender values of life insurance policies . . . upon whatever form, shall not in any case be liable to attachment . . ." that the owner of an insurance policy may withdraw money from an Insurance policy's cash value and as long as that money is not commingled with other assets, it will retain its exempt status.

> Assume that after the judgement creditor sued Ichabod, Ichabod decided to take $200,000 from his insurance policy and open a brokerage account so that he could invest in a type of investment not offered in his policy. So long as the only money placed in the brokerage account was the $200,000 withdrawn from the cash value of his Insurance policy, the brokerage account will be protected from the claims of Ichabod's judgement creditors.

Note that in the above example any future growth in Ichabod's brokerage account may not be protected. If the brokerage account were owned by Ichabod and his wife as tenants by the entireties ("TBE") account (see Chapter 12), the future growth would be kept from creditors by virtue of the TBE protection, however, it would also be subject to the weaknesses of TBE protection.

Effect of Insurance Policy Ownership on Asset Protection.

A potential trap for the unwary is that the insurance policy (or more specifically, the cash value held inside the insurance policy) must be owned by the Insured. If it is not, at least one case has held that the Florida statute that protects the cash value of an insurance policy will not apply. Therefore, if an insurance policy is owned by someone other than the Insured, do not count on it providing any asset protection. The most common scenarios that involve an insurance policy being owned by someone other than the Insured are listed below.

Insurance Policy Owned by a Child. Some individuals transfer their insurance policy(ies) to a child or children for estate tax reasons. In general, when someone owns an Insurance policy insuring their own life, when that person dies, the entire Death Benefit is included in the decedent's estate and subject to estate taxation. In the event someone other than the Insured owns the Insurance policy, then the

Death Benefit escapes estate taxation. While an estate tax benefit can be garnered using this strategy, there are many downsides. One of the largest of these downsides, is that if the child is ever sued, the cash value in the Insurance policy could be subject to the claims of the child's creditors. Therefore, even though the parent provided the money to pay all the premiums and the Insurance policy insures the life of the parent, a lawsuit against the child could result in the loss of the entire cash value of the policy. This, in turn, usually results in the termination of the insurance policy itself (which may be difficult or impossible to replace depending on the age and health of the insured when the policy terminates).

Split Dollar or Split Ownership Arrangements. Some people have used "split dollar" structures to split the ownership of insurance policies so that the death benefit is owned by a life insurance trust and the cash value is held by the spouse of the Insured or the Insured's employer, for example. This could result in the loss of the policy's cash value in the event the spouse or employer is ever sued. While a complete discussion of these types or arrangements are beyond the scope of this book, be careful when structuring the ownership of a life insurance policy where the cash value is owned by someone other than the Insured.

Insurance Policy Owned by a Revocable Trust. In the event a cash value life insurance policy is owned by your revocable trust, the Insured is technically not the owner of the policy. While this distinction may be thought by some to be hypertechnical, a similar argument was made in the homestead context (see the case of In Re Bosonetto discussed in Chapter 9) which resulted in Mrs. Bosonetto losing the protection of the Florida homestead exemption and her home. There is no compelling reason to have a revocable trust own a life insurance policy, therefore, it is almost never a good idea to risk losing the asset protection benefits granted to insurance policies by owning it in your revocable trust.

Insurance Policy Owned by a 419 Plan. Certain insurance professionals are marketing something called a "welfare benefit plan" or "419 Plan" (named after the section of the Internal Revenue Code authorizing them). These plans are typically set up by business owners to provide certain employee benefits to themselves and their employees. Many of these plans (but certainly not all of them) are abusive and should be closely scrutinized before you invest your hard earned money. A complete discussion of 419 Plans is beyond the scope of this book, however, suffice it to say that if you are being promised a huge up-front tax deduction by participating in one of these plans, be very careful. These plans will oftentimes invest the contributed money in a cash value life insurance policy. It is important to note that these 419 plans are oftentimes not afforded the same protection as retirement plans (see Chapter 10 regarding protecting retirement plan assets). Therefore, there is an argument that a 419 Plan does not provide any asset protection. In addition, since the insurance policy is owned by the 419 Plan and not the Insured, there is an argument that the protection of life insurance cash value offered under Florida law will likewise not apply. 419 plans are oftentimes marketed by people making claims that asset protection is a benefit to be garnered by participating in these plans. This is most likely not the case.

Note that in the last two examples (i.e., the revocable trust example and the 419 Plan example), there is an argument that the beneficiary of the revocable trust and the plan participant should be treated as the owner since they are the beneficial owner of the underlying assets, however, it is only an argument and one that you may lose.

Protection Offered by Annuities.

Similar to the protection afforded to the cash value of life insurance policies, Florida Statutes Sections 222.14 also exempts annuities from the claims of creditors. This statute reads in relevant part as follows:

> The . . . **proceeds of annuity contracts** issued to citizens or residents of the state, **upon whatever form, shall not in any case be liable to attachment, garnishment or legal process** in favor of . . . any creditor of the person who is the beneficiary of such annuity contract, **unless the . . . annuity contract was effected for the benefit of such creditor.**

Before proceeding with a discussion of the asset protection benefits of annuities and the corresponding "traps for the unwary," it is important to understand a little about how annuities work in general.

There are two basic types of annuities: (i) "immediate annuities," and (ii) "variable annuities." I will first discuss immediate annuities and then move on to the topic of variable annuities.

Immediate Annuities.

With an "immediate annuity," an individual pays an insurance company a lump sum of money and the insurance company, in turn, agrees to pay the individual a certain amount each month or year for as long as that individual lives or for a term of years (i.e., 10 years). If the individual will receive payments over their life span, the annuity company will calculate the size of the annuity payments based on the person's age and the interest rate being offered under the annuity contract.

> Ichabod decides to take $100,000 and invest in an immediate annuity that will pay him an income stream for the next ten years. The annuity provides for a 5% interest rate. Each year (for the next ten years) Ichabod will receive a check from the insurance company of roughly $12,500. If Ichabod dies before the ten year period has elapsed, his wife will receive the rest of the payments. No creditor of Ichabod will be entitled to reach any portion of these payments.

Now lets review the terminology. In the preceding example:

1. Ichabod is the **Owner** of the annuity contract since he has the right to exercise control over the annuity.
2. Ichabod is the **Annuitant**. The term "annuitant" in the context of an immediate annuity means two things. First, the annuitant is the person entitled to receive the payments under the annuity (similar to a beneficiary). Second, the annuitant is the person whose age is used in the actuarial calculations that determines the size of the annuity payments in the case of an annuity that makes payments over someone's life span.
3. The ten year period over which Ichabod will receive annuity payments is called the **Term** of the annuity.
4. Ichabod's wife is called the **Beneficiary** since she will receive the annuity payments if Ichabod dies before the end of the ten year term.

Private Annuities.

The 1988 case of **In Re Mart**, stands for the proposition that you can purchase an immediate annuity not only from an insurance company, but also from a family member or trust established by a family member. These types of arrangements are typically called "Private Annuities."

> Ichabod decides to purchase an immediate annuity from his adult child. He transfers property worth $100,000 to his child and they both sign an annuity contract where the child is contractually obligated to pay Ichabod annual payments of $12,500 per year for the next ten years (i.e., the same terms as the above example where Ichabod purchased an immediate annuity from an insurance company). These payments are likewise exempt from the claims of Ichabod's creditors.

Structured Settlements.

When someone wins a law suit such as a personal injury suit, wrongful death, or workers' compensation case, and is awarded a judgement, the victorious plaintiff is oftentimes able to choose how they receive the money that has been awarded by the court. One of these options is to elect to have an annuity purchased that will make payments to the plaintiff over their lifetime or for a term of years. These annuities can be structured so that the payments increase over time and pay out additional sums every third or fourth year, for example. In addition, the annuity can provide that in the event the plaintiff were to die before a certain age, his or her beneficiaries would receive a specified amount. These types of annuity arrangements are commonly referred to as "structured settlements."

There can be numerous benefits to using structured settlements, including asset protection. Florida courts have ruled that even if the annuity is part of a structured settlement, the payments received by the plaintiff are protected from the claims of their creditors, so long as the plaintiff is a direct beneficiary under the annuity contract. In the 1995 case of **Guardian Life Ins. Co. v. Solomon**, an annuity was purchased as part of a structured settlement, however, the annuity listed the defendant as the beneficiary of the annuity, and the defendant then turned around and paid the amount they received from the annuity to the plaintiff. The plaintiff later filed for bankruptcy and claimed that the payments from the defendant were exempt as proceeds from an annuity. The court held that the payments were unprotected because the plaintiff was not a direct beneficiary of the annuity and the settlement agreement alone did not constitute an annuity. Structured settlements should be explored in the event you anticipate receiving an award stemming from the type of law suits described above, however, make sure and consult an attorney knowledgeable in the area of asset protection to avoid any unpleasant surprises in the future.

Lottery Winnings.

In the event you ever have the good fortune of winning the lottery and are faced with the decision of whether to take the lump sum or take payments over the next thirty years, beware that these payments are not considered annuity payments and are, therefore, not protected from the claims of creditors. If you win the lottery at a time when you are not being sued and no identifiable creditor is on the horizon, you should consider taking your winnings in a lump sum and then taking measures to protect those winnings using an asset protection strategy described in this book. If you elected to receive the annual payments and were sued sometime in the future, it could be more difficult to protect your winnings. In fact, if you like the idea of receiving annual payments for the next thirty years or so, you can take the lump sum amount and turn around and invest it in an immediate annuity designed to do just that and those payments would be exempt from the claims of creditors.

Variable Annuities.

The second broad class of annuities is the "variable annuity." These annuities are similar to cash value life insurance in that they have an investment feature. Also, like cash value life insurance, the money invested in the annuity grows on a tax deferred basis (like an IRA) but does not have the possibility of growing tax free like a cash value life insurance policy. With a variable annuity you start by giving the insurance company a sum of money to be held in the variable annuity. The contributed money is then invested in various "sub-accounts" similar to mutual funds. Finally, at a specified age (i.e., 80 or 90) or future date (called the "maturity date"), the variable annuity in essence converts to an immediate annuity and pays out an income stream for the rest of the owner's life or a term of years. At any time before the maturity date, however, the owner of the annuity can withdraw money from the annuity (subject to certain rules and possible penalties discussed below), and can even cancel the annuity and take back the entire "cash surrender value" (i.e., the money in the annuity), again subject to certain rules and possible penalties. Understand that there are a myriad of options with annuities and it is important to understand the product before investing in it to ensure it is right for you. The downsides of annuities will be discussed more completely below.

> Assume that Ichabod invests $100,000 in a variable annuity which provides him the ability to invest the assets in various mutual fund type investments. Ichabod will enjoy tax deferred growth inside the annuity policy and if he is ever sued, he will have access to the annuity's "cash value" without interference from his creditors. If Ichabod dies while money is still in the annuity, the annuity assets will be paid to his wife. If Ichabod lives to age 85 and there is still money in the annuity it will start making payments to Ichabod similar to an immediate annuity.

Now lets review the terminology as it applies to a variable annuity. In the preceding example:

1. The **Maturity Date** of the annuity is the date Ichabod turns age 85. At this point in time, the annuity will be "annuitized" which basically means it converts to an immediate annuity that will pay Ichabod an immediate payment for the rest of his life or a term of years (i.e., 10 years, perhaps). Once the Maturity Date is reached, the analysis on immediate annuities described above would apply.
2. Ichabod is the **Owner** of the annuity contract since he has the right to exercise control over the annuity. One of these rights is the ability to withdraw money from the variable annuity's "cash value." Therefore, in the context of a variable annuity, the initial "beneficiary" of the policy (i.e., the person entitled to receive money from the annuity) is the "owner" prior to the annuity's Maturity Date.
3. Ichabod is the **Annuitant**. Prior to the annuity's Maturity Date, the term "annuitant" refers to the person whose age is used in the actuarial calculations that determine the size of the annuity payments in the case of an annuity that

makes payments over someone's life span. Unlike an immediate annuity, the annuitant is NOT the person entitled to receive the payments under the annuity. While this distinction may seem hyper-technical, it will be relevant when we discuss who is entitled to asset protection; namely the "beneficiary" of the annuity.

4. Ichabod's wife is called the **Beneficiary** since she will receive the assets in the annuity if Ichabod dies before the Maturity Date.

Florida Supreme Court Confirms Variable Annuities Are Protected.

In 2001, the Florida Supreme Court heard the case of **In re Alan L. Goldenberg.** This case involved a physician, Dr. Alan L. Goldenberg, who had been sued for medical malpractice and lost resulting in a judgement against him in the amount of $4,000,629. Dr. Goldenberg had filed for bankruptcy and claimed that seven variable annuities he had previously purchased were exempt from the claims of the judgement creditor. Up until this case, some people questioned whether "variable annuities" were exempt prior to their "maturity date" when the annuity starts paying out a stream of income like an "immediate annuity." Their argument was that the legislature in granting annuities asset protection only meant "immediate annuities" and that a "variable annuity" prior to the Maturity Date is really akin to an investment account with an option to receive an annuity in the future. The court in **In re Alan L. Goldenberg** confirmed that variable annuities **are** protected even before their Maturity Date. This is obviously wonderful news to people who use these financial products to invest their assets.

In stating the court's holding that variable annuities are protected, the exact language they used was:

> "We . . . hold that the proceeds of an annuity contract where there is a surrender penalty are exempt from legal process by virtue of section 222.14. "

Although the court did not elaborate on the underlined language in the court's holding, it seems to indicate that annuities that do not have a surrender penalty may not be protected. A surrender penalty is a fee that the purchaser of an annuity must pay if the annuity is cancelled within a certain period of time after the annuity is purchased. Certain annuities, such as "no-load" annuities , do not impose a surrender penalty, and may not offer the asset protection benefits of annuities with surrender penalties. In the event you are relying on annuities that never imposed a surrender penalty as a means of protecting your assets, you may be wise to convert them to annuities that do if it makes sense financially. It is not entirely clear whether an annuity that had a surrender penalty in the past but which has lapsed by the time the creditor is trying to reach the annuity assets would somehow lose its protection. I do not believe that the court intended this result but was merely referring to the existence of an initial surrender penalty.

The "Beneficiary" of an Annuity is Entitled to Protection.

You may remember that the exact language of the Florida Statute providing protection with respect to annuities is as follows:

> The . . . proceeds of annuity contracts issued to citizens or residents of the state, upon whatever form, shall not in any case be liable to attachment, garnishment or legal process in favor of . . . any creditor **of the person who is the beneficiary of such annuity contract**, unless the . . . annuity contract was effected for the benefit of such creditor.

Under the language of the statute, the person entitled to asset protection is the "beneficiary" of the annuity. As I have explained above, the term "beneficiary" typically refers to the person who will receive the balance of the assets in or payments from the annuity contract when the annuitant dies. In the case of **In Re Ebenger,** Mr. Ebenger was provided an annuity by his law firm that gave him the option of taking a lump-sum distribution from the annuity of almost $100,000. Mr. Ebenger had filed for bankruptcy and Mr. Ebenger's creditor argued that the annuity should not be protected because he was the "annuitant" under the annuity contract and not the "beneficiary." The court stated that "the term 'beneficiary' is not a term of art necessarily restricted to those who receive a benefit upon the death of another." The court then held that Mr. Ebenger should be considered a "beneficiary" for purposes of the Florida statute protecting annuities. Therefore, if you are an "annuitant" or "owner" entitled to receive assets from an annuity, the annuity should be protected.

A possible "trap for the unwary" may exist if the annuity is held inside a retirement plan that is not protected from the claims of creditors (see Chapter 10 of this book for a complete discussion of this topic). If the retirement plan itself is entitled to receive payments from the annuity, the plan may be considered the "beneficiary" not the plan participant. In that case, having the retirement plan invest in an annuity may do little to increasing asset protection. This is not a settled area of law, however, so if investing in an annuity makes sense for other reasons, there may be an added benefit of asset protection.

Distributions from an Annuity can Retain their Protected Status.

The case of **In re Benedict** was similar to the **Faro** case discussed previously in the context of life insurance. In this case, Mrs. Benedict was the beneficiary of an immediate annuity contract. Annuity payments were made to her and she deposited them in her checking account. Mrs. Benedict had filed for bankruptcy and her creditors claimed that the annuity payments that were deposited in a checking account were unprotected. The court disagreed and held that annuity payments that are deposited in a bank account retain their protected character "so long as the funds can be properly traced into the account and are readily accessible to the debtor."

This can create some interesting planning opportunities. For example, assume Ichabod is leery of the stock market and has $1,000,000 in a money market account earning 1% interest. Ichabod goes to his financial advisor who recommends that Ichabod invest that money in an immediate annuity. Ichabod tenders the $1,000,000 to an insurance company and purchases an immediate annuity with an interest rate of 4%. Under the terms of the annuity, Ichabod will receive roughly $225,000 each year for the next five years. If Ichabod places each payment in a brokerage account that is not commingled with other assets, the annuity payments will retain their protected status even after distribution. An even safer technique would be to use these exempt assets to fund a separate asset protection structure, thereby giving yourself a two-tiered defense if sued.

The Upsides and Downsides to Life Insurance and Annuities.

The preceding sections of this Chapter have been spent discussing the asset protection aspects of life insurance and annuities. Now I want to give a general overview of some of the benefits and detriments of using these life insurance and annuity products, so you can make an intelligent decision as to what is right for you. There are some who argue that these financial products never make sense and others who argue that they are always the best way to invest. The truth is that these products can be very valuable in the right circumstances, and can produce negative results in others. The determining factor is usually the thoroughness of the planning prior to making the decision as to what is right for you given your personal facts and circumstances. That being said, on to the upsides and downsides.

The Downsides.

In the wrong situation, using life insurance and annuities may present some problems. Some of these are described below:

1. **Costs.** Not all life insurance policies and annuities are created equal. Some have internal fees and costs that are high enough to make it unattractive as an investment vehicle. With respect to cash value life insurance, one of these costs is obviously the expense of the insurance (i.e., the portion of the policy that will pay a death benefit to the beneficiaries in the event you die). Therefore, if you do not have a need for insurance, this added cost may do nothing but reduce investment return. For example, if the increased cost of investing in an insurance product or variable annuity is 1% when compared to investing outside an insurance product (e.g., a brokerage account, money market account, etc.), you would be paying $10,000 each year for every million dollars invested. Over a ten year period that would amount to $100,000, which makes it an expensive method of protecting assets. In short, make sure you understand the costs of any investment before you sign on the dotted line.

   On the other hand, another calculation that needs to be taken into account is the IRR (i.e., the internal rate of return) you are earning when you compare the premiums paid into the policy and the ultimate death benefit the beneficiary will receive. For example, suppose Barney is 65 years old and purchases a life insurance policy with a death benefit of $2,000,000. The policy requires him to pay an annual premium of $30,000 per year to keep the policy in place. Barney has plenty of savings to live on but wants to make sure his children and grandchildren receive at least $2,000,000 to fund education and provide them with incentives to be hard working and do well in school. Barney establishes a trust that contains these incentive provisions, and purchases the insurance policy inside the trust. If Barney lives to his life expectancy (roughly age 85), Barney will have contributed a total of $600,000 to the trust over that twenty year period and upon his death the trust will receive the $2,000,000 death benefit. If the trust had not purchased insurance but rather invested the $30,000 received by it each year in a brokerage account, the brokerage assets would have had to earn an 11.33% after tax rate of return (remember that the trust receives the death benefit free of any obligation to pay income taxes) each and every year to have the same $2,000,000 when Barney dies at age 85. In other words, the after tax IRR of Barney's investment in the policy was 11.33%. If Barney had died at age 80, the after tax IRR jumps to just over 19%. If Barney ends up living to age 90, the after tax IRR drops to 7.37% which is still a decent rate of return. Obviously, the longer Barney lives, the lower the IRR, however, investing in the policy could give Barney a very respectable rate of return when viewed from this perspective. These numbers may not be so fantastic if Barney was in poor health and had to pay higher premiums, but it is always important to crunch the numbers to get a handle on what you are looking at. I do not sell insurance and have no incentive for my clients to use or not use insurance products. I just consider life insurance to be a tool like any other which sometimes makes sense and sometimes does not.

2. **Cash Flow Restrictions**. As mentioned above, most life insurance policies and annuities contracts have "surrender penalties." These require the owner of a life insurance contract or annuity to pay a fee if the life Insurance policy or annuity is cancelled or if you withdraw more than a certain amount (usually around 10%) in any one year. These penalties usually start high and then decrease to nothing over time (usually between 7 and 15 years although some annuities have shorter surrender penalty periods). Another restriction with certain variable annuities is the imposition of a 10% income tax penalty (on top of any other penalties) if the annuity owner withdraws money from the annuity before age 59 ½ (similar to IRAs and most retirement accounts). Therefore, if the life insurance policy or annuity is being purchased to provide a source of protected cash flow in the event you are ever sued, you need to make sure these

restrictions will not be prohibitively expensive.

3. **Taxes.** As mentioned above, investing in life insurance can actually result in tax free growth if the policy is still in force when you die (remember that the beneficiary does not have to pay any income taxes when they receive the Death Benefit). Other than a ROTH IRA, there is no present investment vehicle of which I am aware that gives the potential to invest in an equities portfolio on a tax free basis. There is, however, a potential trap for the unwary.

   When money is placed in an insurance policy, you are able to withdraw the cash you put into it on a tax free basis. For example, if you invest $100,000 in a life insurance policy and over the next several years it grows to $300,000, you could withdraw the first $100,000 (i.e., your investment in the policy) and not pay any income taxes. Once you exceed this amount you have to pay income taxes. To avoid this negative income tax result, life insurance companies usually permit you to borrow money from the policy which does not cause you to pay income taxes on the borrowed amount. Building on the previous example, assume that you have already withdrawn your initial investment of $100,000, and now want to take out an additional $50,000. If you simply withdrew it from the policy it would be taxed. If you borrowed it from the policy instead, the $50,000 is income tax free. Note that certain insurance companies design policies where the interest rate on the loan, is offset by a guaranteed investment return so the net cost of the loan is zero. If the net cost of the loan is greater than zero, the loan, which compounds annually, can obviously affect the cash value in a negative manner, sometimes significantly.

   With this explanation out of the way, I will now move on to the trap for the unwary. Life insurance policies of this type require you to keep a certain minimum cash value, otherwise the policy can lapse (i.e., terminate). If this happens when there are outstanding loans, you have to pay tax on the amount you previously borrowed at the time the policy lapses. A good financial advisor will help you fund the policy correctly and maintain it to reduce the likelihood of the policy lapsing. In addition, some insurance companies offer something called a "death benefit guarantee" where so long as you continue to make some minimum premium payment, the policy can never lapse. There is obviously a cost for this additional benefit so you will have to weigh (i) the cost of the guarantee against (ii) the tax cost if the policy lapses multiplied by the likelihood that a lapse will ever occur. You will probably see more policies lapsing in upcoming years, since the downturn in the market at the beginning of this century had the effect of substantially reducing the cash value of many individuals' policies.

Variable annuities are taxed differently than cash value life insurance. Assume that you place $100,000 into a variable annuity and that your investment grows to $300,000 over several years. Now assume you want to withdraw $100,000. Unlike the life insurance policy, you are forced to withdraw the growth (i.e., the taxable portion) first before you can withdraw your initial investment (i.e., the tax free portion). In addition, the annuity will convert capital gains (which are presently taxed at 15%) to ordinary income which is presently taxed at rates as high as 35% (and which is likely to rise in the future). Finally, when you die owning a variable annuity, the beneficiary inherits the tax liability in addition to the assets. This would not be the case if you had owned an equities portfolio outside of an annuity. To make matters worse, if the owner of the annuity has an estate that is subject to estate tax, the entire annuity is subject to estate tax including the portion of the annuity that will have to be used to pay income taxes by the beneficiary. There is a tax credit which partially offsets this potential double taxation, however, it is not completely offset.

It is important to note that the explanations described above are general in nature. There are numerous types of annuities and life insurance policies with literally thousands of options, some of which may mitigate a portion of these downsides.

The Upsides.

1. **Asset Protection / Simplicity.** The obvious first benefit is the ability to shelter your investment assets from the claims of creditors. Some people also like the fact that maintaining an insurance policy or annuity is simple and easy to understand. In other words, even if a family limited partnership, offshore asset protection structure, or domestic asset protection structure is less expensive in the long term (and sometimes even in the short term), certain individuals prefer the simplicity of using insurance and annuities to protect their assets.

2. **Taxes.** As noted above, cash value insurance can allow an individual to invest in the stock market and realize tax free growth similar to a ROTH IRA without

the limitations on how much you can invest. Tax free growth on equity investments can obviously be a significant benefit, especially if the market performs well over time.

Annuities offer the benefit of tax deferred growth similar to an IRA. Like an IRA you will ultimately pay taxes, however, the money that would have been used to pay taxes had you invested outside the annuity are available to reinvest. For example, suppose that you invest $100,000 and get a 10% return on your money (i.e., $10,000). If that $10,000 were subject to tax at a 30% tax rate, the tax would be $3,000, leaving a balance of $107,000 to reinvest. In a tax deferred vehicle like an IRA or annuity, the full $110,000 would be available to reinvest (i.e., you now have $3,000 working for you that you would not have in a taxable investment).

How valuable tax deferral is to you will depend on three primary factors. The first of these factors is the rate of return at which your assets are growing. Building on the previous example, if you are a conservative investor and are not likely to earn more than 4%, instead of having a full $3,000 to reinvest, you would only have an extra $1,200. The second relevant factor in determining the benefit of tax deferral is the length of time you plan to invest the assets. Again returning to the previous example, in the event you received a ten percent rate of return, the benefit of tax deferral after five years is roughly $1,500, after fifteen years that number jumps to roughly $38,000, and after twenty-five years, the benefit of tax deferral jumps to $212,000. Note that if the investment return was only 4% instead of ten percent, the benefit of tax deferral after five years is roughly $210, after fifteen years that number jumps to roughly $4,000, and after twenty-five years, the benefit of tax deferral jumps to $15,000. The third factor to consider is to whether the annual return on the assets invested outside the annuity are taxed in the first place (i.e, capital gains are only recognized if a stock is sold, tax free bond interest is not taxed, etc.), and what tax rate would apply if the were taxed (i.e., capital gains are taxed at a top tax rate of 15% versus a top ordinary tax rate of 35% percent). In other words, it may be possible to construct an investment portfolio that meets your individual goals and objectives and that offers an ability to garner significant deferral outside a tax deferred vehicle.

3. **Guarantees.** One of the principal benefits of investing in annuities are the

availability of certain guarantees. For example, many annuities offer a principal guarantee. This allows you to invest in the market and if your money grows then you reap the benefit of that growth. If the market performs poorly, however, and you lose money, when you die your beneficiary is guaranteed to receive the full amount of the principal you initially invested. Another variation on this guarantee will pay the highest value during the preceding year to your beneficiary in the event you die. For example if you invest $500,000 in an annuity. One year later, it has grown to $550,000 but then drops to $450, 000 six months later. If you were to die in month seven, your beneficiary would receive the entire $550,000. Another of these guarantees is called a "living benefit" that does not require you to die in order to get your principal back. For example, assume you invest $500,000 in an annuity with a living benefit. You can invest the assets in the stock market and if you do well and your assets grow, you reap the benefit. If on the other hand your investments perform horribly and you lose money, you have the option on the tenth anniversary date of purchasing the annuity to receive an income stream for the rest of your life (i.e., an immediate annuity) based on your entire principal investment plus five percent compounded annually for the entire ten years. There are many versions of this living benefit, however, this is just one example. Each of these guarantees has a cost, however, many people have lost money in the market in the last few years and in hind sight would have gladly paid to protect their principal.

4. **Permanent Income for Life.** Another principal benefit of annuities is their ability to provide you with an income stream that you cannot outlive. With an immediate annuity or a variable annuity that you can annuitize (i.e., convert to an immediate annuity) in the future (especially if the annuity contract provides for a living benefit as discussed above), the insurance company is promising to pay you a specified sum each year regardless of how long you live. Some even provide for cost of living increases to offset the negative effect of inflation on your buying power. This can be a huge benefit especially if you end up living past your anticipated life expectancy. If you want the peace of mind of knowing that you will have an income stream that will never end so long as you live, an annuity product may be the answer.
5. **Flexible Death Benefit.** Another benefit of a cash value life insurance policy is the flexibility to reduce the death benefit in later years if you feel you do not need the full amount later in life. For example, assume you invest in a cash

value insurance policy that has a $3,000,000 death benefit. This is a sufficient amount to provide for your spouse and children in the event you were to die unexpectedly. Suppose you do not die before retirement age and now have $2,000,000 built up in cash value. You now feel that a $500,000 death benefit is more appropriate given your now current obligations and need for liquidity. You have the power to reduce the death benefit to the $500,000 amount thereby reducing the cost of the insurance which will allow the cash value to grow even faster. If you felt you did not need insurance at all, you could reduce the death benefit to a de minimis amount even further reducing the cost of the insurance.

6. **Non-Garnishable Source of Cash Flow.** Certain asset protection techniques like the family limited partnership can keep assets from the claims of creditors, however, they can also be kept from you. If you need to get money out of the partnership to maintain your lifestyle, the creditor can get access to the distributed money (See Chapter 17 on Family Limited Partnerships). Since part of the strategy of a Family Limited Partnership is the ability to tell a creditor that it will be a long time before they will be able to get at the assets inside the partnership (i.e., the ability to play the "waiting game"), you will need a source of protected money to maintain your life style, otherwise, if the creditor believes you will be unable to play the waiting game for the duration of the judgement (or at least a significant period of time), they will pursue their judgement rather than settling. Life insurance and annuities can be just such a source of exempt cash flow.

7. **Liquidity on Death.** A final benefit to insurance is to provide liquidity upon death. For example, if you own your own business and want to pass it to the next generation on your death, if you do not have the cash to pay the estate tax, the business may suffer or fail to survive. Likewise, if you have partners in your business, insurance can provide your partners liquidity to buy your interest in the business so your family has the liquidity they need to survive.

In conclusion, whether or not insurance is right for you will depend on a number of factors. You may want to use the above explanations of the upsides and downsides of life insurance and annuities as guidelines for asking intelligent questions as you shop for a life insurance policy or annuity. The bottom line is do your homework so you can make an intelligent decision as to what is right for you.

Planning Considerations.

Below I have listed several planning considerations. As you read them, understand that I have made the assumption that you have already analyzed the non-asset protection factors of life insurance and annuities, and have made a decision that one or both of these investment vehicles is beneficial given your personal facts and circumstances.

Who Should Consider Using Life Insurance or Annuities as Part of Their Comprehensive Asset Protection Plan?

People with an Insurance Need. The first individuals who should consider using life insurance or annuities as part of their comprehensive asset protection plan, are people who have a long term insurance need. Since you will be purchasing a death benefit anyway, why not take advantage of the ability to receive a tax free investment account that is also protected from the claims of your creditors.

As a quick aside, I am constantly asked by my clients who are purchasing insurance to provide for their spouse and children "how much insurance do I really need?" This answer is obviously different for each person, however, the real question these clients are asking is "if I had died yesterday and (i) added up my liquid assets available for my spouse and kids to live on (i.e., the home, etc. are not included), and then (ii) added the death benefit of my insurance to that number, how long would it take for my family to run out of money given (a) their present life style, (b) the inflation rate, (c) the rate of return on the assets if conservatively invested, and (d) any income from other sources (i.e., spousal income, social security, etc.)? For example:

> Harold and Maude have three children ages 11, 9, and 6. Harold and Maude have not yet accumulated enough money to retire and Harold is concerned that if he were to pass on, Maude and the kids would be left in financial straights. Maude has been a full time mother since their first child, Glaucus, was born and they want to be sure that Maude can continue to play that important role until their youngest child, Nathan Hale, turns

> age 18. Maude has a college degree but they realize it will take her roughly 10 to 12 years to build a career that will pay a sufficient salary to meet the economic needs of her and the kids. Therefore, they realize that they need to have enough money to support the needs of Maude and the kids for roughly that 25 year period.

I have designed a spreadsheet that allows you to enter the variables relevant to your family to make these calculations. I like using spreadsheets because all of the variables and assumptions are completely transparent and any changes to a variable give you an instant update to the end result. By using this spreadsheet, the process is relatively short and becomes much more educational than using some rule of thumb like 10 times your income (which really makes no sense since it only involves the use of one variable and ignores all of your personal facts and circumstances). If you are interested in doing this type of planning, go to http://www.kirwanlawfirm.com to download the spreadsheet.

Single People. People who are not married have less asset protection options since they cannot use the tenancy by the entireties form of ownership or engage in "I Gave it to my Spouse" planning (see Chapters 12 and 13). For them, using life insurance or annuity products provides a way to protect assets domestically if a more sophisticated asset protection structure is unwarranted given their personal facts and circumstances.

Owners of Family Limited Partnership. As explained above, people with Family Limited Partnerships have a need for protected sources of cash flow in the event a charging order is levied and they do not have access to the partnership assets. Cash value life insurance, annuities, exempt wages, disability insurance payments, and IRAs and protected retirement plans, can all be sources of protected cash flow.

Fraudulent Transfers.

It is important to understand that once a creditor has been identified, a transfer of assets to a life insurance policy or annuity will most likely be deemed a "fraudulent transfer" (see Chapter 5 on Fraudulent Transfers) and, therefore, reachable by the identified creditor. An interesting case called **In Re Kimmel** was decided in 1991. In that case Dr. Kimmel was involved in an automobile accident. **After** the accident occurred, Dr. Kimmel sold his Jaguar and invested the sales proceeds of $22,000 in a cash value life insurance policy. Dr. Kimmel's creditor argued that the conversion of unprotected assets (i.e., the sales proceeds from his automobile) to protected assets (i.e., the cash value life insurance policy) should be considered a fraudulent transfer and the creditor should be able to reach those assets. The court, however, stated that "[Dr. Kimmel] had engaged in a pattern of financial planning dating back to 1978 . . . [and] the evidence indicates that [Dr. Kimmel], on the advice of a financial planner, continued this practice after the date of the accident. Based on these facts, the court finds that the [life insurance policy] was not purchased with the intent to hinder, delay or defraud creditors. . ." In other words, since Dr. Kimmel had established a pattern of investing in life insurance prior to the date of the accident, the continuance of that pattern after a creditor appeared on the horizon was not considered a fraudulent transfer and Dr. Kimmel did not lose the assets in the life insurance policy. One should note that the case was decided before Florida enacted a "fraudulent conversion" statute so the case may not carry the same weight now as it did back in 1991, however, it illustrates the importance of (i) establishing a financial and asset protection plan prior to the identification of a creditor, and (ii) maintaining that plan over time.

Proper Ownership / Beneficiary Designations.

As discussed above, it is important to review the beneficiary designations of all your life insurance and annuity contracts to ensure that they pass to your intended beneficiaries in a manner that maximizes both asset protection and your estate planning objectives. You should also review your beneficiary designations for your retirement plans and IRAs. I cannot tell you how many people I have worked with who were certain that their beneficiary designations were made one way only to discover that they were wrong upon further investigation.

Create a Financial Plan / Cash Flow Needs Analysis.

I am a big believer in proper planning which includes creating a financial plan that sets forth your anticipated cash flow needs over time. Understanding how much you need to maintain your lifestyle and to meet your financial goals and objectives allows you to make intelligent decisions with respect to asset protection planning, estate planning, and whether life insurance and annuities make sense given your individual facts and circumstances. Once you know how much you need and when you are likely to need it, you should examine your sources of cash flow and analyze whether they are protected from the claims of creditors (i.e., cash value life insurance, annuities, exempt wages, disability insurance payments, IRAs and protected retirement plans, asset protection structures, etc.). Once this has been accomplished, you can move on to create an asset protection and estate plan built on this foundation (I call this process Integrated Wealth PlanningK) that will accomplish your specific, individual goals and objectives rather than leaving you with a generic set of legal documents that you do not understand and that may or may not give you your intended result. Remember that whether a plan is "successful" is measured by the results it provides. Therefore, the planning process should always start by identifying what you want (i.e., your desired outcome), and why you want it.

Conclusion.

Life insurance and annuities can provide solid asset protection and in some cases, even provide advantages from an investment standpoint. Use the information in this Chapter to help you determine whether these financial products are an appropriate part of your comprehensive asset protection plan.

CHAPTER 15

Miscellaneous Exemptions

In this Chapter, I am going to briefly review a few miscellaneous exemptions that were not covered in previous Chapters of Part II. The principal exemptions I plan to cover are (i) the exemption for the Florida Prepaid College Program; (ii) the Florida exemption for Section 529 College Savings Plans, (iii) the Florida exemption of Disability Insurance Payments, and (iv) the exemption for Social Security Payments.

The Florida Prepaid College Plan .

The Florida Prepaid College Plan allows parents, grandparents, businesses, and others to pay for a child's college education in a Florida college or university and lock in today's tuition prices. Any money paid into this program is protected from the claims of creditors under Florida Statute Section 222.22. This statute reads in relevant part as follows:

> "Moneys paid into or out of, the assets of, and the income of any validly existing qualified tuition program authorized by section 529 of the Internal Revenue Code of 1986, as amended, including, but not limited to, the Florida Prepaid College Trust Fund advance payment contracts under Florida Statutes Section 1009.98 and Florida Prepaid College Trust Fund participation agreements under Florida Statutes Section 1009.981, are not liable to attachment, levy, garnishment, or legal process in the state in favor of any creditor of or claimant against any program participant, purchaser, owner or contributor, or program beneficiary."

Therefore, both the purchaser (i.e., the parent, grandparent, etc.) and the beneficiary (i.e., the child / future college student) receive protection.

In addition, Florida Statute Section 732.402(2)(c) also protects the assets in the Florida Prepaid Tuition Programs when you die and further protects it from being subject to probate.

Section 529 Plans

529 Plans are named for the section of the Internal Revenue Code that govern them. These plans provide a parent, grandparent, etc. a manner to save for a child's education and receive tax free growth on the invested assets so long as the assets ultimately are used for certain defined educational expenses such as college tuition. As with the Florida Prepaid College Plan, they are given asset protection under Florida Statute Section 222.22.

Therefore, like the Florida Prepaid College Plan, both the purchaser (i.e., the parent, grandparent, etc.) and the beneficiary (i.e., the child / future college student) receive protection.

It is also important to understand that most, if not all, states have a Section 529 Plan. When I wrote the first edition of this book in 2003, the Florida Statute only protected assets deposited in the Florida 529 Plan NOT any 529 Plan. Thankfully, the Florida legislature saw fit to amend the statute to include ALL 529 Plans regardless of which state's law they were established under. If you visited your local Florida banker and asked him or her to set up a Section 529 Plan for you, you may have ended up with a Georgia 529 Plan, or an Alaska 529 Plan, etc. This used to mean that there was no guarantee that a 529 Plan was protected (unless it was a Florida 529 Plan). Under the new amended statute ALL 529 Plans are protected regardless of which state's laws govern them.

I want to add one quick side note regarding the new bankruptcy act (BAPCPA). BAPCPA added provisions which exclude 529 Plans from the bankruptcy estate subject to certain limitations. Since a Florida resident in bankruptcy is forced to use Florida's state law exemptions which exempt 529 Plans in whole (i.e., without any such limitations), the limitations will not apply to reduce their asset protected nature.

Another benefit added by the amendment to Florida Statute Section 222.22, is that now medical savings accounts (tax deferred accounts that are used for paying medical expenses) are protected from the claims of creditors. The new addition also added protection for a "hurricane savings account" which are defined as an account owned by the owner of homestead property holding assets up to twice the amount of an insurance deductible or other uninsured portion of the risk of loss from a hurricane, windstorm, or flood. The new provision states that it will only become effective when the federal government provides tax-exempt or tax-deferred status to such accounts. This has not yet happened so as things stand now, any such account is not yet exempt.

Disability Insurance Payments.

One form of insurance that makes imminent sense for any family "bread winner" is disability insurance. This insurance replaces that person's salary in the event they become disabled and are not able to provide for their family. When the disabled person receives these payments, they are protected from the claims of his or her creditors under Florida Statute 222.18. This statute reads as follows:

> "Disability income benefits under any policy or contract of life, health, accident, or other insurance **of whatever form**, shall not in any case be liable to attachment, garnishment, or legal process in the state, in favor of any creditor or creditors **of the recipient of such disability income benefits**, unless such policy or contract of insurance was effected for the benefit of such creditor or creditors."

Therefore, the statute protects disability income benefits received under an insurance policy from the creditors of the recipient of such benefits.

In addition, at least one case has held that payments received under a worker's compensation settlement are protected from the claims of creditors under a provision of the federal bankruptcy case. Another Florida case, **In re Green**, held that the payments received by an individual that are traceable to workers compensation settlement proceeds, remained protected even after they were distributed. Therefore, like payments from an insurance policy or annuity, if you hold payments from a disability policy or monies received from a worker's compensation settlement in an account that is not commingled with other assets, they will remain protected from the claims of your creditors.

Social Security Payments.

Social security retirement and disability payments are generally not reachable by a creditor of the recipient. This protection is found under the federal law that governs these payments. One exception to this general rule is that social security benefits of this type are still reachable to pay for child support obligations.

Another type of social security benefit is called Supplemental Security Income (SSI). These payments which are based on need (i.e., they are made available to people with little assets or means to support themselves) are also protected from the claims of creditors. Unlike the other forms of social security payments, they cannot be reached to satisfy child support obligations.

Part III

Protecting Assets with Domestic and Offshore Entities

The final portion of the book is designed to give you a deeper understanding of protecting your assets using various domestic and offshore structures. These structures can be excellent tools for sheltering wealth from the claims of creditors, however, as I have explained in previous sections of this book, there is no such thing as a one-size-fits-all planning structure. For individuals with a high net worth, using these structures as part of a diversified, comprehensive asset protection plan makes imminent sense. In addition, many of the means to protect assets using state law exemptions simply do not make practical sense in many situations. For example, single individuals cannot use "Spousal Asset Protection Techniques" such as the tenancy by the entireties form of asset ownership or "I Gave it to my Spouse" planning. For these people, asset protection structures are oftentimes the only intelligent choice to provide a substantial fortress in which to shield their assets. In addition, (i) there are limits to how much one can contribute to an IRA or retirement plan, (ii) life insurance and annuities can be prohibitively expensive in many situations, (iii) divorce or the death of a spouse can completely destroy the asset protection offered by Spousal Asset Protection Techniques, and (iv) certain illiquid assets like real estate, equipment, machinery, and the like are not suitable for protection using state law exemptions. Finally, all domestic asset protection techniques suffer from (a) the uncertainty in effectiveness that future U.S. law changes may bring and (b) the added complexities that arise when someone moves from state to state.

Physicians who own their own practice (and any business owner for that matter), face certain risks and liabilities that can only be mitigated through the use of various business entities. For this unique class of individuals, their first line of defense has to be the intelligent structuring of their businesses, taking into account factors such as tax planning, estate planning, business succession planning, and, of course, asset protection planning. A failure to understand your options in this area can produce disastrous results, not only for the business owner but also for his or her family and the employees who rely on them to support their families.

As the old adage goes, if you fail to plan, you are planning to fail. The following Chapters in this book will arm you with the information necessary to plan intelligently to keep your hard earned assets safe and secure.

Chapter 16 will discuss how to use business entities such as corporations, limited liability companies, and various types of partnerships to shield assets from numerous sources of liability. I will also explain why physicians and other professionals cannot use corporations or other legal entities to shelter themselves from malpractice claims and which type of legal entity is best suited to house your medical practice.

Chapter 17 discusses the benefits and detriments of using the highly promoted "Family Limited Partnership" to protect your assets. I will cut through the copious "hype" surrounding this asset protection technique and give you a solid understanding of their "upsides" and "downsides" so you can make an intelligent decision of whether using an FLP as part of your asset protection plan makes sense given your personal facts and circumstances.

Chapter 18 provides an overview of what trusts are and the terminology used when discussing trusts. It also explains how certain domestic trusts can provide asset protection to the trust beneficiaries. The trusts discussed in this Chapter are those created by one person for the benefit of another. Finally, it describes how to incorporate these trusts into your estate and asset protection plan to increase the plan's total effectiveness.

Chapter 19 discusses how to protect assets using domestic asset protection trusts and how to combine the Family Limited Partnership with these "Self-Settled Trusts" to create a flexible and effective means of protecting your assets and create a powerful estate planning tool. I will also discuss how these relatively new structures may be challenged by a creditor and show ways to strengthen their protection though intelligent structure design.

Chapter 20 discusses the often misunderstood area of offshore asset protection planning. It will explain why a well constructed offshore structure combining a foreign trust with an offshore limited liability company can provide some of the strongest asset protection available. It will also explain why these structures are not a wise choice to protect assets if a creditor has already been identified.

Chapter 21 introduces the topic of equity stripping (i.e., ways to remove sufficient value from an asset so as to render it unattractive to a creditor). Equity shifting is structuring the ownership of an asset or business entity so that any resulting cash flow and/or appreciation end up in a "protected place." Neither equity stripping nor equity shifting are stand alone asset protection techniques but rather involve the use of the other asset protection techniques discussed in other chapters of this book.

Chapter 22 will discuss various means of protecting the assets of your medical practice. It also discusses the weaknesses of the heavily promoted "accounts receivable financing structure" and suggests lower cost alternatives to accomplish the same result.

CHAPTER 16

Using Business Entities to Limit Liability

This Chapter is designed to provide you with an overview of how legal entities can be used to limit your exposure to certain types of liability. Before delving into a discussion of the various types of legal entities, I will first provide you with a deeper understanding of the types of liability you may face and their source. This is important because if the source of a law suit (or other liability) stems from an asset (real estate, for example), and that asset can be sequestered inside a legal entity, the liability can be contained within the entity leaving your other assets protected. Likewise, if the source of the liability is not the type that stems from a "sequesterable" asset or business activity, entities can be used to hold other assets in a manner that makes them difficult for a creditor to reach.

In the next section, I will describe several types of legal entities (i.e., corporations, various types of partnerships, and limited liability companies) and provide an explanation of how each one operates, how each one is taxed, and the asset protection benefits and detriments of each one.

Next, I will explain why corporations and other types of legal entities cannot shelter physicians, attorneys, and other professionals from malpractice claims. I will also discuss the things you should consider in choosing the type of legal entity to house your medical practice and why you may **not** want to establish a P.A. (i.e., a professional association) or a P.L. (i.e., a professional limited liability company) to house your medical practice.

I have devoted an entire Chapter (Chapter 17) to discuss one type of legal entity, the Family Limited Partnership. I do so because it has been so heavily promoted as an asset protection device and because there are various upsides and downsides that need to be clearly understood before you make the decision to use a Family Limited Partnership as your primary asset protection method.

Inside and Outside Liability.

In order to understand how legal entities work to limit liability, it is important to understand two broad types of potential liability; namely, "Inside Liability," and "Outside Liability." Each of these categories of liability is discussed below.

Inside Liability.

The first of these broad types of liability is what I call "Inside Liability." As mentioned above, if you own real estate, the property itself can produce liability. For example, people can sue a property owner if they slip and fall on the property, if they are attacked or raped on the property, or if the ceiling caves in and injures someone, just to name a few. Property that has environmental contamination can also produce liability. Other types of property such as heavy equipment can also be the source of law suits. In many cases, if property that has the potential to spawn liability is held inside a legal entity, the liability can be contained and kept from endangering your other assets. I call this type of liability "Inside Liability" since it is the type of liability that can be contained "inside" a legal entity.

> Assume that Chuck forms a Limited Liability Company (I'll call this type of entity an "LLC" for short) and he and his wife, Belinda, own the LLC on a 50% / 50% basis. The name of their LLC is "Heavenly Havens, LLC." Chuck and Belinda want to buy a parcel of real estate with a building they plan to convert into several small apartment units that they will be able to rent. The property is purchased in the name of Heavenly Havens, LLC, and Chuck and Belinda quickly find renters for all of the apartment units. Shortly thereafter, one of the renters, Ralph, slips and falls on the way into his apartment and breaks his leg. Ralph brings a lawsuit claiming that the sidewalk was negligently maintained and that this negligence caused his injury. This is an example of Inside Liability since the source of the liability stemmed from an asset owned "inside" the entity (i.e., the LLC).

In the above example, assuming that Heavenly Havens, LLC, was properly formed and that the lease and all communications with Ralph made clear that Ralph was dealing with a legal entity (i.e.,Heavenly Havens, LLC), then Ralph is entitled to sue the owner of the property (i.e., Heavenly Havens, LLC), not Chuck and Belinda. Therefore, in the event Ralph is successful in obtaining a judgement, he will be entitled to reach the assets held in the name of the LLC (i.e., the real estate, bank accounts in the name of the LLC, etc.), but not any of Chuck and Belinda's other property that they own "outside" the LLC.

> Assume that Chuck and Belinda had decided not to use an LLC and instead purchased the apartment property in their individual names. Since they knew that asset protection was important, they decided to hold it as tenants by the entireties. They also titled their brokerage account, all bank accounts, and some other properties they owned as tenancy by the entireties. The total value of all these other assets was $2,000,000. Now assume that Ralph again slips and falls and breaks his leg. He sues the owners of the property (i.e., Chuck and Belinda) and gets a jury to believe that his leg will never be the same and that his life long dream of being an Olympic athlete is now hopelessly and permanently dashed. The jury awards Ralph $4,000,000 in damages. Since Ralph now has a judgement against **both** Chuck and Belinda, he can reach all of their property, including their property titled as tenants by the entireties. If Chuck and Belinda had purchased property and casualty insurance in the amount of $1,000,000, that insurance would still leave $3,000,000 of Ralph's judgement unsatisfied and Ralph could move on to take Chuck and Belinda's brokerage account, bank accounts, and other properties.

As is exemplified by the above example, the mere formation of a Limited Liability Company to hold the apartment complex property could have protected Chuck and Belinda's assets and left them $2,000,000 richer after Ralph's unfortunate accident. Note that Chuck and Belinda's assets would have also been protected from Ralph's law suit had they used a corporation instead of a Limited Liability Company.

Piercing the Corporate Veil.

Now that you have a general understanding of how a business entity can protect your personal assets from Inside Liability, I want to discuss the exception to that general rule. Creditors will sometimes attempt to reach through a legal entity and sue you personally in an attempt to seize your personal assets . This is called "piercing the corporate veil."

In Florida it is generally very difficult to "pierce the corporate veil" provided that the corporation or other legal entity is respected as a distinct and separate entity. In the case, **Dania Jai-Alai Palace, Inc. v. Sykes** (1984), the Florida Supreme Court held that in order to "pierce the corporate veil," a plaintiff must prove that "the corporation is in actuality the alter ego of the stockholders **and** that it is organized or after organization was employed by the stockholders for fraudulent or misleading purposes, or in some fashion that the corporate property was converted or the corporate assets depleted for the personal benefit of the individual stockholders, or that the corporate structure was not bona fidely established or, in general, that property belonging to the corporation can be traced to the hands of the stockholders." (citing the case of **Advertects, Inc. v. Sawyer Industries, Inc.**(1955)).

In the Advertects case, the Florida Supreme Court explained that to hold otherwise would be to allow every judgement against a corporation to "be exploited as a vehicle for harassing the stockholders and entering upon fishing expeditions into their personal business and assets." Therefore, unless a legal entity is organized or employed to mislead creditors or to work a fraud on them, they should be respected.

In addition, the Florida Statutes governing corporations and limited liability companies both state that for a corporate director or LLC manager to be personally liable to third parties, the creditor must show that (i) the manager or director breached or failed to perform his or her duties, **and** this breach constituted an act of recklessness, bad faith, malicious purpose, or wanton and willful disregard of human rights, safety, or property. This is also a very high standard for any creditor to prove.

A common misperception is that if you fail to create your annual corporate minutes each year and otherwise maintain your corporate book, a creditor will be able to ignore your corporation and "pierce the corporate veil." This is not the case, however, it is still a good idea to do so since it can serve as a strike against you. What you really want to avoid is having your entity considered to be your "alter-ego." The most common behaviors that produce this result are (i) commingling personal and corporate assets and activities such as paying personal expenses out of the corporation, paying business expenses from your personal bank account, and making distributions without a real business reason, and (ii) not keeping enough assets in your entity to run the business the way an actual business person would do so.

So, if you have a legal entity and (i) keep up on maintaining your minutes, books, and records, (ii) establish a separate bank account for your legal entity, (iii) pay only business expenses from that corporate bank account, and (iv) maintain enough money in the entity to pay its debts and obligations as they come due, then a creditor should have a difficult time "piercing the corporate veil."

The Canavan Case, Hopefully an Anomaly.

Now that I have finished explaining how difficult it is to pierce the corporate veil under Florida law, I need to tell you about the disturbing case of Estate of **Canavan v. National Healthcare Corp.** (2004). Roger Friedbauer and his wife, purchased a nursing home known as National Healthcare located in St. Petersburg, Florida. This nursing home was owned and operated in a limited liability company called 1620 Health Partners, LLC, and Southern Hospitality Developers, Inc. was the LLC's manager. The case states that Mr. and Mrs. Friedbauer were "the only principals or shareholders" of these two entities. Patrick Canavan was a resident at the National Healthcare nursing home. Mr Canavan ended up with several injuries, including pressure sores, infections, malnutrition, and dehydration. Mr. Canavan died and the representative of his estate, sued both the business entities and the Friedbauer's individually.

The defendant produced evidence that Mr. Friedbauer (i) had the responsibility of approving the budget for the nursing home, (ii) functioned as the sole member of the 'governing body' of the nursing home making him legally responsible for establishing and implementing policies regarding the management and operation of the facility and for appointing the administrator who is responsible for the management of the facility, and (iii) ignored complaints of inadequate staffing while cutting the operating expenses. They then argued that Friedbauers' "elevation of profit over patient care was **negligent**" and the court agreed. Based on mere **negligence** (remember all those tough standards enumerated above), the appellate court found that the Friedbauers could be held personally liable even without piercing the corporate veil.

If this makes you a little nervous, it should. In essence it sets a legal precedent for undoing the very thing a legal entity was designed to protect against; namely to prevent individuals from being held liable for negligent acts stemming from a business run through a legal entity. It ignored the standards enumerated in both the Florida Statutes and the holdings of the Florida Supreme court. Hopefully, this case will be considered an anomaly and will not carry much weight in the future, but at the present time it has to be taken seriously. I am still a strong advocate of using legal entities to protect against Inside Liability, but also caution that it is more important than ever to attend to establishing a sound asset protection plan to protect your personal assets from creditors.

Outside Liability.

The second broad category of liability is what I call "Outside Liability." This is where the liability comes from something unrelated to the assets or activities of the entity.

> Building on the previous example, assume that Chuck and Belinda did not form a Limited Liability Company to hold the apartment complex, but rather formed a corporation called Heavenly Havens, Inc. Chuck decides one day to visit his ailing grandmother at her home in Apalachicola, and on the way hits a bus load of highly compensated business executives causing them all to suffer significant injuries. These executives all end up suing Chuck, and are successful in obtaining various judgements totaling $20,000,000. One of Chuck's assets is his 50% ownership interest in Heavenly Havens, Inc. which they quickly

> take. Belinda is now in business with Chuck's creditors, who may be able to force a liquidation of Heavenly Havens, Inc. and a sale of the underlying apartment property.

In the above example, the liability did not have its genesis inside the entity, but rather from a completely unrelated source (i.e, an automobile accident involving Chuck).

Protection from Outside Liability.

As noted in the example, the corporation offered Chuck no protection from Outside Liability and Chuck's creditors were able to take his corporate stock with little to no difficultly. As you will soon see, entities such as LLCs and certain partnerships have a distinct advantage over a corporation in the case of Outside Liability.

> Assume that Chuck and Belinda had formed a Limited Liability Company to hold the apartment property instead of a corporation. Further assume that Chuck was in the same automobile accident described in the last example, and the executives obtained the same $20,000,000 in judgements. Unlike the previous example where the judgement creditors were able to simply take Chuck's stock in the corporation, since Chuck now owns a 50% interest in an LLC, the judgement creditors will not be able to directly take Chuck's interest in the LLC, nor will they be able to reach the apartment property held inside the LLC. They will not even have the ability to exercise Chuck's voting rights in the LLC. Instead, they will be able to obtain what is called a "charging order."

The charging order will be discussed in full in Chapter 17 covering the topic of Family Limited Partnerships, however, I will provide a brief description of the "charging order" remedy here to facilitate a deeper understanding of how your choice of entity can result in significantly different outcomes in the context of Outside Liability. In short, a charging order is a court order which entitles a creditor to the debtor's distributions from the entity if and when made; which can be a very long time since the creditor does not have the ability to vote and LLC owners are, therefore, left in control of making all management and distribution decisions.

> Building on the last example, assume that the injured business executives have obtained a charging order from the court to enforce their judgement against Chuck's 50% interest in Heavenly Havens, LLC. Since Chuck and Belinda are still the Managers of the LLC (i.e., the people entitled to control the LLC), they have control over whether or not to make distributions to the owners of the LLC (i.e., themselves). Therefore, if they collect the rents and instead of taking that money out of the LLC, they leave it in the LLC (perhaps they purchase other rental properties in the name of the LLC), Chuck's creditors will not be entitled to collect any money to satisfy their judgements. If, on the other hand, Chuck and Belinda do decide to distribute money from the LLC, the share that would have been paid to Chuck (50% in this example) would instead have to be paid to Chuck's creditors with the charging order.

Therefore, the fact that Chuck's creditors are limited to a charging order gives Chuck the ability to play the waiting game. Put another way, Chuck has the ability to tell a creditor that has filed a law suit against him (or is considering filing a law suit against him) that the best the creditor could ever hope for is a charging order and that it will be a cold day in hell before Chuck and Belinda will ever authorize distributions being made from the LLC. In such a case, the creditor may want to settle for less than 100 cents on the dollar rather than take the risk of waiting for twenty years (i.e., the length of time a judgement is valid in Florida) and receiving nothing.

There is also some authority (though this is still a gray area of law) that a creditor holding a charging order can be taxed on a portion of the legal entity's income while the charging order is in effect. In short, this ability to make the creditor wait to receive distributions (and potentially incur tax liability in the interim) can give you a big advantage in forcing a favorable settlement. As I will explain in detail in Chapter 17 on Family Limited Partnerships, I do not feel that this shifting of tax liability to the creditor is likely to be upheld by a court if it is ultimately ever tested.

The first obvious downside to charging order protection is that while a charging order is in effect, all distributions from the entity will go to the creditor. Some promoters of Family Limited Partnerships and LLCs have explained that this can be avoided by having the entity make loans to owners or paying the owners a salary or management fee for their role in managing the entity's assets. Unfortunately, this is typically not the case.

Types of Legal Entities.

In this next section, I will provide a brief overview of several types of legal entities together with how they work and their advantages and disadvantages from an asset protection standpoint. In general, I will provide a simple overview of the terminology associated with each type of entity and briefly describe how each one is taxed. In the section on "professional companies" (i.e., P.A.'s. and P.L.'s), I will discuss the options that a physician has in choosing the legal entity that will house their medical practice and why a "professional company" may not be the best option.

Corporations.

Corporations are probably the best known type of legal entity and date back to before America was even founded. It is because of this fact that they are so widely used, however, as you will see, I rarely feel that they are the best choice given all of the available options.

Terminology.

Corporations are owned by people called "shareholders." The units of ownership in a corporation is referred to as "stock." Therefore, the shareholders own stock in the corporation. Each year, the shareholders elect a "board of directors" which have the authority to control the corporation. The board of directors in turn usually elect the "officers" of the corporation (i.e., the president, vice-president, secretary, and treasurer) who are generally vested with the authority to run the day-to-day affairs of the corporation.

A corporation is formed by filing Articles of Incorporation with the Secretary of

State's office together with a filing fee. The Articles contain information such as the name of the corporation, the street address and mailing address of the corporation's initial principal office, the number of shares of stock the corporation is authorized to issue, etc. This information becomes part of the public record. The legal document that governs the administrative activities of the corporation is called the "By-Laws" which includes provisions such as (i) the time and place for meetings of officers, directors, and shareholders, (ii) how many directors will serve, their tenure, and their qualifications, (iii) the fiscal year of the corporation, (iv) how the bylaws are amended, and (v) various rules regulating the approval of contracts, loans, stock certificates, etc. Finally, there is oftentimes an agreement entered into between the shareholders (called a "Shareholders' Agreement" or "Buy-Sell Agreement") which (i) sets forth rules on who a shareholder can sell their stock to, (ii) gives the corporation and the shareholders a right of first refusal if a shareholder wants to sell their stock, (iii) sets forth rules governing the price to be paid for stock in the event someone dies or becomes disabled, and (iv) sets forth rules giving the corporation the right to buy back stock that is lost by a shareholder in a divorce proceeding or to a judgement creditor.

Taxation.

Corporations are generally taxed as either a "C corporation" or an "S corporation." In a C corporation, any income earned by the corporation is first subject to tax at the corporate level. Then, when the corporation makes distributions to its shareholders (i.e., makes "dividend payments"), the shareholders pay a second level of tax. S corporations on the other hand, pay no income tax at the corporate level but pass the tax liability through to the shareholders regardless of whether dividends are made.

Therefore, assume we have a corporation owned 50% / 50% by Sam and Joe. Further assume that the corporation had a net income of $100,000 at the end of its tax year. If the corporation were a C corporation, the corporation would first pay a corporate tax of $30,000 (I'll assume the corporate tax is 30%). If it then paid a dividend to its shareholders of the remaining $70,000, Sam and Joe would have to pay a second tax on the $35,000 dividend each of them received. With an S corporation, the corporation would pay no tax on the $100,000 of income, however, both Sam and Joe would report their proportionate share of the corporate income (i.e., $50,000 each) on their individual tax return (and pay tax on that income) regardless of whether the corporation paid a dividend or not. S corporations are, therefore, referred to as "pass-through" entities since the income tax liability "passes through" to the shareholders. Please note that this is a very, very basic overview of corporate taxation and there are good reasons for using both C corporations and S corporations. Before forming any legal entity, it is best to sit down with your accountant or tax professional and discuss the tax implications of your various options so you can make an intelligent and informed decision as to which entity will best suit your individual needs.

A downside to using corporations from an income tax perspective is that distributions of appreciated property can trigger capital gains tax. For example, assume Cindy buys a rental property for $100,000 and owns it in an S corporation. Over the years the property appreciates to $250,000. Cindy now wants to take the property out of the corporation so that she can contribute it to another entity as part of a lucrative business opportunity. When the property is distributed, Cindy will have to pay capital gains tax on $150,000 (i.e., $250,000 fair market value less $100,000 she paid for the property (her "basis)) despite the fact that the property was not sold. I call this the "Corporate Capital Gains Trap." As you will see, this negative result is avoided in entities taxed as partnerships.

One final point, is that the tax law governing S corporations places certain restrictions on S corporations that do not apply to C corporations. For example, S corporations can only have individuals (and certain types of trusts) as shareholders. S corporate stock cannot be owned by non-resident aliens and can only have one class of stock. These restrictions can limit the estate planning and asset protection options of the S corporate shareholder, and should be considered before forming an S corporation. Unfortunately, I have met literally hundreds of people holding appreciated property in an S corporation because their accountant was comfortable with S corporations and recommended them to everyone. Do not trust the advice of any professional unless you have at least some understanding of WHY they are recommending something. Any good professional will be happy to explain their decision making process and the upsides and downsides of any option they are recommending.

Asset Protection.

As mentioned above, a corporation provides a means of protecting the shareholders' assets from the Inside Liability of the corporation but provides no protection to a shareholder from having their stock taken by a creditor (i.e., no protection from the Outside Liability of a shareholder). For this reason, it almost never makes sense from an asset protection standpoint to use corporations to hold your valuable assets or business enterprises. In addition, the corporate laws require that certain meetings be held, and corporate minutes be maintained. While failure to keep minutes all by itself may not be enough for a creditor to argue that the corporation be ignored (i.e., "piercing the corporate veil"), it is still important to follow these legal guidelines. If you fail to do so, it can be used as evidence against you that you are not respecting the corporation's legal existence and, therefore, should not be able to benefit from its asset protection benefits.

Partnerships.

The next broad class of entities are partnerships. There are general partnerships, limited partnerships, limited liability partnerships, and limited liability limited partnerships. I will start with a general explanation of the general partnership and then distinguish the other types of partnership from it.

General Partnerships. Under Florida law, "the association of two or more persons to carry on as co-owners a business for profit forms a [general] partnership, whether or not the persons intend to form a partnership." Therefore, if Tony and his next door neighbor, Ira, decide one day to start a small business selling popcorn balls to local retirement homes, and they plan to split their profits, they just formed a general partnership regardless if they intended to do so or not. It is also possible to purposefully create a general partnership, however, as you read on you may wonder why anyone would do so intentionally. If a general partnership is intentionally created, the legal document that governs the rights of the partners is called, not surprisingly, a "Partnership Agreement."

The owners of a general partnership are called "partners" and each partner has an equal right to control the management of the partnership business. What each partner owns is a "partnership interest."

Taxation. Partnerships are taxed similar to S corporations in that they are also considered "pass through" entities. While there are some significant differences between the way partnerships and S corporations are taxed, a complete discussion of them is beyond the scope of this book. Like an S corporation the income earned by the partnership is not taxed at the partnership level but is rather "passed through" to its partners. Assuming that Tony and Ira's partnership makes $1,000,000 in their first year selling popcorn balls to retirement homes, both Tony and Ira would have to report $500,000 on their own tax return and pay the associated income tax, even if the partnership did not distribute any money to Tony or Ira.

One benefit of a partnership over an S corporation is that a partnership can make a distribution of appreciated property without triggering the Corporate Capital Gains Trap discussed above. Therefore, in the previous example under the topic of corporations where Cindy purchased rental property for $100,000 which grew to $250,000 in value, if she (and at least one other partner) had owned the property in a partnership rather than an S corporation, when she wanted to take the property out of the partnership she would not have to pay any capital gains tax.

Another benefit of partnerships is that they are very flexible; much more flexible than corporations both from a tax and non-tax perspective.

Asset Protection. The general partnership is probably one of the single worst ways to hold property or conduct a business. First, from an Inside Liability perspective, Florida statutes provide that generally "all partners are liable jointly and severally for all obligations of the partnership . . ." This means that all partners are personally responsible for any liability that stems from the partnership. Therefore, if someone slips and falls on a piece of real estate owned inside the partnership and obtains a judgement against the partnership, the judgement creditor can enforce it against all of the partners, jointly and severally. Building on the example of Tony and Ira, assume that Tony has a net worth of $5,000,000 and Ira has no real money to speak of. Further assume that Ira stupidly enters into a business deal in the name of the partnership without Tony's knowledge and the partnership is later sued for several million dollars due to Ira's actions. The judgement creditors can go after Tony for the full amount of the judgement despite the fact that he was personally not at fault. Therefore, from an Inside Liability perspective, general partnerships are very dangerous.

From an Outside Liability perspective, the partnership does offer charging order protection, however, it is not as protective as one might think. Based on a Florida statute governing the dissolutions of general partnerships, the court in a case called **Schiller v. Schiller**, held that a court could order the sale of a partner's general partnership interest that was subject to a charging order. Therefore, the ability to force a favorable settlement with a would be creditor by threatening to play the waiting game may not be taken seriously by a creditor or potential creditor. Due to the way the Florida dissolution statute is drafted, if a general partnership has a term (i.e., it is specifically designed to last for 20 years, for example, rather than indefinitely), there is at least an agreement that a forced sale should not be allowed.

In conclusion, from an asset protection standpoint, general partnerships are not good entities to hold assets or conduct a business.

Limited Liability Partnerships. Limited Liability Partnerships (sometimes referred to as "LLPs") are basically general partnerships that have filed something called a "Statement of Qualification" with the Florida Secretary of State. The effect of filing the "Statement of Qualification" is to give all partners limited liability with respect to the Inside Liability of the partnership. In other words, if the partnership were ever sued, the partners' individual assets would not be subject to the claims of the creditor as would be the case in a general partnership. Therefore, all things being equal, an LLP is far superior to a general partnership from an Inside Liability perspective. From an Outside Liability point of view, an LLP and a general partnership are equal. In all other respects (i.e., taxation, voting rights, etc.), LLPs and general partnerships are essentially the same.

In addition, it is important when an LLP is formed to have a Partnership Agreement that establishes a term for the LLP (i.e., how long it will last), relevant tax provisions, and language similar to a Shareholders' Agreement in the corporate context.

One final downside to using an LLP is that in the event the LLP does not file its annual report with the Secretary of State, the Statement of Qualification will be revoked and the partnership will lose its LLP status and the protection from Inside Liability that accompanies it. If the Statement of Qualification remains revoked for more than two years before reinstatement is properly applied for, the end result will be that all partners will be jointly and severally responsible for all liabilities of the partnership that arise after the revocation. This is not the case with a corporation or limited liability company who can apply for reinstatement at anytime and receive protection as though the entity were never dissolved in the first place.

Limited Partnerships. A limited partnership is formed by filing a certificate of limited partnership with the Secretary of State together with a filing fee. In Florida the filing fee is basically one thousand dollars. The certificate contains the identity of the general partners, the address of the partnership, the name and address of the partnership's registered agent, and other similar information. Once filed it becomes part of the public record.

The partnership's governing instrument is the "Partnership Agreement." This is a written agreement among the partners that sets forth the rights and obligations of the partners with respect to the management of the partnership including voting rights, withdrawal rights, allocation of profits and losses, rights of the partners on liquidation, and provisions similar to a corporate shareholders' agreement, to name just a few. Because the partnership agreement can be amended by the partners, it provides a high degree of flexibility.

Ownership in a partnership is typically evidenced by issuing units in the partnership, similar to stock in a corporation. Each unit represents a certain percentage ownership interest in the partnership. For example, if the partnership has a total of one hundred units, each unit represents ownership of one percent of the partnership and the underlying partnership assets. Two classes of units are issued: general partnership units and limited partnership units. The general partnership units typically represent a total ownership interest of one percent (or some small percentage) and the limited partnership units represent the remaining 99% percent. The general partners are vested with the authority to control the day-to-day affairs of the partnership. The limited partners do not have the authority to participate in management, but may be granted the power to approve extraordinary decisions of the general partners.

Taxation. A limited partnership is taxed the same as any other form of partnership with certain nuances that are beyond the scope of this book. In general, however, it is a "pass through" entity and does not have the Corporate Capital Gains Trap discussed above.

Asset Protection. The asset protection offered by a limited partnership is based on the protection offered by the "charging order" which is generally stronger than a general partnership or LLP, since it is governed by a separate set of statutes that do not give rise to the same concerns raised by the **Schiller v. Schiller** case discussed above (remember that the **Schiller** case held that a court could order the sale of a partner's general partnership interest that was subject to a charging order). The topic of asset protection as it applies to limited partnerships is discussed in considerable detail in the next Chapter on Family Limited Partnerships.

It is important to note that with respect to Inside Liability, the general partners of a limited partnership are completely responsible for the liabilities of the limited partnership. In other words, if the limited liability company is sued and a creditor obtains a large judgement against the limited partnership, the judgement creditor can reach the personal assets of the general partners. Because of this unsavory consequence, people have historically placed their general partnership units inside a corporation or limited liability company to insulate themselves from the Inside Liability of the partnership. This also gave rise to the entity called the Limited Liability Limited Partnership which is discussed below.

Limited Liability Limited Partnerships. The Limited Liability Limited Partnership (sometimes referred to as an "LLLP") has a relationship with a limited partnership that is similar to the relationship between an LLP and a general partnership. In other words, an LLLP is basically a limited partnership that has filed something called a "Statement of Qualification" with the Florida Secretary of State. The effect of filing the "Statement of Qualification" is to give the general partners limited liability with respect to the Inside Liability of the partnership. In other words, if the partnership were ever sued, the general partners' individual assets would not be subject to the claims of the creditor as would be the case in a limited partnership. Therefore, all things being equal, an LLLP is far superior to a limited partnership from an Inside Liability perspective, because it gives the general partners limited liability without having to form a corporation or limited liability company to hold the general partnership units. From an Outside Liability point of view, an LLLP and a limited partnership are equal. In all other respects (i.e., taxation, voting rights, etc.), LLLPs and limited partnerships are essentially the same.

Limited Liability Companies.

The best way to think of a Limited Liability Company (sometimes called an "LLC" for short) is that it is a hybrid between a corporation and a partnership. The people who own an LLC are called Members. Their ownership interest in the LLC is called a "Membership Interest," however, an LLC oftentimes issues "units" which represent a specified percentage ownership interest in the LLC. For example, if an LLC issued one hundred units, each unit would represent a 1% ownership interest in the LLC. The people who control the affairs of the LLC are called Managers. Some LLCs have Members who are also Managers and some Members who are not Managers (similar to a limited partnership). In other LLCs, all of the Members are Managers (similar to a general partnership). Some states even allow an LLC to have Managers that are not Members.

Like a corporation which can have a single shareholder, an LLC can have a single Member. Partnerships, on the other hand, must always have at least two partners. As I will discuss below, single Member LLCs are not likely to protect the sole Member from Outside Liability, and the single Member LLC (and all the assets held inside the LLC) is likely to be completely reachable by a creditor of the sole Member.

An LLC is formed by filing Articles of Organization with the Secretary of State together with a filing fee. The Articles contain information such as the name and address of the LLC, the names of the Members and/or Managers, etc. The legal document that governs the LLC is called the Operating Agreement which is akin to a Partnership Agreement or corporate By-Laws. Note that the terms of the Operating Agreement will be more like a partnership agreement if it elects to be taxed as a partnership and more like By-Laws if it elects to be taxed as a Corporation (see below). This Operating Agreement will also contain the "shareholders agreement" type provisions that govern the terms of any transfer of LLC units whether by death, disability, or the presence of creditor issues.

Taxation. An LLC is an interesting creature from an income tax perspective. When a client tells me he or she has an LLC, I always ask them how it is taxed. About half the time the person says "You know, its taxed as an LLC." As you will see below, an LLC is never taxed as a LLC because there is no such classification under the Internal Revenue Code. An LLC can be taxed as a corporation (S or C), a partnership, or a "disregarded entity."

As mentioned above, if it is owned by two or more Members, it can either be taxed as a partnership or as a corporation. If the LLC has only one Member, it can elect to be taxed as a corporation or a "disregarded entity." A disregarded entity is basically taxed as a sole proprietorship where the assets and business of the LLC are treated as being owned directly by the sole Member for income tax purposes. For all other purposes, the LLC will not be disregarded (i.e., it will be treated as a distinct entity separate from the sole Member). If the LLC elects to be taxed as a corporation, it will be able to choose whether to be an S corporation or a C corporation and will be subject to the rules discussed earlier in this Chapter under the taxation of corporations. If it elects to be taxed as a partnership, then none of the corporate tax issues will apply and the earlier discussion on the taxation of partnerships will be applicable. Before establishing an LLC it is important to discuss your options with your accountant or tax advisor to enable you to make intelligent decisions given your individual facts and circumstances.

Asset Protection. From an asset protection standpoint, LLCs are similar to limited partnerships in that a creditor is limited to a charging order rather than being able to simply take the Member's ownership interest. When comparing a Florida LLC to a Florida limited partnership, however, the LLC has one potential disadvantage. As will be discussed in the next Chapter, the Florida law governing limited partnerships specifically provides that a creditor's **sole and exclusive** remedy (i.e., method of collecting its judgement) in trying to reach a partner's **partnership** units is the charging order (remember that this allows the partner to play the waiting game). If the charging order is **not** the **sole and exclusive** remedy available to a creditor, the creditor may be able to convince a court to order a sale of the Member's LLC interest or to order a liquidation (i.e., termination) of the LLC itself. In either of these situations the asset protection offered by the LLC would be seriously compromised or eliminated altogether. Unfortunately, there is no Florida statute or case law which establishes that the charging order remedy is the sole and exclusive remedy in the LLC context. It is quite possible that a future court may hold exactly that and follow the partnership cases. Until that case is decided, however, this will remain a grey area of the law. Therefore, all things being equal, a Florida LLLP is superior to a Florida LLC from an asset protection standpoint.

I have always been concerned (for reasons discussed in the next Chapter) that single member LLCs may not receive charging order protection. On April 4, 2003, the bankruptcy case of **In Re Ashley Albright**, held exactly that. Therefore, while a single Member LLC continues to be a helpful tool to protect your personal assets from Inside Liability, it is not wise to rely on it to provide you protection from the claims of "outside" creditors, including medical malpractice judgment holders.

The Delaware Series LLC.

The Delaware Series LLC is a unique type of limited liability company that can only be formed under the laws of Delaware. If you plan to own more than one parcel of property in a limited liability company, you should consider using a Delaware Series LLC rather than a "typical" LLC. The reason for this is exemplified in the following example:

> Jimmy is planning on purchasing five different office buildings, an apartment building, and four parcels of vacant land. The total value of these properties is $15,000,000. Jimmy, having learned the value of using an LLC to protect his personal assets from Inside Liability that may stem from these types of assets, decides to form Jimmy Jones Enterprises, LLC. All ten of the properties are then purchased in the name of the LLC. One year later, the roof of the apartment building caves in seriously injuring several of the tenants. They sue Jimmy Jones Enterprises, LLC, and obtain judgements totaling $20,000,000. While Jimmy's personal assets held outside the LLC are protected, the judgement creditors are able to take all of the assets held in the LLC, which is obviously horrible news for Jimmy.

One way Jimmy could have avoided this result is to have formed ten separate LLCs, and then purchased each piece of property in a different LLC. The obvious downside to this is that Jimmy will have to pay a lawyer ten times more than it would cost to form a single LLC, and then after the LLCs are formed, each year

Jimmy will have to pay ten annual fees to the Secretary of State, file ten separate tax returns (one for each LLC), and file ten separate annual reports for the LLCs. Now enter the Delaware Series LLC.

The Delaware Series LLC is a single LLC that contains individual "series." Each of these series is akin to a separate "sub-LLC" that protects the other assets in the LLC from the liability stemming from property inside a particular series.

> Building on the previous example, assume this time that Jimmy decides to create a Delaware Series Limited Liability Company called Jimmy Jones Series, LLC. Jimmy places each of the five office buildings in their own series (i.e., series one through five), the apartment building in series six, and each of the parcels of undeveloped land in their own series (i.e., series seven through ten). Now assume that the same catastrophe happened and the injured apartment tenants obtain the same $20,000,000 in judgements. This time the judgment holders are only able to reach the property in series six (i.e., the series holding the apartment building), and the properties held in the other nine series remain protected. In addition, Jimmy saved a significant amount in legal fees and only has to file one tax return, pay one annual fee, and file one annual report.

A Limited Partnership (and a Limited Liability Limited Partnership) can also be created with series under the laws of Delaware. I have not found many attorneys in the state of Florida that are familiar with Delaware Series LLCs or Delaware Series Limited Partnerships, however, if you think you may want to form one, you can feel free to contact me.

General Rules in Funding Entities.

When using entities to hold assets, there are some general guidelines to consider to avoid an unexpected and undesirable surprise. Some of these are listed below.

Hot vs. Cold Assets. When funding a legal entity, it is best not to place "hot" and "cold" assets in the same entity to the greatest extent practicable. By "hot" asset, I mean an asset that has the potential to spawn liability such as real estate. By "cold" asset, I mean property that is highly unlikely to spawn liability such as cash, or marketable securities. I have seen this mistake made in the context of a Family Limited Partnership with disastrous results.

> Assume Meursault and his wife, Marie, decide to form a Family Limited Partnership (sometimes referred to as an "FLP") as part of their asset protection plan. After the partnership is formed, the couple transfer an apartment building and $2,000,000 in marketable securities to the FLP. One year later, a tenant in the apartment complex is attacked by a stranger in the parking lot and sues the apartment building owner (i.e., the FLP) for being negligent in not providing adequate security. The tenant wins the law suit and obtains a $4,000,000 judgement. Because the "hot" asset (i.e., the apartment building) and the "cold" asset (i.e., the marketable securities) were all "owned" by the FLP, the judgement creditor, having obtained a judgement against the FLP, can reach all of the assets, both hot and cold.

Therefore, when funding an entity (say an FLP), it is best to either use a Delaware Series Limited Partnership, where hot and cold assets can be separated in different series, or to have the FLP form an LLC (which is owned by the FLP) to hold the hot asset(s).

The Investment Company Rules. While a complete discussion of the Investment Company Rules is beyond the scope of this book, it is important to understand that if you are transferring investment type assets (i.e., stocks, bonds, etc.) into a partnership or an LLC that is taxed as a partnership, and those assets have appreciated in value since the time you purchased them, that unless the transfer is done correctly, capital gains tax could be triggered. Before funding any limited partnership or LLC, it is always important to hire the assistance of a qualified tax attorney or accountant who is familiar with the Investment Company Rules.

Transferring Real Estate Already

Owned by an Individual to a Legal Entity.

Above we have spent considerable time discussing the upsides of holding real estate in a legal entity like an LLC. There are, however, three principal downsides of transferring property you initial purchased in your individual name(s) to a legal entity. Each of these downsides are discussed below.

1. **Florida Documentary Stamp Tax.** Florida Statutes Section 201.02(1) requires anyone purchasing Florida real estate to pay something called "documentary stamp tax." The tax is based on the "consideration" (i.e., the purchase price) paid for the property. The tax rate is 7/10th of a percent or $7 for every $1,000 paid.

   When property is transferred to a legal entity, an interesting Florida Documentary Stamp Tax question is raised. In the past, the Florida Department of Revenue has argued that such a transfer should be treated as a **sale** of the property to the legal entity even though such a transfer is not treated as a sale for federal income tax purposes. For example, if you transfer a piece of Florida real estate worth $200,000 into an LLC, the DOR argued that the property should be treated as having been sold to the LLC in exchange for the LLC membership units which are deemed to have the same value as the property (i.e., $200,000). Under this reasoning, since the property was "sold" to the LLC, the transfer would cost you $1,400 in Florida Documentary Stamp Tax. This could result in your paying a double tax since you will pay Documentary Stamp Tax once when you first buy the property and then a second time when you transfer it into the entity. Of course, if you simply purchase property directly in the name of the legal entity, you would only pay Documentary Stamp Tax once.

   Thankfully, on May 19, 2005, the Florida Supreme Court rejected the DOR's "transfer equals sale" argument in the case of Crescent Miami Center, LLC v. Department of Revenue with two exceptions. The first of these exceptions is that if the ownership structure of the property being transferred is different from the ownership structure of the legal entity to which it is being transferred, the transfer will trigger the imposition of Documentary Stamp Tax on the entire fair market value of the property (I'll call this the Identical Ownership Requirement). The second exception is that if you transfer unencumbered property (i.e., property that is not subject to a mortgage) to a legal entity and the Identical Ownership Requirement is met, the Crescent Miami court held that no Documentary Stamp Tax need be paid "because nothing was exchanged . . .; thus, there [is] no consideration or purchaser in the transaction, just a 'mere change in form of the stockholder's equity in the corporation." It needs to be noted that if the property being transferred is subject to a mortgage, Documentary Stamp Tax is required with respect to the mortgage amount. For example:

> "T. Ferguson owns a rental home in his own name valued at $500,000. The rental home was originally subject to a mortgage of $300,000, but Mr. Ferguson has paid it down so that only $200,000 is left owing to the bank. He decides to transfer it to T. Ferguson Holdings, LLC, of which he also the only owner. When he records the deed to effectuate the transfer, he will owe Documentary Stamp Tax on $200,000 (i.e., $1,400 in tax) since that is the current amount outstanding on the mortgage."

Transfers of non-Florida real estate are not subject to this tax, however, it is always wise to check and see whether the state where the property is located has a similar tax.

2. **Title Insurance Issue When Transferring Property to an LLC**. Another potential problem in transferring property that you previously purchased in your own name to a legal entity is that it could invalidate your title insurance. When you initially purchased the property, a title insurance policy was issued to the owner of the property (i.e., you). If the property is later transferred to an LLC, for example, and the LLC subsequently sells the property, if a title problem arises, the title insurance company may not have to pay since the seller of the property (the LLC) is uninsured. If you plan to transfer property to a legal entity, always check with the issuer of your title insurance policy to ensure the policy will continue to protect you.

3. **Real Property With a Mortgage**. Finally, if you already own property in your individual name and that property is subject to a mortgage, you will need to obtain the permission of the lender before you transfer the property into a le-

gal entity. All mortgages have something called a "Due on Sale" clause which gives the bank the right to immediately call due the entire mortgage balance if the property is ever transferred (including to a legal entity). If the current mortgage is a Fannie Mae mortgage, you will need to refinance.

In addition, even when you directly purchase property in the name of an LLC and want to keep a mortgage on the property, your options will be less than if you purchased the property in your individual name. First, you will not be eligible for a Fannie Mae loan. This stems from the fact that a requirement to obtaining "Fannie Mae" financing is that the property must be owned by natural persons (i.e., not legal entities). In short, Fannie Mae mortgages are "standardized" so they can be bundled together with other Fannie Mae mortgages and sold in the open market similar to commodities like pork bellies or soy beans. One of the standardized requirements is that the property be owned by an individual and not a legal entity. Because a bank or mortgage lender can easily sell the mortgage on the open market (and thereby divest itself of the risk of your possibly defaulting on the loan), the interest rate with a Fannie Mae mortgage is usually slightly lower.

Even with respect to non-Fannie Mae financing, if you want to own the property in a legal entity, the interest rate will typically be slightly higher than if you owned the property in your individual name. Even if you can find a competitive interest rate, other mortgage terms are usually more restrictive (such as having a shorter term (i.e., 10 years rather than 15)). Some banks even refuse to extend mortgage financing with respect to property being purchased in a legal entity. Beware of the bank employee (who will be paid only if your mortgage closes) advising you to close in your individual name(s) and then quit claim the property into the LLC or other legal entity post closing. He is setting you up to all three of the negatives listed above (including breaking the terms of your contract with his employer).

All of the factors mentioned above need to be taken into consideration before you decide whether or not to use a legal entity to hold assets. In most cases, the benefits to be gained by using a legal entity far outweigh the costs, however, this will be a personal decision. I have seen a person decide not to use a legal entity to hold property because they did not want to pay Florida's Documentary Stamp Tax only to be sued later for a significant amount. With the benefit of hindsight, that person regretted their decision to forgo using an LLC to save the Documentary Stamp Tax.

Choosing the Right Entity to House Your Medical Practice.

This final section will discuss your choices in the type of legal entity to house your medical practice. Before moving forward with a discussion of the types of entities, however, I want to explain that unlike non-professionals, professionals are not permitted to use a legal entity to shield themselves from liability stemming from their own malpractice. The court in the case of Lochrane Engineering, Inc. v. Willingham Realgrowth Inv. Fund, Ltd., sheds some light on why this is:

> "The duty of a professional who renders services, such as a doctor, lawyer, or engineer, is different from the duty of one who renders manual services or delivers a product. The contractual duty of one who delivers a product or manual services, is to conform to the quality or quantity specified in the express contract, if any, or in the absence of such specification, or when the duty and level of performance is implied by law, to deliver a product reasonably suited for the purposes for which the product was intended . . . or to deliver services performed in a good and workmanlike manner. However, the duty imposed by law upon professionals rendering professional services is to perform such services in accordance with the standard of care used by similar professionals in the community under similar circumstances."

Due to this heightened level of duty a professional owes to his or her patient or client, the best a professional can accomplish using a legal entity such as a corporation or limited liability company, is to shield their personal assets from the liability of the other professionals with whom they practice. For example, assume Dr. Sartre, Dr. Nietzsche, and Dr. Camus, decide to go into practice together, and form a professional corporation to conduct their practice. Dr. Sartre is then sued for medical malpractice and the creditor obtains a large judgement against Dr. Sartre and the P.A. While the P.A. does nothing to protect Dr. Sartre's personal assets from the claims of the judgement creditor, the personal assets of Dr.

Nietzsche, and Dr. Camus are protected due to the existence of the P.A.

Professional Companies.

A professional company is typically formed by professionals (i.e., doctors, lawyer, architects, etc.) all of which practice in the identical profession. If a corporation is used as the "professional entity" the company name must contain the suffix P.A. (which stands for "professional association") or contain the word "chartered." An example would be "Professional Medical Associates, P.A." If a Limited Liability Company is used, the company name must contain the words "professional limited company" or the abbreviation "P.L." An example would be "Professional Medical Associates, P.L." Understand that the only difference between a corporation and a P.A. (or an LLC and a P.L.) is that the entity is subjected to some additional restrictions set forth under Chapter 621 of the Florida Statutes. In all other respects, a P.A. will be taxed as a corporation (either S or C) and will be subject to the other rules governing corporations. Likewise, a P.L. will be taxed as a corporation, partnership, or disregarded entity (depending or your situation) and will be subject to the other rules governing limited liability companies.

Unlike attorneys, who are required by their ethics code to practice in a P.A. or P.L., physicians are not required to do so. They can, instead, create a "standard," non-professional entity like a corporation or LLC to house their medical practice. This is advantageous because Chapter 621 of the Florida Statutes, which governs P.A.s and P.L.s, imposes additional restrictions on professional entities that do not apply to non-professional entities. For example, Florida Statutes Section 621.09 entitled "Limitation on Issuance and Transfer of Ownership," reads in part as follows:

"No corporation organized under the provisions of this act may issue any of its capital stock to anyone other than a professional corporation, a professional limited liability company, or an individual who is duly licensed or otherwise legally authorized to render the same specific professional services as those for which the corporation was incorporated. No shareholder of a corporation organized under this act shall enter into a voting trust agreement or any other type agreement vesting another person with the authority to exercise the voting power of any or all of that person's stock."

In addition, Florida Statutes Section 621.11 entitled "Alienation of Shares and Ownership Interests; Restrictions," reads in part as follows:

> "No shareholder of a corporation organized under this act may sell or transfer her or his shares in such corporation except to another professional corporation, professional limited liability company, or individual, each of which must be eligible to be a shareholder of such corporation."

These two statutes read together restrict anyone other than physicians practicing in the same specialty from owning an interest in a P.A. or P.L. These restrictions can present limitations in planning. For example, if it made sense for a physician's spouse (or a trust) to own all or a part of a P.A. for estate planning and/or asset protection purposes, these statutes would prohibit such planning. Below, I will give a few examples of the types of planning you may want to consider, however, first I want to dispel a myth that the above statutes actually provide some level of asset protection to the physician.

I have heard it argued that the above statutes prevent the creditors of a physician/shareholder from reaching that shareholder's stock in a P.A. unless the creditor is "duly licensed or otherwise legally authorized to render the same specific professional services as those for which the corporation was incorporated." In other words, unless the creditor is a physician practicing the same type of medicine as the physician being sued, the stock in the P.A. is protected since the above listed statutes prohibits the transfer of stock in a P.A. to a non-physician. Unfortunately, the Florida Supreme Court held to the contrary in the case of Street v. Sugerman. In the Sugerman case, the Florida Supreme Court stated:

> "The fact that the corporation may not voluntarily 'issue' or the shareholders may not 'sell or transfer' their stock voluntarily to a non_professional is not reason to prevent an execution and sale, by law for a judgment creditor. Further, we agree with the District Court that to affirm the holding of the chancellor [who ruled in favor of an asset protection result] would have the discriminatory effect of affording professionals a shelter for their

> assets, which appears to be inconsistent with the spirit of the Act [and would serve] to carve out a judicial 'no man's land' for shareholders in a professional corporation which is not available to shareholders in non_professional groups."

Therefore, in the event a physician is sued and the plaintiff obtains a judgement, his or her interest in a P.A. (i.e., a corporation which remember does not offer protection from Outside Liability) could be reached by the creditor.

If, instead, a group of physicians create a P.L. (i.e., a professional limited liability company) rather than a professional corporation, the "charging order" protection discussed earlier in this Chapter would apply to keep a creditor from being able to directly seize a physician's interest in such P.L. Better yet, if the physician group forms a "straight" (i.e., non-professional) LLC or corporation, the physician's interest could be transferred to his or her spouse, or some other asset protection structure and be completely protected. At the end of this Chapter I summarize my choices for the best and worst entity to house a medical practice.

Why is There a Need to Protect the Physician's Ownership in the Practice?

Despite the fact that I have always considered the answer to this question to be self-evident, I have been asked the following question on many occasions. "If a physician is sued for medical malpractice, the judgement creditor will usually be able to obtain a judgement against the practice entity, so then why should a physician be worried about protecting his or her ownership interest in the practice?" My answers to this question are listed below.

First, if a physician is sued for something other than medical malpractice (i.e., an automobile accident), the physician's ownership interest in the practice could be a valuable asset that a creditor may wish to take.

Another example is if a physician practices through more than one entity. For instance, I recently met a physician who had two separate types of patients. He, therefore, created two separate P.A.s, one to treat patient type A ("P.A. #1") and the other to treat patient type B ("P.A. #2"). Assuming he is ever sued for malpractice stemming from treating a type A patient and that patient is successful in obtaining a judgement, the patient/creditor could (i) take the assets in P.A. #1, and (ii) take his stock in P.A. #2 since it is owned 100% by the physician. If the physician tried to title the stock in his two P.A.s as tenants by the entireties with his wife or have his wife own the stock, any attempted transfer would be ignored resulting in no asset protection. If, on the other hand, the physician had formed a regular, non-professional corporation or LLC, these transfers would be respected and the judgement creditor would not be able to reach the stock.

Finally, as I discussed earlier in Chapter 11, a sole practitioner is prevented from being able to protect his or her wages using a wage account. This stems from the fact that in order for a physician to be considered an employee, the physician must be able to have entered into an arms length agreement with the employer which is impossible if the physician controls the legal entity that employs him or her. If the controlling interest in the legal entity is owned instead by the physician's spouse, or a trust for the benefit of his or her children, it would seem possible to argue that the wage protection statute should apply if an employment agreement exists between the physician and the employer (i.e., the entity). It is always possible that a court may hold that a physician is not really bargaining "at arms length" when their spouse owns the corporation, however, if all other requirements for obtaining the protection of the wage exemption are met and the physician is not a majority (i.e., controlling) shareholder of the corporate employer, there is a chance the physician may be able to exempt his or her wages.

Registration of Non-Physician Owned Medical Practices.

If a physician practice is owned by non-physicians it may be necessary to register the practice pursuant to Florida Statute Section 456.0375. There are, however, several exceptions to this registration requirement. One of these exceptions exempts the following from having to register:

> "Sole proprietorships, group practices, partnerships, or corporations that provide health care services by licensed health care practitioners . . . which are wholly owned by licensed health care practitioners or the licensed health care practitioner and the spouse, parent, or child of a licensed health care practitioner, so long as one of the owners who is a licensed health care practitioner is supervising the services performed therein and is legally

> responsible for the entity's compliance with all federal and state laws. . . ."

Therefore, if the physician owns the practice as tenants by the entireties with his or her non-physician spouse, or if the physician owns some de minimis amount of the practice and the rest is owned by the non-physician spouse, the practice will be exempt from having to register. It is encouraging to see, however, that the statue directly authorizes ownership of a medical practice by "the spouse, parent, or child of a licensed health care practitioner."

Summary of Entity Choices for a Medical Practice.

Given the fact that falling under Chapter 621 of the Florida Statutes adds nothing but a restriction on non-physicians owning a medical practice and further given the fact that these restrictions do nothing to provide additional asset protection, I do not see any reason for using a P.A. or a P.L. My choices of legal entities to house a medical practice from best to worst are:

1. **Regular Non-Professional LLC.** This entity (i) gives the physician the benefit of charging order protection, (ii) allows a non-physician including a spouse, a trust, or other family member to own all or a part of the LLC, and (iii) can be taxed as a partnership, an S corporation, or a C corporation.

2. **Regular Non-Professional LLLP.** This entity has the benefits of a non-professional LLC but without the flexibility to be taxed as a corporation.

3. **Professional LLC ("P.L.").** This entity has the benefits of a non-professional LLC but does not allow a non-physician to own all or a part of the LLC.

4. **A Non-Professional Corporation.** This entity does not provide any protection from Outside Liability, however, it does allow a non-physician to own all or a part of the corporation. It can be taxed as an S corporation, or a C corporation, but not as a partnership.
5. **A Professional Corporation ("P.A.").** This entity (i) does **not** provide any protection from Outside Liability, (ii) does **not** allow a non-physician to own all or a part of the corporation, and (iii) does **not** provide the flexibility to be taxed as a partnership.

Before leaving this important topic I did want to mention another ownership structure which has some serious asset protection downsides, namely the "partnership of P.A.s." Under this structure each physician creates their own personal P.A. of which they are 100% owner and oftentimes the sole employee. These P.A.s then form a partnership (or LLC) which is the primary practice that sees patients. The profits earned at the practice level are then regularly distributed to the individual P.A.s which, in turn, each pay the physician / owner a salary.

The benefit of this structure is that each P.A. can offer its own benefits if the group as a whole cannot agree. For example, assume Dr. Peirce, Dr. Hunnicut, Dr. Burns, and Dr. Winchester decide to form a practice. Dr. Winchester feels that the practice should provide him with a new Porshe and a $20,000 a year continuing education allowance. Dr. Burns thinks that this is outrageous because he drives a Ford Pinto and feels that continuing education is basically a waste of money. Since the four cannot agree on what "perks" the newly formed practice should provide, they decide to form a "partnership of P.A.s." Now, the profits from the group are distributed to their individual P.A.s where they can each provide themselves the benefits they individually feel are appropriate.

These benefits need to be weighed against the asset protection downsides. First, since each physician owns 100% of the company that employs them (i.e., their individual P.A.), they are most likely not going to be able to protect their wages from being garnished if they are ever sued (see Chapter 11 for a discussion of why sole practitioners are unable to protect their wages under Florida law). Second, since they each own 100% of their individual P.A., it may be difficult to impossible to protect their stock in that P.A. from Outside Liability.
Before forming a partnership of P.A.s, closely examine the benefits and detriments of the structure. A closer look may convince you that the asset protection downsides are significant enough to warrant being more flexible in working out the differences between the partners.

Conversion of Entities.

In the event you are currently practicing in the form of a professional corporation (i.e., a "P.A.") and you wish to convert to a "standard," non-professional corporation (i.e., an "Inc."), you simply need to file a document called Articles of Amendment that will (i) remove certain language from the original Articles of Incorporation that stated your intent to have the corporation treated as a professional corporation and (ii) change the name of the corporation to end in "Inc." rather than "P.A." In the event you are currently practicing in the form of a professional limited liability company (i.e., a "P.L.") and you wish to convert to a "standard," non-professional limited liability company (i.e., an "LLC"), you simply need to file a document, also called Articles of Amendment, that will (i) remove certain language from the original Articles of Organization that stated your intent to have the limited liability company treated as a professional limited liability company and (ii) change the name of the limited liability company to end in "LLC" rather than "P.L."

In the event you are currently practicing in the form of an entity other than an LLC and you wish to convert to an LLC, Florida law provides a means of doing so, either through a "conversion" or though a transaction called a "cross entity merger." The laws of Delaware, however, allow the direct conversion of a corporation to an LLC. When a corporation is converted to an LLC, the LLC needs to elect to be taxed as a corporation to avoid adverse tax consequences. While converting entities from one type to another is not complicated for a professional who is well versed in tax and corporate law, it is not something a novice should ever attempt alone.

Conclusion.

There are numerous ways to use legal entities to shield yourself from liability. Armed with the knowledge provided in this Chapter, you will be able to intelligently discuss your options with your asset protection attorney. Be aware that there are planning strategies using combinations of legal entities that are beneficial for all types of businesses. With proper guidance from knowledgeable professionals, you can shield your assets from creditors and accomplish other tax and non-tax objectives such as creative business succession planing and estate planning. The next Chapter on Family Limited partnerships is designed to be read with this Chapter, and will cover certain aspects of planning with entities either not discussed in this Chapter or discussed in greater detail.

CHAPTER 17

The Family Limited Partnership

Since the advent of the Medical Malpractice Insurance Crises, significant attention has been given to the asset protection benefits of using Family Limited Partnerships ("FLPs"). Some have even gone so far as to state that the limited partnership is without peer in the asset protection arena. While Family Limited Partnerships do offer some asset protection to their partners, it is important to fully understand how it protects assets and what its weaknesses are. As I have stated before, every asset protection technique has an upside and a downside and if you do not understand the downside to what you are contemplating, you should not rely on that technique as a principal method of protecting assets.

What is an FLP?

The FLP is a business entity, nothing more, nothing less. More precisely it is a limited partnership. Under Florida law, a "partnership" is defined as "an association of two or more persons to carry on as co-owners a **business for profit** formed under Florida Statutes Section 620.8202, predecessor law, or the comparable law of another jurisdiction." Therefore, when you form such an entity you need to have a valid business purpose. If the purpose of the entity is to invest assets for long term growth and the assets transferred to the FLP are, in fact, investment type assets, you have a valid business purpose.

Many promoters of FLPs tell people that they protect vacation homes, personal boats, and other similar personal use assets. They are unequivocally wrong. If you bought a home for investment purposes, would you likely let someone use it on a rent free basis for any prolonged period of time? Obviously not. If you cannot legitimately justify why someone would buy and hold an asset as an investment asset, it should not be held in the partnership. If you ignore this warning, the court is likely to ignore the partnership altogether with the result being zero asset protection. For example, in the 2005 bankruptcy case of **In re Turner**, the court stated:

> "'Asset protection' is not illegal and is honored if done for a legitimate purpose. For example, an individual may do business through a corporation or limited liability company and will not be held personally liable for the debts of the entity. The assets of the corporation or limited liability company will not be considered the assets of the individual interest holder. However, an entity or series of entities may not be created with no business purpose and personal assets transferred to them with no relationship to any business purpose, simply as a means of shielding them from creditors. Under such circumstances, the law views the entity as the alter ego of the individual debtor and will disregard it to prevent injustice."

So if a so-called asset protection "expert" is telling you that you can form a business entity like an FLP and use it to protect all of your personal use assets, especially if they are trying to sell you some over priced 'do-it-yourself' book, tell them you are not interested or proceed at your own peril. These people are marketing experts, not asset protection experts.

How Does an FLP Protect Assets?

Assuming that the partnership is properly formed and you have a valid business purpose, the next thing you need to understand is how a partnership protects assets. When someone owning an interest in a Family Limited Partnership is sued and the creditor obtains a judgement against the partner-debtor, the judgement creditor is not able to (i) directly seize the assets of the Family Limited Partnership, (ii) take your ownership interest in the partnership, or (iii) acquire your voting rights in the partnership. Instead, the judgement creditor is typically limited to the remedy of a charging order. A charging order, simply put, is an order of the court requiring that future distributions from the Family Limited Partnership, if any, be made not to the partner-debtor, but rather to the judgement creditor who obtained the charging order. The reason the charging order remedy was created rather than allowing the creditor to directly seize the partnership assets is to prevent disruption of the partnership business and the resulting injustice to the other partners.

The example set forth below illustrates how a charging order works:

> Mitthew, Mirk, and Jihn decide to create a limited partnership with the legitimate business purpose of investing in Florida real estate. Several years after starting their venture, Jihn is sued and the creditor obtains a $20,000 judgement. Given the fact that all of Jihn's other assets are protected, the creditor seeks a charging order against Jihn's partnership interest. So long as the no distributions are made from the partnership, Jihn's creditor will just wait and receive nothing. If a distribution is made, however, any amount that would normally be distributed to Jihn if no creditor problems existed, will now pass to the creditor. Once the creditor receives his $20,000 (plus applicable interest), the charging order will dissolve, and Jihn will once again be entitled to receive distributions. Note that throughout Jihn's creditor problems, Mitthew and Mirk have not been inconvenienced.

As exemplified above, assuming that the partnership agreement was properly drafted with asset protection in mind, if the general partners do not make any distributions, the creditor gets nothing. Therefore, if Mitthew, Mirk, and Jihn are all brothers and Mitthew and Mirk are willing to forgo receiving distributions to help Jihn, and Jihn does not need his distributions to live on, the FLP will provide significant negotiating leverage to Jihn (i.e., let the waiting game begin). Jihn will undoubtedly take the posture that it will be a very long time before a distribution is ever made, and therefore, it is in the best interest of the creditor to take a small settlement now, rather than risk getting little or nothing many years in the future. If the other partners are not inclined to hold off making distributions or if Jihn needs the distributions to pay for his day-to-day living expenses, the FLP will provide a much smaller hurdle to the creditor.

To avoid repeating myself, for the rest of this Chapter when I am discussing Family Limited Partnerships, I will assume the partnership agreement was drafted by competent legal counsel with asset protection as a primary objective. Suffice it to say that many (if not most) of the partnership agreements I have reviewed have various shortcomings, many of which destroy any asset protection benefits that could be offered by the partnership. Additional safeguards can and should be added to the partnership agreement to strengthen its asset protection benefits, especially if you are relying on it as your principal means of protecting family wealth.

Is the Charging Order the Sole Remedy?

The next question you should ask yourself prior to establishing an FLP is whether or not the charging order is the **sole and exclusive** remedy or whether there are other ways for a creditor to skin the asset protection cat? In the event the charging order is NOT the sole and exclusive option to a creditor trying to reach the partnership assets, the FLP may not serve its purpose as an asset protection vehicle. Over the past ten years the national trend has been to move away from the charging order as the sole and exclusive remedy available to a judgement creditor. Some courts have even allowed creditors to force a sale of the partner's partnership interest with the sales proceeds then being available to the judgement creditor. Others have allowed a forced liquidation of the partnership which obviously results in a distribution of all the partnership assets to the partners with no further means to keep those assets out of the creditor's reach. This topic is discussed in greater detail below in the section entitled "Judicial Foreclosure Sale / Judicial Liquidation."

Whether the charging order is the sole and exclusive remedy depends in large part on which state's laws the FLP was formed under. Some states (which, thanks to an amendment to our limited partnership statutes in 2005, now includes Florida) provide that charging order protection is the sole and exclusive remedy in their statute. Other state statutes do not address whether the charging order is the sole and exclusive remedy available to a creditor, but case law interpreting the statute states that it is. A statute which clearly mandates the sole and exclusive nature of the charging order remedy is obviously preferable to case law interpreting a less clear statute. Finally, in some states the law states that the charging order is not the only remedy available to a creditor.

New Florida Statute 620.1703 reads as follows:

> "(1) On application to a court of competent jurisdiction by any judgment creditor of a partner or transferee, **the court may charge the partnership interest of the partner or transferable interest of a transferee with payment of the unsatisfied amount of the judgment with interest.** To the extent so charged, the judgment creditor has **only the rights of a transferee** of the partnership interest.
>
> (2) This act shall not deprive any partner or transferee of the benefit of an exemption law applicable to the partner's partnership or transferee's transferable interest.
>
> (3) This section provides the **exclusive remedy** which a judgment creditor of a partner or transferee may use to satisfy a judgment out of the judgment debtor's interest in the limited partnership or transferable interest. **Other remedies**, including foreclosure on the partner's interest in the limited partnership or a transferee's transferable interest and a court order for directions, accounts, and inquiries that the debtor general or limited partner might have made, **are not available** to the judgment creditor attempting to satisfy the judgment out of the judgment debtor's interest in the limited partnership and **may not be ordered by a court.**"

As you can see from the above language, we now have an "exclusive remedy" statute. My hats off to the Florida legislature for the enactment of this new act.

Problems with Charging Order Protection. Notwithstanding the benefits of charging order protection described above (i.e., the ability to play the waiting game), several pitfalls await a person depending on his or her Family Limited Partnership to serve as their principal means of asset protection. The major pitfalls are listed below:

1. **Restrictive Charging Orders.** A charging order can be more than just a court ordered assignment of partnership profits and surplus in favor of a creditor. A charging order can also contain the following additional restrictions and requirements: (i) a restriction on the partnership's ability to make loans to the partners or anyone else for that matter, (ii) a restriction on the partnership's ability to make capital acquisitions without approval from either the court or the creditor, (iii) a restriction on the partnership and/or its partners from entering into or consummating any sale, encumbrance, or modification of any partnership interest without approval from either the court or the creditor, (iv) a restriction on a partner's ability to pledge his or her partnership interest as collateral for a loan, and (v) a requirement that the partnership deliver to a creditor on an ongoing basis upon request by a creditor a full copy of the partnership agreement plus any amendments or modifications, all income tax returns of the partnership, a balance sheet and profit and loss statement, and all books and records of the partnership including the cash position of the partnership. In other words, despite the fact that many promoters make claims that you will be able to personally access partnership assets after a charging order has been issued by paying yourself a management fee, making loans to yourself, having the FLP purchase assets from you, etc. most often this is not the case. The assets may be safely kept from the grasp of a creditor but they are also typically made unavailable to you as well for the duration of the judgement (typically 20 years).

2. **The Waiting Game.** As mentioned previously, the charging order protection offered by a limited partnership enables a debtor-partner to play the waiting game. In essence, the question comes down to who can wait the longest. Since a charging order that is effective to keep assets from a creditor will also keep assets from being used by you, it is important for you to determine whether you can realistically play this game. If you do not need immediate access to the assets, you can use that to negotiate a favorable settlement. On the other hand, if you do need access to the assets, the waiting game comes to a quick end because any assets distributed from the partnership will end up in the hands of the creditor. Therefore, it is important for a physician using an FLP as his or her primary method of protecting assets to only place assets in the FLP that they feel comfortable that they could lose access to for the duration of a judgement (typically 20 years) without suffering financial hardship.

Another very important exercise that should be completed prior to the decision to use an FLP as your primary asset protection technique is creating a personal financial plan. A good financial plan will identify your sources of income in the various stages of your life and what expenses you are likely to face over time. Once these are identified you can determine whether your income sources are exempt (i.e., protected wages (assuming a wage account has been established and you have the type of earnings that can be protected), monies in life insurance and/or annuities, retirement assets (again assuming that they are protected), etc.) or non-exempt (i.e., earnings from an unprotected portfolio, unprotected earnings, etc.). You also need to analyze whether any of these income sources are likely to "dry up" or be diminished. For example, if you become disabled and had the foresight to purchase disability insurance, understand that most of these policies will only pay you a percentage of your income. Will this be enough to cover your expenses? Likewise, if you are relying on monies held in a variable form of life insurance and/or annuities, how are they invested? How much can you lose in the market before your life style is seriously impaired? Furthermore, are there any penalties for withdrawing assets from these insurance products and how large are they? Next, you need to examine your expenses. Will you be paying for a child's college education in a few years? If so, could you afford to pay these expenses using only your exempt sources of income? Understanding your cash flow over time is critical and if you forgo creating a financial plan, you may be setting yourself up for disaster later down the road.

I know someone who had all of the assets they planned to retire on in an FLP for asset protection reasons. At age 63, the husband was sued and the creditor obtained a large judgement. Their FLP was owned 50% by husband and 50% by wife. Now, a full half of every distribution made from their FLP to pay for their living expenses for the next twenty years will go to the creditor (i.e., husband's share). Husband now has to rethink his planned retirement date. In their case, the FLP was not the asset protection panacea they thought it was.

3. **Policy Concerns.** As stated above, the reason for the charging order remedy rather than allowing a direct levy on the partnership assets is to prevent disruption of the partnership business and the resulting injustice to the other partners. This logic makes perfect sense in the case of two unrelated people who start an active business. Consider, however, an FLP solely owned by husband

and wife who are later jointly sued by the same creditor. A judge may not find that the purpose of the charging order (i.e., protecting innocent partners) is being served under these circumstances. In a previous article I co-authored with physician, Jacques Caldwell, M.D., which appeared in the Florida Medical Association Quarterly Journal, I stated that single member LLCs may not receive charging order protection since there are no innocent partners to protect. On April 4, 2003, the bankruptcy case of **In Re Ashley Albright**, held exactly that. If you do have a single member LLC (while a helpful tool to protect your personal assets from liability stemming from the assets held in and/or the activities of the LLC), do not rely on it to provide you any protection from the claims of "outside" creditors, including medical malpractice judgment holders.

Other Potential Problems.

Assuming you have done your homework and determined that given your personal financial plan and cash flow scenario you could effectively play the waiting game, be aware that there are still some other issues of which to be cognitive.

1. **General Partnership Interest Owned by a Corporation**. Note that the charging order protection may be easy to get around if you own the general partnership interest in a corporation, the stock of which may be subject to attachment by the judgement creditor. Once a creditor has the stock (or voting control of the corporation), it has control of the partnership including the right to dissolve the entity or force distributions. Given the fact that you can now form a Limited Liability Limited Partnership (an "LLLP") that provides limited liability to the general partners without the use of a separate corporation or LLC, I do not recommend using this outdated structure. If an attorney is recommending it, make sure they can justify its use over an LLLP.

2. **The KO with the K-1**. Many lawyers and other promoters of FLPs claim that in the event a judgment creditor obtains a charging order, the creditor, not you, will receive the Form K-1 (the Form which informs a partner of his or her share of the partnership income tax liability). So their argument goes, a creditor will not want to even go after a charging order since they will have to pay income taxes while the waiting game is played. IRS **Revenue Ruling 77-137**, and the case, **Evans v. Commissioner**, are often sited as the author-

ity for this contention. The problem with Evans and **Rev. Rul.** 77-**137** is that neither case dealt with a charging order. Instead, in each of these cases, an individual transferred their entire interest in the partnership to someone else (I will call them the "Transferee"), however, the remaining partners did not vote to admit the Transferee as a full partner. In addition, the transferor of the partnership interest in **Rev. Rul.** 77-**137** signed an agreement agreeing to exercise any residual rights they may have in favor of the Transferee so as to vest the maximum amount of dominion and control over the transferred partnership interest in the Transferee. There was a similar legal obligation by the transferor in **Evans**. Under partnership law, a person who holds a partnership interest but has not been admitted as a full partner is called an "assignee" and is only entitled to receive distributions from the partnership but not vote or exercise the other rights of a partner. In both Evans and **Rev. Rul.** 77-137, since the **entire** partnership interest (i.e., complete dominion and control over the transferred partnership interest) was transferred, the Transferee was taxed on their share of the partnership income despite the fact that they were technically considered an assignee.

When a creditor obtains a charging order, the rights of the creditor are much more akin to a lien than a transferee of a partnership interest. The creditor is deemed to hold the rights of an assignee, however, those rights are less than an individual to whom an actual assignment of a partnership interest has been made and the creditor certainly has rights that are considerably less than complete dominion and control absent an additional agreement between the debtor and judgment creditor. The only real right the holder of a charging order has is a right to future distributions, however, only to the extent of the judgement amount including interest. All distributions above and beyond that amount belong to the debtor-partner (i.e., the physician), and the physician still has the right to exercise any voting rights associated with his or her interest, despite the fact a charging order has been issued. In addition, a judgement creditor with a charging order is almost always going to have a claim that is weaker than other general business creditors of the partnership even if the creditor appeared after the charging order was put in place.

In short, it makes perfect tax sense to tax someone to whom all economic rights in a partnership interest has been transferred (i.e., maximum dominion and control), despite the fact that they are technically an assignee, to pay taxes on their share of the partnership income. On the other hand, since very few rights are transferred via a charging order and the original partner still retains substantial control over the partnership interest, it makes very little tax sense to tax the judgement creditor. In addition, the implications of taxing the holder of a charging order on partnership income would create numerous anomalies that make little to no tax sense. It would be like making the bank pay the income taxes stemming from rental income simply because they have a mortgage lien on the properties generating the rental income.

Since this area of the law is still grey and many people believe that the creditor should be taxed on their share of partnership income, threatening a creditor with the possibility of having to pay income taxes may positively influence them to settle their law suit on more favorable terms, however, before the K-1 is actually sent, beware of the implications that action may have. If you do not report the income on your own return and it is later determined that the creditor did not have to pay the taxes, you will have back taxes, interest, and maybe even penalties to pay.

3. **Judicial Foreclosure Sale / Judicial Liquidation.** If a judgement creditor does not receive satisfaction from the charging order remedy, the creditor is likely to pursue other remedies, including a judicial foreclosure sale of the limited or general partnership interests and/or a judicial liquidation of the partnership. It is less likely for a court to order the liquidation of a partnership, however, the laws of some states do give a creditor the right to request a judicial liquidation of the partnership. Unfortunately, the trend over the past ten years has been away from the charging order being the sole and exclusive remedy of a judgement creditor. Ten states (Arizona, California, Connecticut, Georgia, Maryland, Missouri, New Hampshire, New Mexico, Pennsylvania, and Texas) have allowed the judicial foreclosure sale of limited partnership interests. Fortunately, Florida is not included in this list (and with our new sole and exclusive remedy statute probably won't be in the future). In short, if you are the owner of a partnership interest, don't assume it is protected; make sure you know the applicable state law governing that partnership.

4. **Partnership in Bankruptcy.** Another consideration that needs to be taken into account is whether charging order protection will withstand bankruptcy. While an in depth analysis of this issue is beyond the scope of this book, I

do want to provide you with enough of an explanation to understand why a standard off-the-shelf LLC operating agreement or FLP partnership agreement (or ones that are created online without any agreement at all) are not sufficient to provide asset protection if you end up in bankruptcy. Before we proceed, remember that a partnership agreement and an LLC operating agreement are exactly that; namely agreements or contracts between the partners or members to handle various issues relevant to the business of the partnership or LLC in a certain pre-agreed manner.

That being said, our analysis of this issue begins with Section 541 of the bankruptcy code, which includes in the bankruptcy estate "all legal or equitable interests of the debtor in property . . . wherever located and by whomever held . . . **notwithstanding any provision in an agreement, transfer instrument, or applicable nonbankruptcy law.**" This section casts a pretty large net and certainly will include partnership and LLC interests in the bankruptcy estate. Note that "applicable nonbankruptcy law" (i.e., the law limiting a creditor to a charging order), is ignored. In addition, Section 365 of the bankruptcy code states that "[n]otwithstanding a provision in an **executory contract** . . . or in **applicable law**, an executory contract . . . of the debtor **may not be terminated or modified**, . . . solely because of a provision . . . that is conditioned on (A) the insolvency or financial condition of the debtor . . .; (B) the commencement of a [bankruptcy]; or (C) the appointment of a [bankruptcy trustee] before [a bankruptcy is filed]. Finally, another part of Section 365 states that the bankruptcy trustee may not "assume" an "executory contract" without the consent of a party to the contract other than the person in bankruptcy.

Therefore, two things are important. First, provisions of our state law and clauses in an agreement that only operate if someone files for bankruptcy or becomes insolvent are likely to be ignored in bankruptcy. Second, if your partnership agreement is not considered to be an "executory contract," the charging order laws and other provisions in a partnership agreement that are responsible for the FLP being an effective asset protection tool are eviscerated. If it is considered an "executory contract," the charging order laws should continue to provide you with the desired protection.

In order for a partnership agreement to be considered an executory contract with respect to someone in bankruptcy, there must be some material ongoing obligations of each partner that make sense within the stated purpose of the partnership. After including these ongoing obligations in the partnership agreement, the partners need to conduct themselves in accordance with these provisions if they are expected to be upheld. For example, if there are ongoing obligations to make capital contributions, it may be a good idea for some actual capital calls to be made. In the event certain managerial obligations are required of the partners, minutes should be kept documenting that they were actually provided. This area of the law is still somewhat unsettled, but taking steps to increase the likelihood that your partnership or operating agreement is considered an "executory contract" only makes good sense.

Once again, bankruptcy is not your friend in this context. If you can stay outside of bankruptcy, the above analysis is not relevant. If, on the other hand, you find yourself being forced into bankruptcy, you will certainly be thankful if you had your partnership agreement or LLC operating agreement drafted by an asset protection attorney who is knowledgeable in this area.

Benefits of FLPs.

After having spent most of this Chapter pointing out problems with Family Limited Partnerships, it is important to now spend some time explaining some of their benefits. As I describe these benefits I will be assuming that: (i) the partnership is formed under a jurisdiction where charging order protection is the sole and exclusive remedy by statute, (ii) the partnership agreement is drafted by an attorney skilled in the area of asset protection to ensure the partnership agreement and the formation documents contain the provisions necessary to maximize the asset protection aspects of the partnership and do not contain certain provisions contained in standard business partnership agreements that may mitigate the partnership's effectiveness, (iii) the partnership has a valid business purpose and is managed after its formation with that business purpose in mind, (iv) an exempt/non-exempt cash flow analysis has been made by the individual (usually with the aid of their financial advisor) to ensure they can play the waiting game in the event a charging order is issued without financial hardship, (v) the general partnership interests are owned in a manner so a creditor cannot gain voting control (e.g., such as would be the case if the general partnership interests were owned by a corporation controlled or substantially owned by the physician), and (vi) the partnership has been properly incorporated into the physician's estate plan to ensure that the partnership passes to his or her intended heirs on death. If these criteria are met, then a Family Limited Partnership can be a valuable addition to a physician's comprehensive asset protection plan. If any one of these items are missing, the physician should have his or her plan reviewed and revised accordingly.

1. **Ability to Play the Waiting Game**. As mentioned above, the ability to play the waiting game can provide significant leverage in negotiating a favorable settlement. The possibility of having to wait twenty years and risk ultimately receiving nothing will be a considerable negative incentive to a creditor (and the creditor's attorney being paid on a contingency fee basis) which a physician can use to his or her advantage. In addition, although the law is still grey regarding whether or not a creditor with a charging order could be saddled with having to pay the income taxes associated with the partnership interest so charged, the risk of that possible outcome is yet another adverse consequence to a creditor that will provide the physician with negotiating leverage. If the physician demonstrates that he or she can legitimately play the waiting game given their other exempt assets and cash flow, the creditor may consider the cost and risk associated with pursuing a charging order time and money wasted.

2. **Limiting a Partner's Personal Liability**. Similar to a corporation, a Family Limited Partnership can be used to protect a person's assets from liability that may be spawned from a particular asset or business practice. This makes it a good vehicle to protect real estate. Many states now allow the formation of a Limited Liability Limited Partnership which is a Limited Partnership that protects general partners from personal liability and eliminates the need for a corporate general partner. Another new form of limited partnership (and LLC) allows the partnership to have cells in which separate parcels of property can be titled. Each cell acts likes its own mini-partnership so that if liability is spawned from one piece of property, the parcels held in the other cells remain protected despite the fact that they are all owned by the same entity.

3. **Real Estate and Immovables.** If a person has immovable assets such as real estate and that person is not willing to engage in any equity-stripping techniques (i.e., techniques to convert the equity in a piece of property into more liquid

assets that are more easily protected through other means), the Family Limited Partnership may be their best option for asset protection.

4. **Estate and Gift Tax Discounts.** A properly structured limited partnership can be an effective tool for reducing the owner's federal estate tax liability by reducing the value of the assets held in the partnership for estate tax purposes. It is not uncommon to receive discounts ranging from 30% to 40%. Therefore, if $3,000,000 of assets were transferred to a properly structured limited partnership and a 33% discount were to apply, the assets would only be valued at $2,000,000 for estate tax purposes. With a top estate tax rate of roughly 50%, this discount could result in an estate tax savings of $500,000. Similar discounts apply for federal gift tax purposes.

5. **Separating Ownership from Control**. Another benefit of an FLP is the ability to separate ownership from control. As explained above, the general partner(s) generally own only 1% of the total partnership interests, however, that 1% gives them 100% control over the activities of the partnership. Conversely, the limited partners generally own 99% of the total partnership interests but are not given the right to control the management of the partnership. This separation between ownership and control makes the limited partnership useful in numerous situations. For example, a parent can give children or grandchildren limited partnership interests instead of cash or other liquid assets as part of the annual gifting program. In this manner, the parent can make gifts of $12,000 per person per year to reduce their estate tax liability and obtain discounts to move greater amounts of underlying assets from their estate, all without giving children assets that they can squander. Another example involves parents who established Uniform Transfer to Minors Accounts ("UTMA Accounts") for their children when they were young and who later come to the realization that their twenty year old is about to be able to demand assets from their account at a time when fast cars and cool stereos are higher priorities than a college education. A parent can create a limited partnership in which he or she is the 1% general partner. The custodian of the UTMA Account then transfers the UTMA assets to the partnership in exchange for a limited partnership interest. Therefore, when the child reaches the relevant age (eighteen or twenty-one) they receive a limited partnership interest which has no real value to them unless the general partners (i.e., mom and dad) decide to make distributions.

6. **Coupling the FLP with a Trust or Other Protective Structure.** A powerful asset protection technique is to couple an FLP with a trust structure (either foreign or domestic). The physician (or the physician and his or her spouse) will typically own a 1% general partnership interest with the trust owning the remaining 99% limited partnership interest. Unlike a standalone limited partnership, if the physician is sued, he or she only owns a very small percentage of the partnership (0.5% if the spouse is an equal general partner), therefore, the charging order only attaches to that very small interest. If a $100 distribution was made from the partnership on a pro-rata basis at a time when a the physician's interest was charged by a creditor, the physician's spouse would get 50 cents, the creditor would get 50 cents, and the trust would receive $99. The trust can be structured to name the physician and/or the physician's spouse as a beneficiary so the assets can be used for the benefit of those beneficiaries if needed. The fact that the trust's only asset is a limited partnership interest may act as an additional disincentive to a creditor to try and attack the trust because even if successful, the only assets distributed would be a limited partnership interest which, of course, would have charging order protection. These structures are discussed more completely in the upcoming Chapters of this book, but suffice it to say that the addition of an FLP or LLC to other asset protection structures can enhance the benefits to a physician while increasing asset protection.

7. **Single Member LLC Strategy**. While I do not advocate waiting until a creditor appears on the horizon before taking steps to fix the single member LLC problem, there may be something you can do to help mitigate the problem. As you may remember, the reason for the charging order remedy (rather than allowing a direct levy on the partnership assets) is to prevent disruption of the partnership business and the resulting injustice to the other partners. This is why a single member LLC is not likely to provide you with any meaningful asset protection in the context of Outside Liability (see Chapter 16). If you owned a single member LLC and then discovered that someone was going to sue you (or worse yet, already had), you may consider selling a portion of your LLC to someone for full fair market value. Obtaining a written valuation of the interest being sold from a company that regularly values business entities will be a plus. There is a good argument that if the sale is for a fair price, for commercially reasonable terms, and an operating agreement is entered into with the new owner that is appropriately drafted, the creditor will be stuck

with a charging order. There are still some fraudulent transfer considerations, so it would certainly be better to solve the single member LLC problem prior to the discovery of a creditor. For example, you could transfer a portion of your LLC to a trust for the benefit of your spouse, children, or other family members. This would provide you with the desired charging order protection, reduce the fraudulent transfer concerns, and could still allow you to have the LLC taxed as a disregarded entity or S corporation if the trust is drafted to accommodate that outcome.

Conclusion.

Family Limited Partnership's can provide effective asset protection, however, whether one makes sense for you will depend on numerous factors as explained above. Remember that just like everything else in life, if an asset protection structure seems too good to be true, it probably is (or all the details have not been properly explained).

CHAPTER 18

Domestic Trusts as Part of Your Comprehensive Asset Protection Plan

In this Chapter I will discuss the topic of using domestic trusts as part of your comprehensive asset protection plan. I have saved the topic of "Domestic Self-Settled Trusts" for the next Chapter as this topic deserves a Chapter of its own to fully discuss how they work to protect assets. This Chapter instead focuses on trusts that are created by one person for the benefit of another. If you are not reading this book in order and are tempted to skip this Chapter and move on to the Chapter on "Self-Settled Trusts" or "Offshore Trusts," I would advise against doing so since the overview of trusts in general and the associated explanation of trust terminology provided below will be crucial to a complete understanding of the topics discussed in those Chapters.

I begin this Chapter with an explanation of trusts in general and how they differ from other legal entities such as corporations. I then go on to discuss the two principal ways a trust can protect assets from creditors; namely spendthrift protection and discretionary distributions. The benefits and limitations of these trusts under Florida law is then explained. Finally, I provide you with an overview of how these trusts can be incorporated into the asset protection and estate plan of you and your parents, grandparents, and other family members to provide benefits that are often unavailable through other means.

A Brief Discussion of Trusts.

Before explaining what a **Self-Settled** Trust is I want to give a brief description of what trusts are, in general, and explain the players. Unlike corporations which are formed by filing certain documents with state authorities and then exist as a separate legal entity, trusts are actually a splitting of a property's legal and beneficial title. The following example should help demonstrate what is meant by this.

> Pablo is a business man who travels frequently and who has a five year old daughter, Christina. Pablo has just learned that his business will take him to a part of the world fraught with political turmoil and that he must leave immediately. Pablo leaves his daughter with his trusted brother, Henri, and before leaving gives him various valuable assets with the instruction that they are to be held by Henri and used for the care of Christina in his absence. Pablo may not have realized it, but in giving the assets to Henri, Pablo created a trust. Henri is the Trustee and legally owns the property. As the property's legal owner, Henri has the power to sell the assets, and further has the authority to make decisions on how the assets are cared for and otherwise managed. Henri, however, is not entitled to use the assets for his own benefit. This stems from the fact that Christina is the beneficiary, and, therefore, is considered to be the "beneficial owner" of the property. Put another way, the beneficial owner of property has the right to use and enjoy the property even if they do not legally own it.

In modern times, the vast majority of all trusts are memorialized in a legal writing called a Trust Agreement or Declaration of Trust.

> Building on the previous example, assume this time that Pablo is not so pressed for time, and meets with an attorney before embarking on his travels. He places $1,000,000 in trust for the benefit of his daughter, Christina, and names his brother, Henri, as the Trustee. The Trust Agreement states that Henri has discretion to use the money to pay for Christina's health care, education, and to maintain her existing standard of living.

Since Pablo created this trust during his lifetime, the trust is called an "Inter-vivos Trust." Trusts that are created when someone dies are called "Testamentary Trusts." More will be discussed on how each type of trust can be used to protect assets, however, I will primarily focus on inter-vivos trusts.

Before moving on, I will describe some of the terminology used in discussing trusts. Hopefully, this will make the following discussions more meaningful and easier to understand.

Settlor. In the above example, Pablo is the Settlor (i.e, the person who created the Trust). As the trust's creator, he is the one who "settles" (i.e., establishes or creates) the trust. In doing so, the Settlor will determine who the trust beneficiaries are, who the Trustee(s) are, and the terms under which the beneficiaries will receive the assets in the Trust. The terms "Grantor" and "Trustor" are also words used to refer to the creator of a Trust, however, I will use the term Settlor in this book to avoid confusion.

Trustee. In the above example, Henri is the Trustee. The Trustee is the legal owner of the trust assets (i.e., the $1,000,000 in the above example) and has full authority over the assets and how they are managed. The Trustee is considered a fiduciary which is someone who holds a position involving a confidence or trust. As a fiduciary, the Trustee has an affirmative duty to manage the trust assets in a prudent manner and to use the assets in a manner which best serves the beneficiary within the guidelines set forth in the Trust Agreement. If more than one Trustee is named to serve together, they are called "Co-Trustees." For example, if Pablo had two brothers Henri and Patrick, and wanted them to work togther as Trustees, they would be considered Co-Trustees. If a replacement Trustee is named to serve if your first choice dies, resigns, or becomes incapacitated, that person is called a "Successor Trustee." Assume that Pablo has just named Henri to serve as the Trustee of the trust for Christina. If Henri were to die or otherwise become unable to serve as Trustee, he wants his close friend, Otto to take Henri's place. Otto would be called a "Successor Trustee." A Settlor can name numerous Successor Trustees and it is usually wise to do so. In the unfortunate event a Trustee dies and there is no named Successor Trustee, the court typically will appoint one. Their choice may or may not be a choice the Settlor would approve of.

Beneficiary. In the above example, Christina is the Beneficiary of the Trust created by Pablo (the "Settlor"). The beneficiary is the person who is entitled to receive assets from the trust (called "distributions") and the person who is entitled to benefit from the trust assets. For example, assume Christina is now twenty-five years old and wants to buy a house. Further assume that the Trust Agreement was drafted to permit the Trustee to use trust assets for that purpose, and Henri (the Trustee) feels that it would be in Christina's best interest to have her own home. Henri has a couple of options. First, he could simply write a check from the trust bank account to Christina so that Christina could go and buy herself a home. Second, he could go and buy the home in which Christina wants to reside in the name of the trust and simply allow Christina to live in it. Typically, the second option makes more sense from both an estate planning and asset protection standpoint.

Trust Estate. The term "Trust Estate" simply refers to the assets held inside a trust. In the above example, the $1,000,000 transferred to the trust by Pablo would be the Trust Estate. If the $1,000,000 grew over time to $2,000,000, the full $2,000,000 would be considered the Trust Estate. If the Trustee used the $2,000,000 to invest in a combination of real estate, stocks, bonds, and mutual funds, those assets are called the Trust Estate. When I refer to "trust assets" or the "trust estate," I will be referring to assets held in a trust. Though I will not use these terms in this book, the terms "trust corpus" and "trust res" are other phrases used to refer to assets held in trust.

Trust Agreement. The Trust Agreement is simply a written agreement that first identifies the Settlor(s), the Trustee(s), and the beneficiary(ies), and then goes on to define terms that govern what powers and limitations will be placed on the Trustee in managing trust assets or in making distributions to beneficiaries. It is important to note that trusts are extremely flexible and, if drafted properly, can accomplish almost any objective. Just one quick example of this is people with children who may not possess high levels of personal motivation. A parent may be concerned that if they were to die, the money that the child would inherit would pay for him or her to sit around the pool drinking beer rather than assist him or her in being a happy, self-sufficient member of society. In such a situation, the parent may provide that the child's inheritance be held in a trust that will pay for all their health care expenses and provide for some minimum level of existence for the child, but not enough for the child to live an opulent lifestyle. The child is then given an additional right to receive distributions from the trust equal to what they report on their own tax return. In this manner, if a child wants to sit around the pool and drink beer, he or she will be drinking cheap beer. If, on the other hand, they choose to work hard and be productive citizens, they have the opportunity to double their income. Of course, provisions can be added to prevent penalizing a child for choosing a career with significant social value but that does not reflect the importance of the work in a big pay check (i.e., homemaker, teacher, minister, rabbi, peace corp employee, etc.). This is just one example, however, of how a trust can be drafted to help accomplish your goals and objectives (regardless of what they are), even after you are dead.

Protective Trust Provisions.

There are two primary means by which a trust can offer asset protection to its beneficiaries. The first of these two is the inclusion in the Trust Agreement of something called a "spendthrift clause." The second is to give the Trustee discretion over whether or not to make distributions to the trust beneficiaries. Each of these is discussed below. Understand as you read the following discussion, that it relates to trusts that are created by someone for the benefit of another and not a trust created by someone of which they are also a beneficiary.

Spendthrift Protection.

As discussed in other contexts earlier in this book, a general concept in asset protection planning is that a creditor generally cannot take what a person does not have the right to give. That is the basic idea behind a "spendthrift clause." The "spendthrift clause" itself is simply a provision in a Trust Agreement that restricts a beneficiary's ability to transfer, sell, or otherwise give away any of their rights in a trust.

> Assume that Conrad establishes a trust for the benefit of his child, Betty. The trust provides that Betty will receive $50,000 each year for the rest of her life. The trust was not drafted to contain a spendthrift provision. Betty is free to give away or sell her rights under the trust as a beneficiary. Since Betty has this right, if Betty is ever sued and a judgement is obtained by the plaintiff, Betty's beneficial interest in the trust could be taken by

> the creditor which would give the creditor the right to receive the $50,000 per year.
>
> Now assume the exact same facts, however, this time Conrad makes sure that the trust does contain a spendthrift clause thereby forbidding Betty from selling, giving away, or otherwise transferring her rights under the trust. If she is sued by the same creditor, the creditor will not be able to take her interest in the trust which will make it significantly more difficult for the creditor to reach any assets of the trust or distributions therefrom. It is important to note, however, that once a distribution is made to Betty, it is fair game for a creditor to go after.

In 1875 the United States Supreme Court decided the case of **Nichols v. Eaton**, which solidified the effectiveness of spendthrift trusts in protecting an individual's interest in a trust created by someone other than the beneficiary under the laws of the United States.

Florida's New Trust Code and Spendthrift Protection.

During the 2006 legislative session, the Florida legislature gave statutory recognition to spendthrift provisions. Florida Statute Section 736.0502 now reads as follows:

> "(1) A spendthrift provision is valid only if the provision restrains both **voluntary and involuntary** transfer of a beneficiary's interest. This subsection does not apply to any trust in existence on the effective date of this code.
>
> (2) A term of a trust providing that the interest of a beneficiary is held subject to a spendthrift trust, or words of similar import, is sufficient to restrain both voluntary and involuntary transfer of the beneficiary's interest.
>
> (3) A beneficiary may not transfer an interest in a trust in violation of a valid spendthrift provision and, except as otherwise provided in this part, **a creditor or assignee of the beneficiary**

> **may not reach the interest or a distribution by the trustee before receipt of the interest or distribution by the beneficiary.**
>
> (4) A valid spendthrift provision does not prevent the appointment of interests through the exercise of a power of appointment."

Therefore, we now have a Florida statute which gives statutory authority to the validity and enforceability of spendthrift clauses. Of course, spendthrift protection was previously recognized under case law. The statute also restricts a creditor's ability to directly garnish a distribution to a beneficiary from a trust which means that they will have the more difficult task of finding and attaching the distribution directly from the creditor. Finally, the statute states that a spendthrift clause must restrict both the **voluntary and involuntary** transfer of a beneficiary's interest in order to be valid. This requirement does not apply to any trust that was in existence as of the effective date of this new trust code (i.e., July 1, 2007). There was very little authority one way or another with respect to whether a spendthrift clause would be enforced that provided that a beneficiary could withdraw assets but only if they were not having creditor problems at the time. Could this new statute provide a basis for such an argument since the new law which now prohibits this only applies prospectively? Time will tell.

There are some limits to spendthrift protection, however. Florida Statutes Section 1736.0503, states that:

> . . . a spendthrift provision is unenforceable against:
>
> (a) A beneficiary's child, spouse, or former spouse who has a judgment or court order against the beneficiary for support or maintenance.
>
> (b) A judgment creditor who has provided services for the protection of a beneficiary's interest in the trust [i.e., the asset protection attorney].
>
> (c) A claim of this state or the United States to the extent a law of this state or a federal law so provides."

Therefore, the first exception from spendthrift trust protection is with respect to "exception creditors." These creditors include (i) a beneficiary's child with respect to a claim for child support, (ii) a beneficiary's former spouse with respect to a claim for alimony, (iii) anyone (such as an attorney) who has provided services for the protection of a beneficiary's interest in the trust, and (iv) the government. If the trust is also a discretionary trust (see discussion below), these exception creditors may still be thwarted from reaching the trust assets. The second exception to spendthrift protection stems from the fact that a Trustee is prohibited from withholding a distribution required to be paid to the beneficiary under the trust agreement solely to protect the distribution from the beneficiary's creditors. These "held back" mandatory distributions can be garnished from a spendthrift trust.

Do Spendthrift Trusts Only Protect Spendthrifts?

While the term **Spendthrift** implies that the asset protection offered by these trust clauses is intended to protect those who are not capable of handling money wisely, in fact, Spendthrift clauses will protect any trust beneficiary; even those who are very responsible. The reason for this is that the law primarily focuses on the rights of the individual establishing a trust. The Latin maxim "**cujus est dare, ejus est disponere,**" or "[w]hose it is to give, his it is to dispose" is often used when discussing the reason why spendthrift trusts are protective. Put another way, the person who owns an asset should be able to give it away **and** impose restrictions on its use without interference from a court.

The Super Creditor Called the IRS.

Although it probably is so obvious as to not require mentioning, collection efforts by the IRS or other governmental agencies will not be thwarted by a spendthrift trust.

Discretionary Distribution Provisions.

The next broad category of protective trusts are discretionary trusts. As eluded to above, if the Trustee has discretion over whether or not to make distributions to a trust beneficiary, the creditors of that beneficiary cannot reach the trust assets while they reside in the trust. The basis for this is found in a legal Treatise called the Restatement (Second) Of Trusts. Section 155 of the Restatement of Trusts reads as follows:

> "[I]f by the terms of a trust it is provided that the trustee shall pay to or apply for a beneficiary only so much of the income and principal . . . as the trustee in his uncontrolled discretion shall see fit . . . , a [creditor] of the beneficiary cannot compel the trustee to pay any part of the income or principal."

This was reiterated in the case of **Bacardi v. White** where the issue was whether a spendthrift trust can protect trust assets from claims against a beneficiary for alimony and child support. To quote the language of the court "[i]f disbursements are wholly within the trustee's discretion, the court may not order the trustee to make such disbursements."

The New Trust Code and Discretionary Trusts.

Florida's new trust code incorporates and gives statutory authority for the protection of discretionary trusts. Florida Statutes Section 736.0504 reads as follows:

> "(1) **Whether or not a trust contains a spendthrift provision,** a creditor of a beneficiary **may not compel a distribution that is subject to the trustee's discretion,** even if:
>
> (a) The discretion is expressed in the form of a standard of distribution; or
>
> (b) The trustee has abused the discretion.
>
> (2) If the trustee's discretion **to make distributions for the trustee's own benefit** is limited by an ascertainable standard, **a creditor may not reach or compel distribution of the beneficial interest except to the extent the interest** would be subject to the creditor's claim were the beneficiary not acting as trustee.
>
> (3) This section does not limit the right of a beneficiary to maintain a judicial proceeding against a trustee for an abuse of discretion or failure to comply with a standard for distribution."

Prior to the effective date of the new trust code (i.e., July 1, 2007), several Florida cases have held that if a beneficiary of a trust (whether spendthrift or discretionary) is the sole Trustee that the protection ordinarily provided by these trusts will not be effective to protect the trust assets from the claims of a beneficiary's creditors. The above statute changes that by now allowing a beneficiary to serve as the Trustee of their own trust and give them significant asset protection.

In establishing protective trusts, it is usually best to use discretionary **spendthrift** trusts. This belt and suspenders approach provides the best protection since the protections compliment each other.

> Assume that Jerry and Sheila decide to create trusts for their two boys, Stan and Ike. Stan's trust is a purely discretionary trust under which the Trustee has complete discretion to distribute as much or as little to Stan as the Trustee deems appropriate. Stan's trust, however, contains no spendthrift clause. Ike's trust is a spendthrift trust that mandates that no less than $50,000 be distributed to Ike each year (i.e., it is not a discretionary trust). Stan becomes a successful physician and never marries. Ike ends up working in a low paying job as a menial laborer married to Wendy who never really loved him. After several years, Ike's marriage fails. Stan's life also takes a turn for the worse when he is sued for medical malpractice. Wendy is awarded alimony and tries to reach Ike's trust in satisfaction of his alimony obligation. The plaintiff in the suit against Stan for medical malpractice is awarded a $2,000,000 judgement and seeks to enforce it against Stan's trust.
>
> Since Stan's trust is a purely discretionary trust but not a spendthrift trust, the judgement creditor will not be able to reach the assets of Stan's trust so long as the Trustee does not make any distributions, however, the trust assets are now trapped in the trust and, therefore, kept from Stan as well. Had Stan's trust also contained a spendthrift clause, Stan could have had access to the trust assets and kept them from the reach of his creditor. Since Ike's trust is a spendthrift trust but not a discretionary trust,

> assuming Wendy has exhausted all other methods of collecting alimony from Ike, she will be able to reach the assets of Ike's trust to satisfy the alimony payments Ike owes her. If Ike's trust had also been a discretionary trust, the Trustee could have kept the assets away from Wendy by not making any distributions to Ike which could have possibly given Ike more negotiating leverage in the divorce proceedings.

The asset protection benefits of the discretionary spendthrift trust can be substantial, and now, under the new trust code the beneficiary can still maintain significant control by being the Trustee. This works wonderfully so long as the beneficiary/trustee resides in the state of Florida. If, however, the beneficiary/trustee moves to a state whose laws do not provide similar protections, there is a strong likelihood that the trust could be deemed to be governed by the new state's laws and, therefore, these protections would be lost. Careful drafting of a trust can prevent this loss of protection so it is highly recommended that this issue is directly addressed by whoever is helping you draft your trust since the only constant is change and there is a strong likelihood that your children may not spend the rest of their lives as Floridians. The drafter of the trust should also be careful not to add language that gives a beneficiary the right to demand distributions, otherwise the creditor may be able to reach the amount the beneficiary has the right to demand.

Reciprocal Trusts and the Step Transaction Doctrine.

Seeing the benefit of having a trust created for your benefit by another, you may be tempted to try one of the following.

Reciprocal Trusts. You and your spouse are both physicians and would both like a protective trust established for your benefit. You divide your property between yourselves and each create a discretionary spendthrift trust for the other with a third party acting as the trustee. Technically, both of you are now the beneficiary of a trust (i) created by someone other than yourself, and (ii) with a spendthrift clause and discretionary distribution powers granted to the trustee. While there is no case law of which I am aware that prohibits this, there is an estate tax rule called the "reciprocal trust doctrine" which basically states that if two people create trusts for the other, the trusts will be "uncrossed" and each person will be treated as creating their own trust. If this logic were ever applied in the asset protection context, the end result would be that neither of you would receive asset protection because you would each be treated as having created a trust for yourself. As will be explained in the next Chapter on Self-Settled Trusts, if you create a discretionary spendthrift trust for yourself, it provides little in the way of meaningful asset protection. It is my belief that a court would see right through an arrangement like this and deny asset protection to both husband and wife.

The Step-Transaction Doctrine. Assume that you are the primary income earner. Over time you have gifted assets to your lower risk spouse. Your spouse then creates a discretionary spendthrift trust for your benefit with a third party as the trustee. Since all the assets that ended up in the trust for your benefit were earned by you, a court is likely to combine the "steps" (i.e., Step 1- you earn money, Step 2 - you give money to spouse, Step 3 - spouse creates trust for you) and treat the trust as being directly created by you - for you with the end result of no asset protection. This Step Transaction Doctrine is another tax law concept that could easily be applied in the asset protection law arena. It is my recommendation not to attempt something like this as part of your asset protection plan.

Planning With Protective Trusts.

Discretionary spendthrift trusts (and simple spendthrift trusts) can be a valuable addition to your comprehensive asset protection plan. If you are anticipating inheriting assets from parents, grandparents, friends, etc., you should always consider asking them to leave the assets to you in trust rather than leave them to you outright. The same holds true for parents and grandparents who have established gifting programs to reduce their potential estate tax liability. If these gifts are made in trust rather than directly to the individual, the assets can be protected from creditors and provide additional benefits. Finally, when one spouse dies, it is possible to leave assets to the surviving spouse in a protective trust. This is especially important if a physician has transferred property to a lower risk spouse to protect the transferred assets. When the lower risk spouse dies, it only makes sense to use such a trust to keep assets from returning to the physician spouse in a manner that could subject them to the claims of the physician's creditors. Some additional benefits to using these protective trusts are discussed below.

Estate Tax Savings. Trusts established by a third person (i.e., a parent, grandparent, friend, etc.) can be structured to use that person's "generation skipping tax exemption" (sometimes referred to as a "GST Exemption"). While a complete discussion of the generation skipping tax is beyond the scope of this book, suffice it to say that every resident of the United States is given a GST Exemption that allows them to create special trusts (sometimes called "Dynastic Trusts") with a certain amount of assets (i.e., $2,000,000 in 2007). These trusts can be used to benefit a child and then pass the remaining trust assets to the next generation without being taxed in the child's estate.

> Assume that Rhett creates a Dynastic Trust for his daughter, Savannah, and transfers $1,000,000 to it. The trust contains a spendthrift provision. The trust purchases a home and a vacation home in the name of the trust and allows Savannah to use these properties. The trust also provides her with some money, however, Savannah is a success in her own right, so the money in the trust grows to $5,000,000 over her lifetime. When she dies, the full $5,000,000 is passed down to her children without being subject to estate tax at Savannah's death. Even better, Savannah's children can receive the full $5,000,000 in Dynastic Spendthrift Trusts and continue the asset protection and estate tax benefits for generations to come.

Asset Protection.

Beyond the asset protection benefits discussed above, being the beneficiary of a protective trust can provide additional asset protection benefits. Assume for example that a trust was established for you by a parent and now holds $2,000,000. Further assume that you have $500,000 in a brokerage account and were planning on using it as a down payment to buy a new $1,000,000 home. Rather than taking out a traditional mortgage, the protective trust lends you the money to purchase the home and takes back a mortgage on the home and a lien on the brokerage account. Under this arrangement, if you ever default on the loan, the trust is required to first go after the brokerage account. What have you accomplished? First, you are paying interest to a trust for your own benefit which should qualify for the home mortgage interest deduction, thereby reducing the tax cost of the transaction. Second, a creditor is now unable to reach the brokerage account so long as a perfected lien has been granted with respect to the account. The homestead is also protected.

It may also be possible to sell the assets in the brokerage account to the trust in exchange for a private annuity. The annuity payments you receive back from the trust will be protected from the claims of creditors. If the securities or property you sell have a low tax basis (i.e., they have appreciated in value since the time you purchased them) after they have been sold to the trust in exchange for the annuity, it can be sold by the trust without triggering capital gains tax. Instead, the tax will be paid over the period of the annuity, thereby giving you tax deferral.

These are just a couple additional, creative uses of protective trusts to ameliorate your asset protection plan. There are a myriad of other possibilities as well.

Recipient Trusts.

In the event you see the benefits of having someone (your parents, maybe) create a trust for your benefit but do not feel comfortable asking them to make substantial changes to their estate plan, you may want to consider a Recipient Trust. This entails having your spouse (or other friend or family member) establish a trust for you that contains all the estate planning and asset protection provisions you would want. The person creating the trust for you initially funds it with a small amount (say, $100). Thereafter, you can approach your parents and say "if you are planning to leave me anything when you die, could you please leave it to the [name of the trust] rather than to me outright?" If your parents are willing to make this very small change, which should be very inexpensive, your inheritance flows into the asset protected Recipients Trust. I had a client who, in the middle of a law suit, inherited $8,000,000 from his father. The entire amount was left to him outright and unprotected and resulted in him paying a much higher settlement than was initially contemplated. Had he used a Recipients Trust, the entire problem could have been avoided.

Business Succession Planning.

Finally, these protective trusts can solve certain business succession planning issues. Assume your parents died leaving you a protective trust holding $1,000,000. Further assume that you want to start your own business selling certain medical supplies via the internet. Instead of requesting a distribution from the trust to start the business, the trust creates an LLC of which you are the manager/president. Over the years, the business becomes quite valuable and you want to have it pass down to your two children who have become active in the business. If you owned the business in your own name, the estate taxes could be considerable and you may not have the liquidity necessary to pay the estate taxes and pass the business to your children. If the trust owns the business, however, and it was a Dynastic Trust discussed above, the business would not be subject to estate taxes when you die and could pass to your children under the terms of the trust unscathed. Trusts can also be drafted to include something called a "limited power of appointment" that allows you, the trust beneficiary, to change who inherits the money from the trust when you die. In this manner, you could have the business pass to the children who actively participate in the business and have other assets pass to the remaining children.

The Inter Vivos QTIP Trust.

In the event you are the primary income earner and are considering using "I Gave it to my Spouse" planning (see Chapter 13), as part of your asset protection plan, you may want to consider using an Inter-vivos QTIP Trust (don't you just love the names we lawyers come up with). As you may remember, the term "Inter-vivos" refers to a trust you create while you are living (as opposed to one created upon your death) and the term "QTIP" refers to a special type of trust created for your spouse that will not trigger gift tax. The primary benefit of this type of trust is exemplified by the following example:

> Marie is a physician married to Phillip. Phillip is a school teacher with very little occupational risk. Marie wants to title their brokerage account in Phillip's name alone to protect it in the event she is ever sued for medical malpractice. She understands that one of the downsides to this type of "I Gave it to my Spouse" planning is that the assets are all subject to the claims of Phillip's creditors if he were ever sued. Marie knows that Phillip is a horrible driver and she is fearful that if he ever caused an accident, Phillip could be sued and they could lose the bro-

> kerage account in his name. One morning while cleaning her ears, Marie exclaims "I've got it, we can use an Inter-vivos QTIP Trust." Instead of transferring the brokerage account to Phillip individually, she creates an Inter-vivos QTIP Trust for Phillip's benefit (Phillip can even serve as the Trustee under Florida's new trust code). Now if Phillip is ever sued, the trust assets will be protected from his creditors and if Marie is ever sued, since she transferred assets to the trust at a time when no creditor threats existed, the assets will be beyond the reach of her creditors. The trust was drafted so that if Phillip dies, the assets return to her in a protective trust that uses Phillip's estate tax Unified Credit and helps reduce their estate tax liability.

There are two potential downsides to this type of planning. First, if Phillip ever divorces Marie, the assets in the trust will be his alone, and will not be subject to being divided between them upon divorce as would be the case if Marie simply titled the brokerage account in Phillip's individual name. Second, there is an argument that if Phillip were to die, the trust that would be created for Marie's benefit upon Phillip's death (I will call this the "Testamentary Trust") could be considered a "self-settled" trust and, therefore, not protective. While I feel that there are good arguments that this should not be the case, it may be safer to have the Testamentary Trust governed under the laws of a State or foreign country that protects self-settled trusts (see Chapters 19 and 20).

Using Trusts to Plan for Your Children If They Are Forced to Grow Up in a World Without You In It.

While this does not directly relate to asset protection planning, I felt it was important to cover some of the types of planning you should consider with respect to leaving assets to your children. As you begin the process of creating your individual estate and asset protection plan, one of the single most important aspects of that plan will be creating the environment in which your children will develop if they are faced with growing up in a world that does not include you in it. Of course, we always hope for the best, however, if you do not take steps to plan for the worst, your children are the ones that will pay the price.

Your Children's Trusts.

If you had died without any planning in place, the person who is ultimately appointed by the court to serve as your child's guardian will typically be in charge of their inherited assets as well. As the child grows up, the inherited assets are used to pay for the costs of raising the child including the child's education and medical expenses. The guardian will have significant discretion to determine what expenses are reasonable and appropriate given the child's individual situation. When the child reaches age eighteen (18), the child is entitled to receive all the inherited assets that were not used for his or her care as a minor. The majority of people I have worked with over the years (and myself as well) do not feel that giving an eighteen year old a large sum of money is necessarily in their best interest.

Now enter the trust. An alternative to having a guardian care for the assets passed on to a child is to provide for a trust to be created for the benefit of each child upon the death of the last surviving parent (i.e., both mom and dad have passed on). Trusts have numerous benefits most of which can be summed up in a single word "FLEXIBILITY." Trusts can give you, the parents, significant control over (i) who will be in charge of the trust assets (this will be discussed in greater detail below when we discuss trustees), (ii) how the assets will be invested, (iii) when and for what purposes money can distributed to your children, (iv) whether creditors of your child (including a divorcing spouse) can reach the trust assets (which most people want to avoid), (v) who will receive the assets in the trust if a child dies or fails to meet a requirement you felt was important (such as graduating from college), and (vi) the extent to which the trust assets will be taxed upon the death of your child. In short, the options offered by trusts are as limitless as the parents' imagination. Philosophically, some parents are opposed to the idea of "parenting from the grave," while others see customized trust planning as providing important incentives and important tangible and intangible benefits above and beyond the mere inherited assets. Where you fall on the continuum should be a personal choice that takes into account the individual characteristics of your children and your family and personal moral values.

Below I have given you a few examples of some of the things my clients have requested with respect to the provisions of their children's trusts over the years. Remember as you read through them that they are intended to be food for thought and that you always have the option of making modifications or personal improvements given your individual goals, objectives, and insights. First, I address some issues that will affect your children while they are still minors. Then I will move on to trust planning that will affect your children during the adult stages of their life.

Planning For Minors.

When a child is a minor, I feel it is often best to give considerable discretion to the trustee to make decisions with respect to which expenses make the most sense for the well-being of your children. This gives the trustee the flexibility to adjust to the changing needs of your children as they go though the many stages of young life. That being said, it is oftentimes preferable to state your specific intent with respect to any number of topics to guide the trustee in their decision making. Some of the issues that you may wish to address in planning the specifics of your children's trusts are:

1. **Guardians**. To what extent do you want the guardians of your children compensated for serving in that capacity. For example, do you want to specify that above and beyond compensating them for their out-of-pocket expenses, they should receive payments to compensate them for their contribution of time, hard work, and patience in raising your children? Would you want the trust to pay for a larger home for the guardian and their family (which now includes your children) to live in while your children are minors? Should the trustee be permitted to pay for the addition of a room or wing to be added to their existing home? If you answered yes to any of the above questions, do you wish to place a cap on the amounts that could be paid out of the trust for these purposes? The answer to all these questions will depend in part on how much money is likely to end up in the trust were you to die unexpectedly and what you estimate the cost of raising your children will be until they reach an age where they will leave the guardian's home (which may be older than age 18). In making these decisions, a comprehensive financial plan that crunches these numbers based on your input can be invaluable.

2. **Education**. If you have a strong preference that your children attend public or private schools as they grow up, or that they attend a school that emphasizes a

particular religious perspective, letting the trustee know will aide them in making decisions as to how money should be allocated given your preferences.

3. **Miscellaneous.** There are numerous other topics you may want to cover including whether the trustee should pay for travel to visit family members that live in other states or countries, whether being involved in extra-curricular activities that may involve additional expenses are desired, whether you want them to have a car at age 16 or upon graduating from high school, or whether there are any limitations on how the trust assets are invested while the child is a minor, just to name a few. In short, take the time to think through any expenses or thought processes that the trustee may not think of (or understand the importance of) if you do not point them out.

Planning for Young Adulthood and Beyond.

After your child has reached a certain age or achieved a specified goal, you may want to start turning control over the trust assets to him or her. This desire has to be weighed against the fact that giving a child a large sum of money can sometimes do more harm than good given the child's maturity level and general ability to manage the inherited assets. In fact, if the child is addicted to drugs or some other destructive behavior, a large sum of money placed directly in their control can even be deadly. Trust planning, however, goes far beyond simply determining what ages your children will receive their assets. It is amazing to me how the vast majority of the trusts I have reviewed over the years that simply require trust assets to be distributed to the child outright and free of trust at certain ages. The most common scenario is for trust assets to be distributed one-third at age 25, one-half of the balance at age 30, and the balance at age 35. As I have outlined below, careful consideration should be given to numerous topics in planning the specifics of your children's trusts. Think through what you want for your children and what would serve their best interest.

1. **Asset Protection.** One of the most valuable gifts you can give your children is an asset protection trust to house their inheritance throughout their lifetime. Rather than providing for the trustee to distribute say one-third of the trust assets directly to the child at age 25 (where they would be subject to the claims of his or her creditors), you can instead provide for those assets to be transferred to a special trust over which the child has considerable control (i.e., the child

can even serve as trustee), but that has provisions that can serve to protect the inherited assets from the child's creditors, including a divorcing spouse (I'll call this type of trust a "Beneficiary Controlled Trust"). If a child inherited $1,000,000 outright and free of trust at age 25 and used the money to start a business or purchase a home, a creditor or a divorcing spouse could end up taking your child's home and his or her livelihood. If instead, the $1,000,000 were held in an asset protected Beneficiary Controlled Trust, the child's home and business could be owned by that trust. The child could be the president and CEO of the business, earn a large salary, and control when the company is sold without directly owning the business and without subjecting it to the claims of his or her creditors or the divorcing spouse. Likewise, if the home is owned by the Beneficiary Controlled Trust and a divorce ensues, the child's spouse, not the child, will be the one moving out of the home. This can also provide a child with a means to protect their home even if they live in a state that does not have Florida's generous homestead exemption. John D. Rockefeller once said: "Own Nothing, Control Everything." This was excellent advice back in his day and is even better advice today. In a world where asset protection planning has become a necessity, you can give your child the advantage of an asset protection trust that will protect their inheritance and provide them with a tool to ameliorate their own planning as well.

2. **Estate Planning.** In addition to the asset protection benefits of creating a Beneficiary Controlled Trust to hold the child's inheritance, if it is also drafted to be a Dynasty Trust (see the discussion above) there can be significant benefits from an estate tax perspective as well.

3. **Incentive Provisions.** Another benefit of leaving assets to your children in trust is the ability to tailor how the children will receive their money in a way that provides them with incentives to do any number of things. Again your choices are as limitless as your imagination.

Incentive Provisions.

It has always been my opinion that the trusts you establish for your children if you were to pass on unexpectedly should attempt to mimic the decisions you would make if you were alive to make them yourself. If your son or daughter came to you on their 25th birthday asking for $1,000,000, you may or may not give it to them. If your daughter had graduated with honors, was the picture of maturity and responsibility over the past several years, and had a well thought out business plan in her hand detailing the financial projections for a new business she was exited to start, you would probably stroke the check if you were able to do so. If on the other hand she had dropped out of community college, had no direction in life, spent money like water, and spent most of her time sitting around the pool drinking wine coolers with her equally ambitious friends, you would probably laugh out load at her request for the $1,000,000 and go in the other room to share the joke with your spouse. If your thought pattern was something like what I detailed above, why would you draft your trust to give your child a large sum of money simply because they attained a certain age.

Below are a few popular options with respect to providing incentives to your children that will serve as food for thought as you go through the planning process.

1. **Education Incentive.** One popular option is to provide a child an incentive to better themselves through education. For example, you could provide for the child to receive one-third of their inheritance at age 25 (through an asset protected trust), however, in the event the child has not graduated from college by that age, they only receive ten percent (10%). You could even tie the percentage to their academic performance. If a child graduates with a 3.9 grade point average ("GPA") or better, they would receive 50% of the trust assets. If they graduate with a GPA between 3.0 and 3.9, they would receive 33% of the trust assets. If they graduate with a GPA between 2.5 and 3.0, they would receive 20% of the trust assets and if they graduate with a GPA of less than 2.5, they receive 10%. Instead of percentages, you could also provide for set sums of money to be distributed to the child upon the same milestones. Provisions such as these provide the child with an incentive to not only go to college, but also to perform academically.

2. **Incentive to be Self Sufficient.** A concern of many parents is not that the child will not receive enough but that the child will receive too much. As stated above, you need to ask yourself whether giving a child a full one-third of the trust assets at age 25, for instance, will help them or provide them with an incentive to not work and instead sit around the pool with friends drinking beer all day. Many parents assume that this is not a concern because they are

not wealthy enough, however, consider the following. A family has two young children (ages 3 and 5). They own their own home worth $350,000, have savings of $500,000, and a $2,000,000 term life insurance policy. The total assets available for the children were both parents to die would be $2,850,000. If the trust earns just 5% per year it will produce an annual income of $142,000 per year. Many children will not come close to needing a full $71,000 each to meet their annual needs so the trust assets will continue to grow. If each child actually needed $30,000 per year (i.e., $60,000 between the two of them), by the time the three year old reaches age 25, his or her trust will be worth almost $3,150,000 (i.e., $6,300,000 collectively for both children). One-third of this amount, therefore, would be $1,050,000. Remember that at age 30 they will receive the next installment of $1,250,000 each and at age 35 each child will receive almost $1,450,000. Even if the trust did not grow at all, each child would still receive almost a full $500,000 at each milestone age. You need to ask yourself is this really going to be good for your children or does a 25 year old receiving something between $500,000 and $1,050,000 scare you a little. If it does you may want to consider the following type of incentive trust.

When your child reaches age 25, the trust will start paying him or her the sum of $25,000 per year (or some other sum that would allow them to live a decent but not opulent life). You could also decide to provide them with no annual payment (remember that the trustee can always use the trust assets to provide for the health care needs of your children), or have the annual payment disappear after age 30 or 35. In addition to each annual payment, if any, the child could receive an amount equal to what they report on their own income tax return. Therefore, if they are a professional, business owner, or otherwise earning a good salary, they have the opportunity to double their income. If they work at the local fast food joint, they will earn double minimum wage. Therefore, they will have an incentive to work hard and be productive, otherwise they will receive very little from their trust. Remember that since the purpose of this type of trust is to provide an incentive to be a self-sufficient person, you could provide that the restrictions will be removed and the child can receive all of the trust money if they earn in excess of some amount (say $80,000) each year for five consecutive years. In this manner, even if the child did lose the money in their trust, at least they have proven their ability to be productive at that level.

I also want to point out that a well drafted incentive trust will provide for various "exceptions to the rule." For example, what if a child decides to become a full time homemaker and devote their life to raising their children. We all know that this is one of the most difficult and important jobs a person can have, however, they simply do not receive a paycheck. In this scenario, the trust could provide that the homemaker will be deemed to earn a salary equal to that of their spouse or you could define a set amount they would receive each year (e.g., $125,000 per year; inflation adjusted, of course). Another consideration is what if a child is passionate about pursuing a job as a teacher, a minister, a peace corps worker, or some other full-time job that just does not pay very well. In this circumstance, the trustee could be given the authority to increase the multiplier (e.g., perhaps an annual payout of 4 times income rather than a 1 to 1 income match) so that the child is not penalized for choosing a career that they love but is not lucrative. There are obviously numerous variations to the themes I have pointed out above and many that I did not mention. You need to consider what is important to you and whether an incentive trust makes sense given your personal facts and circumstances.

3. **Incentive to be Charitably Inclined.** One of my clients was a true philanthropist and wanted to pass a desire to give back to the community on to his children. He created a trust that set aside a sum of money that was controlled by a group of five people in the charitable world he had worked with and trusted. After he died, the five individuals were to work with the children to continue the work their father had begun. Every four years the five trustees would meet and determine which of the children had been most active in their philanthropic endeavors. The winner received a plaque and a check for $250,000. There were also gifts to children who had made an earnest effort. This is just one example of the type of personalized planning you may want to consider.

4. **Incentive to Stop Abusing Drugs or Alcohol.** In the event a child is ever addicted to drugs or alcohol, the child's trust can give the Trustee broad discretion to withhold making distributions to the child until and unless the child submits to drug testing and/or undergoes treatment and ongoing counseling. The trust can even provide harsher penalties if the child refuses to go along. For example, the child could suffer the permanent loss of all or a portion of the trust assets which would thereafter only be available for his or her medical expenses. Obviously giving an addicted child a large sum of money would not

only be unwise, but could also be deadly.

5. **Forced Retirement Savings.** Another option you may want to consider is setting aside a portion of the trust assets after a child has reached age 21, for example, to be invested for the child's retirement. If 20% of a trust holding $1,000,000 was set aside for the child and invested to produce a 5% return until the child reached age 60, the child would have retirement assets of a little over $1,400,000. If the assets produced a 7% rate of return, the amount waiting for the child at age 60 would be just over $2,300,000. This is obviously a huge benefit to provide for a child, especially one that may be less disciplined in saving money than you would have hoped. Of course, if the child or his or her children ever need the money for medical needs, it could also be used for that purpose thereby giving them a safety net that the government may not provide in the future.

6. **Incentive to Save.** In addition to setting aside money for their retirement, you could also structure incentives for them to establish good habits when it comes to saving money. Again, by instilling good habits at an early age, you will help them to become self-sufficient, happy grown-ups.

7. **Providing for Health Care.** In all trusts created for your children, especially those that have restrictive provisions, you always want to make sure that the trustee can pay for the health care needs of your children from the trust assets. Obviously, if a child has a serious medical condition or is in a life threatening accident, your first consideration is maintaining their health and safety and the other trust provisions will take a back seat to this concern. You may also want a trust provision that requires the trustee to pay for a child's health insurance regardless of whether they are acting responsibly or not. You would be surprised how many trusts do not address this issue.

8. **Providing for Your Child's Children.** Once your children have children, you may want to have a provision in your child's trust that would permit for distributions to be made for the benefit of your grandchildren, especially for their health care and education. You could also establish separate trusts for grandchildren rather than leaving everything directly to children, especially if your children are already adults and doing well. All the things you would consider

relevant in planning for your children's trusts would be things to consider in planning for your grandchildren's trusts.

9. **The Importance of Crunching the Numbers.** As you have seen in many of the above examples, having a clear understanding of exactly how much money would pass to the next generation is practically a necessity when it comes to making intelligent decisions with respect to your children's trusts. If you can estimate how much it will cost to provide for your children's needs as they grow up (which of course requires you to quantify what those needs are), you can make sure there are sufficient assets through life insurance, if necessary. If you already have enough assets to provide for your children's needs after taking into account estate taxes and other related costs, then you have more options in how and to whom the excess assets will be distributed. I strongly recommend working with your financial advisor to create a financial plan that crunches the numbers so that you know what number you need to have to accomplish your objectives. When going through your children's needs think about (i) where will they be living and will there be a need to help pay for their living quarters, (ii) who will their guardians be and did you want them to be compensated from the children's trusts, (iii) do your children have any special health care needs that could be costly to treat, (iv) how much will their health insurance cost (and how much will co-pays and deductibles cost in a worse case scenario), (v) do you want them to attend private grade, middle, and high schools or at least have the option to do so, (vi) do you want to provide your children with the ability to participate in any extra-curricular activities such as participating in sports, attending camps, etc., (vii) do you want them to have a car at age 16, (viii) what will be the cost of your children's college educations, (ix) do you want to provide them with enough extra money to make a down payment on a home or to serve as seed capital to start their own business, (x) do you want to provide your children with enough money to fund a retirement trust as discussed above, and (xi) do you want to leave enough to provide any benefits to future grandchildren, including money to assist with their health care and education? This list is obviously not inclusive but should provide you with a good beginning point. Remember to think about YOUR children, YOUR family values, and the people and places where your children will be growing up if you are not there.

Whether or not an incentive trust is right for your children is a personal decision that should be given careful consideration. I encourage you to take the time to **visualize** your children's future and the many challenges they may encounter as they grow up and then to craft a trust that truly serves their personal best interests, whatever they may be.

The Trustee.

The trustee of your children's trusts will play a very important role in ensuring that your children are given every opportunity to succeed despite the fact that you are not around to help them. The **trust**ee will be the person in charge of managing the assets in your children's trusts and making decisions about when distributions should be made from the trust and for what purpose. As the term trustee implies, it is important that you have a significant degree of trust in that person or entity to not only prudently manage the trust assets, but also to keep in close enough contact with your children to enable them to make intelligent decisions about their financial needs. Below are a few points to consider before naming the trustee of your children's trusts.

1. **Interplay Between the Trustee and the Guardian.** The person you name as your guardian can be the same person you name to serve as the trustee of your child's trust. For example, assume your sister, Sally, is a loving person who you know will take wonderful care of your children were you to die so you have named her as your children's guardian (i.e., the person they will live with and who will serve as a surrogate parent). Further assume that she is organized and has a keen understanding of money matters. She could also be the perfect choice to serve as the trustee of your children's trusts. If, on the other hand, she has a hard time balancing her checkbook despite the fact that her mothering skills are extraordinary, she would probably not be the best choice as trustee. In such a case you may want to have another family member or a corporate trustee serve in that capacity. Another advantage to naming a trustee who is different from the guardian is that it establishes a system of checks and balances. When large sums of money are involved and the proverbial fox is guarding the hen house, the guardian may be more apt to spend the money in a way that benefits him or her if she knows that noone is overseeing the account. When these two people are different, the guardian can demand to see the financial statements and receive accountings of the trust assets on behalf of the children, and the trustee can require receipts for expenditures to make sure

that the money is being properly spent on behalf of the children. You may also consider naming the guardian as a co-trustee (i.e., one of two or three trustees) to give the guardian some input as a trustee but not sole control over trust assets. The decision is obviously a personal one that will be based in large part on trust. If you are skeptical as to a person's ability to resist being in charge of a large sum of money without supervision (and let's face it, money can change people), consider naming a separate trustee.

2. **Corporate Trustee vs. Individual Trustee.** Many clients have asked me whether it is better to use a corporate trustee or an individual family member to serve as the trustee of their children's trusts. Each has their upsides and downsides. The primary upside of using a family member to serve as trustee is that they are more likely to be maintaining a close relationship with the children and can, therefore, make good decisions as to how the trust assets should be spent to best benefit the children. If the family member is (i) skilled at managing money and maintaining the necessary records for the trust, or (ii) can hire good financial advisors and accountants and properly supervise them, they may be a good candidate to serve as trustee. A principal downside to using an individual as trustee is that if they were to mismanage or pilfer trust assets and a law suit were brought against them, the law suit may not be worth much to the child if the trustee is broke. Again, you must have a high degree of trust in the individuals you choose to name as trustees. The upsides of a corporate trustee are (i) they have experience in managing assets, (ii) they are set up to maintain the proper accounting, bookkeeping, and tax accounting records, and can prepare the tax filings for the trust, (iii) they do not die, and (iv) they are deep pockets in case they are ever sued for mismanagement or pilfering of trust assets. The principal downside of using a corporate trustee is that they may not be as able to maintain a close relationship with the children as an individual family member. This will make it harder for the corporate trustee to make distribution decisions based on the personal needs of the children as they will need to rely on the guardian for that information. Oftentimes, the best solution is for a family member to serve as a co-trustee with a corporate trustee. The family member can make distribution decisions based on his or her close relationship with the beneficiary and the corporate trustee can manage the trust assets and take care of the administrative and record keeping duties. If a corporate trustee is used, many people like giving the child (or the guardian while the child is a minor) the right to remove the corporate trustee

and choose another corporate trustee. Therefore, the child cannot replace a corporate trustee with an individual, however, in the event a particular corporate trustee was ever to act inappropriately, the child has the ability to get rid of that trustee and name another corporate trustee willing to be more reasonable. When it comes to costs, the corporate trustee will charge a fee which is usually based on a percentage of the trust assets. If a Trustee charged a 1% fee and the trust assets were $2,000,000, their annual fee would be $20,000. This may seem high at first glace, however, you have to remember that if a family member were serving as trustee, they would have to hire (i) an investment advisor (who would also charge a fee based on a percentage of the assets they were managing), (ii) an accountant to prepare the tax returns and trust accountings, and (iii) usually an attorney to advise them with respect to the proper means of conducting the administration of the trust. Since a corporate trustee's fees usually includes most or all of these services, the cost is not as high as you may initially think.

3. **Co-Trustees.** You can always name more than one trustee of a trust (called "co-trustees"). When you do so, you need to take several things into consideration. Understand that if there are two trustees, they typically must agree on decisions regarding the trust otherwise there is a stalemate which sometimes requires legal action to settle. This being said, it is important to choose co-trustees wisely. Sometimes people choose a person from the husband's side of the family to be co-trustee with someone from the wife's side of the family. If these two can be reasonably anticipated to get along, the pairing of these two co-trustees may make perfect sense. On the other hand, if these two have a history of not getting along or simply have opposing points of view on important topics (e.g., one is a miser and the other thinks you should enjoy money) you may not want to have them serve together as co-trustees. It is sometimes helpful to name a third co-trustee who could break a stalemate or name a third party who is not a full fledged trustee but who is given the power to vote when the other two trustees cannot agree. In short, be pragmatic and make sure the co-trustees you are choosing are the right fit, otherwise, your children may be the ones who suffer.

4. **Successor Trustees.** As with guardians, you need to plan for the contingency that your first choice for trustee of your children's trusts, may not be willing or able to serve in that capacity when the time comes or may die while serving.

Therefore, it is equally important to choose as many alternate trustees as possible. In the event you were to run out of trustees, a court would most likely need to appoint a successor trustee unless you provided for another method in the trust. For example, you could allow the child to choose a successor trustee if he or she were at least 18 years old (or some older age if you so choose). If the child were still a minor, the guardian might be given that right. You could also name one or more nominators who could be given the power to choose the successor trustee.

5. **The Importance of Education.** While choosing the right trustee(s) and guardian(s) is an important step, it is equally important to educate these people with respect to anything you would want them to know as they raise your children. I recommend picturing yourself dead looking down (hopefully) at your children. God says to you, "I will allow you to return to earth for one hour for the limited purpose of telling your guardian and trustee anything you feel might be helpful to them in raising your children." If you could turn to God and say "Thanks for the offer, but I've got it covered. Let's get this show on the road," then you are doing great. If you would take advantage of that hour, you may want to take steps to educate your trustees and guardians now (since you may not get that hour later). Now go back and think about all the topics you might cover in your one hour talk:

    a. Does your guardian already know your children's (i) blood type, (ii) medical history, (iii) family medical history, (iv) allergies, (v) regular medications, if any, etc?
    b. What religion do you want your children raised in?
    c. What religion **don't** you want your children raised in?
    d. Do you want your children educated in public or private schools? Do you feel strongly one way or the other?
    e. What geographic location do you want your children raised in?
    f. What family members do you want your children to visit? How often?
    g. What are each child's strengths or frailties?
    h. What are each of your children's likes and dislikes?
    i. Have your children expressed anything to you about their inner most feelings that they may not tell a guardian or trustee but would be important for them to know?
    j. What is the best way to motivate and communicate with each child?

This list is obviously limited and only you as your children's parents truly know your children well enough to create a comprehensive and meaningful set of information tailored to help create the best environment possible for each of your children as they grow up in a world that does not include you in it.

It is also a good idea to write all this information down in a letter to the trustee and guardian. First, remember that your first choice may not end up being the trustee and/or guardian and you may not wish to educate all of your successor trustees and guardians at this point in time. Second, if a court ends up appointing the trustee or guardian, you may not know who these people will actually turn out to be. Finally, even those of us with the best of memories will appreciate having your wishes memorialized in a letter they can refer back to. This letter can be kept with your estate planning documents.

6. **Excluded Persons.** There may be some people you wish to exclude all together from ever being able to be the guardian of your minor children or the trustee of their trusts. This does not mean that these people are evil (although sometimes they are), it may just mean that they have a very different viewpoint when it comes to raising children or handling financial matters. If this is the case, you can simply have language added to the guardianship nomination or trust document that states "While I have a great deal of love and respect for Uncle Tony, he shall be considered to have predeceased me for all purposes under this trust agreement and shall not be able to serve as a trustee or guardian for any reason." Remember that a brilliantly drafted trust run by a bunch of incompetent or morally bankrupt people is a horrible plan.

Your Children's Emotional Legacy.

The final issue I want to address is the single most overlooked aspect of planning for your children's future if you cannot be there for them; planning for your children's emotional well-being. I think we all know that the most important things you give your children are not ipods, gameboys, cool clothes, toys, and the numerous other material benefits you bestow upon them on a regular basis. The real treasures we give our children are things like:

1. The feeling that they are deeply loved by you simply because they are your children;

2. The knowledge that you are proud of them and the self-confidence and inner-strength that accompanies that feeling;

3. The comfort of knowing they have a soft place to land when their world treats them harshly;

4. The often not-so-welcome push to do something that you know will make them grow when they are scared to take that first step (or maybe not just very motivated);

5. A work ethic and moral foundation that comes from you and the example that you set; and

6. A deep understanding that they absolutely have what it takes to be happy, fulfilled, successful individuals in a world filled with obstacles and where the only constant is change.

This list is obviously not all inclusive but is representative of some of the things you as parents have given your children. Several years ago I was approached by a client (I'll refer to her as Betty) to represent her interest as a beneficiary under her mother's will. Her mother died with a considerable estate that left Betty and her siblings all millionaires several times over. I later learned that prior to her mother's passing, Betty never had much of a relationship with her mother and had felt that she never quite lived up to her mother's expectations. Her mother was very stoic in nature and there had always been distance between them regardless of their physical proximity. I learned all this after Betty received a series of letters that were written to her by her mother. Betty's mother had provided in her will that certain letters be given to Betty at certain ages in the event she had passed on. Some of the letters were old and some had been penned relatively recently. It was impossible to explain the emotional reaction Betty had as she first started to read the letters. The letters expressed how proud her mother was of her and how much she loved her. Her mother went on to detail much of her own past that explained her stoic nature and how alone she felt in the world. Everything

Betty had thought and felt about her mother dramatically changed in a matter of hours as she read through the letters. Afterwards, Betty told me that she had the letters framed and that they were hung in a special room in her home. Betty also explained how much better her life had become since she was no longer burdened with the feelings of inadequacy that stemmed from her perception that her mother had been disappointed in her. These letters changed her life.

I tell you this story in hopes that it affects you the way it affected me. Take a few minutes and just think about your children; who they are and what they mean to you. Now think about the prospect of them first losing you (the most important people in their life) and then growing up in a world without you in it. As great and warm and loving as your chosen guardian may be, if you are gone they can never replace you and your love. Think how special it would be for your children to receive a letter, tape recording, or video tape (or nowadays a high definition quality DVD) from you even if the only message communicated was that you loved them and were proud of them. Regardless of the medium used, if the message gets through it will most likely change their lives for the better.

Although it is not a legally necessary part of your estate or asset protection plan, you may wish to create letters (or tapes, etc) to be given to each child at specified ages or life events. For example, you may want them to receive a letter just after you have passed on to help console them in their time of loss. If they are very young, you may want them to receive a letter at the age you feel they can first understand who you are. You may want them to receive a letter upon starting grade school, or high school, or college. These letters could prepare them for what they will face and encourage them to do well. You may want them to receive a letter at their wedding to let them know more about their parent's relationship, what marriage means, and just give them your words of congratulations and how happy you are for them. If a particular holiday was especially meaningful in your family, perhaps you could write each child a letter to be given to them on that holiday. Children's birthdays, graduations, confirmations or bar mitzvahs; the list goes on and on. You could explain your family heritage and pass on wisdom that you learned from your grandparents. You may even want to pick an age well into adulthood after they have had a chance to grow and mature into an adult. Obviously, the dates, ages, or life events that you choose have to be personal to you and your children. Again, picture yourself looking down at them overtime after you have passed. If given the chance to come back down for brief moments, what moments would you choose and what would you say? Once these letters are written, they can be incorporated into your estate planning documents so that they are safeguarded by the trustee of their trust or by some other trusted person. The movie, My Life, staring Michael Keaton and Nicole Kidman is an excellent example of how a parent (the Michael Keaton character) can play an active role in a child's upbringing even after they have passed on. Another recent movie with a similar theme is the Ultimate Gift. I highly recommend both of them.

One final reason for writing these letters that many people do not think about stems from the fact that we do not always conduct ourselves with the emotional control we would want. Everyone has seen a movie or televison scene where a parent and a child get into a terrible fight, the parent screams something hurtful to the child and later dies without the opportunity to say they are sorry and that they did not mean what they said. A less dramatic example is simply knowing that you could die without letting them know everything that is in your heart which you may not feel comfortable expressing or which your child may not be able to understand at their stage of life. If you have sat down and placed those words in the letters I have described above, those words will instead be the last words they hear (or read) and the last thoughts that are communicated to them. Think of it as "Last Words Insurance."

Conclusion.

As you can see, protective trusts have many uses. If you have the opportunity to discuss your parents' estate planning with them and feel comfortable asking them to create a protective trust for you rather than leaving you your inheritance outright, it can be a valuable tool in protecting your assets, reducing various taxes, and complimenting your own estate plan. You may also consider having a Recipients Trust established (as discussed above) if you do not feel comfortable asking them to do this for you. Also make sure your own estate plan creates these trusts for the benefit of the surviving spouse and your prodigy. Please note that these types of trusts are NOT typically included as part of a "standard" estate plan using revocable trusts. Do not think that because your estate planning documents set up trusts for your spouse and/or children, they will be able to provide the benefits discussed above. It is important to use an attorney who understands complex estate planning and asset protection issues and sit down and discuss these issues with them. This book should provide you with enough basic information to ask intelligent, open ended questions and enable you to ascertain whether the attorney you are thinking about using may be qualified based on his or her responses. Asset protection is a burgeoning area of the law and there are very few attorneys who are truly skilled in this area. Do not base your decision on which attorney to hire on the fact that they work for a large law firm, a boutique firm, or a solo practice. These are not indicia of whether a lawyer has the requisite skills. Interview the attorney using the knowledge you have amassed by reading this book and then carefully review the attorney's work to ensure it makes sense to you. Talking the talk and walking the walk are two completely different things.

CHAPTER 19

Domestic Self-Settled Trusts

In this Chapter I will discuss the topic of "Domestic Self-Settled Trusts." These trusts can be powerful asset protection devices (especially if combined with an entity such as a Family Limited Partnership), however, like every asset protection strategy discussed in this book there are upsides and downsides that you should be aware of prior to making the decision to use it as a means to protect your hard earned assets from the claims of creditors. Please note that this Chapter builds on the last, and you are advised to read that Chapter first if you have not already done so.

I begin this Chapter with an explanation of what is meant by the term "**Self-Settled** Trust" and how they are generally ineffective under Florida law (and the laws of most states) when established to provide the trust's creator with asset protection. I will also briefly discuss a few types of Self-Settled trusts such as Charitable Remainder Trusts and Qualified Personal Residence Trusts. Some lawyers and other professionals have stated that these trusts provide asset protection to the people creating them, however, I generally disagree and will explain why.

Next, I explain how the laws of a select few states allow one to establish a trust for their own benefit and derive asset protection with respect to the assets transferred to that trust. I also explain how combining a Family Limited Partnership with a Self-Settled Trust can allow the creator of the structure to maintain management control and increase the asset protection afforded by the structure. I will also discuss some of the potential weaknesses of these "Onshore Asset Protection Trusts" and how to structure a Self-Settled Trust to mitigate some of the potential downsides. Finally, I discuss who should consider using these structures to protect their assets.

What Is a Self-Settled Trust?

As eluded to in the previous Chapter, a Self-Settled Trust is simply a trust that is created by someone (the "Settlor") who is also a beneficiary under the trust. A familiar example is the basic revocable trust many of you have probably already established as part of your estate plan.

> Earl and his wife, Lucinda, decide to engage in some estate planning so that their assets can pass to their two children, Sammy-Joe and Tony, without paying estate taxes and without going through the probate process. Given the size of their estate, revocable trusts will allow them to accomplish both of these objectives. Earl creates a revocable trust (he is the "Settlor" of the trust). He and Lucinda are the Trustees of the trust, and Earl is the primary beneficiary of the trust. Lucinda creates a similar trust under which she is the primary beneficiary. Since the trusts are "revocable," each spouse has the ability to terminate the trust at any time and also has the power to change the terms of the trust (i.e., how their children will receive their inheritance, for example). When one spouse dies, trusts are created for the survivor and when the last spouse dies, trusts will be created for their two children, Sammy-Joe and Tony.

Since Earl is the Settlor of his trust and he is also a beneficiary of his trust, his trust is a "Self-Settled Trust." Likewise, because Lucinda is the Settlor of her trust and she is also a beneficiary of her trust, her trust is also a "Self-Settled Trust." As will be explained below, if either of them is ever sued, their trusts will do absolutely nothing to protect the assets transferred to them.

You may be thinking that it makes sense that a trust that can be unilaterally terminated by the beneficiary should not provide asset protection; and you are absolutely right. Unfortunately, the same "no asset protection" result would still be the outcome even if the trust were irrevocable (i.e., it could not be revoked or changed by the beneficiary or Settlor).

> Assume that Earl is a neurosurgeon and is concerned about protecting his assets. He decides to create an irrevocable trust (i.e.,

he is the "Settlor") and he names a third party to act as the Trustee. Earl then transfers $1,000,000 to the trust. Earl, Lucinda, Sammy-Joe and Tony are all beneficiaries. The trust agreement is drafted to give the Trustee absolute discretion when it comes to making distributions. In other words, the Trustee could decide to make no distributions at all, to make distributions only to Lucinda and/or the kids, or to make distributions to Earl. The trust also contains a spendthrift clause to add additional protection.

Unfortunately, this trust is also a "Self-Settled Trust" since Earl is the Settlor and is also a beneficiary under the trust. Like the revocable trust in the first example, if Earl is ever sued, the trust will do nothing to protect the trust assets from Earl's creditors.

Before moving on to the explanation as to why these Self-Settled Trusts provide no asset protection under Florida law, I just want to reiterate that **Revocable Trusts do NOT offer ANY asset protection**. I am asked this question often and am surprised how many people are under the false impression that they do protect assets. Sadly, one individual I met did not find out the unpleasant truth until after he was sued and a judgement had been handed down against him. At that point he was left with virtually no asset protection options.

Why Don't Self-Settled Trusts Protect Assets Under Florida Law?

When I wrote the first edition of this book, my explanation of why a Self-Settled Trust provided no asset protection with respect to the Settlor involved (i) an analysis of case law discussing the limits of spendthrift protection, and (ii) an explanation of the"Maximum Permissible Distribution Rule" based on Section 156(2) of a legal treatise called the Restatement (Second) of Trusts.

With the passing of Florida's new trust code, the result is basically the same, however, the analysis became a whole lot simpler. Effective July 1, 2007, Florida Statutes Section 736.0505 now provides the following statutory rules:

"(1) Whether or not the terms of a trust contain a spendthrift provision, the following rules apply:

(a) The property of a **revocable trust** is subject to the claims of the settlor's creditors during the settlor's lifetime to the extent the property would not otherwise be exempt by law if owned directly by the settlor.

(b) With respect to an **irrevocable trust**, a creditor or assignee of the settlor may reach **the maximum amount that can be distributed to or for the settlor's benefit**. If a trust has more than one settlor, the amount the creditor or assignee of a particular settlor may reach may not exceed the settlor's interest in the portion of the trust attributable to that settlor's contribution."

Therefore, Florida Statutes Section 736.0505(1)(a) now specifically states that a revocable trust is to be ignored and the assets held in such a trust are no more protected than they would be if directly owned in the name of the settlor. Florida Statutes Section 736.0505(1)(b) now contains what has been referred to as the "Maximum Permissible Distribution Rule." In other words, going back to the example of Earl and the **irrevocable** trust, since the trustee **could** exercise his or her discretion to pay the entire $1,000,000 out to Earl, even if the trustee flatly refused to do so, a creditor of Earl could still reach the full $1,000,000. Note that if the trustee only had the power to distribute up to $100,000 per year to Earl, the creditor could only reach that amount (i.e., the $100,000) per year. Likewise, if the trust provided that trustee could only distribute assets to Earl ten years in the future and/or up to a maximum of $500,000 total, the creditor would be bound by those same restrictions. This is not too much of a comfort to Earl, since the creditor could still reach the assets before Earl ever does.

Charitable Remainder Trusts and Other Specialized Self-Settled Trusts.

This next section begins with a discussion of the asset protection aspects of Charitable Remainder Trusts (sometimes called "CRTs"). I will also discuss another specialized estate planning trust called a Qualified Personal Residence Trusts (sometimes called "QPRTs") and the risks associated with doing so.

While a complete discussion of CRTs is beyond the scope of this book, a CRT is a type of trust whereby the Settlor transfers assets to the trust and receives, in return, a stream of payments for the rest of the Settlor's life or for a term of years (i.e., ten years for example). When the Settlor dies or the term expires, whatever is left in the trust is given to a charity chosen by the Settlor when the trust was created.

> For example, Ernesto decides to establish a CRT. After the trust is in place, he transfers $500,000 to the trust. The trust agreement provides that Ernesto will receive $50,000 each year for the next ten years. At the end of the ten year period, The assets remaining in the trust will pass to the American Cancer Society.

In the above example, note that Ernesto is the one who created the trust (i.e., the Settlor) and will also receive payments back from the trust (i.e., he is a beneficiary). Therefore, the CRT is a Self-Settled Trust.

Ernesto receives an income tax charitable deduction when he sets up the trust of roughly $100,000. If the property transferred to the trust was appreciated property, Ernesto may be able to defer paying the capital gains tax as well. Therefore, there may be some good reasons to establish a CRT, however, asset protection is not one of them.

In the 2002 case of **In Re Brown**, a woman by the name of Jane McLean Brown inherited roughly $250,000 from her mother in 1993. Jane suffered from chronic alcoholism and decided to establish a CRT that would pay her a monthly income for the rest of her life in order to protect her inheritance from her own improvidence. In 1999, Jane filed voluntary bankruptcy and listed the income stream as exempt from the claims of her creditors. Unfortunately, the court focused on the fact that the CRT was a Self-Settled Trust and, therefore, the spendthrift clause was invalid. The court then went on to discuss what exactly was reachable by her creditors:

> "When a settlor creates a trust for her own benefit and inserts a spendthrift clause, the entire spendthrift clause is void as to her creditors. . . . In the absence of a valid spendthrift provision, a beneficiary's interest in a trust is a property right which is liable for the beneficiary's debts to the same extent as her legal interests. . . . As with any other property right, a trust beneficiary's right to receive income for life is an interest which may be alienated or subject to attachment by her creditors. . . . **Where the only interest a settlor has retained for herself under a trust is the right to income for life, it is solely this interest which her creditors can reach."**
>
> In this case, [Jane] transferred assets of $250,000 into a [CRT]. The transfer was irrevocable, and the charities listed in the trust became vested in [those assets] . . .. In establishing the [CRT], however, [Jane] granted herself an interest in the trust in the form of a right to receive 7% income from the trust for life. **As a result, [Jane's] income stream is subject to the reach of her creditors.** The [$250,000], having irrevocably been conveyed to the trust for the benefit of others, is not . . . subject to the claims of her creditors."

Note that while the court applied logic similar to the "Maximum Permissible Distribution Rule" discussed above in reaching their conclusion that Jane's income stream is subject to the claims of creditors, they did not expressly do so. This will be relevant when discussing self-settled trusts below.

It is a shame that Jane decided to use a CRT to protect her $250,000. It does not appear from the language of the case that she was charitably inclined (however, I may be wrong). Her primary motive seemed to be to ensure that she did not squander the money and that she would always receive some income for the rest of her life. This being the case, she could have achieved a better result (both from a financial and asset protection standpoint) by investing the $250,000 in an immediate annuity that would have provided her the desired lifetime income stream and which would have been fully protected from creditors since it would have constituted "proceeds of an annuity" (see Chapter 14).

It is interesting to note that there are two ways to calculate the right to receive income from a CRT. The first payment option is to pick a flat dollar amount that will be paid out each year. A CRT that has this payment option is called a Charitable Remainder **Annuity** Trust or "CRAT" for short. The second payment method is to be paid a percentage of the value of the trust as of a particular date (i.e., 7% of the value of the trust assets as of January 1 each year). The second of these options result in a larger annual payment if the trust assets grow in value and a smaller annual payment if the trust assets decline in value. A CRT that has this payment option is called a Charitable Remainder Unit Trust or "CRUT" for short. Jane chose the second option. Jane appears to have argued that her payment stream should be exempt as an annuity (see Chapter 14), however, the court simply stated "[t]he bankruptcy court rejected [Jane's] . . . argument that her interest in the trust constituted an exempt annuity" and provided no further discussion of the issue. While it is possible that had Jane created a CRAT rather than a CRUT, the outcome may have been different, I would not recommend using a CRT to protect assets until a case clearly indicates that payments from a CRAT constitute exempt annuity payments under Florida law.

A Qualified Personal Residence Trust is similar to a CRT in that one transfers property (in this case their primary residence or a vacation home) to the trust, and reserves certain rights under the trust (with a QPRT, the right to live in it for a set period of time). After the term expires, the house passes to someone else (typically children or a trust created for their benefit). Again, the trust is created by someone (the Settlor) who reserves the right to benefit from the trust assets (i.e., they are also a beneficiary). Therefore, it is a Self-Settled Trust. In the event someone recommends that you place your homestead in a QPRT, please understand that it is possible that doing so would (i) cause you to lose your homestead exemption under the **Bosonetto** case (see Chapter 9), and (ii) risk giving a creditor the ability to seize your right to live in the home before it passes to children, for example.

> Assume Eliza transfers her home into a QPRT and reserves the right to live in it for 20 years. Now assume she is sued and the creditor obtains a large judgement. Since the court in the Brown case stated "[w]here the only interest a settlor has retained for herself under a trust is the right to income for life, it is solely this interest which her creditors can reach," Eliza's creditor

may have the right to seize Eliza's right to reside in the home for the 20 year period, thereby ousting Eliza from the home.

Under most QPRTs if someone ceases to reside in the home, this triggers a sale of the home with the sales proceeds (or a portion thereof) being paid out in installments over the remaining portion of the 20 year term (which again would be reachable by a creditor). Obviously, this is not a good result.

Before leaving this section, I want to mention that if you create a QPRT under the laws of Delaware, you may be able to avoid the problems set forth above. Since a primary problem with the QPRT is that it is considered a domestic Self-Settled Trust, by creating the trust under Delaware law, there is an argument that the right to live in the residence is not subject to the claims of creditors and, therefore, cannot be taken from you. Domestic Self-Settled Trusts are discussed at length below.

I will not go into the details of other types of trusts such as GRATs, GRUTs, CLATs, and CLUTs, however, if you want to learn more about the tax benefits their use provides, you can visit my website (i.e., http://www.KirwanLawFirm.com). Suffice it to say that if anyone is suggesting that you use a CRT, QPRT, or any other above mentioned trust for asset protection purposes, proceed with extreme caution.

Onshore Self-Settled Asset Protection Trusts.

As mentioned above, most states in the United States have laws that (i) prohibit a Self-Settled trust from being a spendthrift trust, and (ii) require the application of the "Maximum Permissible Distribution Rule" which results in a creditor of the Settlor being able to reach the assets of a discretionary trust to the extent that they could be distributed to the Settlor. In April of 1997, however, Alaska was the first state to change its laws to provide that an individual could create a Self-Settled Trust the assets of which would be protected from the claims of creditors (I will refer to trusts of this type as "Domestic Asset Protection Trusts" or "DAPTs" for short). Just three months later, Delaware amended its trust laws to permit individuals to create DAPTs. Since then, Nevada, Rhode Island, Utah, and South Dakota have followed suit. A comparison of the nuances of each state's laws are beyond the scope of this book, however, Delaware and Nevada appear to be the most popular jurisdictions based on the strength of their laws and the availability of numerous trust companies to serve as Trustee. Alaska has progressive laws, however, there is only one trust company that I am aware of that is willing to serve as Trustee of an Alaska DAPT (which can present problems if you ever become dissatisfied with that trust company).

To create a DAPT , an individual will create a trust meeting the following criteria:

Irrevocable Trust. The DAPT will be an irrevocable trust. In the event the trust were subject to being revoked (i.e., terminated) or changed by the Settlor, it would provide no asset protection for obvious reasons.

Qualified Trustee. The trust agreement must name a Delaware Trustee. The Trustee can be an individual or a corporate Trustee authorized to act as a Trustee in Delaware. The Trustee will perform important management and record keeping functions and will also need to be knowledgeable in the area of DAPTs in the event the trust is ever challenged by a creditor. For these reasons, even if your uncle Joe happens to live in Delaware, it is usually not prudent to choose him (or any other individual) over a corporate Trustee. Although this is probably so obvious as to not even require mentioning, the Settlor of a DAPT should never serve as the Trustee.

Delaware law (and other states that permit the creation of DAPTs (I will call these "DAPT States" for short)) typically permit you to appoint another person who is not a Delaware resident to act as a Co-Trustee with the Delaware Trustee. This, however, is not advisable since it may give a creditor greater ease in getting jurisdiction over the DAPT in the event it is ever challenged.

Another consideration in choosing a corporate trustee to serve as the Trustee of your DAPT, is whether they conduct business in the State of Florida. As I will explain later in the section discussing the potential arguments a creditor may try and use to convince a court that the DAPT should not be protective, if the Trustee of your DAPT conducts business in the state of Florida, one of these potential arguments may be strengthened in favor of the creditor. Therefore, if a large bank or trust company that has offices in the state of Florida and also has offices in Delaware, they would not be the best choice to serve as the trustee of your DAPT.

A practical concern in choosing a DAPT State in which to form your DAPT is the number of qualified trustees available in that state. For example, Delaware has numerous qualified trustees who understand DAPTs and several that only maintain offices in the state of Delaware. Alaska, on the other hand, only has a handful of corporate trustees and only one that I am aware of that is knowledgeable in the area of DAPTs. Therefore, in the event you ever wished to change the trustee of your DAPT without having to change the jurisdiction of the trust (i.e., convert the trust from an Alaska DAPT to a Delaware DAPT), it would be preferable to have several trust companies from which to choose.

Some Assets Must Reside in Delaware. Another requirement in order for the DAPT to be protective is that at least some of the assets in the DAPT must actually be held in the state of Delaware. Typically, an investment account will be opened in the name of the DAPT which will hold some of the assets of the DAPT. Below in the section discussing how to mitigate some of the arguments a creditor may have in attempting to pierce a DAPT, I will discuss combining a DAPT with a Family Limited Partnership. If this structure is used and the principal asset of the DAPT is an ownership interest in an FLP, (i) the FLP should be a Delaware FLP since the ownership interests are arguably Delaware assets, and (ii) at least some other assets (i.e., $10,000 or some other significant sum of money) should be held in the trust's investment account.

As mentioned several times before, when deciding how much of your wealth should be transferred to a DAPT, it is best to base your decision on a sound financial plan. Most people want to protect the assets necessary to comfortably retire and meet their ongoing financial goals and objectives. If you can quantify this amount prior to transferring assets to the DAPT by creating a sound financial plan, you will have a written document that can help you in defending the DAPT if it is ever challenged in the future. The financial plan also aids you in determining whether or not you are solvent after transferring assets to the DAPT. As discussed earlier in the Chapter on fraudulent transfers, you do not want to ever make a transfer of assets that leaves you insolvent after the transfer as this will make it easier for a creditor to win a fraudulent transfer law suit against you.

Lifetime Beneficiaries. The beneficiaries of the DAPT during the life of the

Settlor are typically the Settlor's spouse and children, and, can even include the Settlor. Oftentimes, a husband and wife both create a DAPT and, therefore, both of them are considered to be Settlors. The Settlor(s) can even be the sole beneficiary of the DAPT, however, as will be explained in the section discussing how to mitigate some of the arguments a creditor may have in attempting to pierce a DAPT, it may be preferable for the Settlor to not be an initial beneficiary of the DAPT. When the Settlor is a beneficiary of the DAPT, he or she will be a discretionary beneficiary, meaning that the trustee can distribute to them as much or as little as the trustee deems advisable. This offers the greatest asset protection to the Settlor.

Estate Planning. The DAPT also typically serves as the Settlor's principal estate planning document. Therefore, when the Settlor dies, the trust creates certain sub-trusts (i.e., a Credit Shelter Trust, a Marital Trust, Dynastic Trusts for children, etc.). These sub-trusts make sure the assets in the DAPT pass to the intended beneficiaries (i.e., children, for example) in a manner that (i) reduces or eliminates federal estate taxes, and (ii) provides the beneficiaries with tax and asset protection benefits. Since a DAPT is irrevocable (i.e., it cannot be changed by a Settlor) it is common to add what is called a "Limited Power of Appointment" to the trust which allows a Settlor to change (i) the persons who will receive the assets in the DAPT upon the death of a Settlor, and (ii) the manner in which they receive it (i.e., in trust, outright, in a specialized trust, etc.). This allows additional flexibility as time passes. When a Family Limited Partnership is combined with a DAPT, additional estate tax savings can be garnered. Finally, the laws of many DAPT states have been drafted to provide additional estate planning benefits such as the ability to create trusts that can endure in perpetuity, the ability to create protective trusts for your children and other beneficiaries, and the ability to serve as part of many advanced estate planning structures to give them flexibility in a manner that cannot be accomplished in non-DAPT states. Delaware also allows you to include an "in terrorem" clause which provides that if a beneficiary contests the trust (typically in an attempt to get more assets), that beneficiary's share is reduced or eliminated all together. These in terrorem clauses are void under Florida law. Delaware also allows you to restrict a beneficiary's (i) ability to request a copy of the trust agreement, and/or (ii) access to various financial information relating to the trust assets. Therefore, a DAPT not only provides the benefit of asset protection but also serves as a superior estate planning vehicle.

Trust Protector. The trust agreement will usually name a Trust Protector. The Trust Protector is a person (or even a corporate entity) that has been granted the power to do things such as veto the Trustee's decision to make distributions, approve or disapprove of certain decisions the trustee may make with respect to the management of the trust assets, remove the trustee and appoint a successor trustee, add or remove beneficiaries of the trust, amend the trust to make it more protective or to improve its effectiveness in reducing estate taxes in the event of future tax law changes, etc. The Trust Protector can be a trusted friend, family member, or professional such as your accountant or attorney. Having a Trust Protector allows for greater flexibility over time and can make the DAPT more protective as they can exercise certain rights over the trust that you cannot. The Settlor should not be the Trust Protector.

Investment Advisor. Delaware law gives the Settlor of a DAPT the right to appoint someone to serve as the Investment Advisor to the DAPT. This person has the right to instruct the trustee with respect to how the assets of the DAPT should be invested. Since the power of the Investment Advisor is limited solely to providing investment advice to the Trustee and the Investment Advisor does not have the power to instruct the Trustee with respect to making distributions or exercising other trust powers, the Settlor should be able to serve in this position without jeopardizing the DAPT's effectiveness in protecting assets. Of course, the Settlor can also name their financial advisor (or the lower risk spouse) to serve as Investment Advisor. The Settlor can also retain the right to remove them at any time and replace them with a successor Investment Advisor. This second option may be slightly preferable, however, many people creating DAPTs prefer to serve as Investment Advisors themselves.

Divorce Clause. If a husband and wife both create a DAPT and are, therefore, both Settlors, what happens in the event of a divorce? Typically, the DAPT is drafted to split into two separate trusts (i.e., one for husband and one for wife) upon a dissolution of the Settlors' marriage. The split of trust assets can be equal or can provide for some other method of determining how much is allocated to each spouse's separate (post divorce) trust. After the divorce, each spouse has their own DAPT in which the other spouse has no continuing rights. If the DAPT is being established by a single person, the trust could provide for any future spouse to be a beneficiary. In this case the term spouse can be defined in the trust agreement as "the person to whom the settlor is happily married from time to time."

Therefore, in the event Settlor marries and is later divorced, the ex-spouse will cease to be a beneficiary. In other words, the DAPT can be a good prenuptial planning tool, as well.

Duress Clause. A Duress Clause is language in the DAPT trust agreement that removes a person's ability to exercise any power contained in the trust agreement unless the person exercising the power is doing so of their own free will. Therefore, if a court were to order the trustee or protector to exercise a power that would cause the trust to be ineffective in protecting assets, even if they try to comply with the court order (which they should always do), their efforts will be ineffective.

Flight Clause. A "Flight Clause" is a provision in the DAPT's trust agreement that allows a Trustee or the Trust Protector to change the jurisdiction of the DAPT. Assume that future litigation calls into question whether a DAPT formed under the laws of Delaware will be protective as to the creditors of a Settlor. The Flight Clause could be exercised to change the trust from a Delaware trust to a Nevada trust, for example. If the laws of all DAPT states are later found to be ineffective in protecting DAPT assets from the claims of a Settlor's creditors, the DAPT could even be moved offshore. The Flight Clause can even be triggered automatically upon the happening of a certain event such as the Delaware DAPT laws being found to be ineffective in protecting assets by a court of law. If the Flight Clause is only triggered once a suit is filed in the relevant state, however, it is not likely to be respected.

While there are a number of important factors in drafting an effective DAPT, the above should give you a good idea of how a DAPT is properly structured. Understand that there are a number of important factors that need to be considered given your individual facts and circumstances and that you should always use competent legal counsel in creating the DAPT. A good asset protection attorney will also be able to give you advice on the proper maintenance of the DAPT after it is created which is just as important as a properly structured trust agreement.

Combining The DAPT with an FLP.

While this topic will be discussed below when I discuss the ways to mitigate some of the potential arguments a creditor may try and use to challenge the DAPT's effectiveness to shield assets from the claims of creditors, I want to explain how the DAPT can be combined with a Family Limited Partnership (an "FLP") since this structure is commonly used by individuals considering using DAPTs to protect their assets.

In the following discussion on combining a DAPT with an FLP, I will assume that the structure is being created by a physician (you) and your spouse. You and your spouse are both general partners of the FLP and each of you own a .5% ownership interest in the FLP. Therefore, the two of you acting together have the authority to manage the assets inside the FLP and decide when distributions from the FLP should be made. The remaining 99% limited partnership interest has been contributed to a DAPT created by you and your spouse. The DAPT has a Delaware trust company serving as trustee and you have named a trusted friend as the Trust Protector. You and your spouse are also serving as the Investment Advisors to the DAPT. You, your spouse, and your children are all beneficiaries of the DAPT. A graphical depiction of this structure is provided below.

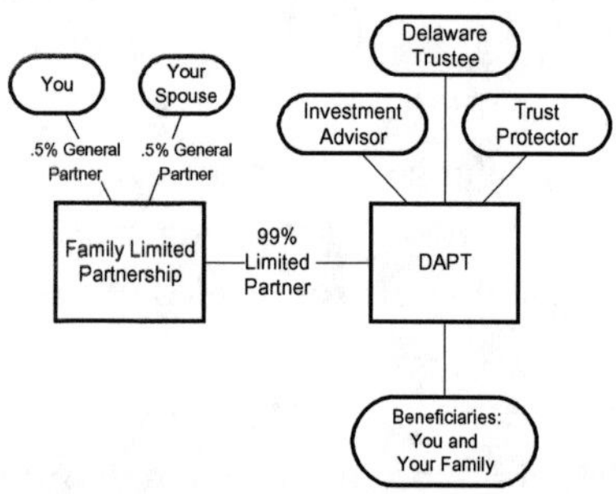

Since you and your spouse only own a total of 1% of the partnership directly, if a creditor were ever successful in obtaining a charging order against your interest in the FLP, the charging order would only be relevant to the small percentage owned by you (i.e., your 0.5 % interest as a general partner). Therefore, even if you made regular (i.e., proportionate) distributions from the FLP, the creditor would only be entitled to receive 50¢ for each $100 distributed by the partnership. The remaining $99.50 would be distributed 50¢ to your spouse and $99 to the trust. The $99 dollars transferred to the trust could then be distributed to the trust beneficiaries or used for their benefit without making distributions.

Another advantage to this structure is that in the event a creditor ever decided to spend the time, money, and effort to challenge the effectiveness of the DAPT from an asset protection standpoint, and was actually successful in piercing the DAPT, the only asset that would be distributed to you and your spouse would be the FLP limited partnership interests which are not reachable by a creditor due to charging order protection. That being the case, you will have significant leverage in negotiating a favorable settlement from the outset since they first have to win and obtain a judgement, then they have to bring another expensive law suit to try and pierce the DAPT, and even if they are successful in that endeavor, they are still limited to a charging order and may never be able to reach the underlying assets. I want to point out that there are other variations on this structure that can add additional layers of protection, however, they are beyond the scope of this book.

Potential Challenges to DAPTs.

Continuing the theme set forth throughout this book that every asset protection structure has upsides and downsides, it is important to understand some of the potential arguments a creditor may try and use to challenge the DAPT's effectiveness to shield assets from the claims of creditors. As mentioned above, the first DAPT laws were enacted just ten years ago in April of 1997. Since that time, the effectiveness of these Onshore Asset Protection Trusts have not been tested. Therefore, some degree of uncertainty is one of the downsides of the DAPT. That being said, there are many very good agreements as to why these DAPT laws should be upheld, especially if you have taken the potential arguments against their effectiveness into account when creating the DAPT. As mentioned in Chapter 7, under the new bankruptcy laws, DAPTs that have been in existence for 10 years or more should be considered exempt, and, therefore, fully protected. Below are the primary arguments a creditor is likely to use to challenge the effectiveness of a DAPT to protect assets together with a discussion of how effective I think these arguments are.

Conflicts of Law / Public Policy Arguments.

The first argument a creditor trying to reach the assets held in a DAPT is likely to assert is based on a body of law called "Conflicts of Law." A "conflict of law" is a situation in which laws of more than one state are applicable to a potential lawsuit or interpretation of a document and seem to be inconsistent or in conflict. The obvious conflict we are speaking of here can be summarized as follows.

> Assume Dr. Petty is a Florida resident and forms a DAPT under the laws of Delaware. Dr. Petty is later sued in Florida for alleged medical malpractice that occurred in the State of Florida. The patient is successful in obtaining a judgement against Dr. Petty and now seeks to reach the assets in the DAPT. If a court were to find that Delaware law applies because that was the law specified in the trust document, then the DAPT is protective. If, on the other hand, a court were to find that Florida law were to apply, the trust may not be protective.

The Restatement (Second) of the Conflicts of Law. The Restatement (Second) of Conflicts of Law is a legal treatise published by the American Law Institute dealing with the subject of Conflicts of Law. In deciding cases that involve conflicts of law issues, courts often look to The Restatement Second of Conflicts of Law for guidance, however, they are not required to do so. There are two sections of the Restatement that apply to the asset protection aspects of DAPTs. First is Section 270. This section states that the **validity** of an inter vivos trust is generally governed by the law chosen by the Settlor as reflected in the trust agreement provided that (i) the state has a substantial relation to the trust, and (ii) the application of the law does not violate a strong public policy of the state where the court is exercising its jurisdiction. The first of these provisos (i.e., that the law chosen by the Settlor of a DAPT, (Delaware, for example) has a substantial relation to the trust) should not present much of a problem since the Trustee of the DAPT is a Delaware trust company and all or a portion of the trust assets are held within the state of Delaware. The second proviso (i.e., that the application of the law does not violate a strong public policy of the state where the court is exercising its jurisdiction (i.e., Florida) is of greater concern and is discussed in the next section. It is important to note that this section deals with the **validity** of the trust itself, and not the spendthrift protection offered by the trust (that is dealt with in Section 273 of the Restatement).

The case of **Fehlhaber v. Fehlhaber**, decided in 1988, dealt with a revocable trust where the trust's Settlor was also a beneficiary of the trust. The court stated that "there seems to be little question but that [a self-settled trust] is **valid** under Florida law. . . . [N]ot withstanding the **validity** of spendthrift trusts created by a Settlor who is also the beneficiary of the trust, where . . . the beneficiary has the power to acquire all of the trust [assets] upon request, the [trust assets] should not be exempt from the claims of creditors." Therefore, the court in **Fehlhaber** drew a distinction between the validity of a self-settled spendthrift trust (holding that it was indeed valid) and its ability to protect assets when the Settlor/beneficiary had the unfettered right to demand all the assets in the trust. In addition, the 2002 case of **In Re Brown** (discussed above in the section on Charitable Remainder Trusts) also addressed the issue of a trust's validity. In this case the court stated:

> "Although the spendthrift provision of a trust is void as against a settlor-beneficiary's creditors, the trust itself remains valid. See, e.g., **In re Goff**, 812 F.2d at 933 (holding spendthrift provision was void as against creditors based on self-settlement, but trust itself was valid); **Liberty Nat. Bank v. Hicks**, 173 F.2d 631, 634-35 (D.C. Cir. 1948) (holding settlor-beneficiary was bound by terms of trust, even though its spendthrift provision was ineffective as against his creditors); see also 76 Am. Jur. 2d Trusts §§ 128 (1992) ("[W]here there is a [spendthrift clause in a trust] and the [spendthrift clause] is illegal, the provision fails, but the whole trust does not fail, since provisions like this can ordinarily be separated from other provisions without defeating the purpose of the settlor in creating the trust."). Thus, although a settlor-beneficiary's creditors are not bound by a trust's spendthrift clause, the assets subject to attachment are circumscribed by the trust agreement."

Therefore, notwithstanding the public policy issue, a DAPT should be considered **valid** even if Florida law were to apply.

The next Section of the Restatement that has applicability is Section 273. This Section says that if a Settlor states an intention in the trust agreement that the trust is to be administered under the laws of a particular jurisdiction (such as Delaware), then the laws of that jurisdiction will be determinative in deciding whether the spendthrift clause will protect the trust assets from the claims of creditors. Unlike Section 270, however, there is no public policy exception. Therefore, in spite of

Florida's public policy against self-settled spendthrift trusts, under a conflicts of law analysis based on the Restatement Second of Conflicts of Law, Delaware law would apply thereby maintaining the protective nature of the DAPT.

Alternative Conflicts of Law Theories. Unfortunately, a Florida court may choose to stray from an analysis based solely on the Restatement Second of Conflicts of Law. If it does so it may use a more subjective analysis. Another well known treatise called **The Law of Trusts** by Aston W. Scott and William F. Fratcher discusses the choice of law issues regarding spendthrift trusts. In this treatise the authors state:

> "If the Settlor creates a trust to be administered in a State other than that of his domicile, the law of the State of the place of administration, rather than that of his domicile, ordinarily is applicable. Thus a Settlor domiciled in one State may create an inter vivos trust by conveying property to a trust company of another state as Trustee and delivering the property to it to be administered in that State. In that case, the law of that state will be applicable as to the rights of creditors to reach the beneficiary's interest. This permits a person who is domiciled in a state in which [self-settled spendthrift trusts] are not permitted, to create an inter vivos [self-settled spendthrift trust] in another state where they are permitted and thereby take advantage of the law of the latter state."

This is just one more example of a well respected legal treatise which speaks to the conflicts of law issues surrounding self-settled spendthrift trusts and concludes that a DAPT should be respected.

A court may also take a more subjective approach to its conflicts of law analysis. In addition to the Restatement Second of Conflicts of Law (which is typically thought of as the principal authority in this area of the law), there are two other dominant approaches used in analyzing conflicts of law issues, namely the "most significant relationship" approach and the "governmental interest analysis." While each of these approaches are different in their application, both of these approaches focus on the principal that the law chosen to govern any transaction should be that which has the "most significant relationship" to the transaction and the parties to it. Some of the factors to be considered are:

1. The needs of the interstate and international systems;
2. Application of a court's own local law unless there is good reason for not doing so;
3. Effectuation of the purpose of its relevant local law rule in determining a question of choice of law;
4. Certainty, predictability, uniformity of result;
5. Protection of justified expectations;
6. Application of the law of the state of dominant interest;
7. Ease in determination of applicable law, and the convenience of the court;
8. Fundamental policy underlying the broad local law field involved; and
9. Justice in the individual case.

Under an analysis using one of these more subjective approaches, Florida's public policy would be more relevant. Before proceeding with a discussion of Florida's public policy with respect to self-settled spendthrift trusts, it is interesting to note that some legal commentators have criticized this more subjective approach exactly because it is more subjective and, therefore, lends itself to being misapplied by a court of law. It is also interesting to note that some of the stated considerations deemed important in applying a more subjective analysis (i.e., (i) certainty, predictability, and uniformity of result, (ii) protection of justified expectations, and (iii) ease in determination of applicable law, and the convenience of the court) are better served by a more uniform approach to conflicts of law issues such as that found in Sections 170 and 173 of the Restatement Second of Conflicts of Law. Leaving a court to answer questions such as "what constitutes a strong public policy" and "which state policies are 'fundamental' and which state policies are not 'fundamental'" can basically give a court complete discretion not to enforce a law of another state. It should be obvious that this subjective approach does not lend itself to producing consistent, predictable, and uniform results.

Two cases, **In Re Portnoy** and **In Re Brooks**, both decided in jurisdictions other than Florida, are examples of a court using public policy arguments and a misinterpretation of Section 270 of the Restatement Second of Trusts, to reach a conclusion it felt obligated to reach. Both of these cases involved individuals who had established offshore trusts after identifying creditors that would most likely pursue their assets. Therefore, these cases were really fraudulent transfer cases. The cases also involved attempts by the individuals to secret certain transfers from the court. These cases prove the old adage that "bad facts make bad law." Rather than decide these cases on the basis of the fraudulent transfer laws, the courts in both **Portnoy** and **Brooks**, instead took what it considered to be the path of least resistance and decided the case on a tortured conflicts of law analysis.

Florida's Public Policy. As previously mentioned, the public policy in Florida is that a person cannot create a spendthrift trust for him or herself, and garner the protection of the trust's spendthrift clause. The next obvious question is on what factors is this public policy based? The 1992 case of **In Re Wheat** discusses this very issue. After discussing a line of cases that involve the limitations of self-settled spendthrift trusts the court stated:

> "The Court notes that the cases examined, which prohibit creating a spendthrift trust for oneself, involved settlor-beneficiaries with much more control over their interests than [Mr. Wheat]. . . . **Moreover, the policy against such spendthrift trusts is heavily dependant upon a settlor-beneficiary's control.**" The court then went on to quote the case of **Matter of Witlin**. "[t]here is, of course, a strong public policy that will prevent any person from placing his property in what amounts to a revocable trust for his own benefit which would be exempt from the claims of creditors." The **Wheat** court then concluded by stating "[t]**hus, the stated policy against self-settled spendthrift trusts is not as compelling in situations where, as here, the settlor-beneficiary's control is relatively limited.**"

Based on the reasoning of the court in **In Re Wheat**, Florida's public policy against self-settled spendthrift trusts may not be terribly compelling if a settlor of a DAPT does not maintain any significant control over the trust.

Thomas O. Wells, an attorney practicing in Miami, Florida, drafted an article entitled "Domestic Asset Protection Trusts - A Viable Estate and Wealth Preservation Alternative" which was published in the Florida Bar Journal. In this Article Mr. Wells states that the case of **In Re Brown** (previously discussed above in the discussion on Charitable Remainder Trusts) may also serve as precedent for the argument that the creditor of a settlor of a discretionary self-settled trust established in a DAPT state should be protective. As you may remember, the court in the **Brown** case, stated that the only interest Ms. Brown's creditors could reach were the rights she reserved under the trust. Therefore, if the trust involved was a DAPT and the settlor only reserved the right to receive discretionary payments from the trust, it is only this right a creditor could reach, which Mr. Wells compares to a "charging order" in the Family Limited Partnership context. Since the interest held by Ms. Brown was a right to receive certain specified payments that were not discretionary, the court may not have felt it necessary to discuss the "Maximum Permissible Distribution Rule," however, Mr. Wells does make an interesting argument that could be applied to again argue that Florida's stated public policy is not very strong at all in the context of a DAPT.

When examining the issue of Florida's public policy against self-settled spendthrift trusts, I also think it is important to examine other related public policies enumerated by Florida courts in asset protection cases. For example, in the case of **In Re Goldenberg** that dealt with the issue of whether assets held in a variable annuity should be exempt from the claims of creditors, Florida's highest court, the Florida Supreme Court, stated that:

> "Florida has a long_standing policy that favors liberally construing exemption statutes so as to prevent debtors from becoming public charges. See **Killian v. Lawson**, 387 So.2d 960, 962 (Fla.1980); **Sneed v. Davis**, 135 Fla. 271, 184 So. 865, 869 (Fla.1938)."

The Florida Supreme Court then went on to hold that assets held in a variable annuity were exempt from the claims of a judgment creditor of a physician who was held to have committed medical malpractice. The same language quoted above has also appeared in cases dealing with other forms of exempt assets such as IRAs and cash value life insurance policies. The owner of these types of assets has significantly more control over the assets as compared to a DAPT and has an almost unfettered ability to enjoy the assets held in these investment vehicles. Therefore, if one takes to heart the statement made by the court in the **In Re Wheat** case (discussed above) that "the policy against such spendthrift trusts is heavily dependant upon a settlor-beneficiary's control," how can it state that Florida has a strong public policy against protecting a person's interest in a DAPT and at the same time say that Florida has a strong public policy that protects a person's interest in an IRA or variable annuity?

In addition, the cases of **In Re Levine** and **In Re Kimmel**, discussed previously in the Chapter on Life Insurance and Annuities, stand for the proposition that in certain circumstances, certain types of pre-bankruptcy planning may be considered acceptable by the court "even if the motivation behind the [planning] is to place . . . assets beyond the reach of creditors." These cases could also be used to argue that Florida's public policy leans more toward allowing persons to protect assets rather than the opposite.

Finally, under Florida's new trust code, Florida Statutes Section 736.0505(c) reads, in relevant part, as follows:

> " . . . the assets of an irrevocable trust **may not be subject to the claims of an existing or subsequent creditor or assignee of the settlor**, in whole or in part, solely because of the existence of a discretionary power granted to the trustee by the terms of the trust, or any other provision of law, to pay directly to the taxing authorities or **to reimburse the settlor** for any tax on trust income or principal which is payable by the settlor under the law imposing such tax."

Therefore, there is now a statute that provides a circumstance under which a settlor can receive a distribution from the trust without jeopardizing the asset protective nature of the trust. This may be one more argument that Florida's public policy against Self-Settled Trusts may not be very strong.

Non-Florida Cases.

While a complete discussion of conflicts of law cases decided outside of Florida is beyond the scope of this book, it should be noted that many cases have held that a creditor of a settlor who had created a trust under which he was also a beneficiary, was prohibited from reaching the assets of the self-settled trust. Other cases have followed the express intention of the settlor as stated in the trust agreement as to the law controlling the trust, despite the fact that doing so seemingly conflicts with the public policy of the settlor's state. One such case, **The National**

Shawmut Bank of Boston v. Cumming, involved a resident of Vermont who transferred most of his assets to a trust which the settlor stated in the trust agreement was to be "construed and the provisions thereof interpreted under and in accordance with the laws of the Commonwealth of Massachusetts." The settlor did so to keep his wife from being able to inherit a significant portion of his assets under Vermont law. In holding that the trust was validly governed under Massachusetts law, the court stated:

> "[i]f the settlor had been domiciled in this Commonwealth and had transferred . . . personal property . . . to a trustee . . . for administration here, the transfer would have been valid **even if his sole purpose had been to deprive his wife of any portion of it.**"

Real Estate and Conflicts of Law.

The conflicts of law analysis described above is with respect to something called "moveables." Movables are basically assets other than real estate. While the general rule for movables held in trust in a conflicts of law analysis is that the law of the trust governs, this is not the case with real estate. The rule with respect to real estate held in trust is that the laws of the state where the real estate is located governs. This means that Florida law could apply with respect to an interest in real estate held in a DAPT. This is one more reason to hold the real estate in a Family Limited Partnership and transfer the limited partnership interests (which are movables) to the DAPT. By doing this you have, in essence, converted "immovable" real estate to "movable" property (i.e., a partnership interest). As mentioned in the Chapter on Family Limited Partnerships, there needs to be a legitimate business purpose for doing so, otherwise a court may disregard the FLP and deem the property to be held directly by the DAPT.

As you can see from the above discussion on Conflicts of Law, there are many very good arguments why Florida law should not be applied to determine the protectiveness of a DAPT. Additional steps can also be taken in drafting the DAPT to further mitigate the uncertainty presented by this body of law. These will be discussed later in this Chapter. Of course, before a case is decided that determines the issue one way or another, a person creating a DAPT will have to be comfortable with some degree of uncertainty.

Constitutional Arguments.

Full Faith and Credit Clause. The Full Faith and Credit Clause of the United States Constitution states that "[f]ull faith and credit shall be given in each state to the public acts, records, and judicial proceedings of every other state." The following example shows how this constitutional rule operates.

> Assume Freddy, a Florida resident, sues Debby, a Delaware resident, in a Florida court. Freddy is victorious and obtains a significant judgement against her. The Full Faith and Credit Clause allows Freddy to enforce his judgement in Delaware to the same extent he could have if Debby was a Florida resident.

Many people in stating that a DAPT will not be protective have argued that if a creditor obtains a judgement against a Florida resident with a Delaware DAPT, the Full Faith and Credit Clause allows the creditor to simply go to Delaware and enforce the judgement against the DAPT. The problem with this argument is that there is a big difference between obtaining a judgement against the settlor of the DAPT and obtaining a judgement against the DAPT itself. This issue was the subject of the United States Supreme Court case of **Hanson v. Denckla**. The facts in this case are somewhat complex so I will not go into detail, however, certain Florida residents had obtained a judgement in a Florida court and tried to enforce it with respect to a Delaware trust. In order to enforce the judgement, the Florida court would have to have jurisdiction over the trustee of the Delaware trust. In order to get such jurisdiction, it is necessary to show that the out-of-state trustee has some "minimum contacts" with the state where the judgement was obtained. In the Hanson case, the court stated:

> "The defendant trust company has no office in Florida, and transacts no business there. None of the assets has ever been held or administered in Florida, and the record discloses no solicitation of business in that state either in person or by mail."

Based on these facts, the court held that the Florida Court did not have jurisdiction over the Delaware trustee.

When establishing a DAPT, it is best to choose a trust company that does not have offices in the state of Florida. In addition, having the DAPT own an interest in a Delaware FLP can further the argument that all of the assets in the DAPT are Delaware situs assets. Of course, in this ever shrinking world of ours where the internet allows a trust company's web site to be viewed globally, applicability of the Full Faith and Credit Clause will remain unknown until the United States Supreme Court finally decides the issue. Remember that the conflicts of law analysis would also have to favor the application of Florida law. Also remember that a creditor trying to reach the assets of a DAPT will need to be prepared to spend a significant amount litigating this issue.

Supremacy Clause. The Supremacy Clause of the United States Constitution requires that in the event of a conflict between federal and state law, federal law must prevail. Therefore, if a person is forced into bankruptcy (which is federal law), the issue becomes whether the federal bankruptcy laws will override state law governing the trust. It is important to understand, however, that Section 541 of the Bankruptcy Code states that a spendthrift clause is enforceable for bankruptcy law purposes if it is "enforceable under applicable non-bankruptcy law." It is arguable that a bankruptcy court would follow Section 273 of the Restatement Second of Conflicts of Law and apply the law stated in the trust agreement to determine the enforcability of the spendthrift provision. Since a spendthrift clause is protective with respect to the settlor of a DAPT in DAPT states, the assets in the trust would remain protected. As mentioned above, in the **Portnoy** and **Brooks** cases, the court failed to apply the spendthrift laws of certain offshore jurisdictions and, therefore, held that the assets were included in the bankruptcy estate (i.e., they were unprotected). In addition, most legal commentators feel these cases were improperly decided, and more importantly, neither dealt with a Florida creditor. Again, the result under a conflicts of law analysis will be a large factor in a Supremacy Clause case.

Delaware has a statute that addresses this issue directly. It states that spendthrift protection afforded to the settlor of a DAPT "shall be deemed to be a restriction on the transfer of the transferor's beneficial interest in the trust **that is enforceable under applicable non-bankruptcy law within the meaning of §§ 541(c)(2) of the Bankruptcy Code**. This should provide another argument that a Delaware DAPT should be protective even if the settlor is forced into bankruptcy.

The new bankruptcy laws may also provide an additional argument in favor DAPTs being protective in the bankruptcy setting. Unlike under the old bankruptcy law, self-settled asset protection trusts (like DAPTs Trusts and Offshore Trusts (Chapters 19)) are now specifically mentioned under the new law. Any assets fraudulently transferred to one of these trusts within the ten year period prior to filing for bankruptcy will be included in the bankruptcy estate and, therefore, subject to the claims of creditors. This 10 year "clawback" provision requires actual intent to defraud in order for any such transfer to be considered a fraudulent transfer. Therefore, if the ten year period has passed or if the transfer to the trust was not done so with an actual intent to defraud a creditor, the fact that the new bankruptcy law specifically refers to these trusts provides an addition argument that the DAPT assets should be excluded from the bankruptcy estate. If they were not, why mention Self-Settled trusts at all.

Contract Clause. Article I, Section 10 of the United States Constitution contains what is sometimes referred to as the "Contract Clause." It reads, in relevant part that "[n]o state shall . . . pass any . . . law impairing the obligation of contracts . . .." Put another way, states are precluded from passing a law which significantly impairs the enforcability of existing contracts. The argument is that the Delaware DAPT law should be considered unconstitutional because if the settlor of a DAPT is sued under a contract that existed as of the date the Delaware DAPT statute was enacted, the creditor suing under the contract will not be able to reach the assets transferred to the DAPT (which would assumably have been reachable had the Delaware DAPT statute not been enacted). In my opinion this is not a significant concern because this constitutional argument would only be relevant with respect to contracts that existed at the time the Delaware DAPT statute was enacted. This will obviously be less and less of a concern as time rolls on. It also has no applicability with respect to judgment creditors (only **contract** creditors).

In addition, the DAPT settlor will also have additional arguments. First, the creditor will still have the benefit of the fraudulent transfer laws. Second, even if the DAPT statute had not been enacted, the Settlor could still have protected his or her assets using other means such as tenancy by the entireties, transferring the assets to a life insurance policy or annuity, etc.

Fraudulent Transfer Laws. While it should be self evident at this point, in the event one transfers property to a DAPT after a creditor has been identified, the transfer of property to the DAPT will likely be considered to be a fraudulent transfer and "unwound" so the creditor will be able to reach the transferred assets. Therefore, a DAPT (like all asset protection planning) will be more protective if done in advance of creditor problems, especially given the ten year period set forth in the new bankruptcy laws.

Much of a DAPT's protectiveness will turn on a conflicts of law analysis, however, as explained above, there are many good reasons why a court should apply the laws of the DAPT state rather than the laws of Florida in determining whether the spendthrift protection should be respected. The fact that there is uncertainty in the law is both a downside and an upside. The test case in this area will require expensive and protracted litigation on the part of the creditor with no guarantee of success. If the DAPT's trust agreement is properly drafted and if it is combined with an FLP, this litigation becomes even more difficult and expensive for the creditor. The existence of a DAPT/FLP structure will provide the settlor with substantial leverage in negotiating a favorable settlement with a would be creditor.

Other Potential Downsides of DAPTs.

The following are a few additional considerations to take into account before deciding whether a DAPT is an appropriate structure to include as part of your comprehensive asset protection plan.

Subject to the Jurisdiction of the US Legal System.

Unlike its offshore counterpart, the DAPT is subject to the US legal system. As explained earlier in this book, result-oriented judges and juries can deviate from what is prescribed under the law to reach a result they feel is just under the given facts of a case. The **Portnoy** and **Brooks** cases discussed above are good examples of this. It is understandable in those cases why a judge would want to pierce their asset protection plan given their dishonesty with the court and the fact that the transfers were made after the creditor had been identified, however, the court disregarded the established legal principals in the name of public policy. Any domestic asset protection device may suffer from this shortcoming. As bad as it may sound, I do not place great faith in our country's judges.

Costs. The cost of establishing and maintaining a DAPT is sometimes higher than using state law exemptions, but not always. When one establishes a DAPT there is the initial legal fee paid to the attorney, the ongoing cost of paying a Trustee's fee each year, the cost of preparing a partnership tax return each year, and the state fee and registered agent fee for the partnership. When these costs are compared, however, to the costs associated with certain insurance and annuity products, the end cost can actually be less in many circumstances. In addition, if you view the DAPT as an all perils insurance policy that will protect your assets not just from medical malpractice liability but from practically all sources of liability, the cost is actually not that significant. One final word to the wise - this is not an area to go bargain shopping. While this may sound somewhat self serving, it is important for the DAPT to be structured correctly given your facts and circumstances and the cost of using quality legal counsel is well worth the money, especially if the plan is ever tested.

Divorce and Child Support. Due to the long established public policy that one should pay their alimony and child support obligations, DAPTs will most likely not shield assets from these types of claims. While I personally feel there is considerable justification for this policy (especially in the area of child support), this is another shortcoming you need to consider. Certain jurisdictions, like Delaware, provide that if you are married to someone at the time a DAPT is established, it will not protect the trust assets from alimony claims from that spouse. Other jurisdictions like Nevada and Alaska claim their laws offer protection from these types of claims. I have serious doubts as to whether this would ever be upheld, and personally feel the Delaware law will be considered more reasonable by a court of law.

Super Creditor called the IRS. While this probably does not warrant mentioning, it should be obvious by now that DAPTs will probably NOT protect assets from the claims of the IRS or other governmental agency.

Mitigation of Downsides.

As mentioned several times above, there are ways to structure a DAPT to increase its protective nature given the possible arguments a creditor may use to pierce the structure. I have already discussed combining the DAPT with an FLP so I will not repeat that suggestion other than to say that it is highly recommended.

Importance of Timing. As exemplified in the Chapter on fraudulent conveyances, transfers of assets that take place after a creditor has been identified may not be effective with respect to that creditor. As seen in the **Portnoy** and **Brooks** case, such transfers (especially coupled with being less than candid with the court) can produce additional negative results. This does not mean that you should hold off planning once you have been sued. First, there may be options with respect to an identified creditor to give you some protection. In addition, if you are sued, then create an Integrated Wealth Plan combining estate planning, asset protection planning, and financial planning, and are then sued by another plaintiff, the asset protection plan will be timely with respect to that second creditor.

This being said, however, making transfers to a DAPT may provide some level of protection without the negative contempt of court risks that are associated with funding an offshore structure on an "after-the-fact" basis (this will be explained in detail in the next Chapter). It may also be preferable to transferring assets to an insurance policy or annuity "after-the-fact," due to the high surrender penalties that may be associated with unwinding the transfer if you lose a fraudulent transfer law suit.

In short, the timing of the creation of your asset protection plan will be integral to its success. Always discuss these issues with your attorney. Your planning options will depend on your personal facts and circumstances.

Transfer Exempt Assets. As was discussed in the Chapter on Fraudulent Transfers, transfers of exempt property are oftentimes held to be beyond the scope of Florida's fraudulent transfer laws. Therefore, assume you created a DAPT and funded it with property that you previously held as tenants by the entireties. Since the only thing transferred to the DAPT is TBE property, a creditor will have a hard time arguing that it should be set aside (i.e., unwound) as a fraudulent transfer. You might also consider funding the DAPT directly from a wage account (assuming you are entitled to protection under Florida's wage protection statute; see Chapter 11). You might also consider purchasing an immediate annuity and then funding a DAPT with the income stream derived therefrom. In all these cases, you will frustrate a creditor's ability to win a fraudulent transfer case. There are also additional benefits to combining these strategies. Take the wage account which is only exempt for a period of six months. Take annuity proceeds which retain their exempt status after they are paid out if not co-mingled with other assets - but what about the future growth? Combining these strategies provides stronger, long term protection while giving you the upper hand in a fraudulent transfer case if one is ever brought.

Lower Risk Spouse as Beneficiary. Assume that Barney and Betty are husband and wife. Barney is an OB/GYN and Betty is a full-time homemaker. Barney is concerned about asset protection since he recently had to lower his malpractice insurance coverage. Barney and Betty decide to create a DAPT and transfer $2,000,000 to it. They are both Settlors of the DAPT. Rather than naming Barney as a lifetime beneficiary of the DAPT, only Betty and their children are named as beneficiaries. The trust agreement states that in the event Betty were to predecease Barney, Barney would then become a discretionary beneficiary of the trust. If Barney and Betty were to divorce, the trust agreement provides that it splits into two trusts, one for Barney and one for Betty, and Barney becomes a discretionary beneficiary of his trust.

Now assume that the DAPT has been formed and Barney and Betty are happily married. Barney is sued for medical malpractice and the plaintiff obtains a judgement for $5,000,000. The plaintiff now seeks to reach the assets in the DAPT. Is the DAPT a self-settled trust with respect to Barney? The answer is arguably no. At best Barney has the right to become a beneficiary in the future if certain conditions are met (i.e., Betty dies or Barney and Betty divorce). If the conditions were something that Barney has control over (i.e., the condition that has to be met for Barney to become a beneficiary is that he rub his left elbow three times), then this argument does not work. However, certain tax law cases have held that if the condition to being able to become a beneficiary or to exercise a given right is predicated on a condition such as someone's death or divorce, that the contingency is so remote that the person is not deemed to be a present beneficiary or right holder. Therefore, there is an excellent argument that the DAPT is not even a self-settled trust with respect to Barney. This would result in very strong asset protection assuming no fraudulent transfer issues. In addition, if the Trustee makes a distribution to Betty, she can spend it to benefit the household and since the distribution is made to her, it is not reachable by Barney's creditors.

If Betty is in an automobile accident and the plaintiff in a personal injury law suit against Betty obtains a judgement, the creditor will have the same difficult hurdles to reaching the DAPT assets discussed previously in this Chapter. If Barney is the sole settlor and Betty is then sued, the trust is completely protective without regard to the Self-Settled Trust laws.

Springing Beneficiary at Specified Date in the Future. Another way to add protection to a Settlor of a DAPT would be for the Settlor to not be an initial beneficiary of the DAPT, but instead to become one at some set point in time in the future. For example, assume Barney was not married. He is forty years old and making good money. Barney creates a DAPT that will have certain family members and his wife (if he is ever married) as the beneficiaries. Barney is not a beneficiary. Barney figures that he will retire at age sixty. For the next twenty years Barney will use the DAPT to save for his retirement. In the event he is sued, since he is not a current beneficiary of the DAPT, the DAPT is not a self-settled trust and, therefore, as in the previous example, the creditors will have an even harder time asserting that they should be able to reach the assets of a "self-settled" trust. The trust agreement could also contain language that extends the twenty year period if Barney has an enforceable judgement against him at the expiration of the twenty years. If Barney were to marry in the interim, distributions could always be made to his wife.

Spouse Holds Limited Power of Appointment. As explained in the case of **In Re Wheat**, Florida's public policy against self-settled spendthrift trusts is "heavily dependant upon a settlor-beneficiary's control." You may remember that since the DAPT also serves as the Settlor's primary estate planning document and that to add flexibility the settlor is typically given a "Limited Power of Appointment" which allows a Settlor to change (i) the persons who will receive the assets in the DAPT upon the death of a Settlor, and (ii) the manner in which they receive it (i.e., in trust, outright, in a specialized trust, etc.). This could be a type of "control" a court may use to assert that Florida's public policy against self-settled spendthrift trusts should apply to a DAPT. Building on the previous example of Barney and Betty, if Betty (i.e., the lower risk spouse) is given this power, but not Barney (i.e., the physician), the protective nature of the DAPT can be ameliorated.

Duress Clause, Flight Clause, and Trust Protectors. As discussed previously in this Chapter, the addition of a Duress Clause, a Flight Clause, and a Trust Protector can add additional protection and flexibility to your Integrated Wealth Plan.

Upsides to Using a DAPT.

Expensive to Litigate with no Guarantee of Success. A creditor seeking to reach assets properly transferred to a DAPT will have to be prepared to spend considerable money to try and pierce the DAPT with no guarantee of success. In the event the trust agreement contains some of the suggestions mentioned above to mitigate some of the potential arguments a creditor may use to try and pierce the DAPT, its protection will be even stronger. This being the case, a creditor will likely think twice about suing you in the first place or will be much more likely to settle for a significantly reduced amount.

Exempt Under New Bankruptcy Laws. As mention previously in Chapter 7, any assets transferred to a DAPT more than the ten years prior to filing for bankruptcy will be fully exempt from creditors. In addition, it appears that even transfers made within the ten year period may also be exempt in bankruptcy so long as the transfers to the DAPT are not "fraudulent transfers." If you consider the fact that most law suits take anywhere from three to five years from initial filing to judgement (sometimes longer if an appeal is pursued), if you established a DAPT today and were sued only five years later, by the time a judgement was obtained, the ten year period may have already passed, thereby ensuring the exempt nature of the DAPT assets in bankruptcy. Once again, if you are interested in establishing a DAPT, do it as early as possible.

Likely Backing from Trust Companies in DAPT States. Although no guarantees can be made in this respect, it is highly likely that trust companies in the DAPT states will prepare legal briefs supporting your fight to protect the DAPT assets if you were the test case in determining their protective nature. Therefore, you will likely have access to some talented legal minds, since they also have a stake in maintaining the effectiveness of these laws.

Estate Planning Benefits. As mentioned earlier, the DAPT will serve as a principal part of your estate plan. The laws of many DAPT states have been drafted to provide additional estate planning benefits such as the ability to create trusts that can endure in perpetuity, the ability to create protective trusts for your children and other beneficiaries, and the ability to serve as part of many advanced estate planning structures to give them flexibility in a manner that cannot be accomplished in non-DAPT states. Therefore, a DAPT not only provides the benefit of asset protection but also serves as a superior estate planning vehicle.

Flexibility Due to the Flight Provision. As mentioned previously, the addition of a Flight Clause in your DAPT can give you further flexibility since the DAPT can be moved to another jurisdiction, onshore or offshore, if the laws of one or more DAPT states are found to be less effective than initially thought.

Who Should Consider Using a DAPT to Protect Their Assets?

Persons With a Higher Net Worth. I am often asked the question "How much money do I need to have in order to consider using a DAPT (or a Foreign Asset Protection Trust (sometimes called a "FAPT")?" Unfortunately, it is impossible to give an exact answer to this question. Typically, individuals with a net worth of $1,000,000 will consider using a DAPT or a FAPT, however, even those with less will sometimes consider it especially if they are not married or if there is no lower risk spouse. Of course, in making a cost / benefit analysis, the costs of establishing a DAPT or a FAPT and the costs to maintain it over time are less when expressed as a percentage of the assets protected the higher one's net worth. On the other hand, when a person has less assets, those assets are usually worth more to them. A good asset protection planner will help you with this decision by going over a list of your assets, explaining the various means you have to protect them (including state law exemptions), and then providing you with the upsides and downsides of your various options. If an attorney is pushing a particular asset protection strategy (including a DAPT or a FAPT) without going over your other options, I would consider using different counsel. As mentioned before, there is no one-size-fits-all solution that is best for everyone.

People Seeking Greater Asset Protection and Investment Flexibility. While many of the state law exemptions explained in Part II of this book can be (and should be) used as part of your comprehensive asset protection plan, a properly designed and properly funded DAPT provides (i) a high degree of asset protection without many of the limitations and potential downsides inherent in the state law exemptions, (ii) an excellent estate planning tool to accomplish your goals of minimizing estate taxes, passing on assets to beneficiaries in protective, Dynastic

Trusts, and (iii) a high degree of investment flexibility. Those who choose to engage in "I Gave it to My Spouse" planning or planning with Tenancy by the Entireties are faced with risks such as the lower risk spouse getting sued and loss of asset protection on death. Life Insurance and Annuities have limitations on investment choices and impose certain penalties if monies are distributed under certain circumstances. These limitations are not present in a DAPT. The primary concern with a DAPT is what future cases may determine with respect to their effectiveness. Many of these concerns can be addressed, however, by intelligently creating and funding the DAPT.

Two Physician Households. In the case of a physician who is married to another physician, the lower risk spouse does not exist. Therefore, given the limitations of Tenancy by the Entireties planning ("TBE"), a DAPT can be an excellent tool to protect assets from the claims of both spouses. If the two physicians happen to work together or refer patients to each other, the possibility of a joint judgement would preclude the use of TBE planning.

Single People. When a person is not married, options such as "I Gave it to my Spouse" planning and TBE ownership are simply not available. Other options such as investing in life insurance and annuities may not be attractive to individuals given their possible reduced need for insurance, potential penalties, and investment limitations. For these individuals, a DAPT can be a valuable tool to protect their assets.

Married Individuals Concerned About the Potential for Divorce. While everyone hopes their marriage will last forever, there are some circumstances where a physician will not feel comfortable transferring large sums of money to the name of his or her spouse or using the TBE form of ownership. In addition, in the event the DAPT is formed prior to marriage, it can serve as an alternative form of premarital planning. In these circumstances, a DAPT can provide significant asset protection without requiring a physician to transfer assets to a spouse.

Conclusion.

DAPTs, especially if combined with an FLP, can provide excellent asset protection under the right circumstances. There is still some uncertainty regarding the extent to which they protect assets, however, as I explained above, if properly drafted and funded, many of a potential creditor's arguments for piercing the structure can be mitigated. By understanding the upsides and downsides of this structure, you can make an intelligent decision as to whether they are right for you given your individual facts and circumstances.

CHAPTER 20

Offshore Asset Protection Trusts

A properly drafted, implemented and administered Offshore Asset Protection Structure typically provides the strongest asset protection, due in large part to the fact that it is not subject to the jurisdiction of the U.S. courts. If you have skipped ahead to this Chapter, I strongly suggest your going back and reading the previous two Chapters as this Chapter will build on the foundation established by the previous two.

As with every other asset protection strategy discussed in this book, foreign asset protection planning has its upsides and downsides. I will start by explaining many of the hurdles a properly structured and funded Foreign Asset Protection Trust (sometimes referred to as a "FAPT" for short) will place between your hard earned assets and a potential creditor. I will then give an overview of what a typical offshore asset protection structure looks like combining a FAPT with an FLP or offshore LLC. (Note that I will refer to the structure combining the FAPT with the Offshore LLC as a Foreign Asset Protection Structure or "FAPS"). Next, I will provide an explanation of the law of Contempt of Court to give you an understanding of how certain people who have used offshore asset protection trusts have found themselves in jail, and how best to try and avoid this result. Finally, I will provide an overview of who should consider using a FAPS as part of their comprehensive asset protection plan.

Specific Hurdles Created by Foreign Asset Protection.

So far, all of the previous Chapters in this book have dealt with domestic asset protection strategies. They have included various state law exemptions, domestic entities such as limited liability companies and family limited partnerships, and various trusts including the domestic, self-settled asset protection trust (the

"DAPT"). While they all have various advantages, they all suffer from one common downside; namely, that they are all governed by the laws of the United States and are subject to interpretation (and misinterpretation) by a United States court. This does not mean that many of these domestic strategies do not offer significant asset protection, however, laws can change and a result_oriented judge or jury could twist or misapply the law in the name of public policy in order to achieve what it considers a "just" result. Offshore planning is not completely divorced from the U.S. legal system as you will see in the section on contempt of court discussed later in this Chapter, however, placing assets beyond the reach of the U.S. legal system does have significant advantages. Below, I describe many of the hurdles a potential creditor will face when confronted with a properly structured and funded offshore asset protection structure.

Non_Recognition of U.S. Judgments. The jurisdictions used in creating a FAPS (I will refer to these countries as "FAP Countries") do not recognize judgments handed down by United States courts. As you may remember from the last Chapter, the United States Constitution contains the Full Faith and Credit Clause which allows a person who obtains a judgement in one state to enforce it in any other United State. Since FAP Countries do not recognize U.S. judgements, the creditor's judgement is of no help to him in trying to reach assets in a FAPS. That being the case, the creditor is forced to bring a law suit in the relevant FAP Country. Typically, the only suit available to the creditor will be a fraudulent transfer case, which as will be explained below, is not an easy case to win.

No U.S. Court. As discussed earlier in this book in Part I, the American legal system is flawed in many respects. Plaintiff's attorneys are continually expanding theories of liability to reach the "deep pocket." In addition, the legal system cannot always be trusted to return fair, unbiased verdicts. The "jury of your peers" is not typically made up of true "peers," result_oriented judges and juries often have broad discretion to interpret the law in an unfavorable, and sometimes, unjust manner, and outrageous awards are becoming common. Again, assets protected in a FAPS are placed beyond the control of the U.S. legal system.

Costly and Time Consuming. If you have ever tried suing someone who lives in another state, you probably understand how expensive it is to pursue these out-of-state claims. The legal issues are even more complex when bringing suit outside the boundaries of the United States and the associated costs involved with doing so can be considerable. For example, there is often a requirement in FAP Counties to post a large bond before a law suit can even be filed. The creditor will also have to be willing to spend the time traveling to and from the FAP Country which is usually a long and expensive flight. The Cook Islands, for example, are located smack in the middle of the South Pacific over 5,000 miles away from Florida.

Statute of Limitations. As most of you are probably aware, the term "statute of limitations" refers to the time in which you are required to bring a law suit. If you do not bring the law suit within that defined period of time, you are barred from ever bringing the suit. The laws of many FAP Counties provide that law suits must be brought in a much shorter time frame than what is permitted in the United States. In the U.S., creditors can sometimes bring a suit within a period of time after the transfer to the trust is "discovered" by someone with a claim against the transferor. This is usually not the case in most asset protection jurisdictions. For example, the Cook Islands have a two year statute of limitations which in many circumstances is reduced to one year. Therefore, in almost every case, by the time the judgment is obtained in the United States, the statute of limitations in the Cook Islands has already expired.

Burden of Proof / Standard of Proof. The laws of many FAP Countries require **the creditor** trying to bring a fraudulent transfer case to prove that the transfer of assets to a FAPT was fraudulent, rather than requiring you to prove that it was not. By placing the "burden of proof" on the creditor, the creditor starts their law suit behind the "8 ball." In addition, the "standard of proof" in FAP Countries is typically higher. In the United States, there are three basic standards that may be applied to a person trying to prove something in a court of law. The lowest standard is "Preponderance of the Evidence." This standard is applied in most civil trials and is basically a "more likely than not" standard. The next standard is "Clear and Convincing Evidence." This is the highest standard applied in most civil trials and basically means that the thing to be proved is highly probable. The highest standard is "Beyond a Reasonable Doubt" which is applied in U.S. criminal trials. This standard means "to a moral certainty" or, in other words, "you better be damned sure." Under Cook Islands law, a creditor trying to prove a fraudulent transfer case must do so by the highest standard; "Beyond a Reasonable Doubt." Compare this to the United States which imposes the lowest standard of "Preponderance of the Evidence."

Other Factors. The fact that a fraudulent transfer suit must be brought in a foreign court raises additional disincentives to sue. For example, plaintiffs must hire one or more foreign attorneys who are usually barred from working on a contingency fee basis. This means that the plaintiff has to come out of pocket with no guarantee of prevailing under foreign law. People also have to deal with a foreign legal and governmental system which is oftentimes uncomfortable from a psychological perspective. In addition, remember that these FAP Countries enacted their laws with every intention of enforcing them. Therefore, the court will have a tendency to favor the settlor, since he or she is the individual the asset protection laws were designed to protect. As you will see in the Anderson case explained below, the High Court of the Cook Islands recently ruled in favor of protecting the assets of an asset protection trust from a very powerful creditor, the United States government.

The hurdles a potential creditor must face before being able to collect on a judgement outlined above are oftentimes a huge incentive for the creditor to settle for pennies on the dollar. In addition, once the plaintiff's attorney is aware that there will not be any readily available assets from which to collect on a judgement (and his or her contingency fee) they will likely not be as enthusiastic to take the case through trial given the time and expense involved.

What Offshore Asset Protection Planning is NOT.

Solid asset protection using an offshore structure can be used to accomplish many planning objectives. There are some misconceptions about offshore planning, however, so I thought it was important to explain some of the things an offshore asset protection plan is NOT.

Hiding Assets / Secrecy. A proper asset protection plan will never rely on secrecy or hiding your assets. I believe that it is oftentimes a huge benefit to keep your assets and business entities difficult to discover by a would be creditor and this type of secrecy is often times incorporated in to client's domestic and offshore asset protection planning. That being said, however, many people marketing asset protection strategies will tell you to set up entities that keep you name off the public record (e.g., Nevada LLCs, "bearer share" corporations, etc.). They go on to explain that you should transfer all of your assets to this secret entity and, if you are ever sued, you are asset protected because the creditor will not be able to find any of your assets. This, unfortunately, is not the case. When a creditor obtains a judgement, he or she has significant access to your personal information. They can get copies of your bank statements (which will show transfers to your "secret" company), insurance policies (which will list any assets you have insured), and your tax returns (remember that "secret" or not, the IRS will be expecting you to file tax returns for your "secret" entity). In addition the court will ask you to disclose, under penalty of perjury, (i) everything you presently own or have owned, and (ii) transfers made by you in the past. Relying on a plan that will require you to do anything but be 100% honest with a court or the IRS about what your assets are and the planning you have engaged in is not real planning and may have serious negative implications such as spending time in Club Fed.

Many offshore financial institutions used to attract the business of United States citizens by promising that no one would ever find out about an account opened with them, including the IRS. Much has changed over the past few years and many people who have engaged in this type of planning are finding themselves in trouble. These accounts are being reported to the United States government and if the account holder was not paying taxes on the income generated from the offshore money, they will be facing significant penalties. Finally, if your "secret" Swiss account is discovered (which, as explained above, is a lot easier than many people think), this foreign account by itself offers zero asset protection.

Defraud Existing Creditors. As mentioned many times previously in this book, the maximum benefit from asset protection planning is achieved if there are currently no lawsuits pending, threatened, or expected. If a creditor has already been identified, a FAPS will most likely not be high on your list of options for reasons that will be explained later in this Chapter in the section on contempt of court.

Evade Payment of U.S. Income Taxes. Another misconception many people have is that a FAPS will enable them to avoid paying income taxes on the income earned inside the FAPS. A proper foreign asset protection structure will be income tax neutral (i.e., you will not pay any more or less tax than you would without it). If anyone approaches you to engage in offshore planning promising you the ability to avoid paying U.S. income taxes, run the opposite direction as fast as you can.

Overview of the Foreign Asset Protection Structure.

As you will see below, the structure of a FAPS is practically identical to the structure of a DAPT discussed in the previous Chapter. Like a DAPT, there are alternative structures that can increase their effectiveness, but I will focus on this structure for simplicity's sake. Rather than establishing a self-settled trust under the laws of a state such as Delaware or Nevada, however, you will instead create a trust under the laws of a FAP Country such as the Cook Islands. In the remaining portions of this Chapter I will use the Cook Islands as the example FAP Country since it is one of the strongest offshore asset protection jurisdictions in which to form a self-settled asset protection trust.

To create a Foreign Asset Protection Trust (a "FAPT"), an individual will create a trust meeting the criteria set forth below. If you refer back to the discussion of the criteria that a DAPT will include in its trust agreement (see Page), you will notice a significant number of similarities.

Irrevocable Trust. The FAPT will be an irrevocable trust. Even though the trust is governed in a foreign country, if the trust were subject to being revoked (i.e., terminated) or changed by the Settlor, it would not provide any asset protection. I am often asked "Why do I have to establish a FAPT? Why can't I just open a bank account in Switzerland?" The answer to the question comes down to control. In the event you establish a FAPT (assuming it was properly drafted and funded), if a court orders you to bring the assets back to the United States, you will be able to honestly reply that it is impossible for you to do so. Therefore, you can use your best efforts and do everything possible to comply with the judge's order, however, you will still be unable to bring the trust assets back to the United States. If you simply open a Swiss bank account, you absolutely have the ability to withdraw money from the account or to close the account and bring the money back to the United States. If a court of law ordered you to do so and you told them "No," you will almost assuredly sit in jail until you have a change of heart.

Offshore Trustee. The trust agreement will name an Offshore Trustee. The Trustee will be a trust company authorized to act as a Trustee in the Cook Islands, for example. The Trustee will perform important management and record keeping functions and will also need to be knowledgeable in the area of FAPTs in the event the trust is ever challenged by a creditor. Although this is probably so obvious as to not even require mentioning, **the Settlor of a FAPT should never serve as the Trustee.**

The laws of various FAP Countries typically permit you to appoint another person (even a U.S. citizen) to act as a Co-Trustee with the Offshore Trustee. This, however, is not advisable since it may give a creditor greater ease in getting jurisdiction over the FAPT in the event it is ever challenged.

Your choice as to which foreign trust company to serve as the Trustee of your FAPT is an important decision. There are obviously several factors to take into consideration. You will want to choose a Trustee that is very familiar with offshore asset protection trusts and that has had experience in actually defending a FAPT from the attack of a U.S. creditor. One offshore trust company used by some of my clients defended a poorly drafted FAPT from probably the single worst creditor you will ever face, the United States government. This trust company did a wonderful job and the Settlors of the FAPT recently settled with the U.S. government for significantly less than the assets protected in their FAPT. Another factor to consider is whether the foreign trust company has any branch offices in the United States. There have been several cases where a United States court has had jurisdiction over a local branch office of a foreign trustee or financial institution and imposed huge daily fines on the local U.S. branch until the foreign company complied with the order of the U.S. court. You also want to know (i) which foreign banks and other foreign financial institutions the trust company regularly works with, (ii) whether the trust company is properly insured, (iii) how long the trust company has been in business, (iv) whether the trust company has been confronted with a "freeze order" (called a "Mareva order"), (v) whether the trust company has had experience working as part of a team (including U.S. legal counsel) in connection with a threat against the settlor's assets held in a FAPT, (vi) the backgrounds of the companies key employees, and (vii) whether the trust company itself ever been sued and, if so, the outcome of the suit. There have been news stories of people losing money to less than reputable trustees, however, there are several very reputable foreign trust companies that add significant value as part of your comprehensive asset protection plan.

Lifetime Beneficiaries. The beneficiaries of the FAPT during the life of the Settlor are typically the Settlor's spouse and children and can even include the Settlor. Oftentimes, a husband and wife both create a FAPT and, therefore, both of them are considered to be Settlors. The Settlor(s) can even be the sole beneficiary of the FAPT, however, as will be explained later, it may be preferable for the Settlor to not be an initial beneficiary of the FAPT. This, however, is of lesser concern when compared to a DAPT. When the Settlor is a beneficiary of the FAPT, he or she will be a discretionary beneficiary, meaning that the trustee can distribute to them as much or as little as the trustee deems advisable. This offers the greatest asset protection to the Settlor.

Estate Planning. The FAPT also typically serves as the Settlor's principal estate planning document. Therefore, when the Settlor dies, the trust creates certain sub-trusts (i.e., a Credit Shelter Trust, a Marital Trust, Dynastic Trusts for children, etc.) which make sure the assets in the FAPT pass to the intended beneficiaries (i.e., children, for example) in a manner that (i) reduces or eliminates federal estate taxes, and (ii) provides the beneficiaries with tax and asset protection benefits. Since a FAPT is irrevocable (i.e., it cannot be changed by a Settlor) it is common to add what is called a "Limited Power of Appointment" to the trust which allows a Settlor to change (i) the persons who will receive the assets in the FAPT upon the death of a Settlor, and (ii) the manner in which they receive it (i.e., in trust, outright, in a specialized trust, etc.). This allows additional flexibility as time passes. When a Family Limited Partnership or Foreign LLC is combined with a FAPT, additional estate tax savings can be garnered. Finally, the laws of many FAP Countries provide additional estate planning benefits such as the ability to create trusts that can endure in perpetuity, the ability to create protective trusts for your children and other beneficiaries, and the ability to serve as part of many advanced estate planning structures to give them flexibility in a manner that cannot be accomplished in the United States. Therefore, a FAPT not only provides the benefit of asset protection but also serves as a superior estate planning vehicle.

Trust Protector. The trust agreement will also name a Trust Protector. The Trust Protector is a person (or even a corporate entity) that has been granted the power to do things such as veto the Trustee's decision to make distributions, approve or disapprove of certain decisions the trustee may make with respect to the management of the trust assets, remove the trustee and appoint a successor trustee, add or remove beneficiaries to the trust, amend the trust to make it more protective or to improve its effectiveness in reducing estate taxes in the event of future tax law changes, etc. The Trust Protector can be a trusted friend, family member, or professional such as your accountant or attorney. There are also offshore company's that can serve as Protector in the event a U.S. Protector becomes subject to the jurisdiction of the U.S. Court. Having a Trust Protector allows for greater flexibility over time and can make the FAPT more protective as they can exercise certain rights over the trust that you cannot. **The Settlor should not be the Trust Protector.**

Investment Advisor. The trust agreement typically appoints someone to act as the Investment Advisor. This person has the right to instruct the trustee with respect to how the assets of the FAPT should be invested. Since the power of the Investment Advisor is limited to providing instruction on how the trust assets are managed, and not with respect to making distributions or exercising other trust powers, it is safe for the Settlor to serve in this position. Of course, the Settlor may name their financial advisor (or the lower risk spouse) to serve as Investment Advisor. The Settlor can also retain the right to remove them at any time and replace them with a successor Investment Advisor. This second option may be slightly preferable, however, many people creating FAPTs prefer to serve as Investment Advisor's themselves.

Divorce Clause. If a husband and wife both create a FAPT and are, therefore, both Settlors, what happens in the event of a divorce? Similar to a Delaware DAPT, the FAPT is drafted to split into two separate trusts (i.e., one for husband and one for wife) upon a dissolution of the Settlors' marriage. The split of trust assets can be equal or can provide for some other method of determining how much is allocated to each spouse's separate (post divorce) trust. After the divorce, each spouse has their own FAPT in which the other spouse has no continuing rights. The FAPT can also be used to shelter assets from the claims of a divorcing spouse. The case of **Riechers v. Riechers** illustrates this. Between 1984 and 1988, three separate malpractice lawsuits had been filed against Dr. Riechers. After experiencing these problems, Dr. Riechers began to consider asset protection planning to preserve the family assets, and ultimately formed a Cook Islands asset protection trust. A few years later, Dr. Riechers' creditor turned out not to be a patient but rather Mrs. Riechers. Mrs. Riechers filed for divorce and sought to receive a portion of the assets in the Cook Islands trust. It turns out that the trust had been drafted to exclude Mrs. Riechers. The court, in admitting that it did not have jurisdiction over the trust stated:

> "Assuming arguendo, that this Court had jurisdiction over the corpus of the Riechers Family Trust, which it does not, a cause of action would not [be permitted] to set aside the trust since the trust was established for the **legitimate purpose of protecting family assets for the benefit of the Riechers family members.**"

The court did find another way around the problem posed by the trust, however. Dr. Riechers had significant assets in the United States and Mrs. Riechers was able to satisfy her full claim from those assets.

Note that in drafting a FAPT, the term "spouse" can be defined in the trust agreement as "the person to whom the settlor is happily married from time to time." Therefore, the FAPT can be a substitute or an addition to a prenuptial agreement.

Duress Clause. A Duress Clause is language in the FAPT trust agreement that removes a persons ability to exercise any power contained in the trust agreement unless the person exercising the power is doing so of their own free will. Therefore, if a court were to order the trustee, the settlor, or the protector to exercise a power that would cause the trust to be ineffective in protecting assets, even if they try to comply with the court order (which they should always do), their efforts will be ineffective.

Flight Clause. A "Flight Clause" is a provision in the FAPT's trust agreement that allows a Trustee or the Trust Protector to change the jurisdiction of the FAPT. The Flight provision can also be drafted to automatically change the jurisdiction of the trust without any affirmative direction by the trustee or anyone else. Assume that a creditor tries to reach assets by bringing suit in the Cook Islands. The Flight Clause could move the trust to another safe FAP Country thereby frustrating the creditor's attempt to gain jurisdiction over the trust. There are downsides using Duress provisions and Flight Clause that are beyond the scope of this book, so make sure the attorney helping you can explain these rather than telling you they are all upside.

While there are a number of important factors in drafting an effective FAPT, the above should give you a good idea of how a FAPT is properly structured. Understand that there are a number of important factors that need to be given consideration given your individual facts and circumstances and that you should always use competent legal counsel in creating the FAPT. A good asset protection attorney will also be able to give you advice on the proper maintenance of the FAPT after it is created which is just as important as a properly structured trust agreement.

FAPT Combined With an Offshore LLC.

Similar to combining a domestic asset protection trust with a family limited partnership, a FAPT can be combined with an Offshore Limited Liability Company (referred to as an "OLLC") to provide the same benefits. The assets are held in the OLLC. The OLLC is owned 100% by the FAPT, however, you and/or your spouse will control how the assets in the OLLC are invested by being the Manager of the OLLC. If you are ever sued, the creditor cannot reach any of the assets because you do not own anything.

Another advantage to this structure is that in the event a creditor ever decided to spend the time, money, and effort to challenge the effectiveness of the FAPT from an asset protection standpoint, and was actually successful in piercing the FAPT (which is highly unlikely), the only asset that would be reachable by the creditor is the ownership interest in the OLLC which is also formed in a FAP Country. This interest in the OLLC will not be reachable by a creditor due to charging order protection. That being the case, you will have significant leverage in negotiating a favorable settlement from the outset since they first have to win and obtain a judgement, then they have to bring another expensive law suit to try and pierce the FAPT and even if they are successful in that endeavor, they are still limited to a charging order and may never be able to reach the underlying assets.

A graphical depiction of a typical FAPT / OLLC structure looks like this:

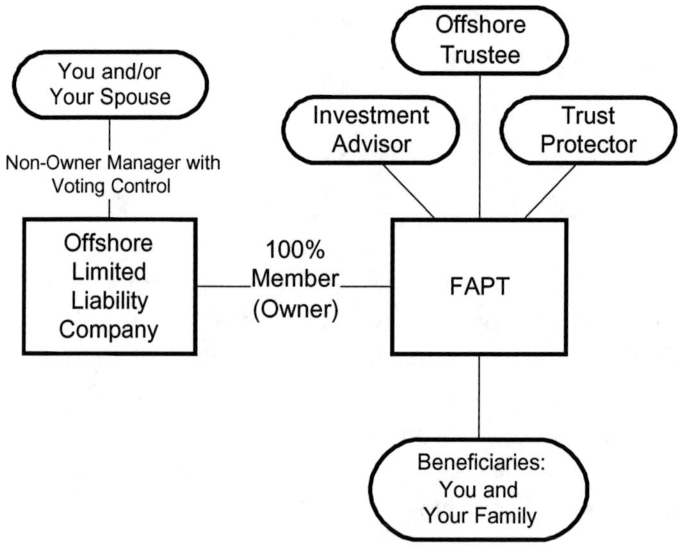

In the event you are ever sued, the Trustee has the power to remove you as the Manager of the OLLC. After you are removed, you can still dictate how the assets are invested, however, all other management functions that could diminish the asset protection offered by the FAPS will be under the control of the Trustee of the FAPT. Therefore, in the event a United States court ever orders you to distribute assets to a creditor, you will be unable to do so.

It is also important to understand that properly funding and then maintaining the plan over time is critical. If distributions are made, they have to be properly documented to show that the structure is being respected. If you simply started paying for personal expenses from the OLLC account, this would not bode well for you in the future if the plan was ever tested. A qualified asset protection attorney will be able to explain the proper "care and feeding" of your FAPS will need over time to provide you with the benefits you expect from the structure.

Also understand that the FAPT/OLLC structure shown above is a basic structure that is helpful in explaining the basics of how it protects assets. There are more sophisticated structures that may make more sense given your individual facts and circumstances.

Location of the FAPT Assets.

Where the assets held inside a FAPS should be located (i.e., the country where they reside) is an important consideration in structuring a FAPS. There are three primary options:

Hold All Assets in an Offshore Account. Probably the safest option is to have the FAPT or OLLC open an account with a foreign financial institution that does not have any branch offices in the United States. There are many fine institutions that meet this criteria including several well established Swiss Private Banks. I would be very leery of a foreign trust company promoting asset protection trusts that wants to custody the assets in the offshore jurisdiction rather than using an established financial institution in a first world country.

If the assets are already offshore and you are sued, there is no additional activity that needs to transpire to move assets offshore. In addition, one of the non-asset protection benefits of using a FAPS is that a FAPS has access to investments that are not available to U.S. citizens. With the dollar falling in value when compared to the Euro and many people's concern about the financial stability of our country, a FAPS can add additional value to your financial plan by diversifying globally.

Hold Some Assets in an Offshore Account. The next option would be to open an account with a foreign financial institution in the name of the FAPT or OLLC as discussed in the section above, however, only a portion of the FAPT or OLLC assets are held in that account. The remaining assets are held in the United States at the financial institution of your choice in an account that is also titled in the name of the FAPT or OLLC. In the event you are ever sued, the onshore assets can be transferred to the offshore account. This should not be a fraudulent transfer because the "transfer" took place at the time the accounts were established in the name of the FAPS. The subsequent moving of assets from one FAPS account (i.e., the onshore account) to another FAPS account (i.e., the offshore account) does not result in a transfer from one owner to another (i.e., the FAPS is the owner at all times). It is possible to structure the FAPS so that someone other than you can effectuate this movement of assets from one account to another which may be more beneficial. Many people, however, would rather not give anyone else this type of control and consider the associated risk (this will be discussed below in the section on contempt of court) a cost of the structure.

Hold All of the Assets Onshore. The least protective option is simply to hold all of your assets in an account opened in the name of the FAPT or OLLC. In the event a creditor surfaces, you will have to go through the process of opening the offshore account in the name of the FAPT or OLLC and then transfer the onshore FAPS assets to that account. Opening a foreign account can take some time and as mentioned in the last paragraph, there is some associated risk.

You should discuss these options with your asset protection attorney who will be able to help you in making the best decision based on your facts and circumstances. Also note that if you hold all or a portion of the assets in a foreign account, you should consider structuring the account so that two signatures, yours and the trustee's, are required to make distributions. This works from an asset protection standpoint since you cannot unilaterally reach the account assets and it provides comfort that the offshore trustee cannot abscond with the assets. Of course, if you are using a quality trustee, this should not be a considerable risk.

Control vs. Protection.

As was exemplified in the previous Chapter on Domestic Asset Protection Trusts, there tends to be an inverse relationship between direct control and the asset protection offered by a DAPT or a FAPT. This is in large part incorporated into Florida's public policy against Self-Settled Trusts providing their creator (i.e., the Settlor) with asset protection. When someone makes a gift to someone else, they typically completely relinquish control over the gifted property. For example, if I were to give you $1,000, once the gift is complete, I do not have any continuing right to tell you how to spend it nor do I have the legal right to demand that you give it back to me. Because of this fact, a creditor of mine is unable to reach the gifted asset (assuming no fraudulent transfer issues exist). On the other hand, if I place assets into a typical revocable trust like the kind used in estate planning, I have taken assets out of my name and transferred them into the name of the trust (i.e., I technically do not own them anymore). However, because I have the legal right to terminate the trust and take the assets back, the assets in the trust are subject to the claims of my creditors. Therefore, the more control you retain over the property that you have given away, the more likely a court will find that you really never made a gift, ergo no asset protection.

In the context of discretionary domestic self-settled trusts (i.e., a trust of which you are both a settlor and a discretionary beneficiary) formed in a state such as Delaware, the focus from an asset protection standpoint will be more on the conflicts of law and constitutional issues outlined in the previous Chapter. In the context of discretionary foreign self-settled trusts formed in a country such as the Cook Islands, these issues are not as relevant since a United States court does not have jurisdiction over the trust. However, with both DAPTs and FAPTs, in the event you retain certain types of control, there could be some serious downsides. These are explained in detail in the following section.

Downsides of Using a FAPS.

Below I have listed some downsides to using a FAPS. Ironically, as will be explained in the section describing the first of these downsides (i.e, contempt of court), one downside stems from the fact that they work so well in keeping assets away from creditors. You will note that unlike most of the previous asset protection strategies, the downside of its not being effective in certain situations is not listed. That being said, however, there are downsides that need to be considered before deciding to use a FAPS as part of your comprehensive asset protection plan.

Contempt of Court. There have been two relatively recent cases involving individuals who have established FAPTs and were incarcerated when the FAPT was tested by a creditor. I will start by giving an overview of each of these cases and then explain the law of contempt of court. Some legal commentators have stated that these cases mark the end of offshore asset protection trusts. Other legal commentators (including myself) are of the opinion that FAPTs work very well to protect assets and, if they are properly structured, are highly unlikely to result in the incarceration of the Settlor. It is important to note that in each of the two cases that will be explained below, the assets held in the Settlor's FAPT remain protected to this day despite the effort of some very powerful creditors.

The Anderson Case. The case of **Federal Trade Commission v. Affordable Media, LLC** (more commonly referred to as the "Anderson Case") involved husband and wife, Denyse and Michael Anderson. The Andersons were involved in a telemarketing venture that offered investors the chance to participate in a project that sold such modern marvels as talking pet tags and water-filled barbells by means of late-night television. The Andersons were successful in raising at least $13,000,000 from investors and kept an estimated $6,300,000 in commissions for themselves. The venture turned out to be a Ponzi scheme where the later investors' investments were used to pay the promised yields to the earlier investors. On April 23, 1998, the Federal Trade Commission charged the Andersons with violating several federal laws under the Federal Trade Commission Act for their scheme to telemarket fraudulent investments to consumers.

Roughly two years before the Andersons began their scheme, they had established a FAPT in the Cook Islands. Under the trust agreement, the Andersons were Co-Trustees with a trust company in the Cook Islands. They were also Protectors under the trust. As Protectors, they also retained the right to determine whether or not an "Event of Duress" had occurred. You may remember that the happening of an "Event of Duress" will trigger the Duress Clause of the FAPT making any attempts by the Andersons to exercise control over the FAPT ineffective. Therefore, under the plain language of their trust, the Andersons could exercise complete control of their FAPT (including the ability to require distributions to be made to themselves) by providing the Cook Islands trustee a written statement to the effect that no event of duress had occurred. To say that the Andersons' FAPT was poorly structured from an asset protection standpoint is an understatement.

Between the months of September 1995 and May 1997, the Andersons received distributions from the FAPT to pay their income taxes. Additional distributions were made between June 1997 and February 1998. These distributions did not bode well for the Andersons either. When a settlor/beneficiary of a FAPT makes frequent requests for distributions and the trustee complies with every request, it appears as though the settlor is controlling the trustee. This is why it is best to only transfer "long-term" money (i.e., money that you do not reasonably anticipate needing for some time, perhaps retirement) to a FAPT and live off the money you earn. You may also want to keep other exempt assets that you could "dip into" if needed such as life insurance, annuities, IRAs, etc.

In May of 1998, the court entered an order which, among other things, required the Andersons to repatriate the assets in the FAPT. At this point the Andersons are still Co-Trustees and Protectors of their FAPT. As such they could have complied with the court's order by certifying to the Cook Islands Trustee that no event of duress had occurred, and, that as a Co-Trustee, they authorized a distribution of trust assets to them. You will probably be shocked to hear that they did not do this. Instead, the Andersons faxed the Cook Islands Trustee requesting, among other things, that the trust assets be repatriated (i.e., brought back to the United States). The fax also noted that they were under court order to make this request. This of course triggered the Duress Clause of the FAPT which resulted in them being removed as trustees and their request for the repatriation of assets to be denied by the Cook Islands Trustee. The Andersons were then taken into custody for contempt of court.

It was later revealed that the Andersons, though no longer trustees, were still the Protectors of the trust. The Andersons then attempted to resign as the Protectors but were not successful.

In November of 1998, the Federal Trade Commission (sometimes referred to as the "FTC" for short) hired Cook Islands legal counsel for advice on how to force a repatriation of the assets in the Andersons' trust. They also created a trust company in the Cook Islands called, FTC, Inc. The FTC's Cook Islands attorney recommended that the Andersons be asked to sign various documents to (i) remove the current Cook Islands Trustee and appoint FTC, Inc. (a trust company created by the FTC) as the new trustee of the FAPT (creative, huh?), (ii) amend the trust agreement to remove the FTC as an "Excluded Beneficiary," and (iii) resign as the Protectors and appoint the FTC as the new Protector of the FAPT. The Andersons did just that and were then released from jail. They were incarcerated for a total of five months.

The Trustee of the FAPT then went to the High Court of the Cook Islands to seek an order that the documents the Andersons had executed were invalid. On August 11, 1999, a judgement was handed down from the Chief Justice of the Cook Islands High Court, Chief Justice Quilliam, which held that all the documents signed by the Andersons were invalid except the one where they resigned as Protectors which was held to be valid.

The Andersons were no longer subject to the contempt order, were free from jail, and the trust assets remained in the Cook Islands. On December 13, 2002, the FTC reported that it had settled the case with the Andersons. The announcement stated:

> "Through the settlement announced today, [the Andersons' FAPT] has turned over to the FTC $1.2 million . . . ending the litigation against it."

This is significantly less than the $6,300,000 that was reportedly transferred to the FAPT. Therefore, the Andersons (i) created a poorly drafted FAPT and transferred somewhere in the neighborhood of $6,000,000 to it, (ii) faced one of the single most powerful creditors, the United States government, and (iii) ended up settling with the FTC for considerably less than the amount held in the trust. Of course, they did spend five months in jail. So, is this a success story? You be the judge.

The Lawrence Case. Stephan J. Lawrence was a successful options trader with Bear, Stearns & Co., Inc. ("Bear, Stearns"). Shortly after October 19, 1987 (the day referred to in the securities industry as "Black Monday"), Mr. Lawrence and his companies experienced a margin deficit with Bear, Stearns, however they disagreed about the exact amount of the deficit. As a result, Mr. Lawrence commenced an arbitration proceeding against Bear, Stearns and Bear, Stearns brought a counterclaim against Mr. Lawrence. The arbitration case lasted 42 months in total. Bear, Sterns was ultimately victorious and was awarded just over $20,000,000. Mr. Lawrence then filed for bankruptcy.

On January 8, 1991, just 66 days prior to the $20,000,000 award being handed down against Mr. Lawrence, Mr. Lawrence established a FAPT. The laws of the Jersey Channel Islands governed the FAPT. The court stated that "the [FAPT trust agreement] appears to be a 'form' document which refers to Mr. Lawrence only once by name, and then only by a typewritten insertion."

One month later, Mr. Lawrence amended the trust on February 7, 1991, (just 36 days before the handing down of the $20,000,000 award) to (i) add specific spendthrift language to the trust which was not included in the original trust agreement, and (ii) change the law governing the trust to the Republic of Mauritius which is arguably more protective than that of the Jersey Channel Islands. In discussing the purpose of Mr. Lawrence's amendment, the court stated "[t]he only conclusion to be drawn from the documents and testimony is that the original trust document did not provide [Mr. Lawrence] with sufficient protection from his creditors, necessitating the subsequent execution of the amendment."

Mr. Lawrence never could produce a signed copy of the FAPT trust agreement which lead the court to question whether a valid trust ever, in fact, existed. In addition, none of the amendments to the trust submitted to the court were signed by Mr. Lawrence. The unsigned copies that the court did have indicated that Mr. Lawrence had retained a substantial amount of control over the trust, including, the right to remove and replace trustees in his absolute discretion.

When asked by the court why he created the FAPT, he stated that it was for his estate planning and retirement security purposes. The court repeatedly asked Mr. Lawrence whether he intended for the FAPT to provide him with any asset protection and he steadfastly replied no. This lead the court to make the following comment:

> "This is absurd, given the fact that absent this shielding effort, there would be no money left for his retirement as creditors would have taken every penny they could find."

The court also inquired as to the specifics of Mr. Lawrence's retirement goals, however, he could not identify any except to state that the money in the FAPT was to "protect him in his old age."

The court then went on to ask Mr. Lawrence a series of questions regarding the facts surrounding his creation of the trust and he provided answers that the court found to be "not credible and not believable." The court went on to state that Mr. Lawrence had been "shockingly less than candid with the . . . Court. . . . This Court concludes that [Mr. Lawrence's] repeated failure to answer the [bankruptcy Trustee's] questions in anything but evasions and half-truths constitutes a willful and bad faith failure to obey this Court's discovery orders."

In July of 1999, the court ordered Mr. Lawrence to bring the assets in the FAPT back to the United States. Mr. Lawrence stated that he requested the trustee of the trust to do so and even attempted to remove the current trustee and appoint the bankruptcy trustee as the replacement trustee. The offshore trustee did not reply, however, due to the duress clause in the trust. Mr. Lawrence was incarcerated in October of 1999 and was finally set free over six years later late last year. His assets remained protected and will be available to him in the future.

Again, Mr. Lawrence (i) created a poorly drafted FAPT and transferred somewhere in the neighborhood of $8,000,000 to it, (ii) did so just sixty-six days prior to the issuance of the judgement, (iii) lied to the court and the bankruptcy court on numerous occasions, (iv) could not even produce a signed copy of the trust agreement, (v) and is now free after spending just over six years in jail. Success story or not?

The Law of Contempt of Court.

The law of contempt of court is a rather complex area of the law. That being the case I will start by giving you a brief overview of the major types of contempt and then explain the type of contempt that is potentially applicable to persons who create FAPTs.

The first major category of contempt of court is the classification of the conduct as either criminal contempt or civil contempt. Criminal contempt is conduct that tends to obstruct or interfere with the administration of justice by the judicial branch of government. It is directed against the authority and dignity of a court or of a judge acting judicially. Civil contempt, on the other hand, consists of failing to do something that a court or judge in a civil case has ordered for the benefit of the opposing party in the case. In the Florida case of **Parsons v. Wennet** decided in 1993, the court stated:

> "[T]he purpose of a civil contempt procedure is to obtain compliance on the part of a person subject to an order of the court."

The second broad category of contempt of court is the classification of the conduct as either direct contempt or indirect contempt. Direct contempt is offensive or improper conduct that takes place in the presence of the court. Indirect contempt, on the other hand, is conduct that occurs at a distance and not in the presence of the court.

Given these definitions, the type of contempt that could potentially be applicable to the settlor of a FAPT is indirect, civil contempt. This was the contempt that both the Andersons and Mr. Lawrence faced.

Impossibility of Performance. A basic tenet of the law of civil contempt is that a court cannot hold someone in contempt of court for failing to do something that is impossible. Put another way, impossibility is a complete defense to civil contempt of court.

In the Florida Supreme Court case of **Bowen v. Bowen**, the court states:

> "As this Court has previously stated, the purpose of a civil contempt proceeding is to obtain compliance on the part of a person subject to an order of the court. Because incarceration is utilized solely to obtain compliance, it must be used only when the contemnor has the ability to comply. This ability to comply is the contemnor's 'key to his cell.'"

Another Florida case, **Parsons v. Wennet**, referred to above, makes an almost identical statement:

> "Incarceration in a civil contempt proceeding is used solely to obtain compliance with a court directive, and even then only when the contemnor has the ability to comply with the directive. The ability to comply is the civil contemnor's 'key to his cell' entitling him to release upon compliance."

The United States Supreme Court has also upheld this tenet of the law of civil contempt. In the 1983 United States Supreme Court case of **United States v. Rylander**, Justice Rehnquist stated that:

> "In a civil contempt proceeding, . . . a defendant may assert a present inability to comply with the order in question. . . . While the court is bound by the enforcement order, it will not be blind to evidence that compliance is now factually impossible. Where compliance is impossible, neither the moving party nor the court has any reason to proceed with the civil contempt action."

In addition, the Ninth Circuit in the 1983 case of **Falstaff Brewing Corporation,**

et al., v. Miller Brewing Company, et al., stated:

> "It is clear . . . that inability – **whether or not self induced** – is a complete defense to coercive civil contempt."

Finally, in the area of contempt of court, the case of **Maggio v. Zeitz** is often referenced. In fact, it was cited in the **Lawrence** case explained above. In this case the court stated:

> "[A] motion to [incarcerate a person who has filed for bankruptcy (the term for such a person is 'the bankrupt')] for failure to obey an order of the Court to turn over to the receiver in bankruptcy the property of the bankrupt is civil contempt and is to be treated as a mere step in the proceedings to administer the assets of the bankrupt as provided by law . . .. While in a sense they are punitive, they are not punishment – they are . . . coercive, and intended to compel, against the reluctance of the bankrupt, performance by him of his lawful duty. . . . Of course, to jail one for contempt for omitting an act he is powerless to perform would reverse this principal and make the proceeding purely punitive, to describe it charitably. At the same time, it would add nothing to the bankruptcy estate."

In summation, since civil contempt of court is remedial in nature (i.e., its purpose is to obtain compliance on the part of a person subject to an order of the court), if that purpose cannot be fulfilled because the thing the court is ordering the person to do is impossible, then to hold someone in contempt of court would be purely punitive and, therefore, wholly improper.

To be in Contempt There Must be a Court Order.

The next important point in understanding the law of contempt of court as it potentially applies to the settlor of a FAPT, is that there has to be a court order to violate before you can be held in contempt of court for violating that order. In the United States Supreme Court case of **United States v. Bryan**, the court stated:

> "There is, in our jurisprudence, no doctrine of 'anticipatory contempt.'"

In other words, until a person fails to comply with a court order, no wrong has been committed.

In the **Anderson** case discussed above, the court states:

> "The standard for finding a party in civil contempt is well settled:
>
> The moving Party has the burden of showing by clear and convincing evidence that the contemnors violated a **specific and definite order of the court.** The burden then shifts to the contemnors to demonstrate why they were unable to comply.
>
> **Stone v. City and County of San Francisco,** 968 F.2d 850, 856 n. 9 (9th Cir.1992)."

While this point may seem so obvious to not need mentioning, it will help later in this section to fully understand the law of contempt of court as it may apply to the settlor of a FAPT.

Self-created Impossibility.

This next section discusses an exception to the general rule stated above that impossibility is a complete defense to contempt; namely that if you create the impossibility so that you are unable to comply with an order of the court, then impossibility is not a complete defense to civil contempt of court.

For example, the court in the **Lawrence** case states:

> "While impossibility is a recognized defense to a civil contempt order, the law does not recognize the defense of impossibility

> when the impossibility is self created."

Before proceeding with the discussion on self created impossibility, lets summarize what we have learned thus far.

1. A civil contempt order is remedial not punitive. In other words, its sole purpose is to compel performance of the court order or, put another way, to make you do something that you can do but don't want to do;

2. If it is impossible for the person subject to a court order to comply, then the person cannot be held in contempt (i.e., impossibility of performance is a complete defense to contempt of court); and

3. There must be a court order to violate before someone can be held in contempt.

Given these facts about contempt of court, the rule that self created impossibility is not a defense to contempt of court does not really make any sense because self created or not, it is still impossible to comply with the court's order. For example:

> Assume Jimmy is ordered to turn over important documents to the court. The court tells Jimmy that if he does not do so, he will be held in contempt and incarcerated until he complies. Jimmy goes home, finds the documents, lights a fire in his fireplace, and burns the documents. He video tapes the whole encounter in the presence of 12 Anglican Bishops who are serving as witnesses. He goes back to court the next day, plays the tape for the judge, and has all 12 Anglican Bishops swear on a stack of bibles that the documents have been reduced to ashes, thereby proving beyond a shadow of a doubt that it is impossible for Jimmy to produce the documents."

And now for the $64,000 question. Can Jimmy be incarcerated for **civil** contempt of court? It is painfully obvious that Jimmy cannot produce the documents and will never be able to do so in the future even if he lives to age 150. It is also painfully obvious that Jimmy is the one who created the impossibility. Furthermore, it is also obvious that the purpose behind civil contempt of court is to get someone to do the thing the court has ordered (i.e., to get Jimmy to produce the documents).

When the court states that "the law does not recognize the defense of impossibility when the impossibility is self created," what do they really mean? Do they mean that we throw out the entire remedial purpose behind civil contempt of court and convert it to a punitive purpose? Will Jimmy sit in jail forever? The answer to both these questions is obviously not.

The case of **United States v. O.C. Jenkins,** which is directly quoted in the **Lawrence** case, sheds some light on what is meant by the proclamation that "self created impossibility is not a defense to civil contempt of court." In this case, the court states:

> "It is well settled that if a court finds that a defendant could **at some time in the past** have complied with a court order, the court **should presume a present ability to comply** and impose on the alleged contemnor the burden of producing evidence to establish present inability. . . . Once the defendant satisfies his burden of production, the burden of persuasion shifts back to the person seeking the contempt order."

Therefore, what is really meant by the statement that "self created impossibility is not a defense to civil contempt of court," is that there will be a strong presumption that a person can really still comply with a court order if the evidence indicates that they were able to comply with the order at some time in the past. Going back to our example with Jimmy, since at the time the judge ordered Jimmy to retrieve the requested documents, the greater weight of the evidence suggested that he had the power to do so, the burden of proving that Jimmy cannot, in fact, comply shifts back to Jimmy. In Jimmy's case, Jimmy should be able to do so through the video tape and the sworn testimony of the 12 Anglican Bishops. Therefore, in Jimmy's case, the court should **not** be able to incarcerate Jimmy for **civil** contempt of court. This does not mean that Jimmy is out of the woods, however, quite the contrary. Jimmy's extreme actions probably violated several laws and were clearly the type of "insult to the court" contemplated by the law of **criminal** contempt of court. Next I want to put this in context with respect to the **Anderson** case and the **Lawrence** case. Then I will move on to discuss the importance of timing in creating FAPTs from the contempt of court perspective.

Before moving on, I want to note that a well drafted, properly implemented FAPT will be much like having Jimmy's video tape and 12 Anglican Bishops, in that it will be very easy to prove (i) that you did not have any improper control over the FAPT like the Andersons or Mr. Lawrence, and (ii) that the impossibility you may need to someday prove is real. In addition, if the FAPT was established more than ten years ago, the new bankruptcy law should cure the problem altogether since it will be considered an exempt asset (see Chapter 7 for a discussion of the new bankruptcy laws).

In the **Anderson** case, as you may remember, the Andersons had significant control over the offshore trust when the court ordered them to repatriate the assets. They were trustees, they were protectors, they had established a pattern of receiving distributions from the trust, and, most importantly, they had the power to declare that an "Event of Duress" had not occurred which was tantamount to a power to repatriate the assets at any time. When the court issued its order to repatriate the assets, the Andersons could, in fact, comply, however, they chose not to and created the impossibility to do so by sending a fax to the Cook Islands trustee that contained language they knew would trigger the Duress Clause.

Therefore, since the Andersons had the ability to comply with the order and then created an impossibility, the Anderson court "should presume a present **ability to comply**" on their part. This shifts the burden back to the Andersons to prove that they could not comply (i.e., that it was factually impossible).

A quote from the Anderson court is instructive:

> "In the asset protection trust context . . . the burden on the party asserting an impossibility defense will be particularly high because of the likelihood that any attempted compliance with the court's orders will be merely a charade rather than a good faith effort to comply."

The Andersons' only proof that the impossibility was real was a response from the

Cook Islands Trustee that it would not repatriate the assets. Therefore, the court found that the Andersons had not made a good faith effort to comply with the court's order and they were incarcerated to see if the lack of freedom could coerce them into finding a way to bring the assets back.

In other words, the relevant issue was not whether impossibility was defense to contempt of court, but rather could the Andersons prove that they could not comply with the court order. Given the high standard stated above in addition to other factors such as the Andersons being less than candid with the court and trying to resign as protectors, the **Anderson** court acted clearly within the law by finding them in contempt. The purpose of civil contempt was being served; namely to coerce the Andersons into bringing the trust assets back to the United States.

Turning to the **Lawrence** case, there were also numerous facts that the court could use to imply that Mr, Lawrence had control over the trust. Mr. Lawrence could not produce signed copies of the trust or the amendments to the trust. When asked by the court to explain various particulars about the trust, Mr. Lawrence's responses were described as "shockingly less than candid." Again, since the greater weight of the evidence supported a conclusion that Mr. Lawrence did have control over the trust just before the court ordered him to repatriate the assets, the court should assume that he can still exercise control over the trust and bring the assets back to the United States. The court described Mr. Lawrence's attempts to repatriate the assets as nothing more than part of his continuing efforts to "hinder, delay, and defraud [his creditors]" (note the court's use of the 'fraudulent transfer' language. Again, given the high standard of proof required of Mr. Lawrence to prove impossibility, in addition to other factors such as his complete and utter unwillingness to be honest with the court, the Lawrence court acted clearly within the law by finding him in contempt. The purpose of civil contempt was being served; namely to coerce Mr. Lawrence into bringing the trust assets back to the United States.

As will be explained in more detail below, the **Anderson** case and the **Lawrence** case do not establish the precedent that settlors of FAPTs will end up in jail for using FAPTs to protect assets. The facts in these cases completely support the results of each one. A FAPT established before a creditor is recognized and that is intelligently drafted by an asset protection attorney that understands the nuances of these cases, will be highly protective and pose very little risk to the settlor of being incarcerated for contempt of court (however, some risk of incarceration will exist given the current status of the case law).

Before leaving this topic it should also be noted that several cases have held that an individual was not subject to civil contempt of court even when the impossibility of performance was self-created. Some of these cases will be discussed in the section below entitled "The Important Issue of Timing."

How Long Can One be Jailed for Civil Contempt?

Due to the fact that civil contempt is remedial in nature and the contemnor has to be given the "key to his jail cell," one cannot be jailed indefinitely in the context of an offshore asset protection trust even if they create a horrible trust such as the Andersons and Mr. Lawrence. The case of **United States v. O.C. Jenkins**, referred to earlier, dealt with an individual, Thom, who was ordered to pay his previous employer the sum of $115,752.68. It seems that Thom had stolen a proprietary process from the employer prior to leaving and was using that process to compete with the previous employer. He had been ordered by the court several times to stop using the process but he continuously disobeyed those orders. Thom had provided his probation officer (he was on probation from an unrelated offense) a probation report that listed over $260,000 in savings and assets. Later, in explaining to the court that it was impossible for him to comply with their order to pay the $115,752.68, he stated he was broke. Thom was incarcerated for civil contempt until he paid the money. In addressing the issue of how long Thom could be incarcerated, the court stated:

> . . . In conclusion, we note that each passing month of incarceration strengthens [the defendant's] claim of inability. . . . for it can be assumed that at a certain point any man will come to value his liberty more than [the benefits of not complying] and the pride lost in admitting that he has lied. Of course, that point cannot be identified in the abstract and we leave that determination to the discretion and good judgement of the . . . judge. We also note that while incarceration for civil contempt can last indefinitely, it cannot last forever. . . . If after many

> months, or perhaps even several years, the . . . judge becomes convinced that, although [the defendant] is able to pay he will steadfastly refuse to yield to the coercion of incarceration, the judge would be obligated to release Thom since incarceration would no longer serve the purpose of the civil contempt order – coercing payment."

The court also stated that regular review of Thom's incarceration would be required to readdress the issue of impossibility. Again, the risk of incarceration is small with a well drafted, well implemented FAPT that is formed when there are no creditors looming, however, if a FAPT is put in place after a creditor has been identified, being jailed is a distinct possibility. The length of the incarceration will depend on how well the impossibility can be established; however, most people want to avoid incarceration altogether. Therefore, establishing a FAPT to protect assets from a particular, presently identified creditor is not something I would ever recommend.

The Important Issue of Timing.

As I have stated numerous times throughout this book, the best time to engage in any form of asset protection planning is before a creditor has been identified. This is especially true with respect to using a FAPT to protect your assets. As was exemplified in the **Anderson** case and the **Lawrence** case, after-the-fact planning can produce some harsh results. Of course, the fact that their trusts were so poorly drafted did not help matters either. In this section I will explain why establishing a FAPT when the "skies are blue" rather than waiting for a creditor to appear can practically eliminate the possibility of being incarcerated for civil contempt of court.

You may remember the Florida case of **Hurlbert v. Shackleton, Jr., M.D.** discussed in Chapter 5 on Fraudulent Transfers. In this case, a physician, Dr. Shackleton, had received notice that his medical malpractice insurance was going to be cancelled and started transferring various assets to him and his wife as tenants by the entireties. During a deposition, Dr. Shackleton was asked why he transferred various assets to him and his wife jointly; he responded "[b]ecause I wasn't able to get malpractice insurance, and I wanted to cover all the bases." In other words, he admitted, quite honestly, that asset protection was a reason for the transfers. Dr.

Shackleton was sued roughly one year later for alleged malpractice that occurred after the transfers were made.

The trial court drew a distinction between "probable" and "possible" future creditors. The court classified the plaintiff as a "possible" future creditor, and then went on to say that it found no cases holding a transfer of assets to be fraudulent as to "possible" future creditors.

Although this case was a fraudulent transfer case, there is a close nexus between the law of fraudulent transfers and the law of contempt of court. Looking back at the Anderson case, the Andersons had control over the assets in the trust right up to the hearing for contempt of court. When they sent the fax to the Cook Islands Trustee that resulted in their loss of control, it can be said that the "transfer" of assets took place then, not when the assets were titled in the name of the trust. Likewise, with Mr. Lawrence. When he established a FAPT after 40 months into the arbitration hearing, and just 66 days before the ruling against him was handed down, I do not think any intelligent person would classify his transfers to the trust as anything but "fraudulent transfers." There was a clearly identifiable creditor when the assets were transferred and you do not need a fortune teller to know that a court "Turn Over" order was clearly a reality in Mr. Lawrence's not so distant future. This close nexus in time between loss of control over the transferred assets was a large factor in Mr. Lawrence being incarcerated for contempt. On this point the Lawrence court stated:

> "We agree with the district court that Lawrence created this Trust in an obvious attempt to shelter his funds from an expected adverse arbitration award. In addition, at the time Lawrence became an excluded person under the Trust he retained the ability to appoint a new Trustee who would have the power to revoke the excluded person status at any time. We . . . must conclude that the district court did not err in holding that Lawrence failed to establish his defense of impossibility."

Therefore, the fact that the arbitration award was expected (i.e., there was a clear relationship between the transfer and the expected "bad thing"), it cannot be said that Lawrence acted in good faith.

Contrast this with Dr. Shackleton who made his transfers with no specific creditor in mind, but with asset protection as an objective. In his case, because there was no causal relationship between the transfers and the later law suit, the transferred assets remained protected.

Additional evidence of the importance of timing is seen in the case of **Ex Parte Chambers**. This case involved an individual, Mr. Chambers, who had transferred certain assets. The asset transfer happened just prior to a court order that would have required using the transferred assets to pay for a court imposed fine. The court held that Mr. Chambers was not subject to contempt. In doing so the court stated:

> "A contemnor cannot be held in constructive contempt of court for actions taken prior to the time that the court's order is reduced to writing. . . . **Chambers had no duty to preserve [the] assets for the payment of fines to be ordered in the future**; therefore, his actions, taken alone, prior to the issuance of the fine, do not raise any inference that he was seeking to avoid the contempt powers of the trial court."

There are several other cases that I will not describe in detail that have also held that civil contempt is not an appropriate remedy even in situations where the impossibility was self created. In summary, the length of time that elapses between (i) a transfer of property that ultimately gives rise to a person's impossibility defense (such as the creation and funding of a FAPT) and (ii) the date the court issues an order or judgement, will be an important factor in determining whether someone can be held in contempt of court. If the timing is such that there is no direct relationship between the event that gave rise to the liability and the transfer of assets, contempt of court is wholly inappropriate. In the event the timing does indicate such a relationship, a contempt of court order may very well be justified.

The New Bankruptcy Laws. As mention previously in Chapter 7, any assets transferred to a FAPT more than the ten years prior to filing for bankruptcy will be fully exempt from creditors. In addition, it appears that even transfers made within the ten year period may also be exempt in bankruptcy so long as the transfers to the FAPT are not "fraudulent transfers." Since most of the civil contempt of court cases concerning FAPTs are bankruptcy cases, if the transfers to the FAPT are more than ten years old, the civil contempt of court issue may be mute altogether since the trust assets would be exempt if you filed for bankruptcy.

Additional Downsides.

Now that I have covered the area of Contempt of Court, I will address some additional downsides to using FAPTs.

Cost. Like a DAPT, the cost of establishing and maintaining a FAPT is sometimes higher than using state law exemptions, but not always. When one establishes a FAPT, there is the initial legal fee paid to the attorney, the ongoing cost of paying a Trustee's fee each year, the cost of preparing a partnership tax return each year for the OLLC in some cases, the annual fees and registered agent fee for the OLLC, and the increased accounting costs due to the additional tax forms that are typically filed each year by the FAPT settlor(s). When these costs are compared, however, to the costs associated with certain insurance and annuity products, the end cost can actually be less in many circumstances. In addition, if you view the FAPT as an all perils insurance policy that will protect your assets not just from medical malpractice liability but from practically all sources of liability, the cost is actually not that significant. One final word to the wise - this is not an area to go bargain shopping. While this may sound somewhat self serving, it is important for the FAPT to be structured correctly given your facts and circumstances and the cost of using quality legal counsel is well worth the money, especially if the plan is ever tested.

Tax Reporting. When one establishes a FAPT, there are increased reporting requirements to the IRS despite the fact that the trust is treated as a "grantor trust" and is, therefore, ignored for federal income tax purposes. This includes filing the following tax forms: Forms 709 (United States Gift (and Generation-Skipping Transfer) Tax Return), Form 3520 (Annual Return To Report Transactions With Foreign Trusts and Receipt of Certain Foreign Gifts), Form 3520-A (Annual Information Return of Foreign Trust With U.S. Owner), and Form TD F 90-22.1 (Report of Foreign Bank and Foreign Financial Accounts). In certain circumstances there may be additional reporting requirements as well. While this may seem somewhat complex, it is really not that burdensome or expensive. Your accountant should be familiar with these forms and can prepare them for you. Your asset protection attorney should have a conversation with your accountant at the time your FAPS is established to explain the reporting requirements so that all of your professionals understand the structure and the ongoing obligations that accompany it.

The Comfort Factor. While there is no reason to believe that using established offshore trust companies and financial institutions place your assets at risk, some people just do not feel comfortable with the idea. I believe that an argument can be made to the contrary. The vast majority of offshore trustees are reputable and take the protection of their clients' assets very seriously. Take for instance the trustee in the **Anderson** case. They took substantial measures to protect the assets in the Andersons' trust all within the boundaries of the law. In addition, the service you receive in many European financial institutions is at least as good as their United States counterparts. Also, by holding at least some of your assets with a Swiss financial institution, for example, you are also diversifying your risk when it comes to political systems and currencies. Looking at how the dollars is holding up against the euro lends even more credibility to using an offshore trust. While I do not want to be an alarmist, the new emphasis on homeland security since the 9/11 tragedy is some indication that all governments, even the United States, can be subject to severe circumstances that may affect your onshore assets. If some assets are held abroad, this risk is minimized.

United States Real Property. Since real estate located in the United States is not "moveable" and is absolutely subject to the jurisdiction of the United States' legal system, holding it in a FAPT will do little to protect it from a U.S. court who chooses not to respect the protective nature of a FAPT. This also holds true of certain other assets such as notes where the person obligated to pay the debt is a United States citizen. In the real estate context, some foreign financial institutions will lend you money and take back a mortgage on the U.S. real estate. The loan proceeds are then held in your FAPT and used as secondary collateral for the loan. The interest rate earned by the loan proceeds held in your FAPT is typically structured to be slightly higher than the interest rate on the mortgage, however, after all of the costs associated with the transaction are taken into account, the net cost is typically between 0.5% and 0.7% of the money borrowed. Therefore, after the transaction is complete, the U.S. real estate is subject to the lien of the foreign financial institution and not available to the claims of creditors. If a potential creditor searches the public record they will see the recorded mortgage and may decide to settle or not bring suit rather than having to pay the legal fees to try and reach the encumbered real estate. I do not know of a situation where this has ever been tested, however, a creditor may be able to successfully argue that the lien imposed by the mortgage should be ignored because the foreign financial institution is over collateralized (i.e, in collecting its money it has the right to foreclose on the United States real estate and the money in the FAPT). The creditor will ultimately be able to understand the structure including the fact that the offshore financial institution is over collateralized. Why? Because when you are questioned about it you will tell the truth. There will also be additional means for the creditor to discover this information even if you were to take Mr. Lawrence's lead and be "shockingly less than candid" with the court. Given that it is arguably less expensive than a conventional mortgage from a U.S. financial institution, it may still be a viable option but it is certainly not without risk.

Mitigation of Downsides.

As mentioned in the previous Chapter on Domestic Asset Protection Trusts, there are many ways to structure a DAPT and a FAPT to increase their protective nature. In the context of a FAPT, these same suggestions will also minimize or eliminate any argument a court may try and use to find you in contempt of court. I have already discussed combining the FAPT with an OLLC above as a means to add an additional layer of protection to a FAPT. My recommendations made in the last Chapter are also applicable to a FAPT so I will not repeat them here, however, I do suggest that you revisit them (they begin on Page). As mentioned above, there are also other types of Foreign Asset Protection Structures that are beyond the scope of this book. One of these involves a "Purpose Trust" or "Star Trust" which does not have any beneficiaries. There are also ways to use Swiss Annuities and Life Insurance that adds even more protection to these structures. Creative and thorough planning will examine all these options to further reduce risk and increase protection. By adding these additional mitigating planning elements to your FAPS, it will be incredibly protective and leave little risk of being subject to contempt of court in the future.

Anderson / Lawrence Cases
Compared to Medical Malpractice Litigation.

Another issue that bears pointing out is that the facts involved in the **Anderson** and **Lawrence** cases are very different from those that the average physician will ever face. First, the Andersons were involved in a Ponzi scheme and knew at the time that the money going into their trust was ill gotten gains. Second, in both the **Anderson** case and the **Lawrence** case, the trust was established with a particular creditor in mind. In Lawrence, he was 40 months into the arbitration hearing and had a pretty good idea what was in store for him. In the **Anderson** case, whenever someone uses a FAPT to shelter ill gotten gains, it can be said with relative certainty that they also have a specific creditor in mind. This is very different from the case of a physician who is concerned about protecting assets from some future claim of medical malpractice, especially in light of the fact that many physicians cannot obtain medical malpractice insurance due to the recent crisis, or, even if they can get insurance, they cannot afford adequate coverage. It goes without saying that no reasonable person would ever believe a physician established a FAPT so they could go out and hurt their patients. Given cases like the Riechers case (see Page) and **Hurlbert v. Shackleton, Jr., M.D.** (see Page), both of which held in favor of physicians who had engaged in asset protection and one of which involved a FAPT, FAPTs can make perfect sense in the physician context.

The Upsides of FAPTS.

As mentioned throughout this Chapter, the addition of a FAPT to your comprehensive asset protection plan can provide substantial benefits. Some of these benefits include the following:

FAPTs Work to Protect Assets. The biggest upside to using a FAPT is that it works. Even under the horrible facts of the **Anderson** case and the **Lawrence** case, where (i) the trusts were terribly drafted, (ii) the settlors retained improper powers, and (iii) the timing was after-the-fact, the trusts both worked to protect the assets from some very powerful creditors. In addition, the new bankruptcy law specifically exempts property transferred to a FAPT provided it was not fraudulently transferred to the FAPT within the 10 year period prior to filing bankruptcy. Therefore, in the event that you want a high level of protection with respect to your investment assets, a FAPT can be an excellent addition to your comprehensive asset protection plan provided it is drafted by a competent attorney and properly implemented and maintained over time.

Expensive to Litigate with no Guarantee of Success. A creditor seeking to reach assets properly transferred to a FAPT will have to be prepared to spend considerable money and time to try and pierce the FAPT with no guarantee of success. As outlined above, the task that lies ahead for any future creditor is so daunting that the mere existence of the FAPT will be a huge deterrent to suing you in the first place. It will also be a huge disincentive for a plaintiff attorney working on a contingency fee since he or she will only receives a percentage of what they can **collect**. Therefore, the fact that they work so well (which even the most ardent opponents to FAPTs can contest), will provide significant negotiating leverage in the event a medical malpractice law suit is ever threatened.

Estate Planning Benefits. As mentioned earlier, the FAPT will serve as a principal part of your estate plan. The laws of many FAP Countries have been drafted to provide additional estate planning benefits such as the ability to create trusts that can endure in perpetuity, the ability to create protective trusts for your children and other beneficiaries, and the ability to serve as part of many advanced estate planning structures to give them flexibility in a manner that cannot be accomplished in most U.S. states. In addition, a well drafted FAPS can also place a barrier between non_family members (e.g., ex_spouses, etc.), and even "problem" family members. In the event you are concerned about someone contesting your estate plan once you have died, a FAPT can be the perfect solution. Therefore, a FAPT not only provides the benefit of asset protection but also serves as a superior estate planning vehicle.

Substitution for Prenuptial Agreement. A well drafted FAPS can allow you to shield assets from the reach of a divorcing spouse without the need for a prenuptial agreement. Unlike a DAPT, there are no public policies in the FAP Countries which could frustrate your efforts in placing assets beyond the reach of a divorcing spouse.

Investment Benefits. Due to the offshore nature of the FAPS, you are able to participate in global markets that are ordinarily not available to U.S. investors, thereby providing you an opportunity to achieve even greater diversification. By investing in one or more euro denominated accounts, you can also protect against the steadily falling dollar.

All Perils Insurance Policy. As stated before, a well structured FAPS should be thought of as an "All Perils Insurance Policy" that: (i) covers all litigation risks, (ii) has low annual premiums and no deductibles, and (iii) contains few or no exceptions to coverage.

Who Should Use a FAPT?

To avoid repeating myself, the same analysis discussed on Page in the context of DAPTs also applies to FAPTs. I highly suggest going back and reviewing that section. To summarize, however, the list included (i) persons with a higher net worth, (ii) people seeking greater asset protection and investment flexibility, (iii) two physician households, (iv) single people, and (v) married individuals concerned about the potential for divorce. While this list is certainly far from complete, it gives you a pretty good idea of the situations where a FAPT could be most advantageous.

Conclusion.

FAPTs, especially if combined with an OLLC, can provide some of the strongest asset protection available. If you are considering using a FAPS as part of your comprehensive asset protection plan, I cannot stress enough the importance of using qualified legal counsel to help you properly structure and implement it. If done correctly, a FAPS can offer strong asset protection while mitigating the downside of contempt of court. By understanding the upsides and downsides of this structure, you can make an intelligent decision as to whether a FAPS is right for you given your individual facts and circumstances.

CHAPTER 21

Equity Stripping and Shifting

In this Chapter I will discuss equity stripping and equity shifting. Equity stripping is simply removing value from an asset by pledging it as collateral for a loan or other legally enforceable obligation. If the loan is large enough, the asset that has been equity stripped loses its value to a creditor. Equity shifting involves structuring the ownership of an asset or business entity so that any resulting cash flow and/or appreciation end up in a "protected place." Neither equity stripping nor equity shifting are stand alone asset protection techniques. Once an asset's equity is stripped, you typically have cash (i.e., loan proceeds) that then needs to be protected. In order to "shift" cash flow or future appreciation, the asset or business interest needs to be owned, in whole or in part, by a trust, business entity, or other "asset protected pot." Therefore, as you read this Chapter, keep in mind the other asset protection techniques discussed in other chapters of this book.

Equity Stripping.

Equity stripping is a technique that is principally used to reduce the attractiveness of an asset to a creditor that is difficult or impossible to protect using trusts, legal entities, or other methods discussed in the preceding chapters of this book. For example, suppose you own a piece of real estate in a country that requires you to own the property in your individual name (i.e., it cannot be transferred to a trust, LLC, etc.). Or what if you already own real estate in your individual name and the property is encumbered by a mortgage. If you were to transfer this property to an LLC, (i) you may have to pay documentary stamp tax (or some similar tax under the laws of the state or country governing the property), (ii) you will need to seek approval of the transfer from the mortgage lender or refinance the loan all together, and (iii) you would further need to buy a new title insurance policy.

The costs involved in such a case may be prohibitive. I will refer to these difficult to transfer assets as Immovable Assets for simplicity's sake.

The primary strategy with respect to such an Immovable Asset is to "lien" or "encumber" it by pledging it as collateral for a loan or legal obligation. Since the person or entity making the loan (the "Secured Creditor") has the first right to the asset(s), the Immovable Asset(s) are generally not available to satisfy the claims of other creditors such as a judgement creditor. As with every other asset protection technique discussed in this book, equity stripping has upsides, downsides, and traps for the unwary. Below I discuss several methods to strip an asset's equity and the various things you need to consider before doing so.

The Bank Loan. Probably the most secure way to lien Immovable Assets is to borrow money from a bank or other financial institution and pledge the Immovable Assets as collateral for the loan. Because an independent, third party bank has a lien on the Immovable Asset, it would be very hard for a creditor to argue that the lien should not be respected and that the creditor should be allowed to reach the assets.

> Assume Barney and Betty own property in the Bahamas worth \$1,000,000. The property is held in their individual names and cannot be transferred to a trust or legal entity without paying a Bahamian transfer tax of over \$100,000. The property is also subject to a \$400,000 mortgage held by Big Bank. Barney and Betty are named in a law suit brought by Fred and Wilma who are successful in obtaining a \$3,000,000 judgement. Fred and Wilma may be able to force the sale of the property in partial satisfaction of their judgement, but Big Bank is still owed \$400,000. Therefore, if the property was sold for its full fair market value of \$1,000,000, the most Fred and Wilma could reach is \$600,000. Had Barney and Betty borrowed \$950,000 rather than \$400,000, Fred and Wilma would likely get nothing after closing costs and attorney's fees.

There are several things to consider with respect to the above example. First, assuming Barney and Betty owned the property outright and borrowed the money from Big Bank to equity strip the property, they would have received a check for the amount of the mortgage (let's say $950,000). If the loan was taken out prior to the problems that led to Fred and Wilma's judgement, that money would have to be protected using some other asset protection technique discussed in the previous chapters of this book. If the "bad thing" had already occurred, any transfer of the $950,000 would most likely be considered a fraudulent transfer. I'll refer to this as the "Fraudulent Transfer Problem."

Second, assuming the assets were transferred to a protective trust, for example, the assets would need to be invested to produce an after tax rate of return equal to or greater than the interest rate under the loan (assuming the interest expense is not tax deductible). This obviously entails taking on a certain degree of investment risk since no low risk investments are likely to produce a sufficient investment return. If the investment return is not sufficient to fully offset the interest due under the loan, the difference would be the cost of equity stripping the asset. This can be expensive over time. For example, if the interest rate under the loan is 7%, and Betty and Barney can only achieve a 5% return on the investment assets (which equals a 3.25% after tax return assuming a 35% effective income tax rate), the difference of 3.75% means an out of pocket cost of $35,625 each year. Over a period of ten years, Barney and Betty would have an extra $367,828.10 in the bank (assuming they could get the same 3.25% after tax rate of return on the saved annual payments). In addition, if Barney and Betty used an interest only loan (i.e., the principal balance of the loan never decreases), the interest rate is typically not fixed so if interest rates increase, so the cost of protecting the asset. I'll refer to this as the "Cost Problem." Of course, if Betty and Barney could achieve an after tax rate of return in excess of the 7% interest rate, they would be richer from the arbitrage. So what will it be? Higher risk or higher costs. The choice, of course, is all yours.

Third, it is highly unlikely that Betty and Barney could borrow a full $950,000 using a $1,000,000 property as collateral. Banks are good at protecting themselves, and almost always leave equity in the property in case the asset declines in value. Therefore, it is almost impossible to fully equity strip an asset using straight bank financing. This problem becomes even more pronounced when the asset you are attempting to strip of value is art, account receivables, or other assets which tend to have values that are more difficult to discern or that can fluctuate dramatically over time. With certain assets, a bank will simply refuse to extend you a loan. I'll refer to this as the "Underfinanced Property Problem."

Fourth, if you are like most people I know, you typically hope your assets will grow in value over time. If Barney and Betty had the good fortune to have their property grow to $1,300,000 before Fred and Wilma obtained their judgement, Barney and Betty would have $350,000 of unprotected equity in their property which Fred and Wilma could seize. In addition to the "problem" of increasing asset value, unless the loan is an "interest only loan," the principal balance of most bank loans will be decreased over time. This also contributes to growing unprotected equity in the "stripped asset." Therefore, if you plan to equity strip an asset, as time passes you need to pay attention to (i) the assets value, and (ii) the principal balance under the loan. As the equity growth becomes substantial over time, you may want to strip the additional equity. I'll refer to this as the "Growing Equity Problem."

Fifth, your credit rating will affect your ability to use bank loans to equity strip an asset. Obviously, if your credit score is too low, finding a loan at an affordable interest rate may prove to be difficult or impossible. In addition, depending on your net worth and income, every time a bank loans you money, you may be reducing your ability to obtain additional financing for any purpose in the future. Most banks base their decision as to whether or not to extend credit to someone on certain mathematical ratios. Once your total debt reaches a certain level, your ratios will cease to fall within the acceptable range and the banks will start rejecting your loan applications. Therefore, there is often a limit on how much value you can strip from your assets using traditional bank loans. I'll call this the "Credit Limit Problem."

As you can see from the above explanation, there are at least five separate issues you need to contend with if you intend to equity strip an asset using traditional bank financing.

Friendly Financing. Assuming using a traditional bank loan is not feasible given your particular fact and circumstances (e.g., to expensive, cannot obtain large enough loan to adequately protect asset, dealing with a non-traditional asset that banks will not lend money against, etc.), you may have other options to strip that assets equity. These options (described below), typically involve private companies, trusts, and friendly individuals. Many of the problems associated with traditional bank financing (i.e., the Cost Problem, the Underfinanced Property Problem, and the Credit Limit Problem) can be reduced or eliminated by using these non-traditional methods to equity strip an asset. Please keep in mind, however, that you can push the limits of these non-traditional methods to a point where they may cease to be effective. A balance must be struck between benefit to you and commercial reasonableness. Remember that pigs get fat and hogs get slaughtered.

Below is a description of the non-traditional options you may want to consider:

1. Individuals. In seeking a loan to enable you to strip the equity from an asset, you may consider having a relative, close friend, or business partner make the loan. They, like the bank, would take back a mortgage or other security interest in the asset you want to equity strip. The main advantages to borrowing money from someone with a close personal relationship to you are flexibility and control. First, the terms of the loan can be tailored to suit your personal needs. For example, the loan may provide a fixed interest rate but remain an interest only loan with a balloon payment far in the future. The loan may require no payments until some time in the future or can be structured so the payments are very small. The loan can also be structured to be nonrecourse, meaning that the person making the loan can only take the property subject to the lien and cannot go after any of your other assets for repayment. They may also be willing to lend you the full value of the asset rather than some lesser percentage as is typically the case with banks. Banks usually do not extend terms like these except under extraordinary circumstances. Second, you have more control by virtue of the fact that the friendly lender is more apt to cooperate with you in the event a creditor is attempting to seize the asset. For example, if a creditor were close to obtaining a judgement against you, the friendly creditor could foreclose on the asset, accept it in full repayment of the debt owned, or seek assets above and beyond the equity stripped asset to remove even more of your assets from the reach of the creditor. The friendly lender will most likely be working with you in the background to ensure they are taking a course of action which will best suit your needs.

   I will discuss the downsides of using friendly lenders in greater detail below, however I do want to point out that you are oftentimes giving your friendly lender significant control and authority over the stripped asset. Therefore, remember that those people that you trust today may be hated by you (and vice versa) in the future. Unfortunately, money does change people so you need to take this fact of life into account when structuring the terms of the loan. If you give them too much power, you may end up with no asset to protect.

2. Closely Held Companies. Another option when equity stripping an asset is to borrow money from a legal entity that is owned and controlled by you and other friendly parties. The advantages and disadvantages of this technique are similar to those when borrowing from an individual, however, your options are more numerous and your control can be greater. Greater emphasis needs to be placed on how ownership of the legal entity is structured as well. For example, I recently spoke to a person who was quite proud of himself for equity stripping an asset by having a corporation of his make the loan against the asset. He had done this himself with no outside help and, unfortunately, it showed. There were several problems with his structure but the biggest one was that he owned 100% of the corporation that extended the financing. Therefore, if someone obtained a judgement against him (which was quite possible in his case since he only came to see me well after a law suit had been filed against him), they could take his 100% stock ownership in the corporation and the asset which was supposedly stripped. His was a classic case of out of the frying pan and into the fire.

   In addition, the business entity making the loan must (i) be properly formed, (ii) have a legitimate business purpose, and (iii) be authorized to engage in lending transactions. The transaction also needs to make sense from a business perspective, otherwise the court considers the whole transaction a sham. None of these hurdles are insurmountable, however, careful and thoughtful attention must be given to all surrounding facts and circumstances before jumping ahead to the loan. If the entity is properly established with the right legal agreements in place, the ownership interests are structured intelligently, and the loan transaction takes into account the relevant facts and circumstances, using a closely held company to strip an assets equity can be an effective asset protection tool.

3. The Bank Front. This is simply a variation on the closely held company option. First, you first take out a loan from a bank (i.e., a well known, unrelated lending institution) which takes back a security interest in the asset whose

equity you want to strip. Next, you ask the bank to sell your loan to your closely held company (this should obviously be prenegotiated with the bank). The bank, of course, wants to profit from the sale of the loan, so there is some costs involved. Once the purchase is completed, all the creditor will be able to find on the public records is the original mortgage issued by the bank. This technique gives the outward appearance of a true, third party loan, with the flexibility of a private loan.

Note that the benefits of this technique are really quite small if a judgement is actually obtained by a creditor. This is because with a judgement in hand, the creditor will have little problem finding the closely held entity that now holds the loan. This does not mean it will not be effective, just that it will not be more effective than using a straight closely held company without the bank. I have found that it is typically not worth the effort given the inherent difficulties in implementing it. Some of the biggest hurdles are practical ones. Most of the large banks are so bureaucratic these days that finding a person with authority to sell you the loan is nearly impossible. In addition, the banks are so heavily regulated by our government that the bank lawyers, in my experience, almost always take the most conservative path which does not include selling loans to people or small companies with no history of buying commercial loans and with whom they have no established relationship. Although it probably goes without saying, your ownership interest in the private company that buys the loan from the bank (if you are successful in doing so) must be protected from creditors.

4. Trusts. One of the best options you have in seeking a funding source for an "equity strip loan" is a trust. This could be (i) a trust that your parents, grandparents, spouse, etc. created for your benefit, (ii) a trust you have created for your spouse, children, etc., (iii) or a domestic or foreign Self-Settled Trust. If you and/or your spouse and children are the beneficiary(ies) of such a trust and the trust has been drafted to the beneficiaries with asset protection, then (i) all of the interest paid under the loan ultimately benefits you and/or your family, (ii) and if the loan is ever called and the asset is taken by the lender (i.e., the trust), the asset then again continues to benefit you and your loved ones. Furthermore, if the trust is drafted to be a Grantor Trust (a special type of trust that is ignored for income tax purposes) then the interest paid under the note is either (i) non-taxable, or (ii) can help reduce estate taxes (this will

be discussed in greater detail in the section on Asset Shifting. Trusts can be wonderful estate planning and asset protection tools and when combined with equity stripping their inherent benefits can be substantially leveraged.

5. Offshore Planning Option. As was briefly discussed in the last Chapter on Foreign Asset Protection Planning, some foreign financial institutions will lend you money and take back a mortgage on certain assets such as U.S. real estate, accounts receivable, and other Immovable Assets. The loan proceeds are held in your offshore asset protection trust which are also subject to a lien held by the foreign bank making the loan. This means that if the foreign bank makes a loan of $1,000,000, it has $2,000,000 of collateral to collect against (i.e., the asset being equity stripped and the account held in your offshore asset protection trust). The interest rate earned by the loan proceeds held in the offshore trust is typically structured to be slightly higher than the interest rate on the loan, however, after all of the costs associated with the transaction are taken into account, the net cost is typically between 0.5% and 0.7% of the money borrowed. Therefore, after the transaction is complete, the Immovable Assets are subject to the lien of the foreign financial institution and not available to the claims of creditors. If a potential creditor searches the public record, they will see the lien and may decide to settle or not bring suit rather than having to pay the legal fees to try and reach the encumbered asset. As stated before, I do not know of a situation where this has ever been tested, however, a creditor may be able to successfully argue that the foreign creditor's lien should be ignored because the foreign financial institution is over collateralized (i.e, in collecting its money it has the right to foreclose on both the Immovable Asset and the money in the offshore trust). How will the creditor ultimately be able to understand the structure and the fact that the offshore financial institution is over collateralized? Because when you are questioned about it under oath you will tell the truth. There will also be additional means for the creditor to discover this information even if you were to take Mr. Lawrence's lead (remember the Lawrence case from the last Chapter) and be "shockingly less than candid" with the court. Given that it is arguably less expensive than a conventional loan from a U.S. financial institution, it may still be a viable option, but it is certainly not without risk if ever tested.

The Problem of Related Parties.

While "friendly financing" arrangements offer increased flexibility, lower costs, and more control, they are not without certain downsides. These are discussed below.

1. Friendly Party Must Have Money to Lend. The first hurdle to overcome in any friendly financing arrangement is that the friendly party, whether it is an individual, legal entity, or trust, must have the money to lend in the first place. Oftentimes this poses no problem since a parent, grandparent, existing business, or trust has plenty of money to lend and your relationship with them is strong. If you are not so lucky, however, your only option may be traditional equity stripping using commercial financing. Many people in this situation, propose just signing a note with no corresponding transfer of actual cash. Unfortunately, this is easily discovered by a creditor and if no money has actually been lent, the corresponding lien will simply not exist regardless of what any paperwork may say. In other words, if money has not actually been lent, friendly equity stripping does not work.

2. Must Trust the Lender. The second major hurdle to overcome when friendly parties are making the equity strip loan, is that you need to trust the people who have ultimate control over the loan. If a friend or family member is able to increase your payments, demand full payment of the loan, impede your ability to enjoy the asset, or otherwise exercise control over the stripped asset, they may do so to further their own interests rather than yours. Remember that any plea in the future that you are being taken advantage of will probably not hold much weight if the legal documents creating the lien have been properly drafted (which is the whole idea in the first place). Therefore, if the asset being stripped is important to you (i.e., land that has been in the family for generations, etc.), unless you have a high degree of certainty that the friendly lender will act honestly and in your best interest, do not use them to equity strip the asset.

3. Heightened Scrutiny. Anytime a transaction occurs between related parties or individuals with an existing friendly relationship, the court will subject that transaction to a heightened level of scrutiny. If all the "i's" are not dotted

and the "t's" are not crossed, the whole transaction may be considered a sham transaction and prove to be completely ineffective from an asset protection standpoint.

4. Need for Clear Documentation and Keeping with Business Standards. To avoid a friendly equity strip from being considered a sham transaction, you must (i) be able to justify the loan by providing reasons for its existence other than pure asset protection, and (ii) you need to clearly document the loan and security interest to the same degree you would if you were dealing with a third party that you have a friendly relationship with. Unfortunately, I have seen people try and equity strip property without the assistance of an attorney with awful results. The loan was not properly documented, they ignored the tax consequences of the loan, they thought a note was sufficient and ignored the fact that no lien was created (or did not know how to create a proper lien), the loan had no legitimate, underlying purpose, and the list goes on and on. In short, do yourself a favor and let a qualified asset protection attorney help you create an intelligent structure that will actually work. Without a well thought out purpose and proper documentation, a friendly equity strip will simply not be respected by a court.

5. Fraudulent Transfer Concerns. Under the fraudulent transfer statutes, the term "transfer" is defined very broadly. The exact language of the statute reads as follows:

   "Transfer" means every mode, direct or indirect, absolute or conditional, voluntary or involuntary, of disposing of or parting with an asset or an interest in an asset, and includes payment of money, release, lease, and creation of a lien or other encumbrance.

   Therefore, since the law of fraudulent transfer will, at least in part, look to your motivation in making the transfer (i.e., did you make the transfer with the "actual intent to hinder, delay, or defraud any creditor"), any type of planning involving transactions between related parties will need to be carefully structured to minimize the potential fraudulent transfer issues. As mentioned above, the planning needs to take into account the personal facts and circumstances of the individuals engaging in the planning. Many will engage in related party techniques but opt for less protection because they do not want to spend the time and money creating trusts or more complex ownership structures. Again, balance is the key.

One Loan to Protect Multiple Assets.

If you already have an existing loan you may consider pledging additional assets as collateral for that existing loan. I worked with a group of physicians who had created an LLC to hold a large medical building. They had a separate corporation through which they provided medical services to their patients. The medical services company then rented office space from the real estate LLC. The physicians had taken out a several million dollar mortgage when they constructed the medical building and the bank required each physician to personally guarantee the loan. One of the assets the physician group was interested in protecting was their accounts receivable. We ended up getting the bank to take the accounts receivable and some other medical equipment as additional collateral for the loan in lieu of the physicians personal guarantees. Therefore, the physicians used a preexisting loan to protect a hard to protect asset at no additional cost to the physicians and got them released from their personal guarantees to boot. If you have existing debt, you may be able to use it to your benefit in protecting assets if the circumstances are right.

Equity Shifting

The next topic I want to cover in this Chapter is Equity Shifting. As mentioned above, equity shifting involves structuring the ownership of an asset or business entity so that any resulting cash flow and/or appreciation end up in a "protected place." While its name sounds similar to equity stripping, the concepts are very different. The best way to describe equity shifting is through an example.

> Assume Dilbert Pickles and Tom A. Toe are both real estate developers in Suwanee county Florida. Dilbert locates a parcel of property which he is sure will produce a huge profit after it is developed. Dilbert forms Pickles Property, LLC, and purchases the property for $1,000,000 in the name of the LLC. Pickles Property, LLC, is owned 100% by Dilbert. The total cost to

develop the property was $500,000. Dilbert was correct in his assumptions as to the profitability of the project and as the development came close to completion, Dilbert was elated. Unfortunately for Dilbert, with just weeks to go until his big payday, Dilbert was sued in connection with a past business deal. With the law suit filed and 100% of Pickles Property, LLC, held by him individually, things were not looking good for old Dil. The profit from the sale of the property was going to be $2,000,000 and it looked as though he was going to lose it all.

Tom also located a parcel of property with huge profit potential. Like Dilbert, the cost of the property was $1,000,000. Tom also planned to purchase the property in an LLC which he intends to call Red Toe Holdings, LLC. Here is where Tom did things a little differently. Tom had purchased a copy of this book and quickly became the brightest person in Suwanee County as he ingested the book's wisdom. He was surprised to find this example (given the fact that his name was Tom A. Toe), but decided to follow its advice. Tom first created a trust for the benefit of his lovely wife, Tanya Toe, and his five strapping boys. Tom then made a gift of $100,000 to the trust. The trust then created Red Toe Holdings, LLC, and contributed the $100,000 previously gifted to it by Tom to the new LLC. The Toe Family Trust, now owned 100% of the LLC and named Tom as the LLC's sole manger. Tom and Tanya then loaned the LLC $1,400,000 ($900,000 to enable the LLC to purchase the property and $500,000 to cover the costs of development) and held the note as Tenants by the Entireties. Tom's venture was also a huge success and as the project was nearing completion, Tom found a buyer for the developed property who was willing to pay Tom's asking price of $3,500,000. Tom was then named in a law suit similar to that of Dilbert. Fortunately, Tom had previously taken steps to protect his other assets and the profits from his Red Toe real estate project were also protected. When the property was sold, the LLC received a check for $3,500,000. It then paid its debt of $1,400,000 to Tom and Tanya, which was protected by Tenants by the Entireties. The remaining $2,100,000 was

> held in the Toe Family Trust which was also protected. Tom's creditors eventually dropped their law suit seeing no assets available to collect.

In the above two examples, you can see how Tom effectively shifted the future profits from his real estate project to a protected trust. An additional bonus was that the full $2,100,000 was shifted out of his taxable estate for estate tax purposes despite the fact that the only gift made by Tom was $100,000. If Tom decides to develop another parcel of land, he now has $2,100,000 to fund a new LLC. Assuming the cost of the new venture is similar to the last, no loan will be needed and the full profits will again accrue to his protected trust.

Equity Shifting should also be considered when starting any new business. For example, I know someone that invested $200,000 in a business he sold less than ten years later for over $15,000,000. The majority of the ownership interests in the LLC had been transferred to a trust prior to the company realizing any significant growth, so when the company was sold the sales proceeds were both asset protected and able to pass to his children free of estate taxes.

> Now think about someone who starts a business that produces significant annual cash flow. By transferring most of the ownership interests in the LLC to a protected trust when the company is first formed (and, therefore, not worth much), very little of their gift tax credit is used. Each year that cash is distributed from the company, most or all of it flows into a protected trust. This has tax benefits, since medicare taxes are saved, and asset protection benefits since distributions are not protected like wages are (see Chapter 11 on protecting your wages for more detail).

These are just a few examples of how equity shifting can be a valuable part of your asset protection, estate tax, and income tax planning. The above examples were simplistic by design for educational purposes, however, there are numerous versions of the equity shifting technique that can produce significant benefits in a number of circumstances. One such technique that deserves a brief discussion is the "Discounted IDIT Sale."

The Discounted IDIT Sale.

The Discounted IDIT Sale is a sophisticated technique that can provide substantial estate tax savings and decrease potential creditors' ability to reach your assets. The paragraphs that follow are designed to give you an overview of how and why the technique works. Whether it may make sense for you will depend on your individual facts and circumstances. If you have any questions as to whether it can provide you with benefits, please feel free to contact my office.

You have already seen the advantages of equity shifting, however, before moving on it is important to understand some of the additional benefits you derive from engaging in this more sophisticated technique. The Discounted IDIT Sale technique accomplishes two principal goals (however other benefits exist as well). First, through the use of a Family Limited Partnership (sometimes called an "FLP"), the assets being used in the transaction are "discounted," or, in other words, made less valuable for estate and gift tax purposes. Discounts typically range from 30% to 40%. Second, the discounted value is "frozen," so that the lion's share of the assets' future income and appreciation are shifted to a trust which benefits your family (and even yourself), and which is not included in your estate for estate tax purposes. Over time, depending on the rate at which the assets grow, a significant amount of wealth can be passed free of estate tax and protected from the claims of creditors. Again, an example may prove helpful.

> For example, assume the Discounted IDIT Sale technique is established by Rick O'Shea, a 55 year old, using $1,000,000. Further assume the $1,000,000 in assets experience annual growth of 10% and the Discounted IDIT Sale was established in today's relatively low interest rate environment. First, Rick creates a Family Limited Partnership (an "FLP") and transfers the $1,000,000 in assets to the FLP. Rick owns a 1% general partnership interest which enables him to control the activities of the FLP. Rick then establishes the IDIT which benefits Rick and his family. A small gift of 10% of the non-voting limited partnership interests is then made to the IDIT and Rick sells the balance of the limited partnership interests to the IDIT in exchange for an interest only promissory note. The promissory note pays a low interest rate and the debt is forgiven if Rick dies

during the term of the note (typically something just short of Rick's actuarial life expectancy). Over time, Rick receives interest payments from the IDIT.

Lets pause a second to look at the numbers. The total value of the 99% limited partnership interests that have wound up in the trust is not $990,000 (i.e., 99% of $1,000,000) but rather $643,500 (i.e., 99% of $650,000). The $650,000 figure is $1,000,000 less a 35% discount. Therefore, Rick's 10% gift of limited partnership interests is not $99,000 (i.e., 10% of $990,000) but rather $64,350 (i.e., 10% of $643,500). The principal balance of the promissory note is not $891,000 (i.e., 90% of $990,000) but rather $579,150 (i.e., 90% of $643,500).

If the promissory note pays 5% (remember this is 5% of $579,150), and the assets in the IDIT/FLP earn 10% (remember that this is 10% of the whole undiscounted $990,000), the difference of $70,043 in the first year alone, accrues to the IDIT. While this may not seem monumental, after 10 years the value of the trust is over $2,000,000; after 20 years, the trusts value is over $5,000,000; and at Rick's life expectancy in year 29, the value of the trust is roughly $11,400,000. Remember that Rick only used $64,350 of his $1,000,000 gift tax credit and an equal amount of his $2,000,000 generation skipping tax exemption. If Rick dies in year 29, then the principal balance of the promissory note (i.e., $579,150) is paid to his estate leaving close to $11,000,000 to pass down to children free of estate tax. In fact, the trust assets can pass from generation to generation without ever being subject to estate tax again. If Rick dies before year 29, the note is forgiven and the trust does not have to pay the $579,150. In addition, all of these assets are protected from creditors, Rick's creditors, his wife's creditors, and the creditors of his kids, grandkids, etc. forever.

If Rick or his family needed assets from the trust during Rick's life, the assets in the trust are accessible. Rick has received note interest from the trust over the years, and given the fact that Rick was also required to pay the income tax on trust income, he has probably been able to shrink his taxable estate and the corresponding estate tax.

Again, the numbers have to crunch and whether this technique is worth implementing will depend on the individual's personal facts and circumstances. As you can see, however, the Discounted IDIT Sale technique is an asset protection technique that can produce significant estate tax benefits.

Conclusion.

Both equity stripping and equity shifting can be excellent asset protection techniques in certain circumstances. If you understand how they work and their corresponding upsides and downsides, each of these techniques can play an important part of your overall asset protection plan.

CHAPTER 22

Protecting Practice Assets

In this Chapter I will discuss some methods of protecting the assets of your medical practice (including the accounts receivable) from the claims of a medical malpractice creditor. I start by discussing the two primary classes of practice assets (i.e., "Movable" assets and "Immovable" assets) and some of the methods to protect each of these classes of assets. I will also explain an "accounts receivable protection strategy" utilizing a bank loan and life insurance products that is being heavily marketed to physicians. It is my opinion that this strategy will most likely not be protective and has many potential downsides which are not being adequately explained by its promoters. Finally, I will discuss the issues involved in closing a physician practice and opening a new practice when the old practice may be subject to liability stemming from a potential medical malpractice judgement. Specifically, I will address the issue of whether a creditor with a judgement against the old practice can enforce it against the new practice. Unfortunately, protecting practice assets is one of the more difficult areas of asset protection planning, however, there are some significant steps that can be taken to ensure that practice assets remain safe.

Protecting Practice Assets.

When a physician is sued for medical malpractice, the legal entity housing the medical practice is almost always named in the law suit as well. For ease of discussion, I will assume for purposes of this Chapter the entity housing a physician's medical practice is a professional corporation (i.e., a "PA"). Therefore, in the event a physician is sued for medical malpractice and the plaintiff is successful in obtaining a judgement, the judgement can typically be enforced against both the physician and the PA. If the PA has significant assets, even if the physician has taken steps to protect his or her personal wealth, the assets of the PA remain at risk. In order to understand how to protect the corporate assets, it is necessary to first make a distinction between two broad classes of assets, namely "Movable Assets" and "Immovable Assets." Each of these types of assets are discussed below.

Movable Assets.

As mentioned above, when looking to protect entity assets, it is best to separate assets into two basic categories, "Movable Assets" and "Immovable Assets." Movable Assets are simply assets that can be retitled (or "moved") to a person or entity other than the PA.

An example of a Movable Asset would be a building that houses the medical practice. If the building were titled in the name of the PA and the PA were subject to a judgement, the building could be seized by the judgement creditor. Since the building is a Movable Asset, however, it is relatively easy to protect it from the claims of creditors. For example, the building could be transferred to a separate LLC or limited partnership and that entity could then lease the property back to the PA. If the PA is later sued, the judgement creditor is unable to reach the building because it is no longer owned by the PA.

Other examples of Moveable Assets are medical equipment, furniture, computers, etc. As a practical matter, assets such as computers and office equipment are usually not very attractive to a creditor due to the fact that there is typically very little resale value with respect to these assets and the cost of collecting, storing, and selling them oftentimes exceeds their value. If the only Movable Assets of a PA are these relatively inexpensive, and, therefore, unattractive, assets, the costs and inconveniences of trying to move them to another legal entity is not terribly practicable.

On the other hand, if these assets had significant value, or if you had previously moved the building from the PA to a separate LLC (or if you were wise enough to do that from the beginning), you may want to consider moving those assets to the LLC holding the building and include them as part of the lease discussed above.

There is a downside, however, to holding assets in a separate legal entity and leasing them to the PA. Under Florida law, lease payments are subject to sales tax. Therefore, if the fair rental value of the office building was $2,000 per month, assuming the sales tax was 6.5%, the cost of protecting the movable assets would be $1,560 per year. (i.e., $2,000 x 12 months = $24,000 per year x 6.5% sales tax = $1,560). Most physicians, however, feel that this is a relatively small price to pay to keep these assets out of the reach of a would be creditor. There may also be authority to avoid paying sales tax at all if the separate entity simply lets the PA use the property, however, whether or not this would apply to you will depend on your facts and circumstances. Additional costs would also include the cost to create and manage another legal entity, but again, in today's litigious society, most physicians feel that this is a small cost to protect the real estate that houses its practice.

If you decide to hold the Movable Assets used by the medical practice in a separate LLC (I will call this type of entity the "Movable Asset Company" or "MA Company" for short) as detailed above and lease them to the PA, it is also important to consider how the MA Company should be owned. Each physician with an ownership interest in the MA Company will need to incorporate the ownership interest into their personal asset protection plan. Since the MA Company will be receiving rent and assumably the rent will be paid out to the owners of the MA Company, you will also need to consider how to protect the cash flow. For example, perhaps a lower risk spouse will own the ownership interest, maybe the physician will own it with their spouse as tenants by the entireties, or maybe a protective trust such as a FAPT or DAPT will hold the interest. Given the relative ease and low cost of protecting Movable Assets, incorporating the equivalent of an MA Company into your comprehensive asset protection plan should be given serious consideration.

Immovable Assets.

The second asset category, Immovable Assets, are assets that are difficult to move to another legal entity such as accounts receivable. In the previous Chapter we discussed equity stripping in the non-business context. With Immovable Assets held in your business, the primary strategy is also to equity strip the assets, however, there are some additional twists. Therefore, at the risk of being a little redundant, I will go over equity stripping in the business context. Remember that when you equity strip Immovable Assets, you "lien" or "encumber" those assets by pledging them as collateral for a loan or obligation made to the company by another person or legal entity (the "Secured Creditor"). Since the Secured Creditor has the first right to those assets, they are generally not available to satisfy the claims of other creditors such as a judgement creditor who sued for medical malpractice. Below I will discuss several ways to lien Immovable Assets. As with every other asset protection technique discussed in this book, there are upsides and downsides to each technique discussed below.

Bank Loan. Probably the most secure way to lien Immovable Assets is to borrow money from a bank or other financial institution and pledge the Immovable Assets as collateral for the loan. Because an independent, third party bank has a lien on the PA's Immovable Assets, it would be very hard for a creditor to argue that the lien should not be respected and that the creditor should be allowed to reach the assets. Think of it this way, assume you buy a new vacation home for $200,000. You put $20,000 down and take out a mortgage for the balance of $180,000. Assume you are sued and the creditor obtains a $1,000,000 judgement against you. The creditor may be able to force the sale of the vacation home, but the bank will get paid its $180,000 before the creditor receives a thing. The same would hold true with respect to the bank's loan to the PA secured by its Immovable Assets.

Unfortunately, there are several downsides to this technique. First, when the bank loans the PA money, the PA now owns the loan proceeds.

> Assume that Dr. Jones, Dr. Smith, Dr. Anderson, and Dr. Geidvilai…ciai, are all partners in Advanced Medical Specialists, PA (referred to as "AMS" for short). AMS has average collectible accounts receivable of $500,000. AMS goes to Local Bank and borrows $500,000 and pledges its accounts receivable as collateral for the loan. After the loan is complete, AMS has $500,000 in cash. In order for Local Bank to "perfect" its lien on AMS' Immovable Assets (to "perfect" a lien means to make it enforceable), a Form UCC-1 will be filed with the Florida Department of State. This form puts the world on notice that the assets described in the Form UCC-1 have already been pledged to someone as collateral and that any new creditor may not be

> available to satisfy their claims from those assets. If a potential creditor sees that AMS' assets are all pledged as collateral for one or more sizable loans, they will typically have a big incentive to settle for less than 100 cents on the dollar (or not to sue in the first place).

The first and most obvious downside is the cost associated with the technique due to the interest payment on the loan. In the event AMS were able to get an interest rate of 7% on the loan, the cost of protecting AMS' Immovable Assets would be $35,000 per year. It is possible that the interest payments would be deductible for federal income tax purposes depending on how the loan proceeds are spent, however, this is still a pretty expensive asset protection technique considering that you continue to pay interest for as long as the loan is in place. Even though interest rates are relatively low as of the date of this book, in the event interest rates go up in the future (which they very well may), this technique becomes even more expensive.

Next, if AMS were subject to a judgement just after the loan transaction were complete, there would be no asset protection because the creditor could take the $500,000 in cash (i.e., the loan proceeds). In order to protect the cash, AMS either needs to spend it or distribute it to its shareholders. In most cases, a medical group does not have expenses large enough to spend down the entire loan proceeds. In addition, most physicians want the money distributed to them so that they can invest it to help offset the interest that is being paid on the bank loan. The problem is that in the vast majority of the cases, when the money is distributed from the PA to the physician owners, it will be taxable to them. Therefore, if the entire $500,000 were taxable to the physicians upon being distributed, assuming it was taxed at an average tax rate of 30%, the physicians end up will only $350,000 after tax to reinvest. That means that in order to break even on the interest payments (remember that the annual interest expense is $35,000), the physicians will have to earn a full 10%. This number may be slightly less if the interest payments by the PA are tax deductible, however, losing $150,000 right from the start is not typically something that people are happy to hear. When the physicians decide to pay off the loan in the future, they will need to come up with the extra $150,000. Also remember that even if the interest payments are deductible (which they may not be), principal payments are not.

Bank Loan to Shareholders. One possible way around the problem of the taxable distribution would be for each physician to borrow money from a bank or financial institution personally and have the PA pledge its Immovable Assets as collateral for the loan as a benefit to the physicians. Using the example above, each of the four physicians would borrow $125,000 (i.e., $500,000 ÷ 4 physicians = $125,000). AMS would pledge its Immovable Assets including its accounts receivable as collateral for the loan. Since these are now personal loans, the interest is no longer deductible, however, the loan proceeds do not have to be distributed from the PA so the taxability problem discussed in the last example will not apply. If you decided to use this structure to protect your PA's Immovable Assets, you will want the loan documents to require the bank to first collect against the Immovable Assets and then collect from the physicians. Many banks will not do this (especially the big bureaucratic banks). If the bank can collect on the loan from either the physicians or the Immovable Assets, a court may order the bank to first collect what it can from the physicians first and only then to collect against the Immovable Assets. This would leave the physicians with a large interest expense and no asset protection. Another downside to this technique is that if a physician were to leave the PA and not repay his or her portion of the loan, the PA's assets are still at risk if the departing physician were to default on the loan.

Offshore Planning Option. As was briefly discussed in the last Chapter on Foreign Asset Protection Planning, some foreign financial institutions will lend you money and take back a mortgage on certain assets such as U.S. real estate or accounts receivable and other Immovable Assets. The loan proceeds are then held in the physicians' offshore asset protection trusts. The interest rate earned by the loan proceeds held in the offshore trusts is typically structured to be slightly higher than the interest rate on the loan, however, after all of the costs associated with the transaction are taken into account, the net cost is typically between 0.5% and 0.7% of the money borrowed. Therefore, after the transaction is complete, the PA's Immovable Assets are subject to the lien of the foreign financial institution and not available to the claims of creditors. If a potential creditor searches the public record, they will see the Form UCC-1 and may decide to settle or not bring suit rather than having to pay the legal fees to try and reach the encumbered Immovable Assets. As stated before, I do not know of a situation where this has ever been tested, however, a creditor may be able to successfully argue that the lien imposed by the secured loan should be ignored because the foreign financial institution is over collateralized (i.e, in collecting its money it has the right to foreclose on both the Immovable Assets and the money in the offshore trusts). The creditor will ultimately be able to understand the structure and the fact that the offshore financial institution is over collateralized because when you are questioned about it you will tell the truth. There will also be additional means for the creditor to discover this information even if you were to take Mr. Lawrence's lead (remember the **Lawrence** case from the last Chapter) and be "shockingly less than candid" with the court. Given that it is arguably less expensive than a conventional loan from a U.S. financial institution, it may still be a viable option, but it is certainly not without risk if ever tested.

Immovable Assets Pledged as Collateral for Building Loan. Going back to the example of AMS, assume the four physicians had established an MA Company to own the real estate that housed its practice. If the building owned by the MA Company is currently mortgaged, the physician owners of the MA Company are most likely personally liable to pay the mortgage upon a default. Therefore, the shareholders of AMS may want to consider pledging AMS' Immovable Assets as additional security for the mortgage. Again, the physicians would want the bank to agree that in the event of a default, they will first accept AMS' Immovable Assets as payment to reduce the debt owed to it, and once those assets are gone, to then foreclose on the property itself, and finally collect on the personal guarantees of the physicians as the last resort. As with the bank loans discussed above, the bank will file a Form UCC-1 to "perfect" its interest in the Immovable Assets. If a potential creditor sees that AMS' assets are all pledged as collateral for one or more sizable loans, they will typically have a big incentive to settle for less than 100 cents on the dollar (or not to sue in the first place).

The principal upside to this technique is that you are liening the PA's Immovable Assets using a preexisting debt, therefore, you are not incurring any additional interest costs and the public record shows the PA's assets being pledged as collateral to a known financial institution. The primary downside to this technique is the problem of the over secured creditor mentioned above in the context of the offshore planning option. Even if the mortgage documents establish that the bank must first exercise reasonable diligence in collecting the Immovable Assets before moving against any other collateral, a creditor will likely try and argue that the lien against the Immovable Assets should be disregarded because the creditor will still be adequately collateralized. There are good arguments why this should not be the case, however, this is still a risk.

Secured Lease Agreement with MA Company. Another possible way to lien a PA's Immovable Assets again involves an MA Company owning real estate or other assets that are being leased to the PA. The lease agreement between the MA Company and the PA can be drafted to provide for a lease term of ten or fifteen years and further provide for a penalty to be paid by the PA (the tenant) to the MA Company (the landlord) in the event the PA ever defaults under the lease. In addition, the MA Company will be able to "accelerate" the lease and demand that the PA pay all remaining payments due under the lease. This will be coupled by a pledge by the PA of its accounts receivable and other Immovable Assets as security for its obligations under the lease. As with the bank loans discussed above, in order for the MA Company to "perfect" its lien on the PA's Immovable Assets, a Form UCC-1 will be filed with the Florida Department of State thereby putting the world on notice that these assets have already been pledged to someone as collateral and that they may not be available to satisfy their claims if they become a creditor of the PA. In the event the PA is ever sued and the owners decide to wind down the PA and form a successor entity (this is discussed below), the assets of the PA can be used to settle the amount due under the lease which should not be considered a fraudulent transfer since the PA is paying a secured creditor.

The upside to this transaction is that the cost is very small since, unlike a loan that bears interest, there is no similar ongoing expense associated with a secured lease. A downside to this technique is that the lease agreement is with an entity that has a similar ownership. This topic will be discussed in greater detail below. An additional downside is that when someone defaults under a lease and the landlord demands all of the remaining payments due under the lease, the landlord is required to exercise reasonable diligence in finding a replacement tenant to mitigate the loss to the defaulting tenant. In other words, a landlord cannot require the tenant to pay fifteen years worth of rent upon default, pocket the money, and then turn around and lease the property to a new tenant. This would be an impermissible windfall to the landlord. Therefore, while this technique has the potential to protect some of the practice assets, it is unrealistic to believe that assets equal to the sum of fifteen years of rent payments will be protected.

Yet another factor to take into consideration is whether the economics make sense. If there are four physicians in a medical practice, but only two of those physicians own an interest in the MA Company, the two physicians without any ownership in the MA Company may not be thrilled to see the PA's Immovable Assets leaving the PA and going to the MA Company.

Secured Severance Pay Package. Another means to lien a PA's accounts receivable and other Immovable Assets is to securitize any obligation the PA may have to provide a physician who has terminated service with the PA with severance benefits. Under many employment contracts, when a physician terminates service with the PA that employs them, they are entitled to receive something roughly equivalent to their share of the collectable accounts receivable received by the PA within a certain period of time following the date of termination. The right to receive these payments under their employment contract could be secured by the PA's Immovable Assets. Similar to the other techniques discussed before, a Form UCC-1 would be filed to put the world on notice of this security interest. There are income tax considerations that need to be taken into account if you plan to use this technique that are beyond the scope of this book, however, your attorney or tax professional will be able to discuss them with you.

The first upside to this technique is that there is no interest cost associated with it unlike the bank loan techniques. Another upside is that at least one case (i.e., **Matter of Southmark**) has held that the payment of severance benefits under certain circumstances may not be treated as a preferential payment in the bankruptcy context and, therefore, is not subject to being pulled back to satisfy the claims of other creditors. Again, the issue of payments to related parties may apply which is discussed below.

Fund Pension Plan in Arrears. Under many pension plans, the obligation to fund the plan can be deferred to the following year. If this is done by a PA, in the event the PA is ever sued and the owners decide to wind down the PA and form a successor entity (this is discussed below), the assets of the PA can be used to fulfill the obligation to fund the pension plan which should not be considered a fraudulent transfer. Again, this is a way to remove assets from the claims of a potential judgement creditor.

Partner Loans. In the event a PA has borrowed money from any of the partners, the loan(s) should be documented using promissory notes and secured by practice assets. If the PA is ever sued, the notes could be paid off thereby depleting the assets of the PA. As you may remember from reading Chapter 5, one type of fraudulent transfer is the payment by a person or company (e.g., the PA) of antecedent (i.e., preexisting) debt to an insider (e.g., an owner of a corporation, LLC, etc.). You probably also remember that there is a shorter, one year, statute of limitations for this type of fraudulent transfer rather than the more typical statute of limitations of (a) four years after the transfer was made, or (b) one year after the transfer was or could reasonably have been discovered by the creditor (this last part, (b), is oftentimes referred to as a 'savings clause'). In the recent (November, 2003) case of **Paragon Health Services, Inc. v. Central Palm Beach Community Mental Health Center, Inc.**, a company had paid antecedent debt to its shareholders after being named in a law suit and by the time the creditor asserted its fraudulent transfer claim, more than one year had elapsed. The creditor tried to argue that they should not be barred in asserting their fraudulent transfer claim by this shorter statute of limitations and that a one year 'savings clause' should apply. The court, however, held that no savings clause was allowed and the creditor was time barred by the applicable one year statute of limitations. This being the case, unless the creditor acts quickly, which it may not be able to do, if the company pays off debts to partners/shareholders it will be difficult to set aside as a fraudulent transfer.

Establish a Management Company. Another possible means to protect practice assets (not only Immovable Assets) is to establish a management company that holds all of the practice equipment and which also holds all of the non-physician employees. The PA then pays the management company to provide it with the services of the support staff, billing services, and other managerial services. The only employees of the PA end up being the physicians and the only real assets of the PA are its accounts receivable and patient files. A complete discussion of all the nuances of this technique are beyond the scope of this book, however, in the event it is properly implemented, it can provide a significant benefit beyond asset protection. As will be explained at the end of this Chapter, if a PA is sued and the owners decide to close its business as part of the plan to protect practice assets, they may very well want to establish a successor PA. The use of a management company can be helpful in doing so by minimizing the likelihood of the new PA being held responsible for the liability of the old PA.

General Downsides to Liening Immovable Assets.

While liening assets may have benefits from an asset protection standpoint, there are also some downsides that must be taken into consideration before a PA decides to do so. Some of these are listed below.

Future Difficulty Borrowing Money. A common downside to any technique that liens Immovable Assets is that the PA will have less available assets when seeking financing from other potential lenders. If the PA does not foresee the need to borrow a large sum of money in the ordinary course of its business, this should not be a major concern. If it does, on the other hand, it will need to take this fact into consideration in deciding whether or not to use one of these techniques. When the lien stems from a lease agreement with an MA Company or in the context of secured severance obligations, it may be possible for the secured party to agree to subordinate their rights to a new creditor (i.e., agree to give the new creditor the right to take the assets before them).

Limited Protection. If a PA's Immovable Assets are greater than the amount of the secured obligations, the assets above that amount will be subject to the claims of creditors. For example, using the example of AMS described above, if Local Bank lends AMS $500,000 secured by their Immovable Assets, over time the loan will be paid down. Assume that three years into the loan the outstanding balance is $300,000. If the Immovable Assets hold their value or increase in value (i.e., assume they are now worth $600,000), the lien imposed by the loan only protects half the value of AMS' Immovable Assets.

The Problem of Related Parties. Anytime a transaction occurs between related parties, the court will subject that transaction to a heightened level of scrutiny. In addition, there are fraudulent transfer issues that need to be examined. Before proceeding lets go back to the example of AMS.

> Assume the physician owners of AMS form a separate MA Company to hold the building that houses its medical practice. The MA Company enters into a fifteen year lease agreement with AMS that provides for total rent in the amount of $600,000 to be paid in monthly installments of $3,333.33 over the term of the lease. In the event AMS ever defaults under the lease agreement, a penalty is to be paid and the MA Company can demand the outstanding rent due under the lease agreement. AMS pledges their Immovable Assets as security for their obligations under the lease to protect the MA Company in the event

> of default. If the default occurs, AMS will consider winding down its practice, paying off its debts (including its obligation to the MA Company under the lease), and distributing whatever is left to the owners. The entity would, therefore, have nothing left for a creditor to reach. The physicians then could consider forming a new practice (this is discussed below), retiring, or going to work for or with different physicians.

You may remember from reading Chapter 5 on Fraudulent Transfers a couple hundred pages earlier in this book, that with respect to a "present" creditor, the definition of fraudulent transfer includes the paying of an existing debt to an "insider" if the person paying off the debt was insolvent at that time, and the "insider" had reasonable cause to believe that the person was insolvent at the time. The definition of "insider" under the statute is drafted very broadly to include many "related parties." For example, the statute states that if a corporation is the one paying off a debt, the term insider includes:

1. A director of the corporation;
2. An officer of the corporation;
3. A person in control of the corporation;
4. A partnership in which the corporation is a general partner;
5. A general partner in a partnership described in subparagraph 4; or
6. A relative of a general partner, director, officer, or person in control of the corporation.

These examples of who is an "insider" provided in the statute are not exclusive. In other words, it is possible that someone or some entity not included in the above list would also be considered an insider.

Therefore, when deciding who should own the MA Company, it is best to avoid having it owned by the exact same people who own the PA because the MA Company would be much more likely to be considered an insider. If that was the case, then the payment by the PA to the MA Company could be disregarded altogether as a fraudulent transfer and the money paid to the MA Company could be reached by a creditor of the PA.

Therefore, from a pure asset protection perspective, a disparate ownership structure when comparing the MA Company to the PA would be more effective because it would be significantly more difficult for a creditor to argue that the secured lease arrangement lacked economic merit and should be set aside as a payment to an "insider." For this same reason, it may be beneficial to have the physician's spouses own the MA Company. Even better would be to have some or all of the physicians establish trusts for the benefit of their spouses and or children, and have the trusts own the MA Company. In the event the MA Company is owned by individuals other than the physicians, the agreement governing the MA Company should be drafted to trigger a buyout of ownership interests in the MA Company in the event a physician terminates service with the PA.

In short, any type of planning involving transactions between related parties will need to be carefully structured to minimize the potential fraudulent transfer issues. The planning also needs to take into account the personal facts and circumstances of the individuals engaging in the planning. Many will engage in related party techniques but opt for less protection because they do not want to spend the time and money creating trusts or more complex ownership structures.

Techniques that Do Not Involve Liens.

Some techniques to protect Immovable Assets do not involve creating liens.

The Fraudulent Transfer to a Protected Homestead. This technique is best described by way of example.

> Assume Dr. Wojciechowski, Dr. Wisniewski, and Dr. Zielinski all go into practice together. They form a PA, WWZ Medical Associates, P.A., through which the practice is run. The total accounts receivable owned by the PA are $1,500,000 and are shared equally (i.e., $500,000 per physician). Further assume that each of the three physicians own their own home that qualifies for homestead protection under the Florida constitution, and each physician has an outstanding mortgage on their home of $600,000. All three doctors have already established a sound asset protection plan leaving their personal assets fully protected. Dr. Zielinski and the PA are now named in a law suit and the physicians all feel that the risk of an adverse judgement is

> high. The three physicians form a new practice (see below for a more complete discussion), and commence to liquidate WWZ Medical Associates, P.A. They collect the accounts receivable, and distribute $500,000 to each physician. Each physician, in turn, uses the money to pay down their mortgage.

Has there been a fraudulent transfer from the PA to the physicians? Yes. Has there been a fraudulent transfer with respect to the transfer of the $500,000 into their homestead. Absolutely, but remember that under the Florida Supreme Court case of **Havoco v. Hill**, the creditor can not reach the transferred assets even though the transfer was made with the specific intent to hinder, delay, and defraud the creditor. Of course, the physicians must stay out of bankruptcy given the 10 year clawback rule under the new bankruptcy act, but if they can accomplish that, the account receivables have been protected. I usually like to couple this type of planning with some of the other techniques discussed above (such as using secured employment agreements).

The Practice Level Offshore Trust. While a thorough explanation of this technique is beyond the scope of this book, a medical practice itself can establish an offshore trust and transfer account receivables to the trust. The beneficiaries of the trust can be the physicians and their families and the trust can serve to provide an additional benefit to entice physicians to continue to maintain employment with the practice. Over time, the trust can provide loans to the practice secured by new accounts receivable to provide a second layer of protection. Since the trust is structured to be ignored for income tax purposes, there is not negative tax ramifications with respect to any transfers to the trust or loans from the trust to the practice. If you are interested in learning more details about this technique, please contact me.

Planning Options I Do Not Recommend.

Next, I want to explain two additional options that I have seen people use. The first of these is problematic from both an asset protection and a federal income tax standpoint. The second is just not protective and creates a trap for the unwary.

The Accounts Receivable Financing Strategy. As I mentioned at the beginning of this Chapter, there is an "accounts receivable protection strategy" utilizing a bank loan and life insurance products that is being heavily marketed to physicians. It is my opinion that this strategy will most likely not be protective and has many potential downsides which are not being adequately explained by its promoters.

The technique starts with a bank lending money to a medical practice with the medical practice pledging their accounts receivable as collateral for the loan. The bank files a Form UCC-1 to "perfect" its interest in those accounts receivable. So far, this is the same transaction mentioned earlier on Page and under the topic heading "Bank Loan." As you will remember from that discussion, one of the problems facing a medical practice using a bank loan to lien accounts receivable will be how to get the money out to the PA's owners without causing the amount distributed to be subject to federal income tax. This technique attempts to solve that problem by having the physicians enter into a deferred compensation plan. After the medical practice receives the loan proceeds from the bank, it purchases life insurance or annuity products (I will call these the "Insurance Products") and then distributes these Insurance Products to the physicians as part of the deferred compensation plan retaining some interest in them. The cash value in the Insurance Products are pledged to the bank as additional collateral for the loan it made to the medical practice. This is a down and dirty explanation of the technique and there are several variations being promoted. All of them, however, have the same significant downsides.

First, from an asset protection standpoint you have an over collateralized creditor (i.e., the bank) so it is very likely that a judge would order the bank to collect its loan against the Insurance Products rather than the accounts receivable. Second, if that does happen, it is likely to trigger surrender penalties in the Insurance Products resulting in an economic loss to the physicians. Even if you are told that the Insurance Products have low or no surrender penalties, since a commission is being paid to the person selling the Insurance Products and all insurance policies and annuities have internal expenses, it is not possible to get back all of the money placed in these Insurance Products until several years down the road and then only if the investments in the Insurance Products perform admirably (which they may not). Third, and of significant importance, is the fact that the non-taxability of the Insurance Products distributed under the deferred compensation plan is based on something called a "significant risk of forfeiture." I do not want to get into a long discussion of the tax rules that apply to deferred compensation plans, however, the "significant risk of forfeiture" that this technique depends on to keep the distributed Insurance Products from being taxable is not directly supported by the Internal Revenue Code but rather by an aggressive interpretation of a "catch all" provision. If the promoters are wrong in their interpretation, all of the money in the Insurance Products will be taxable to the physicians receiving them. The physicians will then have to come up with the money to pay the tax, but wait, the money is all tied up in the Insurance Products. Once again, we are back to the surrender penalty problems.

In short, this technique is great if you are the one collecting the commission on the sale of the Insurance Products, but for the physicians involved it is a losing proposition. Note that some promoters are telling physicians that the plan has been tested and has passed IRS scrutiny. They are referring to one small aspect of the plan, however, the real issue (i.e., the "significant risk of forfeiture") has not been tested to the best of my knowledge. If someone tells you that it has, I would verify their alleged success directly with the IRS.

In short, this is an expensive technique, designed to sell insurance products for the wrong reasons, that in my opinion, will leave your accounts receivables vulnerable. The promoters of this technique also leave out the fact that if it does have any chance of working, the physicians will have to liquidate their practice and pay off the bank loans from the accounts receivable. The impression left with most physicians who have been pitched this idea is that since a lien exists, the judge will simply throw up his or her hands and say "Damn, a lien. I guess I am out of luck. Well you guys, go back to work, keep paying yourselves bonuses, and making distributions to yourselves." If you take the time to think it through, I think you will agree that this will not be the case.

The Line of Credit Strategy. Many physicians are under the false impression that they can obtain a line of credit secured by the accounts receivable of their medical practice and that this will protect the assets of the practice. This is simply not the case. Since the balance due on an unexercised line of credit (i.e., a line of credit that the medical practice has yet to use to borrow money) is zero, none of the collateral (i.e., the accounts receivable) are subject to a true lien. If the line of credit is exercised after the creditor is identified (which a bank may not be willing to do if it knows of the law suit or potential creditor, which you typically have a legal obligation to disclose), the money will be paid to the practice and, therefore, will still be subject to the claims of the creditor. If the money is distributed to the owners (forgetting the income tax issue for a minute), the distribution will most likely be considered a fraudulent transfer. If that is the case, the physicians' income tax liability will most likely not disappear, which would leave a balance due and owing under the line of credit which the physicians will most assuredly be personally liable for under the personal guarantees the bank typically asks for.

The Option of Creating a New Practice.

The final topic I want to cover in this Chapter is the liability a successor legal entity may have for the liability of its predecessor. I will start by building on the AMS example used throughout this Chapter.

> Assume Dr. Jones, Dr. Smith, Dr. Anderson, and Dr. Geidvilai...ciai, are all still partners in AMS. Dr. Smith is named in a medical malpractice law suit together with AMS due to alleged medical malpractice with respect to Patient X. AMS' only real assets are furniture and computers with nominal value, patient records, and accounts receivable. The average collectable accounts receivable are $500,000.
>
> In the event Patient X is successful in obtaining a judgement against AMS, he will be able to reach AMS' assets in satisfaction of the judgement, including the accounts receivable. If the judgement was significant enough, for all practicable purposes, AMS would be put out of business.
>
> Assume further that the physician owners of AMS have consulted with their attorney and feel that there is a substantial risk that they could lose the law suit and that if they did, the judgement could easily exceed $1,000,000.

> The four physicians have used some of the techniques discussed earlier in this Chapter and decide the best course of action is to wind down the business of AMS before Patient X obtains a judgement.

Before proceeding, I want to point out that when a business is wound down like this, there are different means of removing value from the business. Some of them are legally defendable and others are not. The issues the business owners will face are based on a combination of the fraudulent transfer laws and the bankruptcy laws, all of which will be very technical in nature. That being said, this endeavor is not something that anyone should attempt without the aide of competent legal counsel. This typically will mean involving an asset protection attorney, a corporate attorney, a tax attorney, and a bankruptcy attorney. Anyone who attempts an undertaking like this on their own will almost always end up with substantial negative results. If you are ever faced with a situation like this, do yourself a favor and utilize professionals who understand these areas of the law.

Moving on, I will get back to the facts in the example.

As the AMS accounts receivable are collected they are used to pay AMS' various obligations to its regular ongoing creditors, the salary of its employees, and its obligations under the techniques used to lien the accounts receivable. The physicians then abandon AMS once its assets have been dissipated. Note that this process may or may not involve having the corporation file for bankruptcy.

Now that the four physicians have successfully removed all of the value from AMS and have protected the assets via their personal asset protection plans, the obvious next question is where do they go from here. Perhaps Dr. Geidvilai…ciai is near retirement age and decides to return to his homeland of Lithuania. Dr. Jones, Dr. Smith, and Dr. Anderson, however, want to continue the practice of medicine.

> Doctors Jones, Smith, and Anderson, having abandoned AMS, now decide to form The Professional Physicians Group, LLC (referred to as "PPG" for short). They take all necessary steps to establish the new practice including applying for new provider numbers, negotiating managed care contracts, etc. Patient X ultimately prevails in his law suit against Dr. Smith and AMS.

> Dr. Smith had planned well and his personal assets are protected from the Patient X's judgement. Patient X now files another law suit seeking to enforce the judgement he obtained with respect to AMS against PPG.

The obvious questions is will Patient X prevail in his second law suit? To answer this question, I first refer to the 1994 case of **Munim v. Azar.** This case involved two physicians, Dr. Azar and Dr. Munim. Dr. Azar was hired by Munim, PA under a three-year contract. Dr. Munim was the sole shareholder of Munim, PA. Sixteen days before the end of the second year, Dr. Munim fired Dr. Azar. Incidently, this was also just sixteen days before Dr. Azar would have been entitled to a sizeable second year bonus. Dr. Munim stated that Dr. Azar's termination was justified by Dr. Azar's behavior which he characterized as argumentative, undiplomatic and less than satisfactory from a medical standpoint. Dr. Azar countered that his termination was a consequence of Dr. Munim's greed and his overbearing and unsupportive behavior. Dr. Azar ultimately sued Munim, PA for wrongful termination and won. Twelve days after the entry of the final judgment against Munim, PA, Dr. Munim formed a new professional association called Pulmonary and Critical Care Associates of Ft. Lauderdale, PA. Dr. Azar filed a law suit to enforce the judgement he had obtained against Munim, PA against Dr. Munim's new PA.

The court stated:

> "At the outset, we recognize that Florida joins the vast majority of jurisdictions in honoring the 'traditional corporate law rule' which does not automatically impose the liabilities of a predecessor corporation upon a successor corporation unless:
>
> (1) the successor expressly or impliedly assumes obligations of the predecessor,
> (2) the transaction is a de facto merger,
> (3) the successor is a mere continuation of the predecessor, or
> (4) the transaction is a fraudulent effort to avoid the liabilities of the predecessor."

The court first considered the fraudulent transfer issues presented by the change in corporations by Dr. Munim. The court explained:

> "The fraudulent nature of the transaction may be found to exist in the transfer of assets of a corporation without consideration or for grossly inadequate consideration to a successor corporation to the prejudice of creditors **for the benefit of the same individuals who constitute the beneficial owners of each of the corporations involved.**
>
> Here, Dr. Munim simply transferred the assets of one PA, in which he was the sole shareholder, to another PA, in which he was the sole shareholder, without consideration and within days of the entry of a substantial judgment. . . .
>
> To argue, as Dr. Munim does, that the patient files and goodwill of the old PA lack value and therefore, could not be the subject of a fraudulent transfer, misses the point. Patients who called for a follow up appointment after November 30th received appointments with the new PA which then presumably received a fee for rendering these services. The question on the issue of fraudulent transfer is whether Munim, PA transferred its assets to Pulmonary Associates without consideration. **The assets could have minimal value and still be considered a fraudulent transfer** if the result harmed Dr. Azar by eliminating from the old PA its means of earning revenues to pay the judgment."

Based largely on the blatant manner in which Dr. Munim moved assets from the old PA to the new PA (and the timing of those transfers), the court had little difficulty in finding that the transfer of assets from his old PA to his new PA were fraudulent transfers. It should be noted that had the new PA paid for the assets of the old PA, the analysis with respect to the fraudulent transfer issues might have been very different.

The next issue addressed by the court was the issue of whether a "de facto merger" had occurred.

"A de facto merger occurs when one corporation is absorbed by another, i.e., there is a continuity of the selling corporation evidenced by such things as the same management, personnel, assets, location and stockholders. . . . 'The bottom-line question is whether each entity has run its own race, or whether, there has been a relay-style passing of the baton from one to the other.' . . .

Although the words 'de facto merger' were used, clearly the standard being applied was primarily that of 'mere continuation of business.' Applying this standard, we agree that there is no genuine issue of material fact regarding whether the new PA is the alter ego or mere continuation of the business of the old PA. The old PA ceased rendering medical services shortly after the judgment was entered against it. The next day the baton was passed to the new PA which commenced full operations. It provided the same type of medical services in the same office with the same files, patients, nurses, clerical help, office manager and the same major player, Dr. Munim -- the sole stockholder in and president of each PA. . . .

The uncontroverted material facts upon which the trial court properly relied established the following. Pulmonary Associates was incorporated twelve days after the entry of the final judgment against Munim, PA. Within six weeks of the entry of the final judgment Munim, PA stopped seeing patients and rendering medical services. Pulmonary Associates commenced seeing patients and rendering medical services the very next day. Dr. Munim is the sole shareholder of Munim, PA and the sole shareholder of Pulmonary Associates; he is president of and controls both. Pulmonary Associates and Munim, P.A. are located in the same office. Except for newly acquired computer equipment, Pulmonary Associates has the same furniture, medical apparatus and office equipment. Nurses who worked for Munim, PA now work for Pulmonary Associates. The clerical staff and the office manager are the same. The medical records and patient files that were kept by Munim, PA were left in place for use by

> Pulmonary Associates. The medical practice of Pulmonary Associates is essentially identical to that of Munim, PA. Patients of Munim, PA, whose follow-up appointments were scheduled before December 1, 1992, would be seen by Pulmonary Associates. Any payment received for services rendered after December 1, 1992 was given to Pulmonary Associates without payment to Munim, PA. There was no interruption of Dr. Munim's business. Munim, PA gave Pulmonary Associates a "turn-key" medical practice."

Again, given the transfer of assets from the old PA to the new PA within days of the judgement, coupled with the "uncontroverted facts" outlined above, the court found that a de facto merger had taken place. The end result was that Dr. Azar was able to enforce his judgement with respect to Dr. Munim's old PA against the new PA.

The case of **Mason v. Speer** decided in 2003, however, had somewhat similar facts and the court made an opposite holding. The facts of this case are as follows:

> "Charles Mason . . . was employed by E. Speer & Associates, Inc., a Georgia corporation ("ESA Georgia") for approximately ten years when his employment with the company ended in 1991. Mason filed suit against ESA Georgia seeking to recover compensation allegedly owed to him . . .. In November 1996, Mason obtained a judgment against ESA Georgia. However, before Mason could collect on this judgment, ESA Georgia declared bankruptcy.
>
> [Mr. Speer set up a new corporation, ESA Florida,] in November 1996, right before ESA Georgia declared bankruptcy. Similar to ESA Georgia, Speer was the 100% shareholder and controlling agent of ESA Florida. Mason sought to hold ESA Florida liable for his unsatisfied judgment against ESA Georgia under a mere continuation of business theory."

The court directly acknowledged the previously discussed case (i.e., **Munim v.**

Azar). It then explained how the facts in the two cases were different.

> "Mason argues that under **Munim**, ESA Florida should be considered a mere continuation of ESA Georgia because both companies were wholly owned by Speer, both provided the same real estate management services to clients, Speer opened ESA Florida only days after Mason obtained a judgment against ESA Georgia, and ESA Florida used the same office, telephone, stationery and part time personnel that ESA Georgia had used. While all of these facts are essentially undisputed, the instant case is distinguishable from Munim based on the 'assets' that ESA Georgia allegedly transferred to ESA Florida."

The court went on to explain how two main contracts with clients of ESA Georgia were not, in fact, transferred to ESA Florida. ESA Florida continued to work with these two large clients, however, it did so under new contracts.

> "The contract with [Client 1] ended on its own terms and therefore was not an asset of ESA Georgia that could be transferred to ESA Florida. As for the agreement with [Client 2], ESA Georgia was never a party to the agreement and did not have rights in the agreement that could be transferred. In addition, both of the agreements in the instant case were personal service contracts that required performance by Speer."

The court continued to distinguish the facts from the Munim case:

> "The instant case is also distinguishable from Munim, in that ESA Georgia declared bankruptcy and transferred all of its remaining assets (a villa and some cash) to the bankruptcy estate. In addition, there was no real transfer of personnel or equipment from ESA Georgia to ESA Florida. When ESA Georgia declared bankruptcy, Speer was the only remaining employee. For the first two years of ESA Florida's existence, Speer was the only salaried employee. The only connection between the

> companies was Speer. As for equipment, neither corporation had any real identifiable equipment. The nature of the services performed did not require any specific equipment or other assets. In incorporating ESA Florida, Speer set up a new corporate existence through which to provide his services. Based on his reputation, he was able to gain clients for ESA Florida that had previously been clients of ESA Georgia. . . . Speer took the proper steps to dissolve ESA Georgia through bankruptcy and he is not prevented from incorporating ESA Florida as a means through which to provide his consulting services. Therefore, we affirm the trial court's finding and hold that ESA Florida is not liable for Mason's unsatisfied judgment against ESA Georgia."

As you can see in comparing the **Munim** case to the **Speer** case, some rather small details were extremely significant in determining the outcomes of the two cases (the filing of bankruptcy and the lack of gratuitous asset transfers between the old and new corporations, for example). If Munim had (i) used a management company similar to the one described above on Page so that there were no continuity of full time support staff or practice assets, (ii) had the new PA purchase the assets of the old PA (i.e., the patient files) for a reasonable sum of money, and (iii) dissolved his old PA through a bankruptcy proceeding, the outcome may have been very different. Also consider the fact that if instead of using a PA which restricts its ownership to physicians, a Limited Liability Company was used as the successor entity, the ownership structure (and, therefore, the control as well) could be different. This may also have a significant effect on the issue of successor liability. Instead, it appears Dr. Munim felt he could handle matters on his own (or was given terrible advise by his lawyer), and ended up paying the price.
As mentioned above with respect to transferring assets from a PA that is to be dissolved, there are many sophisticated legal issues that accompany moving from one PA to another to protect practice assets. In the event you attempt to handle matters like this yourself, you will likely end up like Dr. Munim rather than Mr. Speer (who had the advice of bankruptcy counsel and possible other advisors). The use of competent legal counsel is well worth the price, especially in light of the important consequences to both the physician and his or her ongoing practice.

Conclusion.

As explained at the beginning of this Chapter, protecting practice assets is one of the more difficult areas of asset protection planning, however, there are some significant steps that can be taken to ensure that practice assets remain safe. There are numerous upsides and downsides depending on the techniques you employ. What is right for you and your practice will be highly dependant on your personal facts and circumstances.

CONCLUSION

I hope you have found the information provided in this book useful in gaining a deeper understanding of what true asset protection planning is and what it is not. Asset protection planning can be of significant value to you especially if incorporated with your life planning, financial planning, and estate planning. Before leaving you, I want to make a few final points.

First, the time to plan is NOW when no creditors are lurking. Once the creditor has been identified your planning options will be significantly reduced. This is more true than ever given the changes to the bankruptcy laws.

Second, there is no such thing as one size fits all planning. Every planning technique you may consider using will have benefits and detriments. Always make sure that your comprehensive asset protection plan is tailored around **your** individual facts and circumstances.

Third, always use a team of competent advisors including legal counsel that is well versed in this specific area of the law. It is always best to have your accountant, financial advisor, and other key professionals work together with the asset protection attorney. In this manner your plan's efficacy will not be compromised.

Forth, always make a cost benefit analysis. Your asset protection options are significant. Make sure you understand what is best for you.

In closing this book, I again want to sincerely thank all Florida physicians for providing their services, especially in these trying times. Your efforts are greatly appreciated